The
Psychoanalytic
Study
of the Child

VOLUME FIFTY-NINE

Kindly submit seven copies of new manuscripts by post
or as an email attachment in MS Word to

Robert A. King, M.D.
Yale Child Study Center
230 South Frontage Road
P.O. Box 207900
New Haven, CT 06520-7900
Phone: (203) 785-5880
E-mail: robert.king@yale.edu

The Psychoanalytic Study of the Child

VOLUME FIFTY-NINE

Yale University Press
New Haven and London
2004

Designed by Sally Harris
and set in Baskerville type.
Printed in the United States of America by
Vail-Ballou Press, Inc., Binghamton, N.Y.

Library of Congress catalog card number: 45-11304
International standard book number: 0-300-10460-X
A catalogue record for this book is available from the British Library.

The paper in this book meets the guidelines for
permanence and durability of the Committee on
Production Guidelines for Book Longevity of the
Council on Library Resources.
2 4 6 8 10 9 7 5 3 1

Contents

TECHNIQUE

THEORY

CONTRIBUTIONS FROM DEVELOPMENTAL PSYCHOLOGY

ALBERT J. SOLNIT AWARD OF *THE PSYCHOANALYTIC STUDY OF THE CHILD*

In 2002, the Editors inaugurated the Founders Award, presented in honor of the three founders of The Psychoanalytic Study of the Child, *Anna Freud, Heinz Hartmann, and Ernst Kris. Beginning with Volume 58 the Editors felt it was fitting to rename the award in memory of Albert J. Solnit, M.D., long-time Managing Editor of* The Psychoanalytic Study of the Child.

Sponsored by The Psychoanalytic Study of the Child *and* The Anna Freud Foundation, *the award is given annually to the author of an original paper that best exemplifies* The Psychoanalytic Study of the Child*'s mission of advancing the psychoanalytic understanding of children from the clinical, developmental, theoretical, or applied research perspective (including neurobiological and genetic contributions).*

The recipient of this year's Albert J. Solnit Award is "From Chaos to Developmental Growth: Working through Trauma to Achieve Adolescence in the Analysis of an Adopted Russian Orphan," by Barbara J. Novak, pages 74–99.

SYMPOSIUM ON HATE

Notes on Hate and Hating

T. WAYNE DOWNEY, M.D.

INTRODUCTION

FIRST, I WILL ATTEMPT TO SEPARATE AGGRESSION FROM HOSTILITY, positive from negative aggression. Then, I will attempt to differentiate negative aggression into usual and pathological forms of hatred and to demonstrate a developmental model of hate. Needless to say, any attempt at defining these terms must fall short because of overlap in dynamics, defensive usages and the ordinary paradoxes of psychological growth.

These writings are notes in several ways. They are brief remarks on a complex subject that deserves much more time and thought than I have been able to devote to it. These are notes in the sense of an attempt to put a proper value on hate in the grand scheme of human mentation. Finally, these are notes in the sense of musical composition. They are attempts at building a theme and a melody, though what I have written is only an approximation of a song about this vital aspect of life. This paper contains familiar psychoanalytic concepts that I have reformulated to accommodate my emphases on the place and development of a spectrum of aggression.

Some time ago, I mentioned to a long time friend that I was working on a paper on hate and hating. I was struck by her response, which seemed just the right question with which to lead off this discussion: "Hate and hating, aren't they bad things for people to have

Clinical Professor of Child Psychiatry, Yale Child Study Center, Yale School of Medicine; Training and Supervising Analyst, The Western New England Institute for Psychoanalysis.

This paper was presented at a Symposium on Hate sponsored by The Western New England Psychoanalytic Society, 8 February 2003.

The Psychoanalytic Study of the Child 59, ed. Robert A. King, Peter B. Neubauer, Samuel Abrams, and A. Scott Dowling (Yale University Press, copyright © 2004 by Robert A. King, Peter B. Neubauer, Samuel Abrams, and A. Scott Dowling).

in them?" she inquired. "Isn't hate like evil, isn't it deadly, and like, pathological?" She went on to say that having recently broken up with her spouse, she was working hard to maintain a respectful attitude toward him for the sake of their children, and not to succumb to the promptings and stirrings of outright hatred. I responded by saying that, as I understood it, hate in an overall sense is part of the human condition where it is admixed and intermingled with love. It is in hate's pathological forms where it is increasingly abstracted and divorced from any connection with love that it becomes noxious, contaminating, and destructive to human relationships. In an overall context, hate seems to be an aspect of a human nature that arises from powerful sources of love and aggression. Hate is an inescapable human passion, though one that can be cloaked in many forms. As the old saying goes, you can't make an omelet without cracking some eggs. It is the rare person who can go through life without creating enemies, either through experience or as a result of projective processes. One of the questions then becomes: Does an acknowledgment of hate and hating inform our compassion, or does hatred become a dictatorial passion that drives our behavior with little or no empathy for the place and mental life of another? It is in this latter state that we identify hate with what is pathological, bad, and evil. More ominously, is the hatred unconscious or turned into an apparently opposite feeling state where there is little or no awareness of either the presence of hate or of its powerful and damaging effects upon others in our lives. To some, the above may appear obvious and self-evident, while as I have come to understand, for many, hate is a constantly morphing entity, hiding behind love, concealed in kindness. In everyday life it presents most blatantly in action films and on the international socio-political stage, or at the family dinner table.

Given the complexities of its character, it is not surprising that there is a multiplicity of theories about the origins of hate. Some, like me, see hatred as resulting from the experience of inner drive states that are necessarily and unnecessarily thwarted in the course of development. Frustration of need or desire is a common factor in the development of hate. Others regard hatred as solely the outcome of environmental interaction. Still others emphasize the internalization of noxious influences in the course of development as both a protective and a defensive way of identifying with the aggressor. According to this model the hated go on to become the haters, though often in occult ways that leave them unaware of their cruelty. Unconscious hatred may stabilize adaptation or it may destabilize adaptation, depending on how it is employed within the individual. For many individuals hate is all of the above. Projection of hatred and the projective identification of hated objects are the split off, critical dynamic mechanisms in many adult situations. In the former instance people are perceived as our nemeses through the unconscious projection of our hatred. In the latter there are many individuals who are prepared and primed by their own experience to step forward with the right hateful qualities to become victims and perpetrators of our projective identifications. In most it is the mixture of love, consummated and thwarted, and hate, along with positive aggression, that joins on the path from pre-ambivalent to ambivalent to the post-ambivalent maturity of a feeling state. It is in its pre-ambivalent and fixated or non-object forms that hate becomes pathological over the years from childhood to adulthood.

THE CONCEPT OF AGGRESSION

This paper is not intended as a scholarly review of the literature on hate. It is more a personal snapshot of hatred in its various varieties as I have experienced it and come to understand it personally and clinically. Aggression is one of the major sources of psychological energy that, by and large, serves as an energic precursor from which hatred emerges as distinct and indistinct entities. In "Beyond the Pleasure Principle" Freud (1920) came up with a dual instinct theory for human psychology when he posited an aggressive instinctual drive that he paired with the libidinal drive theory that he had introduced more than half a generation earlier. He framed his description of this new aggressive drive state with metaphors that primarily referenced hostility, destruction, and death. In doing so he also placed his new theory of destruction and hatred in another realm from that which he had used to categorize the libidinal drive to love and be loved. "Destrudo" or "Thanatos," as it was sometimes called, was not considered to have affirmative, life enhancing characteristics that I consider part and parcel of the spectrum of aggressive drive manifestations.

The death drive, as aggression was referred to, was considered to be anti-affirmative, primarily about hostility. As such, it was lacking any true symmetry and parity with libidinal development other than the symmetry of negative to positive. Whereas the instinctual energies fueling love and life were thought to have distinct reference points to various muco-cutaneous junctions of the body, the death instinct, as Freud presented it, seemed more like gravity, a natural force working in and on the body but with no developmental progression, no points of reference or foci within the body. There were no physical areas of clinical relevance that could be easily inferred or derived from Freud's bio-philosophical construct of the death instinct. Furthermore, this new instinct was presented as lacking the plasticity, dynamism, and burgeoning opportunities for the exploration of the mind that his earlier proposals for love, life, and self-elaboration had found a language for in libidinal theory. In this regard, aggression was viewed as a negative force that had more in common with what I am addressing as the realm of noxious aggression and hatred. In fact, the net result was that this paper created a clinically and theoretically indigestible bone of contention within the field of psychoanalysis.

This quandary is in part born out by the fact that for over a span of nearly sixty years, when we search the psychoanalytic journals, we can only find six analysts—Jones, Balint, Winnicott, and Greenson among them—who have attempted to directly address the problems of hate so inherent in the early conceptualizations of aggression, hostility, and the death instinct. The contemporary examination of hatred began in the 1960s, notably with Parens' series of systematic analytic and developmental observations of the vicissitudes of aggression and hatred in children. In reviewing them, I found that they are quite consonant with what I have attempted to extract from my clinical work. A similar statement could be made about Kernberg's striking conceptualizations of the dynamics of hatred as they have arisen from his work with borderline and narcissistic individuals. Many other analysts have embarked on the study of this negative affective entity in recent years; I single out only one, Shengold (1989, 1999).

In 1984, in an essay on aggression, "Within the Pleasure Principle," I attempted in my own fashion, to bring the concept of aggression, so frozen in the ice of death instinct theory, into a more parallel and consonant state with libido theory. I employed a psychoanalytic shorthand, using clinical examples from child analysis and analogies from literature that placed aggression on a spectrum of pleasure-unpleasure. This was a departure from Freud and from the Kleinian emphasis that equated aggression with hostility and hatred. This approach placed it in the spectrum of the pleasure principle. My premise was that, as with libidinal energies for life and loving, from infancy on, aggression could be conceptualized as a positive force in human development. Central and positive growth effects in the life of the individual could be identified in day-to-day manifestations such as object seeking behaviors, and paradoxically differentiation from others, self-assertiveness, and also in the economy of self esteem. In my definition, all these related to positive aggression. Negative aggression is a term that I reserved for fantasies and behaviors that have the physical and psychological harm or destruction of self or object as its aim as in hatred, spite, and hostility.

In putting a positive spin on aggression, there was no intention of discounting the negative drive manifestations such as violence, murder, hatred, and hostility in the inner and outer worlds of individuals and their cultures. It seems to me that it is as development proceeds that frustration, infantile omnipotence, and defensive measures against passivity and helplessness, turn part of the aggressive energies into hostility and hatred and ultimately, if the conditions of frustration and neglect are right, into psychopathology. According to my developmental model positive aggression is socially refined and sublimated over the first two decades of life. Aspects of it may become conflict free. This may or may not happen with developing hatred, as well. A houseful of young children may be a stage or a battleground for all sorts of practicing behaviors involving competition, rivalry, dominance, and submission toward peers and parents. Aggression in the same settings also plays a major role in turning passive experiences into active opportunities for mastery and prowess.

A Definition of Hate

Hate is an omnibus term and affect. The Eskimos have more than three dozen words for snow. In our culture it would seem that we, like the Eskimos, have nearly as many representative terms for hate. Acrimony, mendacity, envy, jealousy, vindictiveness, abuse, rivalry, soul murder, "gaslighting," rape, Machiavellianism, racism, hate crimes, demagoguery—all are part of a list that evaporates into a snow of syntax. All these terms mean slightly different things, but all have hatred as an inherent common denominator.

Hate defines a state of enmity toward an object that in one way or another has frustrated pleasure or desire, that is, an object in reality or fantasy is construed as having contributed to the hater's unpleasure. The desires of the young child may have been actively or passively thwarted by circumstance or those around him. This may lead the child to hate the object of his or her intense needs or to hate the drive state that puts him or her in such a state of helpless frustration. This definition of hate is quite close to the biopsychology of infancy in which we attempt to capture such a pleasure–un-pleasure state with such metaphors as good object and bad object or "good" or "bad" mother. The mother who frustrates by misreading the infant's condition, the mother who under or over gratifies her child, or the

mother who, with her transference wishes for that child, obscures the
child that is objectively developing, or the absent mother, either in
body or spirit—these are all qualities of usual and unusual mothering that may become part of the imago of the hated and/or hateful
mother. In the course of normal development, the child's omnipotent expectations will automatically exceed the mother's capacities
from gratification, let alone her ability to be in several places at the
same time. Situations of frustration and helplessness that engender
shame also lead to the development of hate. All of these possibilities
for a positive loving or negative hating image of the mother can become locked away in the part-object lacunae of the unconscious.

The early analytic term "imago" captures this representation best
for me. Imago, as Laplanche and Pontalis (1973) defined it: the unconscious or partially unconscious figure of an "important other," as
it is originally built up through the filter of the infant's idiosyncratic
perceptions of the social world of the mother's feelings and behavior
as they are interpreted by the infant. In this process of internal and external perceptual flux, the infant's wishes, impulses, and behavior are
both projected and introjected through the medium of an external
persona. What finally emerges during the second year of life is object
constancy and the child's first constant object. The important quali-
fier here is that these early epochal figures, these self-objects, with
their affective constellations of good, bad, hated, or beloved figures,
or an admixture, may continue to dwell in the unconscious. In the
case of unconscious hate, these imagos may be represented by semi-
independent, partially split off object states that can come to the surface, triggered by affective storms, emotional fatigue and regression,
to finally present a very different and contradictory facet of a person's character. By independent, I mean somewhat separate functionally from the overall representational complex that we term the
constant object. In the case of hateful imagos, they may be built up
predominantly through the processes of non-verbal and largely unconscious identification with the aggressor. In the consulting room
they can emerge suddenly when the patient jarringly introduces a
different mindset, a different set of self beliefs apart from usual functioning. There is a sense that the railed against parent has entered
the room and that the analyst is now in the role of bewildered child
in the face of an onslaught of hostility that is delivered with conviction but not with any sense of responsibility. Whether or not we are
aware of hatred in our minds, most of us carry it around in our
hearts. The great attorney Clarence Darrow, renowned for his participation in the Scopes monkey trial, said on the subject of homicidal

trends in everyday life: "I have never killed a man, but I have read many obituaries with great delight."

DEVELOPMENTAL ASPECTS OF HATE

Out of such preliminary definitions of some of the mental phenomena of hate and hating, further questions arise. Where and how throughout childhood development does hate manifest itself? How does it morph and mold in response to the child's individual development and the social forces of family and environment? However, we need to keep in mind that in the early epochs of development, as described by Mayes (1999), the forces of growth are proceeding steadily, unevenly, sporadically, spontaneously, and surprisingly across a wide range of vistas in the infant's mind and body. It is at once the infant's agency, the manner in which mother interprets that agency, and how the infant further interprets the world's and the mother's response to his own crying out for agency that leads to the laying down of various imagos in his psyche.

Klein and Riviere (1937), following Abraham's lead, cast early infants as being born with a full-fledged capacity for hating their mothers. This would seem not to be one of the most enduring analytic concepts, though many would argue this point. From direct observation and clinical reconstruction, it would seem more salient to view the early infant as in a relatively objectless, albeit pre-adapted object seeking state. In such a state what is infantile discomfort, need, alarm, or distressful crying out should not necessarily be personalized or adultified by the theorist or the parent as rage. What an infant may experience as aggressive in the service of an early form of mastery of his environment should not be read by the adult according to his frame of reference or level of discomfiture as strictly hostile. The capacity to be full of hostility and hate, or fully loving of another, for that matter, comes later. This development occurs when, as a result of aggressive object seeking capacities, a fuller inner world, more differentiated from the outer world, becomes defined by the early representations that I am referring to as imagos. However, having said that, the idealized images of babies awake and babies asleep, so full of love and tenderness, may distract grownups from the realities of child rearing. It distorts an appreciation of the hard work, maternal preoccupations, and round-the-clock efforts that are so much a part of infant care.

The assumption is that the capacity for hating, and a capacity for hate without much in the way of action, emerge in tandem with a developing capacity to love, but perhaps hating anticipates loving by some little bit of timing and affect. The capacity for hate emerges first in the imagination rather than in the functional forum of inflicting psychological or physical hurt upon objects. Usually, the development of the mind and its emotional life outstrips the physical and motile capacities of the child. This leads to hating acquiring a number of defensive functions. Hate comes to counter helplessness and paradoxically, it both expresses frustration at the same time that it defends against it in fantasy. Observationally we may see the emergence of hate intensified and verified when the infant develops the motor powers that enable him to toddle. Here we are talking about hate as it serves motivation and adaptation. Perhaps in most individuals, hate emerges before love comes fully into bloom. This may be why we see hate accounting for very contradictory phenomena. Hate may contribute to the mastery experienced when passive and helpless experiences are transformed into active ones. Hate may also come to account as a force to be nullified by the ego when active experiences are defensively turned into passive ones, and the end result is a reaction formation or an inhibition. Love has more interpersonally vulnerable and needy qualities that may call for defensive measures, but love is not usually initially defensive per se. It is an adaptation to social need and connectedness.

It was Anna Freud (1972) who, in discussing the major features of child analysis some thirty years ago, pointed out the prominence of aggressive dynamics over the libidinal dynamics that her father had discovered and first emphasized. However, it is more than just aggression, as it is broadly defined, it is the particular negative (again, in terms of the intended effect upon the object) forms of aggression that are deeply rooted in developmental and neurotic structures of hate and rage. These may finally contribute to pathological hate of the sort that Kernberg so vividly described. As therapists, we must be ever alert to a feeling state that goes far beyond the superficial displays and trite dynamics of anger. As the child develops speech, hate becomes a powerful word that can now be employed to back up and project the emotion of hate. When children say that they hate their mother, father, or siblings, depending on how ambivalent or pre-ambivalent they are in their love-hate development, they may or may not intend it in the purely destructive form of a death wish, as a parricidal act. The child may hate with or without regret, depending upon her level of conscience formation and the power of her hateful emotion. A likely outcome of intense hate is that it verges on pathology that causes the hate to be projected outward. In the child's mind the offended object becomes the offending object. The child's or adult's own rage becomes justified as a defensive-protective and necessarily reactive measure because of outside negativity.

On the other hand, as Loewald (1979) indicated, guilt, and the hate accompanying guilt, provides a conscious and unconscious base for the glue of social bonding that is variably present depending on emotional temperature and regressive pulls in the mind. Here, again, the parent's response may be determinant in terms of whether the condition of hate remains unbridled, whether it too becomes choked off by guilt, or whether the hate is permitted a controlled burn. Does the parent fight the child's campfire of emotion with a counter inferno? This event could lead to the child's following the parent's example through identificatory processes and countering with his own affective inferno of rage. Alternatively, it might lead to the child's guilt engendering apparatus gearing up. What commonly follows is that through identification, there occurs an internalization of the inhibitory functions of the parent in the child's conscience. These superego characteristics will remain there as a restorative and quelling force to counter hate and rage. This may subsequently lead to inhibition of aggression, in both its positive and negative senses, depression, and lowered self-esteem rather than to a more sublimatory result where conflicting affect states, in broad terms love and hate, can be felt and identified within the same experience. The net effect of becoming capable of guilt and its counterpart shame may be that hate will come to reside in the mind in a variety of seemingly isolated conscious and unconscious forms.

Before proceeding further, a few remarks on hate and therapeutic action seem indicated. It is often the function of therapy or analysis to untangle the confused skein of the different levels of hate that have developed in the service of both self-defense and interpersonal defense. Psychological treatment, emphasizing as it does the discovery of clear sources of passion in the forms of love and hate, leads to vast clarities of the individual's psychological terrain. In an optimal treatment the individual's capacities for loving and for murderousness should become clearer, both in the moment and durably over time. This should emerge in relation to the two major developmental areas of object relations that I have been addressing, the dyadic realm of self/other and the oedipal space of the mother/father/child triad.

When Freud talked about the resistance inherent in transference, he emphasized that it stems from drive dominated, distorted infantile needs that are repeated in relation to the therapist/analyst. We might now say that the dimension of true love and true hate are states of feeling that emerge with mature clarity as a result of analysis. Analysis clears away the defensive detritus and morbid wishes of earlier love-hate states. Paradoxically, the end result of analysis or maturation processes may be that the individual becomes not only more tolerant of ambiguity and the necessity for ambivalence, but they become more clearly and maturely capable of being un-ambivalent. This capacity for clearly distinguishing between love and hate should not be mistaken for pre-ambivalent regression, but it should be understood as the post-ambivalent development of a more mature mind that is capable of holding several contrary feeling states in consciousness simultaneously and assessing them in terms of intensity and need for action without succumbing to the defense of confusion or immobilizing anxiety.

Returning to a main point in this paper, central to all of this is the merger of an ontogeny of aggression with the phylogeny of hate. This merger begins to occur more fully during a critical period in self/other, me/not-me differentiation. We can conceptualize this developmental nidus as occurring in the second year of life, the exact timing or course varying from individual to individual and dyadic unit to dyadic unit. In current times, with fathers assuming more active child care responsibilities, fathers participate in this as well as mothers. This is the period in which Klein (1940) described the crystallization of the depressive position, but it is much more than that. This critical period in the development of the mind is also a time when transitional objects, such as blankets, teddy bears, and the like (Winnicott, 1953), are "invented" as a physical manifestation of the child's emerging sense of oneness and otherness, love and hate. The transitional object becomes a salve and a symbolic substitute for the anger engendered by the mother's absence or imperfection. In that period, self and other, me and not me, appear as part of the establishment of *relative* (and the watch word is relative) object constancy. It is an era when the child, in his own mind, begins to experience his potential for destruction and murderous rage in addition to productive social belonging. Fear of the loss of the object and loss of the object's love comes to the fore, driven in part by the child's increasingly rageful discomfort at not having the pleasurable, gratifying parent at hand. We can infer that simultaneously the child becomes keenly aware of the dependent quality of his love for the providing mother and invents a transitional object to soothingly bridge the gap between needy self and a constant but sometimes absent mother. What were initially parallel tracks in the development of love and hate now merge into the ambivalence of the depressive position. Pre-ambivalence gives way to ambivalence. "Either/or" gives way to "perhaps/ maybe." The infant becomes a child who is capable of a range of hostile displays from preverbal whining and irritable pleading, to fits of crying and tantrums, to assaults upon themselves and others with their teeth and hands. In an emotional crisis he will run away from the currently loveless and hated object, or collapse depressively in deep despair.

During this period, there is the dawning of depression as a syndrome and as a natural event in the development of the mind. Depressive dynamics stop time. They deny painful realities while inflicting substitute, but largely defensive pain. The child, and later the adult, becomes capable of pulling the transitional blanket of depression over her figurative head, and denying the forward march of events of loss. This adds another dimension to the meaning of the transitional object. If the child is of relatively healthy constitution and has had a "good enough" environment in which to grow, he/she also becomes capable of experiencing glimmers of the painful, challenging, but enlivening state of mourning. With the emergence in fuller form of both the capacity for depression and the capacity for mourning during this period, the child awakes to a world full of three dimensional affective experiences in inner and outer psychological space, and over time. Memory becomes a constant contributor to self/object constancy.

The child may also become more prone to repressing and otherwise turning inward murderous wishes and hateful intentions. As we know, the child's turning hostility onto the self leads to self hatred, depressive dynamics, nightmares, "bad" dreams, and the potential for phobic development. These inward/outward options may comprise variants of normal development. However, the child's inward turning of hostile aggression may preserve his object world at the expense of his sense of a positive self. The turning occurs when the shadow of beloved and censorious object is cast onto the self. The outside dimension, on the other side of the developmental coin during this critical epoch, is that the "terrible two" year old child appears in full battle gear. At this juncture we can often see in even very casual circumstances the imbalance of hate and love in the affective economy of children at this age. In the two-something child hatred arises more specifically in response to not being loved as much as he desires and when he demands it. Even as he is hateful at not receiving all the love he wants, he is likely to be stingy with his own affection. This general description varies with the temperament of the child and, of course, the emotional and nurturing qualities of the family climate in which he is raised. The child of this early age of differentiation, with constant but variable object relations, is often an emotional, matricidal, and parricidal extremist. In addition to being genuinely loving, he may have fits of being demanding and disobedient, obstinate and contrary. He shows himself as someone who is prone to running away from objects that are simultaneously being hated and beloved. Upon retrieval, the child will collapse into his parent's arms. In other words, children at this age use their neuromuscular apparatus and their voice to act out the politics of hatred. In conjunction with this they appropriate the use of various libidinal orifices. These orifices are turned into sphincters, actually and metaphorically, to sadistically withhold or expel the products of their disposition to negativity, whether those products are glares, screams, growls, words, feces, urine, or clenched or open fist.

It may seem that I dwell too much on this period and these developments. I do so because the characteristics of hate, and love, that I have been describing persist throughout adult life in relatively unchanged form. Having a developmental prototype to refer to is something that I have found invaluable for treating these "children of all ages" and their morbid fixations of rage that were established so early. If we are alert, we could see in grownups the depressive position, the infantile despair, and the separation anxiety that are carryovers from early childhood, when love and hate war over and with the ego for control of the child's mind. This realization is just as we can spot the persistence of infantile colic, not as a physical entity, but as a psychological remnant that shows up as a certain kind of crankiness, irritability, and unsoothability.

HATE AND ITS DISPLACEMENTS

As I have been indicating, displacement is an important defense in the economy of hatred. When displacement in and from the interpersonal realm of loved or ambivalently held "important others" occurs, often the end result may be the placement of the negative affect onto a safer object where the intensity of the feeling remains the same but a subject further up or down the pecking order is selected. This would apply to husbands and wives regular dislike of mothers-in-law, bosses, or the people next door. This is much the same dynamic of displacement that we may encounter when the hatred of sibling rivalry develops. Note my emphasis on hatred. The term "sibling rivalry" places the emphasis on competition between brothers and sisters while it so often is less a matter of competition and more a matter of hatred of the strange new other. In this sense, the term "sibling rivalry" is little more than a trivializing cliché. When there is real sibling hatred, and this is not an inevitable developmental state, there is great ambivalence toward the parent who has dared to bring other children into the world and to love them. This hateful situation is discharged and leavened with the hatred displaced onto the sibling successor. The competition with the new child may be ceaseless and the constant downplaying of the newcomer may amount to a vicious onslaught. That new child is now hated by the older child, both for being a successor and for the unconscious purpose of keeping such guilt ridden and odious acrimony off the parent. Love is also an important component of sibling emotional economy. If a third child should come along, that newcomer may be invested with intensified fawning, split off love by the oldest, again at the expense of the second child.

HATE AND IDENTIFICATION WITH THE AGGRESSOR

Let us now look at things from the point of view of the development of defense mechanisms. By the time that identity and object constancy are coming to a first coalescence, mourning and depression, hatred and love are also emerging as dynamic entities in the mind of the child. By this time, the primary defenses, projection, denial, displacement, and turning things into their opposite, are usually well tempered and omnipresent, provided that there was good mothering. With the fuller development of object relations we start to discern the emergence of object related defenses, which include reaction formation as counter-compensation for various identificatory defenses, including, in particular, identification with the aggressor. It is my impression that the role and importance of identification with the aggressor tends to be undervalued and underestimated. This may be partially attributable to the everyday manner in which Anna Freud (1936) introduced it into psychoanalytic theory.

Earlier, I made a point that both deserves repeating and further elaboration. I cautioned that the experience of the child and his sense of what was traumatic or problematic for him must be measured by taking into account a number of factors that lead to the building up of an imago. For example, there is the child's perception, filtered through the medium of his inner world, of a nurturing event and of the feeling state of the mother as she is in this exchanging state with the child. Is the perception that the mother is relaxed, calm, and satisfied with events herself, or does she come across to her infant, over hundreds of repetitions, as irritable, distracted, or otherwise out of sorts? Then, and all of this may happen serially or with simultaneity, there is the regular event of the infant's projecting his own feelings and wishes onto the primary object, the mother, in the outer world. Accordingly, we expect a subsequent re-internalization of that expression in a manner which culminates in the building up of an imago of the significant other that has a significant resonance with external reality. This is the usual fundamental sequence.

There is another type of sequence for internalization that does not rely mainly on conflict resolution or other internalizations arising out of conflict. It seems that in some individuals, particularly those who have been reared in extreme circumstances of emotional deprivation and parental hate, a different dynamic is apparent. In this dynamic, processes of adaptation, working subconsciously through the functions of the ego create a defensive conformity with the aggressor who may be actually more powerful or more actively hating toward the child. This is not always the case among survivors of such extreme conditions, but it is often the case. This identification with the aggressor has a different quality and appearance clinically from most other defensive operations. It is rarely, if ever, an object of conscious thought. It involves a patterning of the ego rather than conflict resolution between drive and object. It makes its presence known as a defensive style of the ego and the organism. As such, it is a product of the adaptive potentials of the ego. It is not quite "if you can't beat them, join them." It is more like, "in order to survive, I must take on the adaptive characteristics of threatening objects and environment and dwell in a state of preparedness that looks like strength, even if it isn't."

In an earlier paper (2000) I proposed that "actual neurosis" be applied to the realm of blocked and highly frustrated object relations rather than blocked libidinal discharge. This may lead to a shunning of attachments or to attachments that have an "as-if" quality because of inherent hate. Instead of making attachments, attachments are hated and activity is pursued at all cost. For such adults and children, any strong sensation gives them focus and a certain relief, whether the sensation is of a painful or pleasurable nature. Others have identified something similar in describing the contents of declarative and non-declarative transference phenomena, or cognitive and non-cognitive memory. Further examining identification with the aggressor sheds light on our understanding of this shadowy theoretical and clinical area.

Freud (Anna) and Dann (1951) described the effects of hate that entered the lives of children raised in a concentration camp on the very edge of existence. I revisited this group (Downey, 2001) to attempt an understanding of such children in contemporary terms. These children of Bulldogs Bank (the site of their habilitation by Freud and Dann) identified with a negatively aggressive environment and acted out accordingly. This identification with the aggressor is a commonly observed event that warrants further clarification.

Fairbairn (1941) described another set of circumstances where what is to be adapted to and identified with is on a spectrum from the parent with shortcomings to the mal-parent, the malignant mother or father. He described how, to avoid object loss or approbation, the child takes upon himself in the form of guilt, depression, and low self-esteem, and self-blame and self-hatred, the unconscious burden of hating the mal-parent. Perceptions about the inadequacies or the major or minor malevolencies of the primary parent were kept out of consciousness. In doing this, the child avoids losing hope and replaces conscious criticism of the faulty or malignant parent with the hope that the child, through self-improvement, may one day enter the parent's good graces. In cases of gross failures of nurturing, there are obvious indicators that the child has attempted to do just that, take the blame, so to speak, while simultaneously, on another topographically split-off sector of the psyche, he may rail against the negative parenting of the parent. To see the malignant parent as he or she objectively is would be to admit to the horror of the child's young life. In addition to the risk of losing hope and succumbing to marasmus, psychosis, or psychopathy, to see the parent as he/she actually is, or has been, would mean seeing an aspect of the child himself, where he has internalized the aggressor, the hostile and bad object. In our culture, the potential of parents for having hateful and infanticidal inclinations toward children, and vice-versa, may be hard to grasp. And yet, if we look closely at the adaptations and inner life of individuals born into extreme circumstances, we see that from very early on, they often have had a keen sense, without conscious perception, of the deep hatred that they encountered either in the mother that they are attempting to love or in the impersonal motherless circumstances that they were futilely scanning for a constant, nurturing partner. Their defensive efforts to deny that perception include deep and rigid repression of such identifications and require long and patient therapeutic work to bring clearly to the surface. This coincident identification with the aggressor permits and compulsively impels the individual to unconsciously act out the role of the hateful parent upon others. Individuals are also prone to displacement of the perceived hate onto the world and other objects in it, school for instance. This gives them the illusion that they are living in a hostile and threatening external world rather than a hostile and threatening family. As indicated in a different context, their own hateful efforts are easily rationalized as defensive and self-protective, rather than what they unconsciously are, provocative and initiating of conflict. Along with all this, since such defensive remedies are always only a partial solution, their hatefulness is turned back upon the self in the form of self-hate and self-injurious and self-destructive behaviors, which, among other things, serve as further defensive barriers to the self-esteem and self-integrity that comes with taking on the responsibilities of self-knowledge.

I will conclude with some summary statements about what I have been trying to express about the ways of hate's and hatred's concealments. Adults, to avoid adding insight to injury, promise and pledge that they would never treat anyone in the hateful way that their parent or parents treated them when they were children. These individuals are quite adept at projective identification for enlisting rageful agents to carry their hate around 'out there' for them. Their last line of defense is identification with the aggressor in which the person comes to realize that the mother (or father) they have been unable to visualize is in them and that they may not have been able to defeat the aggressor, but that they can certainly join them. As Walt Kelly stated it in his Pogo comic strip some 50 years ago, "We have met the enemy and he is us."

What saps the vitality of such traumatized and ultimately hateful individuals is that since they began to individuate, they have been forced to develop a motion oriented defensive ego style verbally, in their thoughts and in their actions. They are not manic because their mood rarely moves past the confines of anger, anxiety, and depression. This allows the illusion, if only barely, that they are surviving and not succumbing. The resultant ego state is akin to that of the shark that, myth has it, must forever swim and never sleep lest it die. It has to keep in motion, forcing oxygen-rich water through its gills in order to stay alive. There is a constant compulsive need to stay in action while maintaining their distance from most people in their lives to protect themselves from immanent hate and pain and to protect others from their expressed or implied hatefulness. This also provides the basis for a powerful reaction formation against passivity and guilt that can make these individuals appear quiet, generous, self-sacrificing, and productive in their lives outside their immediate quasi-intimate family situations. Yet, each day is a repeat version of Sisyphus pushing the boulder up the existential mountain only to have it tumble back down to the bottom, pushing hate away only to have it tumble back down for the next day. There is much more that could be elaborated about hate, as others have. Hatred's relation to superego functioning and superego pathology, and by extension the role of rage in the psychology of many groups are topics for further study. Were there time and space, clinical examples from children and adults would be of great interest. I hope that this limited exposition answers some questions about hate, as I think it has for the schoolteacher whose questions organized my response in this paper.

BIBLIOGRAPHY

DEUTSCH, H. (1942). Some forms of emotional disturbance and the relationship to schizophrenia. *Psychoanal. Quart.,* 11:301–321.

DOWNEY, T. (1984). Within the pleasure principle. *Psychoanal. Study Child,* 39:101–136.

———— (2000). Little Orphan Anastasia: The opening phase of the analysis of a five-year-old encopretic adopted Russian girl. *Psychoanal. Study Child,* 55:145–179.

———— (2001). Early object relations into new objects. *Psychoanal. Study Child,* 56:39–66.

———— (2002). Little Orphan Anastasia, Part Two: Developmental growth, love, and therapeutic change. *Psychoanal. Study Child,* 57:218–244.

FAIRBAIRN, W. (1941). A revised psychopathology of the psychoses and psychoneuroses. *Int. J. Psychoanal.,* 22:250–278.

FREUD, A. (1936). The ego and the mechanisms of defense. *W.* 2.

———— (1972). Comments on aggression. *Int. J. Psychoanal.,* 53:153–171.

———— & DANN, S. (1951). An experiment in group upbringing. *Psychoanal. Study Child,* 6:127–168.

FREUD, S. (1920). Beyond the pleasure principle. *S.E.,* 18:3–64.

KERNBERG, O. (1991). The Psychopathology of Hatred. *J. Amer. Psychoanal. Assn.,* 39(supplement):209–238.

KLEIN, M. & RIVIERE, J. (1937). *Love, Hate, and Reparation.* London: Hogarth Press.

KLEIN, M. (1940). Mourning and its relation to manic-depressive states. In *Love, Guilt, and Reparation.* New York: Delacorte Press.

LAPLANCHE, J., & PONTALIS, J-B. (1973). *The Language of Psychoanalysis.* New York: Norton & Co.

LOEWALD, H. (1979). The waning of the oedipal complex. *J. Amer. Psychoanal. Assn.,* 27:751–775.

MAHLER, M. (1968). *On Human Symbiosis and the Vicissitudes of Individuation.* New York: Int. Univ. Press.

MAYES, L. (1991). What makes development happen? *Psychoanal. Study Child.* 54:169–192.

PARENS, H. (1991). A view of the development of hostility in early life. *J. Amer. Psychoanal. Assn.*, 39:(supplement)75–108.

SHENGOLD, L. (1989). *Soul Murder: The Effects of Childhood Abuse and Deprivation.* New Haven: Yale University Press.

—— (1999). *Soul Murder Revisited: Thoughts about Therapy, Hate, Love, and Memory.* New Haven: Yale University Press.

WINNICOTT, D. (1953). Transitional objects and transitional phenomena. *Int. J. Psychoanal.*, 334:89–97.

Discussion of T. Wayne Downey's "Notes on Hate and Hating"

LINDA C. MAYES, M.D.

T. WAYNE DOWNEY AND I WERE RECENTLY TALKING ABOUT THIS ACA-demic ritual of paper and response. How might we think about the different styles of responding—agreeing, highlighting, supportive responses, raising questions, unrelated but interesting responses, and surely responses completely outside the individual or even general thrust of the paper. We decided that one style had a particular appeal—musical improvisation, much like a jazz or bluegrass group where one musician sets a key, a melody or harmonic line and another does a riff using one or several of these elements as a starting point. So here's my riff to the wonderfully harmonic line Wayne Downey (Coltrane, Armstrong, Marsalis) has set before us.

The key to begin on is set by the simple but eloquent question posed by Wayne's friend—"Isn't hate always hateful, always alien to our humanity?" Shouldn't hate always be discussed in one of the darker minor keys, non-pentatonic modes, or an atonal throbbing that capture the "not me" self-deceiving quality of those individuals caught in the deepest, imprisoning web of unconscious hating and moving steadily, inevitably toward their own and others' destruction? This is the stuff that evil is made of, from which we recoil in horror and vow to destroy in the name of righteous goodness and purity lest

Arnold Gesell Professor of Child Psychiatry, Pediatrics, and Psychology, Yale Child Study Center; Faculty, Western New England Institute for Psychoanalysis; Visiting Professor, University College, London; Member of Directorial Team, Anna Freud Centre.

This paper was presented at the Western New England Psychoanalytic Society Symposium on Hate and Hating, New Haven, Connecticut, February 7, 2003.

The Psychoanalytic Study of the Child 59, ed. Robert A. King, Peter B. Neubauer, Samuel Abrams, and A. Scott Dowling (Yale University Press, copyright © 2004 by Robert A. King, Peter B. Neubauer, Samuel Abrams, and A. Scott Dowling).

it infect us as an incurable plague. This is the hate that we do not possess but rather crops up in the subhuman, alien souls who are not of us but are regretful, frightening accidents of nature—the axis of evil, the evil empire, the Mongolian hordes, the Islamic fundamentalist, the savage Apache, the thieving cattle rustler, the neighborhood drug dealer, the physically abusive parent. We go to war to rid ourselves of this hateful element and perhaps of our hating of it—we can feel good about destroying that which is hateful without always recognizing the slow, insidious destructiveness of our own hate of the hated. For as Wayne makes so clear, the capacity for hating and the roots of hate are in all of us. It is ironically a part of our humanity and most paradoxically of our capacity for love and need for relatedness. This is the line that separates tragedy from horror—hate as an inevitable byproduct of always trying to love and never giving up on loving versus hate pathologically cut off from love. We come to hatefulness, hating, and hate out of our need to protect our loved ones, to find secure, even intimate, membership in groups, to remain whole ourselves and not burdened by any sense of our own inferiorities and perceived deficits, all of our dark sides and our own capacities for murder and callous destructiveness.

Trying to understand how hate comes from love, how the hate within us all potentially strangles our compassion and blinds us to our own and, even more importantly, others' frailties and vulnerabilities is the subject of many short stories, novels, poems, and films. Writers as the voice of our collective humanity put before us the struggle to abhor hate, while at the same time they show us that although hatefulness and hating is revolting and alien, it is not just outside us. Hate is both from without and within, and denying that which is within us all only fuels its growth like a whiff of air on a smoldering dry forest floor. We ignore the capacity for hate and hating within ourselves at our own peril, for once inflamed, all that is constructively loving may be consumed. In the cultural parlance of Star Wars, we, like Darth Vader, go over to the dark side.

Here are a few examples from our collective cultural voice. In the classic western novel, the *Ox-Bow Incident,* a gang of the righteous, so hateful of those who would steal, end up themselves murdering the innocents, and in so doing, they murder their own decency and destroy their sense of community. In the epic poem, "Brother to Dragons," Robert Penn Warren imagines Thomas Jefferson struggling to understand how his two nephews, born out of the goodness and love of his sister, could have so brutally and coldly murdered a slave for not responding quickly enough to their call for food and wine and then mutilate his body and scatter the pieces across the family land. Jefferson, as constructed by Warren, lamenting the murder that went without prosecution and stained his family and his own conscious struggle about the hatefulness of slavery, angrily insists that had he known, he would "reject, repudiate, and squeeze from my blood the blood of Lilburne" his nephew. Through Lilburne's inconceivable cruelty, Jefferson sees the fragile, thin veil dividing love and hate in every man. Warren writes, in the voice of Jefferson:

> I've long since come to the considered conclusion
> That love, all kinds, is but a mask
> To hide the brute fact of fact,
> And that fact is the un-uprootable ferocity of self. Even
> The face of love beneath your face at the first
> Definitive delight—even that—
> Is but a mirror
> For your own ferocity—a mirror blurred with breath,
> And slicked and slimed with love—
> And even then, through the interstices and gouts
> Of the hypocritical moisture, cold eyes spy out
> From the mirror's cold heart, and thus,
> Self spies on self
> In that unsummerable artic of the human lot. (p. 33)

Years later, Will Campbell played on Warren's title and theme in his "Brother to Dragonflies," in which he describes his own recognition that even as a liberal activist in the civil rights movement dedicated to freedom and civil liberties—all that is good—his hatred for the right wing opposition groups, such as the Ku Klux Klan, is as crippling to him as their hatefulness was to those they terrorized and to the civil liberties movement itself. One evening at a rally, he watches a young man, a member of the wizardry Klan hierarchy, who on this occasion was not wearing his ghostly disguise, try to learn how to march, and he realized that the young man stuttered in his gangly embarrassment, was awkwardly unable to fall into the left-right march step rhythm, and could barely read and write. Horrifically hateful in his nighttime raids as one of a group, he was as frightened and vulnerable when standing alone as those he tried so often to isolate and terrorize when he was within the strength of his clannish clan. His hate, veiled under a real and imagined sheet, hid his own perceived inferiorities and gave him justification to intimidate and murder those he *needed* to see as even more inferior than he. The writer-liberal-activist understood in that moment that in his deep hatred of the Klan, he was not just closed off to his own compassion even as he fought for a compassionate cause. Rather, his fury was as incendiary as those he hated, and most profoundly the hater and the hated were each capable of indescribable hatefulness that threatened their humanity.

And a fourth example: In John Steinbeck's *East of Eden*, he tells the saga of the intergenerational transmission of hate beginning in the murderous rage of an older sibling toward his younger brother, whom he literally tries to bludgeon to death by the side of the road late on a dark, wet, cold night. The younger brother, Adam Trask, goes off to the Indian wars but years later returns home to help his brother on their jointly inherited rocky New England farm, only to be driven off again, but this time by a woman who is herself coldly hateful and destructive and who has murdered her own parents. Blinded by his need for love and redemption, Adam sees only frail goodness in his wife, Kate, who also tries to kill him, much like a snarling animal lashing out toward a would-be, humane protector. Escaping to the closest town, Kate murderously takes over a brothel and turns her business into the hateful side of loneliness, a house of love without love, dark and deadened by hate and despair. And so the stage is set for the tension of the novel—Will her twin sons learn of their hateful, hating heritage, will they go over to the inevitable family history of hating and paranoid tinged isolation passed down from their uncle and their mother, or will they make another choice to take the risks of living amongst humanity, however flawed, and of intimacy and love? Throughout Steinbeck brings on stage characters who can speak and act the tensions of hate and love, as with Joe Valery, the wily, resourceful hit man doing Kate's dirty bidding of blackmail and extortion. As Steinbeck writes:

> Joe Valery got along by watching and listening and, as he said himself, not sticking his neck out. He had built his hatreds little by little—beginning with a mother who neglected him, a father who alternately whipped him and slobbered over him. It had been easy to transfer his developing hatred to the teacher who disciplined him and the policeman who chased him and the priest who lectured him. Even before the first magistrate looked down on him, Joe had developed a fine stable of hates toward the whole world he knew.
>
> Hate cannot live alone. It must have love as a trigger, a goad or a stimulant. Joe early developed a gentle and protective love for Joe. He comforted and flattered and cherished Joe. He set up walls to save Joe from a hostile world. And gradually Joe became proof against wrong. If Joe got into trouble, it was because the world was in angry conspiracy against him. And if Joe attacked the world, it was revenge and they damn well deserved it—the sons of bitches.

So the key of our riff changes from a dark, ominous minor mode with a single harmonic line—the foreboding two bass notes of the music to *Jaws*—to more complex augmented and diminished sevenths and fifths, chords and harmonies touched with dissonance, sometimes sadness, sometimes excitement and soaring triumph, sometimes sobered, muted resilience, each pointing to the tragedy of all our individual struggles with our hatefulness. The change in key brings us to ask in more detail, How is it that hate and hating are so much a part of relationships and a byproduct or product of efforts to love and be loved? Surely, we say this seeming contradiction must come from failures in the earliest loving relationships between parents and their children, when currencies of disappointment, frustration, and rage are not tempered by protection, satiation, and love, a point Wayne makes especially clear in his clinical material with Anastasia, and Steinbeck brings home with Joe Valery, Kate, and others. As clinicians focused on the minds of our patients, we are accustomed to thinking that a vigorous capacity for hating is the unfortunate residue and inevitable precipitate of a nurturing relationship gone barren or cruelly hurtful. Profound failures in parenting come to be transformed into the Anastasia's and Joe Valery's of the world who are so wary and mistrustful of any whiff of human kindness and see the world as a hateful, dangerous place in which everyone hates each other—the only contest is to avoid being killed before killing. But how are the behaviors of caregiving transformed into the child's mental capacities for hate (or love)? To speculate on this developmental question, we need to consider not just what a parent does in response to the child's behaviors but also how a parent interprets a child's needs and attributes thoughts and feelings to the child. In other words, the text is not just one person's behavior in response to another's behavior but also mind to mind.

Consider the following commonplace moment: A six-month-old just starting to sit up is playing with a set of keys and drops them to the floor. A parent might say "Oh, you dropped your keys. Do you not want them anymore?" In this most everyday of interactions, the parent comments on the baby's desire, his state of mind. Even a step further might be to add after wondering about the baby's desire, "Would you like daddy to get them for you? Daddy so enjoys playing with you," even as the parent hands the keys back to the baby. This slight addition notes their relationship and shared interaction and adds a comment about how the baby makes the parent feel. This is not fancy or deep—it's the stuff of thousands of moments between parents and children. Take the same moment and change the script.

The baby drops the keys and the parent either misses the moment or simply hands the keys back with or without looking at the baby, with or without a resigned or even more forcefully disapproving sigh. Rewrite the script one more step and add this text, "There you go again. Mommy doesn't have time to play now. Can't you see how tired mommy is?" In either of these rewrites, what happens is that there is no link to the baby's mental needs or the baby's state of mind, but rather a perception that it is the baby's task to adjust to the parent, to read the parent's mind.

Or consider an even more extreme example from a recent clinical consultation with a young depressed mother trying to raise her son on her own. During a home visit, her son, just having learned to crawl, tries to follow her everywhere she goes. He crawls quickly into the kitchen where she sighs, "no, not in the kitchen Alex," and then steps over him much as if he is a pile of dirty clothes on the floor. He swiftly turns and follows her into the living room, beginning now to whine. Louder she says, "Oh stop, no, no, Alex," and disappears into another room, leaving her son crying and rocking on the floor looking toward the closed door. He picks up a discarded plastic bottle and rocks back and forth whimpering. After what seems like a very long time, his mother returns with a pan of water. He stops whimpering, crawls rapidly to her, and tries to pull himself up the cabinet where she has placed the pan. She says, "No, Alex, how can I get anything done with you in my way?" By her light, Alex just cannot leave her alone for a moment—he is nearly a real persecutory object for her. Perhaps most difficult is not her frustration or her overwhelmed loneliness but her inability to reflect on his needs as well as her own, to see his mind as a separate individual, to reach out in even the barest of ways: "Alex, I know you want me to hold you but I can't right now. Sit right here and I'll be right back." Perceived as persecutory for the mother, the stage is set for Alex's sense of himself as hateful and hated and the world as a dangerous and persecutory place. What Alex might say as an adult is that his mother always seemed angry and had no time for him, that she was never around, even though in reality she and he were painfully together all the time. But his mental experience, and thus his internalized imago, might be of absence in the sense of her trying to understand his mind and hence his inability, both as defense and developmental failure, to understand her mind filled as it is with ambivalent hatred of him.

This is familiar stuff in our clinical literature, but let's take one step further to make explicit this "mind to mind" point of view. Children learn to reflect on their own minds, to localize themselves and others in a mental world in these tens of thousands of moments in which they experience adults thinking about their minds. It is a developmental achievement for children to appreciate that understanding what another person desires, believes, or feels is key to understanding, even predicting their behavior and if all goes well, children are most concerned about what is on their parents' minds, and by extension, the minds of other people. With care that attends as much to their minds as their physical needs, children move from a mental orientation that Fonagy and colleagues have called "psychic equivalence"—where what a child feels and believes is assumed to be the same for everyone around him—to a capacity to think about interpersonal experiences in the rich language of different feelings and desires with clear boundaries between real and pretend, self and other, inner and outer. When children do not experience such care, they may not reach a steady or comfortable ability to think about their own minds as different from others and may indeed remain in a state in which what they think becomes what they feel certain is another person's reality. Feeling hated, they believe others are hateful and hating—Joe Valery, Anastasia, for example.

Or at least this is one developmental model for a line from failed or despairing love to hate that seems especially applicable to the accumulating data from the study and treatment of individuals who have been raised in circumstances where hostility is the primary, even if ambivalent, text of their early caretaking experiences. But how much does this model inform our understanding of how it is that the capacity for hate is in us all and not just following circumstances of profound parental failure. This really brings us to the question, How is it that love and hate emerge in tandem and co-exist even in the presence of arid or hatefully colored early care and surely in the absence of either? To borrow again from Steinbeck, How is it that love "goads and stimulates" hate?

Hate, or at least those precursors that prepare the psychic ground, takes hold in those inevitable moments when a child feels helpless, hungry, and cold. These moments have their bodily templates that come to be represented as states to be avoided, states that are hateful in their discomfort and by extension, any person or condition bringing us to those states must be hated. (Of course, how these templates come to be "hard-wired," as it were, is a vitally important area to understand and one into which we are making some empirical headway—but that's another story.) Even in the most loving and caring of parenting relationships, these helpless states are unavoidable and thus, hate has a nidus. In other words, hate like love springs from the well of relations with others, and when we take the chance to care for and love others, we are inevitably going to make mistakes. Or as Jefferson's sister, Lucy, again through the voice of Robert Penn Warren, says, "the human curse is simply to love and sometimes to love well, But never well enough. It's simple as that." (p. 18). It is not just that in the absence of love or when love blatantly and ambivalently comes and goes that hate takes hold, but instead, that a part of our developmental thrust toward a separate self has as a necessary byproduct those templates on which a capacity to hate has a form.

In the language of mind, as parents are able through their own caring to bring their children to an ability to think about their own and others' minds, these hateful capacities, always present, are nonetheless kept bounded by relationships with others. As Wayne suggests, only when hate and hating lose this connection with human relationships do these become the cold evil that we often associate with the hatefulness we want no part of. Once the hater of whatever age fails to develop, loses, or forgoes the ability to see the world through the mind and eyes of another, hate is divorced of relatedness. There is no longer any thought about the other or guilt for the impact of one's hateful thoughts and deeds—hate is no longer feared and defended against. Once divorced of love, of relationships, hate and hating are embraced as a necessity for self-preservation—get them before they get you, trust no one, run lean, mean, and alone, strike first.

So this is an essential empirical and developmental question, the clinical dilemma, and the human struggle that Wayne has laid out for us—How does our inevitable capacity for hate remain a part of our efforts to love and be loved across our lifespan? Note the subtle difference from the way we usually implicitly ask the question about hate and love. Instead of suggesting that the developmental ratio of the capacity for hating to loving is akin to the final sum on a ledger balancing expense and income with one diminishing the other, we ask instead what allows us to maintain the tie between the two. What are the developmental conditions that preserve the link and the capacity to bind hate within relationships, and what are the challenges across development that threaten to leave hate objectless and thus mindless, dead and deadening? I do not offer answers but only the recast questions as a stimulus for clinical study, and Wayne has offered us beginning data for such studies in his presentation of Anastasia. Their accounts are as clear a statement as any of what Steinbeck calls "the one story in the world . . . the warp and woof of our first consciousness . . . the fabric of our last . . . the never ending contest in ourselves of good and evil." (pp. 411–413).

BIBLIOGRAPHY

Steinbeck, J. (2002 [1952]). *East of Eden.* New York: Penguin (first published Viking Press), p. 498.
Warren, R. P. (c. 1979 [1953]). *Brother to Dragons.* New York: Random House, p. 44.

Thoughts on Hate
and Aggression

ERNST PRELINGER, PH.D.

The phenomenon of hate is explored from two perspectives: in terms of intensive bodily arousal and mobilization, and as a form of active but paralyzed aggression. Aggression, in this context, is viewed not in terms of discharges of drive energies but rather as reinforced effort aimed at the removal or destruction of barriers that impede the organism's movement, in real or symbolic space. Winnicott (1950) already had emphasized how the basic fact of the child's motility, its activity, lies at the source of what becomes aggression. Encounter with 'reality' brings interference with 'free', unrestricted movement at first in actual, physical space, then gradually within the representational world. Inasmuch as such additional mobilization finds intrapsychic representation which, in turn, comes to be coupled with an 'injured' response from a loved or valued object, an intrapsychic representation of what the person experiences as his own aggressiveness emerges. Aggression thus derives from accumulating 'inevitable' collisions between adaptive motility and objects (real and symbolic barriers, obstacles) in the way. Aggression plays its part in the development of object relations. If aggressive mobilizations are sufficiently interfered with to block any further movement but continue to be stimulated in pursuing valued actual or symbolic goals, hate emerges as a form of active but paralyzed aggression. Selections from two patients' material illustrate these issues clinically.

Chair of faculty, Western New England Institute for Psychoanalysis; Clinical Psychologist, Division of Mental Hygiene, Yale University Health Services; Clinical Professor Psychology and Psychiatry, Yale University.

This paper was presented at the Western New England Psychoanalytic Society Symposium on Hate and Hating, New Haven, Connecticut, February 8, 2004.

The Psychoanalytic Study of the Child 59, ed. Robert A. King, Peter B. Neubauer, Samuel Abrams, and A. Scott Dowling (Yale University Press, copyright © 2004 by Robert A. King, Peter B. Neubauer, Samuel Abrams, and A. Scott Dowling).

HATE AND AGGRESSION MAKE FOR A WELL-CHOSEN AND TIMELY TOPIC. Perhaps no more or less, though, than at any other time in humanity's history. As it is, we sense ourselves surrounded by hate and its violent expressions. Our personal memories and consciousness are burdened with images of World War II, the Holocaust, Vietnam, genocides in Cambodia, Africa, the Balkans, and of the many forms of segregation whether by gender or race. Bitter and deadly stalemates dominate the Middle East; ever new issues of terror and war are being forced upon us. Hate crimes of worldwide magnitude confront us as well as those committed within a classroom. Conflicts everywhere seem to elude resolution, spring ever again from hatreds between groups of all kinds; there are no signs of exhaustion. Ethnic, economic, social, religious, and historical differences, incompatible and contradictory interests—all are factors in this. Our understanding of their nature and interplay is still far from sufficient. Their apparent irreconcilabilty itself inflames hatred in the people who are affected by them because it is an obstacle to progress and reform. In my comments here, however, I wish to focus on hate as an event within an individual's life, considering its development and how it is experienced by the person and plays a role in his adaptation. Studying hate in the individual might contribute to an understanding of its violent expressions on larger scales.

The experience of hate is powerful and absorbing. Body, clearly, is intensely involved. Hate is arousal, mobilization, tension, vigilance, and concentration focused upon the hated object. Hate is affect, feeling, relation. It has force. Hate may feel different in each hating person's inner world. There is hot, burning hate in some; in others it is cold, hard, seemingly sober, and abstract. Hate can feel sharp and jagged but also dull, leaden, burdensome, and oppressive. It is a painful emotional state but at times, or for some, it can provide pleasurable, lustful sensations; there hate may be sweet, even joyful, rather than bitter. Hate can fill, absorb, and dominate a person, crowd out other preoccupations or commitments. It can drive an obsessional pursuit. Hate may feel as a painful mounting of body tensions, of urges to pout, yell, strike, hit, torture, and kill. It sharpens the person's sensitivity to relevant cues, especially to those that represent aspects or pieces of a hated object. Stimuli from the external world can enliven a sense of hating as well. Take designs with hard edges and sharp points intruding on our perceptions, combined with bright reds or deep, featureless blacks—they make clearer reference to rage or violence than do softly rounded images filled with pastel shades. But things depend on context. Red, within the rounded shape of a Valentine heart, brings warmth, a sense of fullness, containment, and love!

Hate, no doubt, belongs with such phenomena as anger and rage, envy, jealousy, the seeking of revenge. Clearly, we sense them all to be different manifestations of aggression. Let us consider theory for a moment. Their manifestations share similar states of physical arousal with variations due to the context in which they occur, and with varying degrees of potential intensity.[1] All involve a person's special mobilization of resources in the face of hindrances or obstacles he meets while moving on a path of pursuing the satisfaction of a "drive" or motivation of whatever kind. Such mobilizations can be viewed as efforts to continue the interfered-with movement, but they also serve the purpose of possibly overcoming or eliminating the obstacle. This "*additional mobilization* (and intensification of the motive pursued) *in the face of resistance or barrier, I suggest to be the root phenomenon and fundamental definition of aggression*" (Prelinger 1988).

Essential items in the theory of aggression are concepts relating to space and to movement applying to both a person's outer and inner world. Words like "path" and "obstacle" point to the spatial context within which to place the elements we refer to in talking theoretically about aggression. Such theory is not too far from the material, however. Winnicott (1950) emphasizes how the basic fact of the child's motility, its activity, lies at the source of what will become aggression. But movement alone is not aggression. A potential for aggression develops when parts of his body encounter contact with real, "hard" objects, and movement is slowed or stopped. Intensification of movement in an effort to complete it might push the object out of the way. While to begin with objects may be hindrances, continued sequences of at first random, later intentional movements lead to establishing sensory-motor maps of paths to desirable and important objects. In the course of such interference objects come to be known. They become located in relation to internal images of the body, its still or moving parts. These relations begin to define space. Space become the mind's stage. Eventually "mind" places itself into the map it has created. Metaphors of internal, symbolic space and of locations, distances, directions, and movements within such space, I believe, are deeply involved in representing our motivations, their objects, aims, direction, and progress. Spatial meanings attributed to "mental" events in ordinary language reflect this. The word 'motivation' itself

1. Kernberg (1991), among others, offers a detailed taxonomy of the members of the aggressive spectrum as does Parens (1991)

is an example. We sense things in ourselves that make us move; they are "drives"; we want to "get somewhere" in our enterprises; a patient resisting our inquiry protests: "I don't want to go there." Some aims are experienced as farther away than others. Still others can't be approached directly, are even covered up; they may require a roundabout detour before they can be reached. The notion of "progress," (even of an analysis) too, suggests movement, as travel of a sort, in symbolic space. Sensations of locomotion and images of the essential nature of objects as "things that are thrown against us" seem deeply and bodily rooted in muscular knowledge of our legs, arms, and of eyes that learned of shapes and distances. Literally speaking, "getting in touch," first of all with the objects of the physical world including parts of one's own body, means experiencing moments of reduced freedom of movement caused by such contact, however gentle. That movement, so to speak, had wanted to continue. Most living things strive to move. When restraint is met, additional force is stimulated to move the object, aimlessly or determinedly, to push it out of the way, to take it apart, ultimately perhaps to eliminate it altogether. These are universally occurring events, experienced by and affecting every growing human being, yielding information about the nature of objects encountered as well. Their apparent inevitability and universality of collisions may have contributed to the idea of a universal, innate aggressive drive.

Rather than to a "drive" (which it is difficult to attribute uniformly to all the kinds of living beings) I would propose that "aggression" seems to refer to a class of events, *inevitable collisions,* that are characterized by what we sense as implying violence or destruction (of whatever degree) of objects or entities located in physical or symbolic space. That sense, in turn, seems to depend on something like a fleeting identification with the object being aggressed. Such identification ultimately rests on sensations of and within our own body, especially also sensations of pain. Recognizing an event as aggressive depends on the arousal of an *"injured response."*

This consideration also applies to the transition from the young child's "non-destructive" aggression to aggression in the mature person (Parens 1973, 1991). Principally, aggression is reinforced movement to get at things. Non-destructive aggression is aggression only in the mind of an observer who notices things that he values being wrecked by the small child. The child itself is merely active; it has no internal representation of itself as being aggressive. Such representation depends on being brought about by the internalization of "injured responses" by loved, libidinally valued important persons whose "injury" would threaten the child's certainty of continued care and love. Such internalizations provide the basis for the child's capacity to "rue," to feel regret, to empathize (Winnicott 1950).

Obstacles, hurdles, barriers, and other impediments are elements critical to understanding events of aggression.[2] They may be material things, fences in the way, machinery not working; circumstances in outer reality such as poverty, lack of opportunity, or discrimination; also items in symbolic space: a prohibition, a principle, a rule, injustice; there are barriers in interpersonal space: Rejection by others, being contradicted, deceived, cheated, excluded, demeaned, most important of all: being attacked. *Anything experienced as a barrier is a cause for pain* and it will mobilize the person, stimulate aggression, to try to remove such cause. Aggressive mobilization takes several forms: *Rage* brings rapid arousal and hard action by word, deed, or planful management, a reaction proper to an obstacle that can be affected, modified, or disposed of. Other varieties of aggression are particularly defined by the nature of the barriers that stimulate them. In *envy* someone else possesses the desired goods; he is therefore in the way. Special efforts will be aroused to remove him. In jealousy a third object becomes a barrier to full access by the first to the second and will invite hate. There is *revenge* against those who took our love object away or who insulted us. *Hate,* on the other hand, involves a person's emotion and thought in confronting an immovable obstacle, one that defies alteration or disposal. It shares with the others the element of arousal, of concentration of the person's feelings and thought in confronting an object that interferes with movement toward a desired satisfaction. "Hate" denotes an intense emotional state, an affect, if you will. But it cannot be viewed simply as a vehicle for "discharging" a quantity of pure aggressive drive or "instinct." Hate cannot be "abreacted." Hate contains an agenda. The hating person has his reasons. Already Freud (1915) saw hate (as well as love) in broader terms as "relations of the total ego to objects." In order to reach the objects sought for the satisfaction of the person's desires, the path to them has to be clear. If effective action is impeded, that satisfaction cannot be reached. The intent, however, is held on to by patience and fierce persistence. It may be pursued in fantasy, in fruitless planning or in partial, perhaps disguised action. *Hate is a condition of active but paralyzed aggression.* The state of physical arousal engendered when encountering the obstacle may continue as persis-

2. Some of the following formulations, developed independently, coincide very well with some put forth by Buie, D. H. et al. (1983).

tent bodily tension. The impeding obstacle (whether an internal condition or the representation of an external thing or circumstance) becomes itself a target of hate, and hate a drive aiming at its removal. Complications can occur. If, for example, the desired object itself contains the obstacle, it may come to be hated as well as desired. Think of the lover rejected by the beloved. He may dramatically change his view of the former object: now, there is nothing good about it anymore. Its former virtues are found faulty and rotten. The object the lover had cared for, tried to further and enhance, he now wishes to kill or hopes it might simply evaporate. In hating, though, he continues a relation with an object he has "lost" in external reality. The formerly "beloved" has become an internal object and, most likely, a burdensome one too. It is not easily gotten rid of; another paralysis adds to the person's situation: the hated object becomes a persecutor itself.

While a person's hate may reach its most dramatic heights when intense and longstanding needs are blocked from satisfaction, its strength and particular quality are affected by his past. The very fact of hating's intimate involvement with the body and its functions speaks for that. Hating has its particular forerunners and precedents. It reaches back to the infant's earliest experiences with caregivers and their care, to subsequent deprivations, disappointments, and insults, to resulting aggressions, and their resolutions. A piece of that history may sometimes come to be conscious to the person. Mostly, though it lives in the person's muscles and bones, stomach and heart, in corners of his brain. Occasionally such history of the past provides resources for coping with paralysis at the present. As well, however, it offers paths, facilitations, and invitations for regression, for returns to modes of adaptation that served in coping with obstacles of earlier times or implement earlier fantasies. The experience of helplessness is of particular importance here. It in itself acts as a significant barrier to the person's ever-present efforts to maintain hopes and illusions of competence, of ability to master things, of self-confidence and pride. Needing help may impair the person's sense of independence and identity. As helplessness leads to despair, it may favor returns to increasingly primitive forms of adaptive functioning. The harsher the person's present paralysis, the deeper and more probable may be regressions in his organization of thought, feeling, imagination, and of relatedness to others. Thinking may become more single-minded, concrete, and absolutistic. Subtlety of judgment suffers as well as the sharpness of reality testing. Things come to be seen in stark contrasts of black and white, right and wrong, good and bad.

The person's inability to resolve his paralyzed state makes him feel surrounded by barriers everywhere. Control over affects lapses. He may feel driven *"just to do something,"* to lash out indiscriminately in order to regain some sense of freedom of movement. Unrestrained use of motility and force provides lustful illusions of mastery and power, opens paths for cruelty, attempts to dominate, to revolt even against internal restrictions, for sexual or moral sadism, for torture and slaughter. Helplessness and despair of any change mean unmovable barriers to individuals or groups and are ready sources of extreme, destructive, hate-driven actions. Cruelties against civilians by retreating or encircled armies, situations like My Lai, and other instances in Vietnam, atrocities committed by opposing forces in the Near East conflict, may have many reasons but coalesce into regressions driven by helplessness and despair, by an inability to recognize the roots of fundamental barriers or to modify them. Accustomed efforts at adaptation fail then, regression to primitive modes takes place, accomplished socialization is renounced, perhaps lost.

There is a familiar range of prominent needs and motives which will lead to hate when seriously prevented from finding satisfaction. Love is among them. Freud (1915) viewed love's turning into hate as one of the basic vicissitudes of instinct (turning into the opposite). Rejection, abandonment, or humiliation by the partner represents barriers in the way of the lover's satisfying his passionate and sexual desires. Hate is the aggressive result when no way can be found to move such obstacles out of the way while the desire continues. Kohut's (1972) discussion of "narcissistic rage" talks of hate in its emphasis on "narcissistic injury," as due to obstacles to and failure to reach gratification of needs for self regard and recognition. Fundamental human needs encountering powerful obstacles become sources of hate. The following case excerpt serves as illustration.

CASE F.

F. came to therapy because of difficulties in her work situation. She wanted to understand what was happening there and was in conflict over whether to stay or leave her job. A single woman in her late thirties she appeared to be in robust health, neat, practical, and unadorned in her appearance. She had never been in psychotherapy before. Her speech was forceful, articulate, and direct but tinged with a bit of self-righteousness. As an educator with a good deal of specialized experience she felt capable of doing her job well. She was proud of her very respectable "credentials," which she was eager to describe and document. In fact they were a good deal more advanced than her present position required. With the young people who were her charges she seemed to have no difficulties but there were considerable though vague problems with her colleagues. Of them she was critical, thought them superficial, not serious enough in their work, of lower caliber than herself. For her supervisors and higher officials she had contempt and thought not much of their "credentials." In a somewhat proud manner she felt quite isolated and excluded and suspected that people talked about her behind her back.

In general she felt little happiness in her life. As an only child she had grown up in a strictly Catholic, middle-class family with many relatives on her mother's side, none on her father's. F. made no bones about hating her mother by whom she had felt hated from birth onward and whom she viewed as a selfish, demanding, and hypocritical woman just like her mother's several sisters, a closely knit group of narrow minded, sanctimonious witches who went to church, thought sex disgusting, and exploited, dominated, and denigrated their husbands. Her father, on the other hand, she remembered as a gentle and open-minded man to whom she felt close and who gave F. the only affection she knew. They seemed to be comforted by their relationship with each other and to have formed something of an alliance against her mother, which the latter clearly resented and contributed to her hatefulness toward F. Her father died during F.'s teenage years of a protracted illness during which she alone nursed him. Her mother, although in good health, forced F. to manage the entire household and serve mother's personal requirements as well without ever providing any signs of acknowledgment or appreciation. Overcoming her mother's protests and rage, F. finally left home, found work, continued her education, and became self-supporting. Active, conscientious, even obsessional work and study became the center of her life. Personal relationships remained restricted to those connected with work but even there F. made no close friendships or intimate connections. A few sexual contacts were brief, superficial, and unconvincing. As the therapy proceeded a repetitive pattern began to emerge. After good beginnings in any of her work situations sooner or later some apparently paranoid ideas would emerge. She felt that colleagues made fun of her behind her back, lacked appreciation of her work, were cynical of her "credentials," and viewed her as "uppity." In several instances she would one day (sometimes at night) simply clear her desk, take her things, and leave work without giving notice or speaking to anyone. When she did so on later occasions, even in the course of the therapy, I as well received no indication of what she was about to do. There were interruptions of the therapy until she had resettled herself and found new work. But it would not take long before the pattern repeated itself.

After some initial mistrust, signs of positive transference began to appear in the therapy. F. began to think well of me as a therapist and seemed to look for a closer relationship. She proposed setting up a joint practice in our related professions and became offended when I explained we had to preserve the other work we were doing and declined She reproached me for not taking her "credentials" seriously enough; these "credentials" clearly serving as objectively based supports for her sense of self worth. The therapeutic relation itself she often depicted as one of my serving as a consultant to her professional work.

Another interruption of the therapy occurred when her old mother fell ill and F. went back to nurse her. She did so with a mixture of anxiety, rage, and a determination to do her best and to finally gain some signs of approval from her mother. As I heard when F. returned several months later, she had been treated miserably. F. was criticized, insulted, and reproached for whatever she did. F. fully recognized the rage she felt but could not even think of leaving mother's care to any other relative. Rage turned into hate. In her mother's presence, however, she managed to maintain a patient and caring attitude. This, however, was a complicated matter. F. realized how, on the one hand, she was striving to attack her mother by demonstrating moral superiority ("I take loving care of you which you never did of me"), also hoping that mother would feel punished by her own guilt. She did not succeed in this regard. On the other hand, F. was yearning desperately for her mother's yet relenting in her lifelong rejection of her. Each day she waited for a word of gratitude, a sign of reconciliation, some expression of love. None came forth; her mother died in cold hostility and disdain and left all her property to distant relatives. When F. returned to therapy her work situation had deteriorated. She did manage to find new jobs and kept them for a while, but they were of ever lower grade. F. never tried to obtain letters of recommendation even when she could have done so. She insisted that her "credentials" would always speak for themselves. She managed her money badly, began to default on her small fee. She tried to make it up by paying me in barter. Skilled in various handicrafts, she brought objects. When she brought some quite expensive ones, I explained that I could not accept them: she left them behind and felt rejected and offended. She was deeply insulted when

I once suggested that she could apply her handworking skills to make quite a good income. She felt humiliated and let me know of my limitations. Needless to say, I found myself quite frustrated by her at times, sensing that she made demands for a kind of love which I could not give. I experienced the quality of her insistence as a definite obstacle to my efforts at trying to be helpful to her. I noticed traces of "hate in the countertransference" (Winnicott 1947). It was clear that in the transference she replayed her relation with her mother. As she had desperately tried to entice if not force her mother into giving in to loving and accepting her, she attempted to make me feel obliged, to recognize her "credentials," to praise her accomplishments. I did the latter on occasions to express my respect for her professional accomplishments or her courage and adaptability during various crises. However, to my efforts at interpreting the connections between what was happening in the transference and her past relation with her mother, she would listen but remain untouched by them. Her unforgiving hatred of her mother continued as did her suspiciousness of people in her surroundings. It played out in other theaters of her life as well, affecting her body in the form of multiple problems without organic basis, and after a number of interruptions and resumptions finally led her to abandon the therapy in the same manner that she had left her jobs. She never resumed treatment. Over the following years, however, she contacted me on widely spread occasions to let me know of changes in her life and how she had been able to cope with them.

From early on in her life, satisfactions of F.'s needs for love and care, support, recognition, and respect had met with profound obstacles in the form of her mother's scorn and rejection, one possibly caused at least in part by F.'s loving alliance with a father who, himself, was despised by mother and the wider family. F.'s attempts to impress and please her mother or to force her into appreciating F. brought no results. In that rejection F. encountered an insuperable obstacle in her demand for acceptance, a demand she never could give up. Her rage and hate, however, also kept her in a tight internal bondage to her mother, an ambivalent and conflicted one until death parted them. Her frequent changes of residence, of abandoning jobs, of dropping in and out of therapy may have served to assert some freedom of movement and to follow a hopeful illusion. But it was a footloose freedom, reflecting the continuity of her hate and an impaired ability to establish unconflicted ties.

Parental rejection is a common obstacle to children's pursuit of secure and loving attachment, of being valued and recognized. Passing disappointments may stimulate anger or rage in the child. Broad attitudes of disdain, remoteness, and distance may act as irremovable barriers on the path to finding acceptance and thus they may lead to hate in the child. The following case example provides another illustration.

CASE M.

M. arrived for consultation and possible psychotherapy on the urgent recommendation by a concerned friend. M. had been discharged from the hospital a few days before. There he had undergone a procedure requiring total anesthesia. After recovery he had developed delusions, thought his doctors might have been malicious and had done harm to his body. He seemed similarly afraid of what I might do to him, something he might not even be able to notice. He was frightened and suspicious and informed me that under no circumstances was he ever going to enter a hospital again. This was in part his response to a recent recommendation that he be psychiatrically hospitalized that had preceded his being referred to me. M. was a single man in his early forties, professional, well educated, and employed in doing advanced scientific work. Despite carrying considerable responsibilities in his workplace, he had remained rather isolated and separate there. Nearness of other people distracted and disturbed him. At our first meeting he voiced his doubts of my intentions and abilities and was reluctant to tell about his family and circumstances. Only slowly did he let me know that he was the only child of a very successful professional, but extremely demanding father who exercised stern authority over the family, of whom he was afraid, and who became a major topic of our conversation for some time. After some weeks M. decided that he would give me a chance to work with him, and we arranged to meet regularly three times a week. Overt delusions began to diminish. His thinking, though, remained highly convoluted, extremely lofty, and complex. At times he seemed to speak in riddles. But while still distrustful and suspicious, he settled into the work in a rather reserved manner and was exact and punctual about his appointments. As far as I was concerned, however, he found fault with anything I would ask or remark. He constructed many proofs of my supposedly not understanding him and not rarely he may have been right. This culminated one day when once again I had apparently said something quite inadequate. Emphatically he asserted: "I have to train you to be my therapist!" While I thought of this as expressing a kind of defensive omnipotence, I also saw in it a sign of a developing relationship and transference. He seemed to feel that something worthwhile could happen in our work and appeared to be giving it some effort.

Shortly after that he began to tell me in very indirect and ambiguous hints that he was seriously thinking about suicide. He might not do it, he said, but he surely would if I were going to try to hospitalize him. I told him of my continuing willingness to work with him but that I needed his presence for doing so. Gradually he gave fewer indications of remaining suicidal. Nevertheless, for a goodly number of subsequent weekends I spent my time in discomfort and unease. He had refused any kind of psychotropic medicine but I knew of his collection of pain medicines which he had been unwilling to surrender to me. He talked of the hatred he felt for his father who, he believed, had wanted him dead. He described his father's intrusions on and domination of M. His father had strictly controlled the boy's hygiene monitoring his (good) health continuously. Often he had intruded into his son's privacy, and, as M. gradually told me, into his body as well. Aside from such physical "intimacies," however, he had disregarded M. completely, treating M. as non-existent when company was in the house and did not talk to him for weeks on end. While remembering these events the patient again became suspicious of me. He returned to reproaching me for not understanding him, insisted that I hated him, wanted him to commit suicide, indeed wanted to murder him. When I remarked I was not aware of any such intentions he rose from his chair, stared at me and yelled: "That's because it is unconscious!!" I responded that I couldn't know about that but that he must have been aware that the work was not easy. It was clear we had a highly mixed relation. He had made me his only resource, refused hospitalization, maintained a threat of suicide, but came to his appointments faithfully despite my supposed incompetence. He seemed to be depending on me but also tried to dominate me in every respect. He refused and scorned any interpretations I offered concerning possible transferences onto me of feelings for his father. Then, one day in the midst of another complicated hour he sat back and very seriously said: "Do you have any idea what we are doing?" I told the truth when I admitted: "Frankly, I really don't know anymore!" A real nadir experience for me but one of victory for him. "Good," he responded. "Now we can begin." With that a remarkable recovery began in the context of a growing positive transference. A wealth of memories and a rich fantasy life came into the range of exploration. Much of M.'s hate seemed to have disappeared. A great deal of further improvement finally led to successful termination of his therapy.

What might have gone into such an outcome? It seemed to me that his father's powerful and cruel authority had for much of M.'s life been a powerful barrier against any form of self-assertion and recognition. His inability to fight his father had turned into lasting and bitter hate. In the course of the therapeutic work this barrier was disposed of by his aggressively driving me to the point of suffering evident defeat. M. saw that not only had I not been trying to "put something over on him" but that truly I would have been unable to do so. He exerted power over me as he also had done in trying to "train me to be his therapist." In this context, I think, he seemed to be identifying with his father, the aggressor, intruder and cruel "trainer," drawing some of his power from him. Such partial identification with his father's aggressiveness enabled him to overcome his paralyzing hate by convincingly defeating me in the transference without fear or experience of threatening revenge. By identifying with the aggressive father he was able to defeat him. Consequently he gained freedom to move and to be, to make another start to go on with his life.

I find it impossible to conclude this essay into the subject of hate without looking briefly at the subject on a larger scale. The phenomenon of regression provides the link from the individual to the study of the group.

A person in a situation of sensing himself completely surrounded by barriers and despairing of his resources is liable to regress to a state of helplessness, to become vulnerable to outside influences, may in fact even seek them out to draw resources from them. He encounters others in a similar condition; their common experience ties them into a growing group. The members communicate their hatreds to each other. In their regressive state, hate proves infectious. Someone among them who has preserved a wider view, or an outsider who wishes to exploit the group for his own purposes, arrives; he articulates the situation for them, explains it in simplified terms. He raises their consciousness of certain issues, provides meaning, creates an ideology. Once the blocked aggressions are focussed into hate against a suggested enemy the group becomes radical. Concentrated hatred narrows thought and perception, other considerations lose importance. They may include those of the group members' personal well-being or safety. The comradeship of the group supersedes individual self-concerns. Concretized thinking reduces time perspective to the immediate moment. The future is left vague or disappears. *Aggression* is likely to review ways and means and resorts to flexible trial and error. *Hatred* has only one object and aim: the destruction of the barrier most immediate as an object of restraint. Only less-regressed individuals, remaining to some degree external to the group, might be able to see the group's purpose in a wider context, coordinate realistic action, and find constructive and relieving resolutions. That such individuals, groups, organizations, even states, could succeed in such efforts is, I think, our great and common hope. Hate, in this world, will not disappear by being "discharged" nor can it be disposed of by the exercise of "overwhelming power."

BIBLIOGRAPHY

BUIE, D. H., MEISSNER, W., RIZZUTO, A. M., & SASHIN, J. (1983). Aggression in the Psychoanalytic Situation. *Int. R. Psycho-Anal.*, 10:159–170.

FREUD, S. (1915). Instincts and their vicissitudes. *S.E.*, 14.

KERNBERG, O. (1991). The psychopathology of hatred. *J. Amer. Psychoanal. Assn.* 39S:209–238.

KOHUT, H. (1972). Thoughts on narcissism and narcissistic rage. *Psychoanal. Study Child*, 27:360–400.

MEISSNER, W. W., RIZZUTO, A. M., SASHIN, J. I., & BUIE, D. H. (1987). A view of aggression in phobic states. *Psychoanal. Q.* 56:452–476.

PARENS, H. (1973). Aggression—a reconsideration. *J. Amer. Psychoanal. Assn,* 21:34–60.

———— (1991). A view of the development of hostility in early life. *J. Amer. Psychoanal. Assn.* 39S:75–108.

PRELINGER, E. (1988). The function of aggression: Old concepts and new thoughts. *Austen Riggs Center Review.* No. 1.7–10, No. 2.4–7.

WINNICOTT, D. W. (1947). Hate in the counter transference. In *Collected Papers,* New York: Basic Books. 1968. 194–203.

———— (1950). Aggression in relation to emotional development. In *Collected Papers.* New York: Basic Books. 1968. 204–218.

Discussion of Ernst Prelinger's "Thoughts on Hate and Aggression"

EDWARD R. SHAPIRO, M.D.

The author suggests that hatred may be a narcissistic phenomenon, a transformation of "I need someone I can't have" into "I hate this person whom I now irrationally completely understand, feel contempt for and must destroy." This transformation removes the other as potentially available for learning and attachment and transforms a potential relationship into an impermeable barrier. It may be the result of an unconscious identification with a parent experienced as prematurely and pathologically certain about the child's experience. The therapist's premature interpretations or limit setting can evoke this negative transference. The patient's recreation of the hated narcissistic object in the transference requires the therapist to undergo an empathic regression in order to identify with the patient's projections. Interpretation of the patient's hatred requires the therapist to discover and tolerate the kernel of truth behind the negative transference and an ability in role to survive this identification with a hated object.

AT THE AUSTEN RIGGS CENTER, WHERE I AM THE MEDICAL DIRECTOR, we spend a great deal of time thinking about hatred. Many of our patients are incredibly angry—in fact, it often takes significant atten-

Medical Director/CEO, The Austen Riggs Center; Associate Clinical Professor of Psychiatry, Harvard Medical School; Training and Supervising Analyst, Psychoanalytic Institute of the Berkshires.

Presented at the Western New England Psychoanalytic Society Symposium on Hate and Hating, New Haven, Connecticut, February 8, 2003.

The Psychoanalytic Study of the Child 59, ed. Robert A. King, Peter B. Neubauer, Samuel Abrams, and A. Scott Dowling (Yale University Press, copyright © 2004 by Robert A. King, Peter B. Neubauer, Samuel Abrams, and A. Scott Dowling).

tion and hope on our part to get through their hatred to their long-ing. Here we focus on hate and, through Dr. Prelinger's paper, to the barriers that evoke it.

Let me briefly restate some of his central ideas. Dr. Prelinger suggests that the child's mobilization to overcome barriers is the root of aggression. He defines different types of aggression mobilized by particular obstacles, and suggests that *hatred* arises from the individual's need meeting an *immovable* object—that it arises from some form of "collision." Dr. Prelinger lists many causes for such immoveable barriers, including loss, rejection, rivalry, insults, humiliation, competition, defeat, restriction, and persecution—all of which block needs for love, passion, sex, self-regard, pride, possession, power, being respected and recognized. The resultant intolerable helplessness experienced by the individual in response to such immoveable barriers is managed by hatred, described by him as, "patience and fierce persistence in the maintenance of unchanged purpose." He defines hatred as a "condition of active but paralyzed aggression."

Dr. Prelinger states that hate has an agenda, a motivation, and becomes a kind of drive in itself; it cannot be abreacted. If the barrier cannot somehow be eliminated, free and effective aggression cannot be unleashed and the person remains stuck in hatred. Structural changes in the relationship between person, obstacle, and original object must be accomplished to dissipate hatred. He states that the intensity and quality of this state are affected by the past, and indicates that the state of hatred results in regression in thought, feeling, imagination, and relatedness to others. It blunts judgment, conceptual thinking, and reality testing.

To illuminate these ideas, Dr. Prelinger presents two cases. But before we turn to these, I will explore his idea of barriers a bit further, particularly as the mobilizers of aggression.

We know that interpersonal barriers to the child's unimpeded movement can be thought of as the building blocks of character, defined as the ego's adaptation to the shape of the interpersonal world. In this discussion, I will propose that when the child responds to such unmovable barriers with hatred instead of adaptation, this outcome is a dynamic creation, originating in family life and involving complex projective and introjective processes and a dynamic I have described as *pathological certainty* (Shapiro, 1982).

Kleinian authors describe hatred as an outcome of projective identification: the conscious disavowal and unconscious interactive mobilization in another of some aspect of the self that cannot be integrated, and the enduring narcissistic use of the other as a hated aspect of the self. We hate that which we cannot discover an empathic connection to, that which is experienced as "not me." It represents a blind spot in our self-understanding, an internalized identification that cannot be owned and must be projected. The barriers Dr. Prelinger presents are ultimately barriers within ourselves: both the irresistible force and the immovable object reside within, internalized from failed early relationships.

What is the link between identification and hatred? In the absence of identificatory links, "pathological certainty" (Shapiro, 1982) takes the place of curiosity, exploration, and inquiry. The other becomes a hated known, not object for learning and exploration. Pathological certainty emerges as a dynamic in both of Dr. Prelinger's cases, and is regularly present around issues of hatred. It marks the complex dynamic transformation of "I need something I can't have," into "I hate what I now irrationally completely understand, feel contempt for, and must destroy."

Dr. Prelinger notes the regression that accompanies hatred. This is accompanied by the replacement of tentative exploration and cautious moral assessment with asserted knowledge and merciless judgment. This hateful transformation makes the other unavailable for learning and attachment; the resultant rigid relationship constitutes a barrier to development.

Dr. Prelinger reminds us that narcissistic rage stems from obstacles to gratification of needs for self-regard and recognition. He differentiates narcissistic rage from the hatred that stems from loss, rejection, defeat, and persecution, but I am less clear about this distinction. My view is that the transformation of all of these insults, injuries, and defeats into impermeable "barriers" and hatred stems from particular aspects of early family relationships. The basic impermeability derives from a quality of *pathological certainty* in the early mother-infant dyad.

I have described a stage in the earliest mother-child relationship, midway between the validation of the child's "true self," described by Winnicott, and the accurate, empathic, mirroring response described by Kohut. In this transitional space, the mother must not know too well what the child needs. She must be open to surprise, to learning something from her child that she has not guessed. This is particularly important when their relationship is dominated by aggression. So, for example, the child screams and refuses the mother's breast at the end of a long day, when the mother is irritable, tired, and upset. The infant's rejection of her and her own identification with him evoke her childhood recollection of feeling unaccepted and unloved by her own parents. At this moment, the mother has an unconscious choice: to confuse the image of her child with that of her mother and react with the rage that this overlapping experience and memory evoke, or to suspend her reaction long enough to consider that the infant's rejection is precipitated by something other than her inadequacy, something within her child that remains unknown to her.

The parent who can tolerate uncertainty and remain open to new information provides the child with an implicit message that some territory belongs to him and remains totally in his control. This parent communicates the limitations of her omniscience and offers the child the freedom to create his own internal world, which he can ultimately, at his own volition, choose to share with the parent and others. The parent who cannot provide this space intrudes into the child with pathological certainty and creates in him a mirror of what she cannot stand in herself. The child's desperate effort to maintain his parent as potentially caretaking leads to identification with these projections and begins a process of becoming the child that the parent needs. This deprives the child of a space for development and is internalized as an impermeable barrier to communication and need gratification.

Here are my questions for this discussion: Is this kind of narcissistic invasion of the vulnerable child by parental projections the origin of the kind of barrier Dr. Prelinger is describing? To what extent is hatred a narcissistic phenomenon resulting from the collision of the child's developmental thrust with parental intrusion? To what extent does hatred represent a failure of the possibility of empathic connection because of rigidly internalized parental relationships? And, what are the implications for treatment, when these early relationships are recreated in a hating negative transference?

I raise these questions, in part, because these dynamics appear in both of Dr. Prelinger's cases. The first patient, F., has a "tinge of self-righteousness." She looks down on her equals and has contempt for her superiors. She abandons her job without notice when she becomes paranoid about her colleagues. She hates her "selfish, demanding and hypocritical" mother, in part, for her devaluation of her beloved father. In her work, she demonstrates her unconscious identification with her mother's contemptuousness. In the treatment, she initially attempts to develop a paternal transference, inviting Dr. Prelinger into a "joint practice from their related professions." He "declines and explains we have other work to do" and she is offended. She thinks that he has not taken her credentials seriously enough; she is not good enough for him. It is not clear in the material whether he offered any space for an interpretive inquiry about her invitation as a metaphor about her wishes about treatment, but it seems clear that his limit-setting response evoked her negative maternal transference. The patient then nurses her dying mother, hoping to get through mother's narcissistic barrier by being a better mother to her than her mother was to the patient. She fails to resolve their relationship and mother dies in cold contempt. She continues to fail at work, in part because she cannot ask for recommendations. She tries to pay her analyst through barter. When Dr. Prelinger does not accept, and he suggests she could make a living by selling her wares, she is deeply wounded and tells him about his limitations. In response to her scorn and devaluation, he feels what he calls "a trace of hate in the countertransference." She attempts to get him to praise her accomplishments, admire her credentials. He interprets her effort to coerce his love and acceptance as she had done with her mother. The interpretations are not useful to her and she abruptly quits the treatment.

While we don't know enough about the work to fully assess this impasse, there is sufficient information to allow for speculation. F.'s early relationship with her mother was deeply affected by mother's narcissism. Despite F.'s efforts, she could not discover a loving mother. Mother's self-preoccupation and contempt created the barrier that Dr. Prelinger describes, but the child,identified with this, took the mother inside and re-created the relationship in the transference with roles reversed. Her unconscious effort was to become the mother and learn from Dr. Prelinger's response to the transference how to re-establish contact with this difficult mother. To help her, Dr. Prelinger would have to discover an alternative solution within himself for the hatred evoked by the seemingly immovable barrier the patient created. His task was to manage his hatred long enough to discover his role as the child in the transference and find an empathic link to the vulnerability behind the patient's demeaning attack.

Not having a language for this struggle, the patient presented her dilemma in dramatic form: she suggested, in a coercive way, that they become allies in business and that Dr. Prelinger accept her creations as payment for his work. In both circumstances, Dr. Prelinger responded with limit setting—and both limits injured and enraged the patient. It is not clear from the material how much space Dr. Prelinger provided for the mutual exploration of the fantasy of a joint practice, but it seems likely that the patient's proposal represented her idealized wish for a good maternal relationship. She may have experienced his limit setting in the negative transference as a reassertion of the mother's "selfish needs." In this context, Dr. Prelinger's reasonable effort to clarify the frame can be seen as a defensive countertransference reaction to the intensity of her demanding, and coercive longing. Similarly, the patient's wish to have her productions valued, when met by Dr. Prelinger's suggestion that she sell her wares, may have been experienced by her as a hurtful demand from her mother to "take her wares elsewhere."

The second case study, M., develops hallucinations about his body after undergoing total anesthesia in the hospital. An isolated man, he is a bit odd, speaking in riddles, withholding, suspicious, and devaluing. In the context of suicidal preoccupations, he reveals his hatred of his father, who he experienced as unempathic, controlling, and intrusive. In an unconscious identification with his father, the patient treated Dr. Prelinger contemptuously, managing him through paranoid projections and devaluing every effort at interpretation. With pathological certainty, he interpreted Dr. Prelinger's unconscious hatred of him, dismissed his efforts and controlled him. With relentless pressure, he drove Dr. Prelinger to admit his helplessness—and at that point began a genuine collaboration. Dr. Prelinger feels that the patient "disposed of a powerful barrier by driving me to a point at which I was convincingly defeated and could not put anything over on him."

Both cases underline the issue of unconscious identification with the hated narcissistic object. The narcissism of these parents presented an impermeable barrier to the child's desire. In both cases, both the barrier and the desire were reconstituted within the patient and re-created in the transference. For the first case, the patient was unable to discover a loving connection to a narcissistic mother. In the second, the patient could not find a way to discover an independent space in the face of narcissistic paternal control.

In the first case, the barrier persisted and destroyed the treatment. Were Dr. Prelinger's limits too much for his patient to bear? Was there a bit of her that Dr. Prelinger could not see in himself, evoking his "trace of" hatred? Did he, by reaffirming the framework, seem like the patient's mother, who focused too much on her own needs? Was there too little intermediate space negotiated between them for an interpretive inquiry? For these and perhaps other reasons, the patient's re-creation of the maternal relationship in the transference could not be borne, survived, and interpreted.

In the second case, the patient/analyst pair was able to work through and contain the massive projections long enough for Dr. Prelinger to grasp and accept his helplessness in the face of the patient's pathological certainty and still stay in the work. Dr. Prelinger states that unbearable helplessness in the face of an immovable barrier is managed through hatred. In this case, in the countertransference, he was able to contain and accept the helplessness that the patient could not stand without having to mobilize his hatred of the patient. Only at that point—when Dr. Prelinger said, "Frankly, I don't know any more!"—could the patient recognize him as a potentially helpful analyst (instead of a too knowledgeable and potentially intrusive father) and establish a working alliance in which they could learn together.

The patient says, "I have to train you to be my therapist." Dr. Prelinger sees this, in part, as the patient's effort at defensive omnipotence. But don't *all* of our patients have to train us to understand them? Don't the barriers to mutual understanding that derive from both roles require negotiation to overcome? And, isn't it a given that the therapist is initially ignorant of the patient and relatively helpless in the face of the need for joint work? After all, *all* we have are our analytic tools and ourselves; we are totally reliant on the patient to join us. If all of this is true, what evoked the feeling in Dr. Prelinger that acknowledging his ignorance was a defeat, a "nadir experience?" He felt the patient had defeated him—but what was the war? Was he caught in a countertransference effort to become the knowing father?

Dr. Prelinger felt the patient exerted power over him in a successful effort to defeat the powerful father in the transference. He suggests that the patient's victory over him allowed the patient to be free to move and go on with his life. I have a different perspective. I think this was an enactment in the transference and that the transition to collaboration was a non-interpretive one, managed through containment and survival of projected rage and helplessness. In this case, unlike the first one, Dr. Prelinger's interest and curiosity about the patient survived his hatred, overcoming the barrier of his patient's paternal identifications. But, I suspect that an interpretive inquiry might have added to this patient's understanding of the struggle. For we never actually defeat our parents, even in their death: we come to terms with their roles and let them go.

Though it goes beyond the focus of this particular paper, I want to just mention one other form of hatred—that which arises out of triadic conflict. The argument I've just gone through is based on a dyadic formulation. One other entry point into hatred is around the Oedipus. Facing the conflicted possibilities of complexity, passion, surprise and excitement in a triangular situation, some patients back away and into a regressive dyadic solution. For some, this takes the form of pathological constructions of victimization. Rather than taking the conflicted risk of joining a triadic fantasy, some patients exclude the third, and regress to a familiar and hating feeling of worthlessness, abandonment and victimization. The other is seen with pathological certainty as uncaring, abandoning, and dismissing. The hatred around this constellation looks similar to the dyadic one, but represents a regression from a more advanced level of development.

Dr. Prelinger has offered us an entry point into the dynamics of hatred and the unconscious origins of this powerful and crippling affect. In my own clinical experience, to help patients move beyond hatred as a solution requires a deep immersion and regression on the part of the therapist. In this empathic regression, the therapist must discover his own identification with the hated object reawakened by the negative transference. To allow our patients to openly and fully hate us does not allow for our customary defenses. Interpretation of such hatred requires discovering and tolerating the kernel of truth behind the transference and an ability in role to survive our unwillingness to see ourselves as hated objects. Interpretation is a tool that allows our patients to move through these seemingly impermeable barriers. They only seem impermeable because of our patients' regression and re-experience of their childhood experience of helplessness. But in cases of hatred, we often must wait a long time before we can interpret. Many of these patients experience interpretation as the too rapid manipulative penetration of the narcissistically certain parent. My experience, as in Dr. Prelinger's second case, is that we often must simply contain, survive, and attempt to clarify the transference-countertransference re-creation while we tolerate our relative helplessness—until the patient develops a psychological skin and enough internal space to consider the possibility that we are allies.

I thank Dr. Prelinger for his focus on the seemingly impermeable barriers that evoke hatred and on his courageous presentation of two extremely difficult patients. We have the luxury at the Austen Riggs Center to have others on the staff to help us bear our patients' hatred. The solitude of the consulting room can leave us much too alone in the face of the unbearable failures of family life.

BIBLIOGRAPHY

SHAPIRO, E. R. (1982). On curiosity: Intrapsychic and interpersonal boundary formation in family life. *Int. J. Family Psychiat.* 3:69–89.

CLINICAL CONTRIBUTIONS

Further Reflections
on the "Watched" Play State
and the Role of "Watched Play"
in Analytic Work

SUSAN P. SHERKOW, M.D.

This paper expands upon the concept of "watched play," a play state in which the mother silently but attentively watches her child play. The regulatory presence of the "watching mother" is introjected and internalized through the child's development of mental representations of mother's latently interactive presence, contributing to the development of self-regulatory mechanisms. By contrast, the consequences of failed "watched play" are disorganizing play disruptions which foster ambivalence and affect disregulation. The introjection of the "watching mother" during play contributes to the child's growing capacity to mentalize others' behaviors. Finally, "watched play" is consistent with the paradigm of the passive, albeit attentive analyst in both the adult and child analytic modes.

IN THE CONCLUSION TO HIS COMPREHENSIVE PAPER, "A PSYCHOANA-lytic View of Play" (1987), Solnit proposes that we add the concept of a "play state" to our repertoire of psychoanalytic concepts. By this he means that play, in both its manifest and latent functions in promoting psychic growth, is a necessity to normal development. In keeping with Solnit's concept of the importance of the play state, I have de-

Supervisor, Child and Adolescent Faculty, New York Psychoanalytic Institute; Assistant Clinical Professor of Psychiatry, Albert Einstein College of Medicine.

The Psychoanalytic Study of the Child 59, ed. Robert A. King, Peter B. Neubauer, Samuel Abrams, and A. Scott Dowling (Yale University Press, copyright © 2004 by Robert A. King, Peter B. Neubauer, Samuel Abrams, and A. Scott Dowling).

scribed a type of play interaction between mother[1] and child that I call "watched" play, and elaborated upon its relevance for normal ego development (Sherkow, 2001).

My experience has led to the observation that there is a type of children's play that is distinct from the more commonly observed play states of either reciprocal play or playing alone. Thus, I have distinguished the "watched play" state from reciprocal play, where a mother and toddler take turns in using a toy or creating and enacting a fantasy. In reciprocal play, the mother and child are mutually engaged in an active way, and learning takes place through the use of the mechanical, sensorimotor, and cognitive modalities in the course of play (Sherkow, 2001). In such play, the reciprocal process between mother and child is as important as the content of the child's fantasy, allowing for identifications to take place in the elaboration of the pretend play. This form of play, reciprocal play, has been thoroughly described and investigated in our literature and practice.

In a very different situation, what I refer to as "watched play," the young child wants mother to "participate" in his play by quietly observing him. He wants her undivided attention focused on him while he plays, though she is to remain silent. Whether he plays with a toy, or enacts a fantasy story that he is creating with his playthings, he appears to want mother to watch him without her trying to engage reciprocally in the play. Indeed, should she try to engage with child-plus-toy, or even speak, she will be ignored, rebuked, or perhaps be told to "keep quiet" and watch. Some children use body language to ignore mother; others behave as if they were lost in a fantasy world or are too "busy" with their toy or game to hear her trying to engage them. Because these play states can be difficult for the mother to tolerate and are often likely to make her feel bored, restless, or annoyed by the toddler's apparent insistence on her silence and passivity, play interruptions ensue upon mother becoming distracted and losing focus on her toddler. She may turn away to use the time "more constructively." These play disruptions then create tension and annoyance on the part of her toddler. He

---

1. Though I will refer to "mother" as the primary caretaker throughout this paper, this does not exclude the possibility of another person—a nanny, a grandparent, an adoptive parent, etc.—acting as the primary caretaker for the child. It is conceivable that there can be a substitute for the mother in watched play if the caregiver meets the criteria for relational representation and is thus a substitute identificatory model for the child. However, it is of note that the identificatory process discussed below is facilitated by the presence of a single primary caretaker, so that variations of this situation (for example, two or more primary caretakers or a single-father household) may involve psychic processes different from those I describe (e.g., variations in identification).

wishes, expects, and needs her to sit silently, to focus her undivided attention on him, and to watch him play (Sherkow, 2001).

Indeed, we know that a mother needs to be present when her child encounters frustration, fear, anxiety, or disappointment in the course of his play, in exploration of books, television and his environment, in meeting new people, and in encountering new experiences. But, as obvious at it seems, most parents do not associate the child's need for their presence when their child appears to be happily playing alone. "Watched play," like reciprocal play, is interactive, despite being less visible. From the child's perspective, the mother is fully engaged in the play, although her engagement, her interaction, occurs on the latent level. In other words, while in reciprocal play the role of the mother is manifestly *apparent,* in "watched play" play the role of the mother is manifestly *inactive* (Sherkow, 2001).

In normal infant development, the play state is intrinsic to the processing of external stimuli, at first facilitated through reciprocal play, particularly in the form of imitation and repetition (Sherkow, 2001). Reciprocal responses elicited by bids from either the infant or the mother are part of the essential process of turning passive into active in the course of the child's mastery of impulses, outside stimuli, and positive and negative affective states (Waelder, 1932). These social interactions are "playful" (Tronick and Gianino, 1986), and even in the first few weeks, when parents are predominately concerned with caring for the infant's physical needs, playfulness is bound up in the psychological experience of mother and infant. For example, a mother may interpret a smile or eye contact from her child as responsive and act in turn, creating the rudimentary setting for a play state.

As the infant enters the toddler stage, "watched play" becomes an additional part of the play repertoire between mother and child. In this paper, I will elaborate further upon the process through which "watched play" is internalized, expanding upon the role of mental representation and attributional capacity. Additionally, I will look at the role of the mother in the possible interference with "watched play" and give examples of difficulties in creating a state of "watched play." The parallel between "watched play" and some aspects of the analytic model will also be discussed.

"Watched play," per se, is not an entirely new concept. Winnicott (1958), in his paper, "The Capacity to Be Alone," addresses the positive aspects of this capacity, which he calls "playing alone in the presence of mother," and refers to the necessity of playing alone in the development of emotional maturity through adulthood. He hypothesizes that the capacity to be alone develops while the child is in the presence of the mother and refers to this state as a "paradox"; he attributes this capacity to be alone to the child's ability to successfully process emotions aroused by the primal scene. In my earlier paper, I stated my impression that this capacity is facilitated not by working through the primal scene, but rather by the child's ability to introject, internalize, and identify with the non-interrupting, watching mother in play, a primary state of being that is not, in my opinion, a paradox at all (Sherkow, 2001).

The internalization of the "watched play" state, in addition to the internalization of the ego-supportive presence of mother as described by Winnicott (1958), is a latent and gradual process of positive identification, in which the child first perceives the mother's watchful, quiet, accepting presence, then introjects this non-interrupting mother in "watched play" and "finally integrates this state with the other cognitive, pleasurable aspects of the play itself, leading to a positive identification with mother's 'watched play state'" (Sherkow, 2001, p. 536).

This process appears to begin in toddlerhood, when the child is in the process of acquiring the capacity for self-object differentiation. At about 15 to 17 months, toward the end of the phase Mahler (1979) has described as the practicing subphase, the toddler begins to show anxiety at those moments when he realizes that mother is not physically present, and he cannot yet conjure up the internal representation of her hovering presence to soothe him. This moment is, to my mind, the first indication of "play disruption" for the toddler. His play halts, and he is suffused with negative affect, on the alert for mother's presence and unable to soothe himself until he is reunited with her through visual or auditory contact. This stage of the process of differentiating the mental representations of self and object and the "good" and "bad" selves is a cognitive process, and only at this point can the toddler "know" that he and mother are separate. With this recognition that mother is apart from him, the toddler begins the internalization of her watchful presence in his play. In other words, for the child, the development of the "watched play" state, and thus the child's internalization of the "watching mother" in play, are dependent upon his ability to begin to differentiate between self and object, between "mommy" and "me."

Thus, in addition to the frequent, everyday activity of reciprocal play, the toddler begins to demand that the mother focus on simply watching him play, and this is when "watched play" begins. Mother must suspend her playfulness so as to sit quietly and watch, which, for the child, is a validation of the identificatory fantasy already formed at this age. At this point, he has internalized her soothing quality, her playfulness, her curiosity, and her perceptions, all of which are manifest elements of her reciprocal play. The child has various options in terms of his play fantasy; he may choose to represent himself and his mother by one or two toys (the former option would correspond to the earlier, symbiotic "mommy-me"), or he may play "as if he were her," that is, in a state of imitation or identification with her. And, in order for the child's fantasy to be played out to completion, it is important that mother sit and watch, rather than interrupt the play.

As development proceeds into the second and third years, the child's cognitive, libidinal, linguistic, and symbolic tasks are to encode the mental representations of the mother, the representations of maternal patterning, and the representations of interactions with her, all within the child's self-representations, gradually building the structure of the child's mental apparatus. This building of the mind, so to speak, requires encoding, processing and retaining the child's constitutional and environmental experiences at each phase of development. It also requires navigating the challenge of modulating impulses and creating useful defenses. The next step on the road to symbolic functioning and expression of sophisticated fantasy play is language development, which, as Galenson (1971) so aptly noted, arises out of these affect-specific creative play moments grounded in drive derivatives. She noted that mental experimentation, which is then translated into actions, appears at a time when language is still very rudimentary.

In addition, play allows for the fantasy elaboration which accompanies locomotive, cognitive, neurological, and emotional development, leading to "playful" experimentation with representations of the toddler's internal and external world of people and objects. This process of experimentation with fantasy play is an intrinsic and very important component in the toddler's development of mastery over his bodily functions, such as eating, spitting, biting, hitting, banging, urinating, defecating, and genital play. Such fantasy play is, in fact, often explicitly visible to the observer. Mother's presence as a supportive but unobtrusive observer of this experimentation and fantasy elaboration is as much a normal requirement as is reciprocal play, where mother manifestly engages herself in the child's fantasy world. "Watched play," therefore, via the mechanism of internalization, provides structure and support for the child's affective state while it simultaneously provides justification for his play fantasy.

"Watched play" is also relevant in situations involving television or video, such as when a child wants his mother to watch him watch television, just as if she were watching him play (Sherkow, 2001). Because of the sociological, sexual, and aggressive themes emphasized on television and video, even in media developed specifically for children, the mother's watching presence may be even more important when her child is watching television than when he is playing with toys. The mother's presence regulates affect, controlling overstimulation and providing a role model that the child can identify with and internalize, beginning the process of superego formation (e.g., when the mother prohibits a child from watching a certain program or movie).

Fonagy and Target (1998) have also elaborated upon the important role that the parent plays in facilitating mentalization, a reflective function that allows children to interpret and respond to others' behaviors. These authors cite the parents' inability to think about their child's experience in a meaningful way as detrimental to the child's symbolic use of affect, attributional capacity, and self-other differentiation. The child internalizes or "re-presents" an image of the caregiver, who, in an ideal dyadic relationship, reflects the child's changing emotional states. I propose that "watched play" is another form of necessary—though latent—mutual exchange, which must also be present for the child to properly introject and internalize the image of the caregiver. Both forms of internalization are necessary for the child to master autoregulation of emotion, suitable defense mechanisms, stable self-representation, and linguistic/symbolic capacity.

If the child achieves mentalization, mental states are then experienced as representations, and he is able to relate internal experiences to the external world and differentiate between the two (Fonagy & Target, 1998). Fonagy and Target emphasize the mother's role in this process; the child is able to access representational emotions if the mother sufficiently reflects his emotional states. My observations suggest that the child is also able to access a representation of the "watching mother" if the mother does not reflect the child's emotions that he is expressing in his play at those times when he demands that she sit and watch him passively, providing regulation from without.

For Fonagy and Target (1998), the child's ability to represent emotion symbolically, if properly achieved, is always an ability to meta-represent emotion. This theory derives from the recent focus on metacognition in the cognitive science literature and holds that "all mind is presentation, but representations are themselves represented in the mind" (p. 92). Normal and neurotic functioning incorporate the ability to refer to, access, and functionally utilize a symbolic network or cognitive schema system, whereas incapacity or disorganization in these processes signifies disorganized or psychotic functioning, among other impairments. This is evident in those patients whose mentalization we label "concrete," absent the playful state of being able to represent fantasy and recognize fantasy in others.

It is perhaps the case that the "watching mother" makes possible a different sort of internalization than the mother who simply reflects the child's emotional states. For example, it may be that the child, upon seeing the watching mother, understands that mother is able to comprehend and represent the child's own actions and emotions in her mind. The mother does not need to mirror the child's behavioral gestures; here, such action would be detrimental to the child's growing ability to understand that mother mentally comprehends his emotions and actions, even when she simply watches him, without mirroring. In this way, the child's understanding of his mother's meta-representational capacity is the necessary component that facilitates his own capacity for mentalization.

Thus, I suggest that the child's capacity to play alone is dependent upon an internalization of his mother's capacity for mentalization. Developmentally, then, it could be said that the child's growing ability to mentalize, corresponding to ego development, is a function of an internalization of the mother's mentalization itself. In the same way, the child's internalization of the "watched mother" in play is an internalization of the patient, focused, watching mother's cognitive processes, including the ego functions of affect regulation and compensatory stabilization. The internalization of "watched play" and the internalization of mentalization coincide in two ways: first, both involve an introjection of the mother's mental state as it relates to the child, and second, it is not necessary in either case for the child to understand the mother's actual mental state—in "watched play," for example, the mother may successfully conceal her boredom while sitting still. One could say that, chronologically, internalization of the watching mother not only follows but acts as a function of the capacity to mentalize, as a child without the capacity for mentalization will undoubtedly encounter attributional difficulties in understanding the symbolic meaning of the "still" but "alert" watching mother.

The internalization process involved in "watched play" is also relevant for the understanding of ego development. Inasmuch as the growth and stabilization of the regulatory functions of the ego are dependent on both the child's ability to differentiate between self and other (which comes to the fore during the anal stage) and his ability to master this differentiation such that an identification can be made with the mother, the phenomenon of "watched play" highlights the difficulty of the attributional aptitude required of the child. The capacity to mentalize in the child as well as the adult is not necessarily accompanied by attributional accuracy; the emotions and mental states of others are not always correctly identified and attributed.[2] Thus the internalization of the watching mother in play cannot be distinguished from the internalization of the mother's mental states as perceived by the child; in other words, perception of the mother's mental state may be distorted by projective identification.[3]

The function of "watched play" in the development of fantasy and in affect regulation was exemplified by a mother who consulted me about her child's sleeping difficulties. Mrs. W. revealed her concern that she was extending her child's bedtime so that she would have time with her after Mrs. W.'s arrival home from work. In her worry that she had too little time during the workweek with her child, she found herself trying to interact with her two-year-old son in a reciprocal fashion nearly nonstop for two to three hours each evening. She observed that, particularly during bath time, when she would constantly try to engage with her child in playing with the bath toys, her son would become cranky and irritable, indicating that he wanted her mother to stop and "sit." After reporting this to me, and my explaining the possibility that this toddler wanted his mother to watch him play instead of engaging in reciprocal play at every moment, the mother tried sitting patiently next to the tub the following evening. To her amazement, she reported, the toddler developed a rather elaborate fantasy about the toy duck and his adventures in the water, revealing not only more complex ideation than the mother thought the child was capable of, but also more vocabulary words than the

2. This, of course, excludes the pathological and generalized inability to comprehend emotional states in others, as seen in autistic spectrum (axis I), antisocial, and narcissistic personality disorders (axis II), among others.

3. For a comprehensive discussion of the role of the mother in affect-mirroring, which builds both internal and external attributional capacity, see Gergely and Watson (1996). These authors develop a social biofeedback model in which the infant learns to distinguish the parent's *marked* and *realistic* displays of emotion, the former corresponding to the baby's own affective state as the parent mirrors it in a particular, exaggerated way, and the latter corresponding to the parent's affective state. In normal development, the infant learns to differentiate between these two emotional states on the basis of the external social cues and behaviors preceding and following an affective event.

mother knew he had. Soon thereafter, Mrs. W. shared her revelation with her spouse, who had similarly found himself distressed during bath time because their son would roll a car across the tub endlessly, while his father was made to "sit and watch," feeling bored and left out. Upon some enlightenment as to the possible positive nature of their son's play, he began to take an interest in watching his son and discovered that his son had elaborate fantasies about Daddy and son cars that "zoomed" and "collided" and competed for the Mommy car's attention.

To what extent does the process of internalizing the focused but manifestly passive parent contribute to the defense of turning passive into active? As Waelder (1932) has stated, this early defense of children is a ubiquitous component of many defensive processes, such as obsessive-compulsive defenses and repetition compulsion. Turning passive into active seems to be intrinsic to the use of fantasy in play to master aggressive and libidinal drive components.

The use of play for fantasy elaboration has historically been attributed to older children, but it behooves us to understand how it evolves in infants. Solnit (1987) defines play in toddlerhood as requiring certain specific capacities, including suspension of reality, creation of illusion, practicing, assimilation, and mastery. Regarding the suspension of reality in play for toddlers, Solnit, like Freud, describes play as a trial action of a different sort than "thinking," without expectation of consequences or responsibility for one's behavior. Such play occurs in the atmosphere of suspended reality.

However, the play of infants and toddlers is different. In my experience, toddlers process reality by playing, and playing includes trial "thinking" and problem-solving, although we cannot see the cognition as clearly as when a child puts his fantasies into words. We can see the basic elements of the suspension of reality developing in toddlers, but as they process reality by playing, their differentiation of fantasy and reality is not fully developed, as it is in older (oedipal and post-oedipal) children. The play of toddlers has not yet arrived at a point where reality is suspended. The difference between toddler play and that of oedipal and latency-aged children is twofold: first, neurological, affective, cognitive, and motor development, all of which facilitate symbolic capacity, are at the most rudimentary stages in the very young child; second, the super-ego is just forming in the young child, and thus the sense of consequence and responsibility is in formation, in flux. Toddlers are being taught rules and boundaries as *they play*, whereas older children play in order to suspend rules and boundaries that they have already been taught. For example, when a child is experimenting with breaking things apart and then putting them back together, whether the underlying meaning of the play refers to anal loss or to castration anxiety, the toddler is building an organizational structure and integrating his affect, cognition, and self-object differentiation; all the while he is engaged in pleasurable activity. The integration process in turn gives him pleasure, clearly visible to those watching him engaged in the repetitive play.

For example, a 20-month-old girl, Jill, entered my office with her parents, who had come for parent counseling. Jill had not been in my office in some months, and her mother noted that although she seemed a bit wary of me, she played on the furniture, making herself comfortable in the surroundings, and then approached the basket of toys. As Jill was beginning to take the toys out of the basket, her mother remarked with great pleasure that Jill recognized the toys and really enjoyed playing in my office. As Jill then removed the toys one by one and played with each—a telephone, a set of nesting boxes, a small drum and drum sticks—for a few moments, as if reacquainting herself with their function, her mother remarked that both she and her husband were concerned that Jill's creativity might be stifled if she were made to draw images rather than create her own abstractions, and that when mother drew butterflies for Jill to color in, Jill would often "get bored" and run away. This discussion of how to help Jill learn to draw—to be an artist like her mother—continued as Jill played with the toys and made increasing contact with me.

Each time Jill picked up a toy, she looked at me intently, not smiling, although I smiled back. She then put all of the toys carefully back in the basket, except for a stacking ring toy, which she put on the couch, and she repeatedly tried to put the rings back on the central pole. When her mother tried to help, Jill directed Mother to just sit and watch. Then, Jill turned and began to offer me the rings, but she did not give them up. And then, to my surprise, she began to line the rings up on the crossbar of her stroller, which was just thick enough to hold the rings, if balanced perfectly. When she saw that the bar could not hold more than three rings, she moved them onto the stroller itself and lined them up in a row.

Why is this bit of play so fascinating? It reflects a number of elements important to our understanding of the development of play, its multiple functions, and the role of mother in the process of mentalization that is facilitated by play. It illustrates what Solnit (1987) points out about the pretend nature of play: "Play is pretend, an indirect approach to seeking an adaptive, defensive, skill-acquiring, and creative expression" (p. 214). Jill's play illustrates the element of experimenting with the toys for their function, which gives her mastery, and the defensive and adaptive actions of taking toys out and putting them back, which defends against loss of object in the bodily, or urinary/anal sphere at this age. It also defends against loss of maternal object, in that Jill is in the middle of the separation anxiety phase of separation-individuation, with nightly wakening and tearfulness upon separation from her mother during the day. The toy is also used by Jill to reacquaint her with a nearly new object, me, via the pretend gifts of the rings.

This play helps to develop structure for the ego, with its repetitiveness, sequencing, and development of the capacity for interpretation, each of which are all-important for adaptation. But the play becomes truly "creative" when Jill lines up the rings on the bar of her stroller, a unique use of the toy, one that moves the play beyond the realm of mastery and defensive adaptation and into the realm of illusion. Here, her play begins to meet Solnit's (1987) requirements of suspension of reality, creation of illusion, practicing, assimilation, and mastery. It is clearly proto-symbolic, because it is so suggestive of meaning beyond the realm of concrete play. What does it mean? Jill is making a connection between the rings in my office and her stroller, which she uses to come and go. Lining up things is an activity in which toddlers typically engage as a way of keeping objects together, an early normal obsessive-compulsive defense. Putting the rings on her stroller brings us together, while simultaneously suggesting that we will soon separate, and that, moreover, she and I are separate.

Another important aspect of Jill's play, aside from its repetitiousness, is Jill's introjection of her mother's preoccupation with creativity. Just at the moment that Jill's mother speaks of creativity, Jill begins to create, using the rings in a proto-symbolic fashion. This process of introjection on the part of the toddler is also central to our understanding of one of the functions of play. In play, the child processes mental representations of every element of his experience. As he moves beyond mirroring, which takes place during infancy, both conscious and unconscious internalizations pervade all aspects of the mother-child relationship, not just the feeding and playful aspects of the dyadic relationship. The infant "picks up" his mother's fantasies, conflicts, impulses, and defenses through a sequential mode of internalization: incorporation, introjection, and identification (see Moore & Fine, 1994). In the first year of life, the baby incorporates part-objects or aspects of the mother, mainly through taking in relatively undifferentiated representations of the mother via pre-verbal processing.

The pleasure that Jill takes in her repetitious play demonstrates Freud's theory that the repetition compulsion is coupled with the libidinal pleasure in children's play, much like that which happens in the working-through phase of an analysis. The importance of "watched play" for the development of symbolic capacity can be seen, in fact, in the role of the repetition compulsion. Because repetitive play often involves symbolic leaps, so that a narrative that a child develops in play can be continued despite the reiteration of one or more of its elements—or created from the sequencing of one similar event after another, the presence of repetitive play evidences the child's growing capacity to symbolize.

For example, Tyler's play in the following sequence demonstrates the evolution of mastery through watched repetitive play. Tyler is a four-year-old boy who came to treatment for developmental delay. His mother was deeply distressed by his being less than perfect, so that the social appropriateness (or lack thereof) of his behavior was a central problem to be addressed in the dyadic work. Thus I was also helping him to reinforce superego aspects of his development, especially social appropriateness (see Sherkow, 2002). Although mother was present for the first two years of Tyler's four-times-per-week analytic treatment, by the end of the second year, she came to only half of his sessions. In a session in which his mother was absent, Tyler played with the toy cars on a floor-mat with a city scene. Each car contained two passengers, himself and a little girl in one, his brother and another little girl in a second car. He drove these cars around the mat, making them stop at various locations, such as the "pizza shop" and the "car wash."

Our first sequence of play with this play-set was reciprocal. At each stop on the mat, Tyler had me pretend that I was the purveyor of the location. He would act like he was trying to buy something for which he would give me money, and I would say at the end of the interchange, "Thank you very much," whether it was for a hot dog or for a purchase at the sports store. Also, at each stop, Tyler made sure that his car arrived before his brother's car, with constant attention to the competition, which included a race to the end of the racetrack on the mat. A few sessions later, when mother was present, Tyler repeated this play without engaging mother or myself, making both of us watch him. He also, significantly, made a shorthand of this competitive and social play by taking his car, stopping at each point, and saying, "Thank you very much, thank you very much," without going through the actual act of purchasing or visiting that we had done previously. His mother seemed puzzled at the play, and I said that he was repeating what we had done before, this time taking the symbolic shortcut. This signaled to me that he had incorporated the social niceties and was demonstrating to us that he had gotten that message.

In subsequent sessions, Tyler continued to play in this fashion, having me watch him while he competed with his brother and using the shorthand "thank you" play to organize his aggression and to reinforce the development of socially appropriate behavior. This play thus signaled that Tyler was able to recall the semantic value of the statement "thank you very much" and create a new narrative in which his repetitive play was exhibited through language—in other words, symbolically. This he did within the context of a narrative game in which the social conventions of everyday life—in this situation, saying "thank you" after a purchase—were integrated, and in such a way as to suggest his comprehension of the arbitrariness of linguistic signifiers. There seemed to be no pejorative denotations associated with Tyler's play, though he may have been pulling my leg or teasing his mother. (Her emphasis on propriety in my office occurred more often than would be expected.) Its good-humored quality conflates pleasurable affect with repetition compulsion, as would be expected from a pre-oedipal child; moreover, its highly symbolic nature (Tyler's actions referred not only to the act of purchasing but also to the generalized context of our earlier session) coincides with the process of internalization as aforementioned. The process of internalizing the watching analyst/mother began in the first session, was repeated in the second session, and was reinforced through repetition in many subsequent sessions. In other words, his experience with "watched play" facilitated his capacity to manage his competitive fantasies and his guilt over successfully swiping mother away from brother.

The above example of Tyler represents a situation in which "watched play" was successful; however, this is not always the case. One of the primary impediments to "watched play" is its vulnerability to interruption, which occurs for many reasons. As aforementioned, mother may not recognize the importance of engaging with her child in this way, and she may prefer to do something else or to play reciprocally and actively with her child. Personality factors play a large role in determining how each individual mother will respond; a depressed mother, for example, may be unable to attend to her child's play, though she may appear to be "watching." Other mothers may feel bored or left out. Additionally, derivatives of mother's own conflicts—be they sexual, aggressive, or narcissistic—may be aroused by the play, bringing close to the surface unacceptable fantasies or wishes. She may be overwhelmed by her own aggressive or libidinal responses to the situation, making it difficult to be manifestly patient and calm.

Typically, when play is interrupted, aggression appears in the form of a play disruption. Such disruptions can occur in a therapy hour, just as they do between mother and child. Every child therapist experiences how his patient loses focus when play is interrupted by a misplaced interpretation. In another case I saw in supervision, Teddy, age 6, was reacting to the loss of a beloved relative by climbing the shelves in his therapist's closet and endangering himself, engaging in acts of brinksmanship, such as getting too close to breaking the lightbulb and perching himself on a high shelf. His therapist had difficulty watching this play, feeling concerned for his safety to such an extent that she could not get enough distance from him to interpret why he was inviting disaster, or how sad he felt about the loss. Nor was she was able to distract him by eliciting reciprocal play. Her constant expressions of anxiety about Teddy's safety interrupted his "brinksmanship" play and led to his directing his aggression toward her by challenging her to a showdown, declaring that she "couldn't make me move!"

It also occurred to me, listening to the material, that the therapist's countertransference as a protective mother, which made her unable to watch him play, is similar to what a mother experiences when her child endangers himself when he is still too immature to distinguish between real and imaginary danger. Every mother struggles with this "brinksmanship" aspect of play, for example, in the playground, on the swing-set, or in the swimming pool. Risk-taking and success require some degree of "watched play," with a hovering parent who nevertheless does not participate.

In contrast, another therapeutic session with Teddy illustrates the difference between "watched play" when the child is in actual danger and "watched play" when the danger is displaced onto a toy or a game. In the latter circumstance, the play is rendered symbolic by definition, it is being one step removed from the physicality of active play. This is as true for toddlers as it is for older children. In this second example, the same therapist was wondering how she should manage Teddy's aggression when Teddy insisted on playing chess, controlling both the black and white pieces so that he would win. Whenever the therapist would try to make the play reciprocal and enter into the game with Teddy by moving the pieces, he would become assaultive, telling her to "shut up." He was verbal enough about his play with the chess pieces to announce more than once that he would inevitably win, saying to her, "You know I'm going to win, I always win." She felt threatened and challenged, in her inexperience, not knowing how to address his competitiveness and his need to win. Because this play was displaced from his physical body onto chess pieces at war with each other, even though the defiance seemed palpable to the therapist (who helped him to be defiant in rejecting her), it nonetheless shows more structure of his ego and capacity for metaphor and symbolic functioning, because he knew that he set up the game to win. He equally knew that he required her to watch him so that he could unconsciously express his aggression while she unconsciously hovered and protected him from his aggression. As long as the therapist experienced herself as being threatened, challenged, or left out of the play, she was not able to help him go further in his treatment and to address the conflicts that underlay his competitiveness. Once she understood, however, that he needed her to silently watch his play and unconsciously contain his aggression, as well as protect him without drawing attention to his aggression or his needing to win, he was able to hear her interpretations.

While it is my impression that "watched play," like reciprocal play, arises in the course of normal development, it is clear that for some children, the wish or need to be watched arises from a deficiency in the relationship between mother and child. Some children demand to be watched in play because their mothers are present but chronically distracted, are multitasking while playing, are altogether uninvolved in their child's play, or are absent or negligent during play times, etc. We all know mothers who say, "I simply hate playing with my child. I leave that to the nanny," or, "my child is perfectly happy playing by himself." In this case, a demand for "watched play" may be an attempt by the child to correct a negligent situation. Furthermore, some children may be too passive, or, when older, too guilty to leave mother out.

What happens to those children whose mothers will not sit quietly and give their children undivided attention, and those whose mothers chronically create play interruptions? Are these the children who will have less capacity to separate, to focus, and to evolve in language and in symbolic functioning? The following are two examples.

Melanie's mother was able to play reciprocally with her in our playroom, sitting at the Play-Doh table and helping Melanie make Play-Doh bagels. If Melanie needed assistance, such as when the playdoh factory broke, mother would respond, verbalizing, "You want mommy to fix it." However, equally often, Melanie made bids for her mother to *watch* her play, to which her mother did not respond. In one instance, Melanie was playing on the floor at her mother's feet with a toy garage, running cars down the ramp, not requiring mother to play with her, although mother was at her side. Mother stopped watching after a moment, stopped focusing on her daughter's play, and turned to talk to another adult nearby. When a car came off the ramp, Melanie would call to her mother to watch, but mother seemed not to notice. After several such bids for her mother to watch, Melanie ceased the organized play and regressed to disorganized play, becoming irritable and whiny.

In another instance, Melanie began a reciprocal play sequence at the slide, a game in which Melanie slid herself down the slide, holding a puppet in her hand and calling to her mother, saying, "Mommy, hold hands." Mother responded, taking Melanie's hand. After several repetitions of this play, Melanie went to the top of the slide with the puppet, this time taking turns sliding herself and then the puppet down, a clear beginning of representational play that imitated the reciprocal play with mother. It would have been developmentally in Melanie's interest for mother to have encouraged this practicing "mommy-me" representational play, both to internalize the "mommy-me" experience and to achieve motor regulation through the slide play. However, mother, unable to focus and watch this new play, interrupted Melanie's play with the puppet by reaching her hand out toward Melanie, as if still playing reciprocally. Melanie started to take her mother's offered hand, but then pulled away and went down the slide by herself. She then interrupted her play altogether by going to the toy garage, seeking a car that had two covers, and in a sequence of sad, anxious play, switching the car covers back and forth, apparently distressed by her ambivalence or indecision, as she couldn't have both the red and blue versions at the same time. This was a representation, perhaps, of the ambivalence created by mother's inability to watch her slide play.

Melanie's distressed and disorganized behavior suggests a disruption in the nascent identification with the regulatory process of the internalized mother in "watched play." Melanie's play then takes on a manipulative and sad quality, lacking pleasure in playing in either the reciprocal or watchful play mode.

David, aged 34 months, a child observed in a normal nursery setting, provides another example of a mother's failure to engage in watched play. David was aware that he was about to move to a new apartment, and he expressed his feelings about the change by clutching onto his toys. When he entered the nursery, he pulled his mother to the toy cupboard and selected the nesting boxes. He asked his mother to sit next to him on the floor and watch him play with the boxes. She did not respond to his request, but sat on a chair nearby. Although I then sat on the floor next to him and tried to play with him myself, he repeatedly begged his mother to sit next to him. Becoming increasingly more agitated, he did not want either of us to play with him, but only wanted his mother to watch him. Eventually, with my prodding, his mother did move to the floor near her son, and he was able to be soothed and then to play. David's bid for mother to watch him sort the nesting boxes seemed laden with symbolic meaning. He appeared to want to use the in / out play to master what must have felt to David like a very disorganizing experience for him. He was using the age-appropriate defense of turning passive into active by organizing the nesting boxes, managing his affect about moving, about separation, but could do so only under the condition of mother's focused, regulatory presence.

Generalizing from these examples, one might assume that such failures to establish patterns of "watched play" might lead to decreased symbolic functioning, decreased capacity of the ego, decreased use of language, and decreased ability to be and to play alone. Moreover, in a treatment setting, "watched play" might be an important ingredient in the ability to form and to use transference.

The therapeutic relationship in work with dyads also resembles elements of "watched play." For example, Emily's mother expressed concern, during the course of a nursery session, that four-month-old Emily wasn't producing guttural sounds. While Emily was lying in a carrying seat, her mother was attempting to engage her in play. Emily responded with cooing when her mother shook a rattle, and mother cooed back, trying to elicit differential sounds from her baby. Emily's agenda appeared to be quite different: she engaged her mother with more complex vocalizations, reinforcing mother's shaking of the rattle. Then, Emily reached for the rattle. Mother remarked to us on Emily's reaching for the rattle, and began, in my presence, to practice playing with Emily. Mother soon became transfixed, taking pleasure in her daughter's responsiveness. Although mother seemed at first to be a little awkward, the more Emily fixed her eyes on her mother's face, the less anxious mother became in our "watchful" presence, and mother satisfied herself that Emily's range of vocalizations was within normal limits.

This state of engagement, preliminary to many aspects of development, whether one is thinking in terms of "object relations," "basic trust," "oral incorporation," "cognitive development," "patterning," "language development," "attachment," or "attunement," came about in the moment I was watching their play. I watched them add something to their repertoire that was not there before. As the "watcher" for this dyad, I could help foster the process of internalizing the "mother-me" playing.

In child analysis, we frequently encounter such "watched play" states, whether watching the mother and child play together in dyadic work or watching an older child play alone in our presence. During the course of analytic work, it is necessary to explore the question of when such play is part of the child's developmental growth, when it represents a transference reaction to neglect, when it is meant to act out aggression, rejection, turning passive into active, or when it signifies a step in the direction of ego growth. When a child in analysis requests, verbally or non-verbally, to be watched while playing, it would be interesting to speculate whether this is a child recovering a memory of being watched in play, or if the child is making a new demand, signaling growth.

Moreover, there are further interesting parallels between the mother's nonjudgmental, passive presence during "watched play" and the analytic situation in general. I have already suggested that the person who has had sufficient experience with a parent who has watched them in play may have a more positive analytic experience than a person who did not have the experience of a passive, but attentive parent who could engage in "watched play" (Sherkow, 2001). In adult analysis, the passive analyst may facilitate a transference situation in which the attentive parent of "watched play" is evoked. In child analysis, the analyst may experience problematic discomfort similar to that of the mother, as described above in the example of Teddy's therapist.[4] It begs the question as to whether or not an analyst can provide the "watched play" necessary for internalization in the historical absence of a sufficient parental model. Yet it is clear that for short periods of time, at least, a focused, watching, manifestly passive but latently "interactive" child analyst can provide enough regulatory support for a child to play in a safe environment.

In conclusion, the question of the role that the analyst plays in the child's intrapsychic development extends beyond "watched play." However, the role of "watched play" in the process of internalization

---

4. I am grateful to Rolf Kunstlicher and Nathaniel Karush for the suggestions that inspired these thoughts.

and of the structural development of the ego is significant, as is the role of "watched play" in dyadic development, and surely there is more to be learned about the influence of the analyst on intrapsychic development from further examination of "watched play," be it clinical or empirical.

BIBLIOGRAPHY

FONAGY, P., & TARGET, M. (1998). Mentalization and the changing aims of child psychoanalysis. *Psychoanal. Dial.*, 8:87–114.

GALENSON, E. (1971). A consideration of the nature of thought in child play. In: *Separation-Individuation*, ed. J. B. McDevitt & C. F. Settlage. New York: IUP, p. 41–59.

GERGELY, G., & WATSON, J. (1996). The social biofeedback theory of parental affect-mirroring. *Int. J. Psycho-Anal.*, 77:1181–1212.

MAHLER, M. (1979). *The Selected Papers of Margaret S. Mahler: Volume Two: Separation-Individuation*. New York: Jason Aronson.

MOORE, B., & FINE, B. (1994). *Psychoanalytic Terms and Concepts*. New Haven: Yale Univ. Press

SHERKOW, S. (2001). Reflections on the play state, play interruptions, and the capacity to play alone. *Journal of Clinical Psychoanalysis*, 10:531–542.

SHERKOW, S. (2002). Multiple transferences in the psychoanaltyic dyadic group setting, presented at the NYP Society, Feb. 2002.

SOLNIT, A. (1987). A psychoanalytic view of play. *The Psychoanalytic Study of the Child*. New Haven, Conn.: Yale University Press, 42:205–219.

TRONICK, E., & GIANINO, A. (1986). Interactive mismatch and repair: Challenges to the coping infant. *Zero to Three*, 6:1–6.

WAELDER, R. (1932). The psychoanalytic theory of play. *Psychoanalytic Quarterly*, 2:208–224.

WINNICOTT, D. W. (1958). The capacity to be alone. In: *The Maturational Processes and the Facilitating Environment*. New York: IUP, 29–36.

From Chaos to Developmental Growth

Working through Trauma to Achieve Adolescence in the Analysis of an Adopted Russian Orphan.*

BARBARA J. NOVAK, M.D.

Winner of the Albert J. Solnit Award, 2004

In seven years of treatment beginning with an extended evaluation/ psychotherapy phase of one year's duration followed by a six-year analysis, a picture emerged shedding light on the resilience of this child who had at first appeared too disturbed and intellectually limited to benefit from an analysis. Her first seventeen months of life were spent with her mother in the otherwise deplorable physical conditions of a Russian

Supervising and Training Analyst and Associate Supervisor in Child and Adolescent Analysis, Baltimore-Washington Institute for Psychoanalysis; Clinical Assistant Professor of Psychiatry, Georgetown University School of Medicine.

Shorter versions of this paper were presented at meetings of the Virginia Psychoanalytic Society and The Association for Child Psychoanalysis. I am grateful to colleagues, particularly Drs. Anita Schmukler, Ruth Fisher, Jack Novick, Barry Landau, Robert Gillman, and members of the Writing Study Group, for comments that were helpful in the final preparation of this paper.

I had the opportunity to discuss Dr. Wayne Downey's paper on the analysis of an adopted Siberian-Russian refugee presented at a Scientific Meeting of the Baltimore-Washington Society for Psychoanalysis in the spring of 2002. I am grateful to Dr. Downey for inspiration to present my own case, using process material from sessions to illustrate details of the analytic work.

prison cell. From there she went to at least two different orphanages be-
fore being adopted by American parents when she was seven and a
half. With analytic treatment, Nikita evolved from a traumatized child,
whose inner world reflected the many losses and abuses she had suf-
fered, to a competent adolescent equipped to use the loving relation-
ships her adoptive parents offered her. Analysis of defense, labeling of
affects, and use of the analyst as a developmental object all contrib-
uted to the therapeutic action and to my patient's modification of sado-
masochistic and narcissistic defenses allowing her to fully develop her
capacity for mentalization.

INTRODUCTION

"NIKITA" IS A SEVENTEEN-YEAR-OLD TALL, ATTRACTIVE, AMBITIOUS,
and engaging young woman who began intensive treatment with
me at the age of ten and a half. Her traumatic history and difficulties with learning and language posed major diagnostic questions
from the beginning. The presenting symptoms included impulsivity
(sometimes self-destructive), poor judgment, idiosyncratic thinking, and a tendency to sustain herself through fantasy. These symptoms raised questions about her ego capacity: Were the symptoms
representative of deficits in ego functioning and a liability to serious regressions that could not be worked with analytically? How
limited was she intellectually? After working with her for a year at a
frequency of twice a week, and then three sessions a week of psychotherapy, I came to the conclusion that these symptoms were representative of a traumatic neurosis with sufficiently resilient ego
strength to allow regression in the service of the ego, and therefore
could be worked with analytically. I have been treating her in four
sessions a week of psychoanalysis for five and a half years at the time
of this writing.

Using analytic process from her analysis, I illustrate therapeutic
change through interpretive modification of defenses and facilita-
tion of ego growth leading to mastery. Similarly the harshness of the
superego was modified and sublimated as Nikita, traumatized, institutionalized, and terrified since early childhood, matured into a
lovely, competent young woman over the course of treatment. As her
ability to understand and reflect upon her own and others' mental
states matured, that is, in developing a "theory of the mind," her experience of the aggressive intentions in both herself and others
evolved (Mayes and Cohen, 1993). She acquired a more differenti-

ated use of aggression in the service of both self-definition and relations with others.

The work was extremely difficult in the beginning. Without details of the history, knowledge of the culture and the practices within a narrow frame of that culture (i.e., orphanages), I was frequently operating in the dark, without an average expectable environment that I might know in this day and age in this country, even with orphaned children. Working, as it were, blinded or without grounding in detailed knowledge of history that is often available in working with children, I was at times more vulnerable to over-identifications with this child, who felt alien, dislocated, and lost. If one can struggle through these difficulties, the rewards can be tremendous, not only for the child and the analyst, but for the family and community as well.

This was not a child who one would anticipate could benefit from defense analysis. Her inner world was chaotic, overwhelmed as she often was by rage, sadness, fear, envy, guilt, and longing for closeness that was always frustrated by the dangers it aroused. Similarly, her self and object representations were at times disorienting and confusing, tinged with images of evil, cruelty, and loathing, reflecting the overwhelming trauma to which she had been subjected from a very early age. Reality testing was compromised by an omnipotent view of herself with the accompanying magical thinking, at one time adaptive in warding off experiences and feelings of helplessness and denigration in the orphanages. Defense interpretations helped to identify the reasons why these internal and external experiences were dangerous. In the context of the new experiences within the transference, these dangers were addressed and elaborated, allowing Nikita to initiate and develop changes in her psychic structures and functioning to accommodate the previously unacceptable experiences (Fonagy, et al., 1993). In addition to defense interpretation, use of the analyst as a developmental object (e.g. in setting limits on the aggression), use of play allowing a safe place to work on ideas and fantasy, and the labeling of affects, often in the context of understanding defenses, were all vital to the therapeutic action. I hope to raise questions in readers' minds about accessibility for analytic treatment and awareness of potential advantages in not relying on symptomatology alone in considering psychoanalytic treatment for both children and adults.

HISTORY AND EVALUATION

Born in Russia, where she lived until age seven and a half, Niki's early history was marked by severe deprivation, traumatic separations, physical illnesses, and physical and sexual abuse. She was the fifth child born to her mother, who was serving a prison sentence for stealing at the time of Niki's birth. Reportedly, the pregnancy and delivery were normal; her birth weight was 6 pounds, 10 ounces. She was likely breastfed, as she had been allowed to remain with her mother in prison. At 17 months, she was taken from her mother (who never attempted contact thereafter) and placed in a large, regional orphanage. All of her siblings (ages 16 through 20, at the time of Niki's adoption at age seven and a half) were also raised in orphanages, although presumably not in the same facility. Incomplete medical records indicate that Niki suffered numerous illnesses, including pneumonia, cardiopathy, anemia, and rickets between birth and 17 months, and recurring ear infections throughout childhood. Identified as having "delayed psycho-speech development," she was transferred to a smaller orphanage at four and a half and, at age six, was treated for the speech problems in a neurology clinic for two months. Her "gang upbringing" (Downey 2005) by multiple, interchangeable caretakers included unsupervised struggles with fellow orphans, at least one of whom pushed her from a ladder as she was climbing to take food from a pantry in the orphanage. This fall resulted in several facial cuts requiring sutures.

There were documented reports of several attempted local adoptions in the three years in the smaller orphanage where she was placed at age four and a half. All of these attempts were shortly terminated. Her first adoptive mother returned her to the orphanage presumably due to Nikita's tantrums and out of control behaviors. Another attempted adoption ended when Nikita herself requested she be returned to her orphanage home. It came out in the course of the analysis that the adoptive mother's boyfriend had raped her during her short stay in this new home. Her American parents, with their own rescue fantasies, adopted her at age seven and a half. Within a few days of meeting her, they brought her to their home in the U.S.

Niki's adoptive parents, both in their mid-fifties, decided to adopt a child who would be about the age of a "child" the mother had miscarried (one of several miscarriages early on in pregnancy) in her attempts to conceive a child assisted by fertility treatments. Although married for 18 years, the couple had never tried to have children until the mother was 45 years old. Both parents were highly educated and in academic-related professions, but were naïve about the difficulties they were taking on in adopting a child with Niki's history.

The adjustment to her new home and family was extremely difficult. Niki spoke no English, and her departure from everyone she knew and depended on took place over a few days with the sole assistance of a translator. Her parents, overwhelmed at times by Niki's tantrums and impulsivity (e.g., she ran into the street from the playground when upset at school), sought help through educational and medical avenues. Since age nine, she has attended two schools for learning disabled children and has gone on to matriculate at a competitive public high school.

Diagnosed with Attention Deficit Disorder, she began taking Ritalin at age nine, a year prior to seeing me. The medication helped her with her tantrums, oppositional behavior, and difficulties concentrating. Psychological testing at age ten showed a possible inability (at times) to distinguish reality from fantasy. Although her thinking was "disrupted by breakthroughs of unmetabolized, intense feelings related to rage and worries about starvation, abandonment, and death," she quickly suppressed such thoughts, often dealing with them through denial. There was no evidence of psychotic thinking on structured or unstructured tests. Her IQ scores reflected a 20-point increase in the Performance IQ (to 93), but not the Verbal IQ (70), from age 8 to age 10. Although her Full Scale IQ (78) was "technically" in the borderline range of mental functioning, it was concluded that her current intellectual functioning was "depressed due to a combination of poor early education [she had no formal education in Russia], severe learning disabilities affecting her verbal and written language skills, and emotional factors relating to early trauma and institutionalization."

I noted that in contrast to her IQ scores and presumed learning disabilities, Niki learned to speak English in four months and, in other ways, showed a very bright and capable mind. Her teachers were also impressed with her ability to form meaningful attachments, her adaptability to new situations and her resilience, despite the many frustrations and failures she encountered. She was referred to me for intensive treatment at ten and a half years to help with issues of low self-esteem, poor academic achievement, and the many symptoms previously noted. A prior attempt at psychotherapy with a male therapist/analyst resulted in her refusal to go to sessions. After our first meeting, Niki's motivation for treatment and hopefulness were captured in her exclamation to her father, "Have I found the therapist for me!" In the initial two consultation sessions, I was somewhat surprised (given the history) to meet a lively, vibrant, engaging, related little girl who used play for symbolic communication of important themes with the continuity of these themes demonstrated over several days.

Specifically, in play and with words, Niki acted out a drama, using the bears, tigers, lions, and other animals, that viciously fought with each other. When I inquired what they might be fighting about, she told me they wanted the rabbit (a furry puppet) and were fighting to see who would get the rabbit, both to eat and keep warm. Using the toy blood pressure cuff, she measured to see if the rabbit was "fat" enough to eat. She removed herself from the fray to care for the baby doll, which she nurtured with tissue-blankets as she told me, "I don't fight with the other children (verbal slip)—animals." I said, "You take care of the baby instead." Since she seemed so eager and able to communicate with me, I added, "Perhaps you care for the baby in a way that you would like to be cared for." (I was hesitant to make this interpretation, since these were consultation sessions, but she seemed eager and I was curious about how she might respond. In retrospect, I may have also been "taking care" of her by helping her to understand, i.e., responding to my maternal countertransference to her desire to be taken care of. That she so easily conveyed to me her wish to be taken care of also demonstrated an aspect of her engaging personality.) She listened to my words and seemed to be actively taking them in. Elaborating, she explained that she knew something the others didn't know, "The baby will get the rabbit fur and stay warm, and all their fighting will be useless." In the second session, several days later, she took up where she left off, repeating many of the same themes. This time, however, the animal/children were not fighting, but rather lined up in squares of territory on my couch. At the end of the session, just before leaving my office, she explained, "In the end, the baby dies and no one gets supper for a month!" I thought the timing of her comment just as she was leaving my office showed "healthy" (albeit action-oriented), appropriate defenses; specifically, she distanced herself from the emotional intensity of her statement by taking the action of physically leaving my presence. Although the material certainly seemed raw or unguarded and even "primitive," I thought it might also reflect her experiences and wondered if, in fact, there had been infants who had died in the orphanages. Her comment as she was leaving my office may also have reflected feelings she had about separating from me, since "hungry" feelings and thoughts of death were frequently associated with separations; and the traumatic separation from her mother when she was "the baby" was likely experienced as a death.

Nikita impressed me as a child suffering from a "severe psychoneurosis," characterized by Phyllis Greenacre (1967) as an illness seen in patients who are generally, and mistakenly in her view, diagnosed as "borderline cases" (p. 113). In these cases of severe psychoneuroses, traumas exert intense undermining influences in the years of pre-genital development. Such trauma, particularly if it disturbs the mother-infant relationship in the first twelve to eighteen months of life, "interferes then with the very foundations of object relationship, increases and prolongs primary narcissism, and tends to damage the early ego in its very incipiency with special harm to the sense of reality and often to the beginning sense of identity, based as it is in the growing awareness of the body" (p. 138). Furthermore, such trauma, impacting the immature developing sense of reality, "promotes a greater than ordinary confusion of actual experience with fantasy and enhances ideas of omnipotence and magic" (p. 141).

Unlike Downey's case, "Little Orphan Anastasia" (2000), and the children in American orphanages studied by Provence and Lipton (1962) in the early 1950s, Nikita spent her first 17 months of life with her mother in prison. This paradoxically fortunate circumstance provided her with enough psychological and developmental equipment to survive the traumatic loss of her mother and the subsequent traumas to which she was subjected in the orphanages, experienced by her through the formative lens of this original loss (Greenacre 1967). Just as Spitz reported in his studies on "Hospitalism" (1945, 1946), the intensity of this mother-infant relationship, enforced by confinement to a prison cell, seemed to compensate for the destructive aspects of institutional care for baby Nikita in her first 17 months of life. The various medical illnesses she suffered were indicative of the sub-optimal living conditions of a cold, dark, damp prison cell. The profound impact of this early mother-infant relationship, both positive and negative, was not clear to me until much later in the analysis.

Complicating the diagnostic picture was the impact of the experiences of the orphanages, previous failed adoptions, and Nikita's status and self-image as a "late" adoptee and immigrant in her new home. In her short life there had been multiple experiences of humiliation, denigration, emotional and physical deprivations, rejection, dislocation, victimization, as well as having been "specially chosen," all contributing to overwhelming affects and narcissistic vulnerabilities[1] Her character reflected these vulnerabilities, and narcissistic concerns complicated her learning difficulties.

1. For detailed discussion of narcissistic vulnerabilities in adopted children and other problems associated with adoption, or effects of "late" adoptee status see also: Brinich (1980); Cohen (1996); Frankel (1991); Schechter (1960); Sherick (1983); Wieder (1977a, 1977b).

Some of the problems resulting from her life experiences and their psychological manifestations were illustrated in a session from a week at the end of the sixth month of the psychotherapy/extended evaluation period. In the third and final session prior to my two week vacation, Nikita, absorbed in her drawing told me about her friend, "Earle," whom she had jokingly teased about his hair: though it seemed "like a wig, it was real." She then told me that "Susie" (later explaining that Susie had also been adopted from Russia) would lie and steal if she came to my office. I said she seemed to think I was lucky to have Niki with me and not Susie. She agreed, adding that she also used to lie and steal, but no longer did that. I noted that something had changed. She said, "It's not right, so I don't do that." She commented that she didn't like the eyes of the figure she was drawing because they were "nasty, angry." She added that sometimes she wanted to steal and maybe she would take something and later put it back, because it's wrong to steal and she doesn't do that. She continued, "Susie says mean things. She teases me and says I went to 1000 orphanages. I did not. I went to one and got scared because there were ghosts in the bathroom and my mother came and took me to another one and I stayed there. Susie didn't go to different orphanages." Not commenting on the various aspects of reality and fantasy that seemed confused and confusing, while also narcissistically protective, I said, "Susie hurt your feelings with what she said." She agreed.

I continued, "There are different kinds of teasing, some mild and joking, which seem okay and some, mean and hurtful, which are not okay." I said that ideas of right and wrong, lying and stealing, and angry hurt feelings were also coming up as we approached a break in our meetings and would not see each other for two weeks. Defensively, she complained of feeling tired and withdrew briefly. I noted to her that thoughts of the separation seemed to interfere with her work. She quietly resumed her drawing until the end of the session. As she left she said, "I hate ending." I asked, "Especially when we won't meet for awhile?" "No," she replied, "I always hate ending." In this comparison with Susie, as Niki related it to me, I silently agreed that Niki was making the better adjustment.

From the beginning I was impressed by Niki's responsiveness to defense interpretations, elaborating and expanding themes through the use of play, drawings, and words. She explored ideas about adoption, death, growing old, loss, disappointment, and anger with parents, wanting to do well at school without making an effort, conflicts with peers whom she cared for by being "the cop" and, later, "the psy-

chiatrist," and so on. She exhibited anxiety in relation to these conflicts, which she tried to manage with defenses of denial and turning
passive into active, useful also in serving her strong need to be the
one "in control." The conflicts and defenses that I observed in working with her were consistent with the diagnosis of traumatic neurosis.
She demonstrated good ego strength in relating some past memories, and an ability to modulate what she could affectively tolerate in
sessions (e.g., talking with her parents about her nightmares, but not
with me). She demonstrated the creative use of fantasy to compensate for and master trauma. Also during the year-long course of psychotherapy, Niki made considerable gains in her academic performance (e.g., reading at a second grade level at the end of fifth grade
versus an inability to read), and put up less resistance to demands
that she make an effort.

Following an initial resistance to moving from twice weekly to
three times weekly sessions, Niki quickly settled in, announcing, "I
like what we do here." In addition to a sense of interruption in our
work at the three times a week frequency, I thought the continuity
and intensity of a four sessions a week schedule would allow the further elucidation and interpretive exploration of defenses and transference themes. I knew from the outset that psychoanalysis was the
treatment of choice for optimal working through of a traumatic neurosis. Given the uncertainty that Niki's symptoms might represent
deficits in ego functioning and a liability to serious regressions that
could not be worked with analytically, a trial of psychotherapy as an
extended evaluation seemed appropriate. Niki introduced the idea
of more frequent sessions before I did when she announced one day,
"This is my office, too," and later explained that, in her work as the
"psychiatrist" to her friends, she saw them "everyday." As she entered
the sixth grade at age eleven and a half, she also began her analysis.

THE ANALYSIS

Niki showed little resistance to the change to four sessions per week
except for an intensification of the frequency with which she engaged in action as a mode of expression.[2] In addition to themes of

2. For children whose constitutional vulnerabilities interact with developmental
factors, such as early parental loss, Fonagy and Target (1998) note an increased impairment in impulse control and self-regulation as their attachment to the analyst becomes more intense. They cite research linking this temporary impairment of mentalization "to the activation of traumatic responses triggered by closeness to or
separation from attachment figures" (p. 106).

angry, biting, controlling feelings (e.g., wanting to tie me down so, as I said to her, she might restrict my movements after the summer absence), she was also motivated to "show" me the changes occurring in her body. She twirled around so that her over-sized T-shirt lifted enough to expose the bra she was wearing. She talked about her period, wearing tampons and fears of growing up. There were subtle references in these communications to early sexual abuse, but since it had not come up directly in the treatment, I did not attempt interpretation at this time.

AGGRESSION IN THE ANALYSIS

Niki's predominant defense was turning passive into active, a defense typical of trauma. She acted this out with me, commanding me to be the "slave" to her master, to be the "student" to her teacher, to be the "victim" (with lice) to her perpetrator (having given the lice to me). To illustrate aspects of our early analytic work I have included several vignettes.

In a poignant sequence played out over several sessions early in the first analytic year, she commanded me to do some drawings and then graded me on my work. I said, "You do to me what your teacher does to you." She told me that I had to work very hard to go up to another level in fashion design school, and that there were 12 to 20 levels, each one harder than the next, and that she was going to push me. When I inquired what my motivation might be to work so hard only to have to work harder, she said I would do it to graduate. If I didn't, I would be a dummy and I didn't want that. Furthermore, if I did all the work, I would go to heaven and die. If I didn't do the work, I would go to hell and be killed. I interpreted, "It seems I just can't win—if I succeed or fail, either way, I will die." She thought about being between her parents in bed, when her mother read her a story. (I understood this to be another conflict about what growing up and being competent meant to her. I did not relate it to her since she was primarily engaged in telling me something else and I thought she might hear such an interpretation as a criticism and would be unable to work with it at this time.) She then remembered her terrible fear of coming to the United States on the plane and not being able to speak English (perhaps fear of another "death"/loss that might come with better circumstances). Narcissistic issues involved in the learning difficulties were also evident on occasions when she brought in her spelling work and I had the opportunity to interpret her wishes to be perfect, and to be special and different from the other students in not having to practice her work very often to achieve perfection.

A recurring theme developed related to separations (due to vacations, interruptions to the schedule, and weekends) in which physical hunger and emotional hunger (missing feelings) seemed intertwined and she acted out erotized sadomasochistic struggles with me. I interpreted that her feelings of missing me and wishes to be close to me got all mixed up with the hungry, growling, scratching, kicking, poking, biting, and hugging feelings, all of which she tried to inflict on my body (too often, successfully). Further, when I didn't hug her as she requested, she felt rejected and angry with me and wanted to retaliate. The work could be difficult and trying, especially while undergoing physical assaults on my body and office that did not stop with interpretation.

Before words and play are available as alternatives to the action it may not be desirable to forbid the assaults in the interest of elaborating and understanding the underlying conflicts. In these situations it is a difficult task to know when to institute and how to set limits. I worried if I stopped the assaults while she still seemed unable to verbalize the thoughts and feelings, I might inadvertently restrict further exploration by shutting down her only means of communication. On the other hand, by not firmly setting limits on the aggression directed against my body and office, I risked overstimulating her by gratifying the impulses already heightened by abuse. Such intense stimulation might overwhelm her, leading to her refusing to talk to me. I was usually successful, at least, in containing the attacks before there was physical injury to either of us. These physical assaults provided opportunities to label feelings in the context of defense interpretations. For example, I might say, "You want to push me away with the angry kicking feelings at the same time you want me to get closer to you by touching you to protect both of us (as she kicked my hands, extended to guard my body)." There were also opportunities to address the inhibition of her empathy for me as I interpreted, "You don't want to think about how I feel getting hit in the eye with a ball of paper." Often these struggles included eruptions of aggression that delayed leaving at the end of the session. I interpreted, "You want more time with me, maybe to make up for the missing feelings and not seeing me for several days." When her difficulty leaving seemed more connected with wanting to control me, I said, "Your difficulty leaving is a way of being in control of when things end here."

Further insight into the dynamics related to her regressive, sado-masochistic struggles connected with separations became apparent in the transference seven months into the analysis in a session (in a week following a separation from her mother) in which she told me, as she ordered me around like her "slave," that I was like her boyfriend. Later, as she (somewhat affectionately) spit down on me while exhibiting her body in a seductive pose across my desk, she remembered the first time she had "French kissed" her boyfriend. "We didn't like it so we spit it out. We went, 'Yuk!' and spit it out." She then wanted to telephone her boyfriend. I interpreted, "Maybe you want to call him at a time when you are feeling so close to me and might feel more comfortable having him between us." She asked, "Are you saying I'm gay?" Putting her face down on the desk, hiding her face with her hair, she told me, "I'm not gay!" I said that perhaps it was confusing when feelings came up toward me that she had toward her boyfriend and that, as she knew, sometimes she had feelings toward me like with her father, and sometimes like with her mother and others—that the feelings change and perhaps that's confusing. She became curious as to whether or not I was married, inspecting my fingers for rings, and then said she thought that I shared my body with my husband. She wrote out the phone number of her boyfriend and several other numbers of potential boyfriends, including the current boyfriend of one of her girlfriends (about whom I said perhaps there were jealous feelings as well). At the end of the session she insisted on taking the phone numbers with her as she left my office. I said, "You don't trust me with your boyfriend's phone number." The separations, which brought up tremendous hunger and longing for lost love objects, were closely connected with sexual curiosity and feelings, as illustrated here.

Her worries about being "gay" reflected the strong pull toward a nurturing woman, which would get confused for her with sexual feelings and wishes to be close to a man. For example, in the session described above in which Niki remembered, as she spit down on me, the first time she "French kissed" her boyfriend, this memory was also associated in a several months previous session with the memory of the first time she had kissed her adoptive mother. In this earlier session, she came into my office and complained, "It stinks in here." And then, "Your breath smells like my father's." Later she told me about her boyfriend, whom she liked to tease by calling him "Juanita," a feminine variation of his name. She further noted he had a "rat's tail" (pony tail) which she "just hated." Mischievously, she said she had been French kissing him. When I said it wasn't clear what she meant by "French kissing" and she insisted that "you know," I said, "I may have an idea about what it means, but I'm not sure my idea is the same as your idea." She said, "Well, we touched each other's tongues, but it was yucky and we both spit afterwards." Pausing, she added, "When I first came from Russia, my mother kissed me and I didn't know how to kiss, so I stuck my tongue in her mouth and my mother went, 'Oh, yuk!' and spit and said, 'Oh, Niki! Don't do that!'" I repeated her words, "You didn't know how to kiss," adding (mistakenly), "You hadn't kissed before." She said, "No," but seemed embarrassed, and busied herself finishing her paper doll in a defensive retreat, as though memories of the sexual abuse were just below the working surface. I said she seemed to get so busy with her work that she had stopped talking about her boyfriend. She agreed and finished her cut-out, saying, "You can tell the boy dolls from the girl dolls because the girls have longer tails." I learned to be more careful with the way that I phrased my comments to her, keeping in mind that some of the traumas she suffered were as yet unknown to us in our work together.

As a result of her traumatic experiences, castration themes were prominent. Her worries about losing body parts seemed to intensify through her experiences with other separations and losses of relationships with important caretakers, and sexual abuse further compounded the losses. In drawing her animal paper dolls (e.g., a "panther" woman or a "leopard" woman clad in a red bikini), she would make a "mistake" and draw two tails and then cut one off as she cut out the completed drawing. I said, "If there are two tails, I guess 'they' don't have to worry about losing one." She agreed. Other times she assured me, as she cut off an arm of the (male) "octopus," "It doesn't matter because the tentacles grow back." I said, "Then the octopus doesn't have to worry about being hurt and losing his tentacle since it will grow back." Several months into the analysis, she began to consider drawing "human" figures rather than animal figures. Invariably, she turned the "person" into an animal, fully equipped with a tail. I interpreted her conflict, "I guess one advantage of being an animal rather than a human is that the animals all have tails." She agreed that this was true.

Also, during the first several years of analytic work, Niki exhibited gender confusion and conflict[3] that was particularly clear in her

---

3. Greenacre (1967) notes the likelihood of body image distortions and the pres-

drawings. Her first attempt to draw "a man" early on in the psychotherapy phase of treatment, was of an octopus, with many tentacles that "grabbed and poked." In her "paper doll" creations, I noted to her the absence of male figures. Weeks later, she might attempt to draw a male figure and quickly, through a "mistake," turn it into a female figure. I said, "Something gets in the way of your thinking clearly about a man and being able to draw a male figure." She denied this, saying it was a mistake or that she had decided not to draw a man or "there are only girls here." Eventually (after many months of working interpretively on this problem), she proudly showed me she could draw male figures, "green aliens" who had antennae and others, also with antennae, whose chest muscles closely resembled women's breasts (albeit with six to eight breasts per chest). Toward the end of our third year of work at age thirteen and a half, she was able to draw human male figures that appeared masculine and clearly differentiated from the human women/girl figures. She also moved the "humans" to the front of her notebook that we used to store her prolific collection of paper dolls. I said, "Maybe the humans seem more important than the animals now and you want to give them a special place in the front of your book." She agreed. I think this action signified her growing comfort in her relationships with others, including her relationship with me, and her ability to relinquish some of her reliance on fantasy as a way of coping with conflict and trauma. That she could acknowledge my importance to her by placing the human figures in their prominent position just as we approached the summer vacation was further evidence of her growing tolerance for maintaining loving feelings in the face of more negative feelings aroused by loss and abandonment.

Several weeks following the third year's summer break, quiet and somewhat withdrawn, Niki had been making collages of cutouts from old *New Yorker* magazines she had previously brought in from my waiting room to keep in the cabinet designated for her things. Eventually she told me she was making these collages for her art teacher. I said, "You want to take supplies from my office to share with someone, as though you feel uncomfortable having the time with me all to yourself." She said it was good to share, and resumed her quiet cutting of a magazine cover that showed the opposing heads of two elegant women, one haughty and scowling, the other serene and content. As

---

ence of perversions in patients who have suffered severe pregenital trauma. Cohen (1996) also found the trauma of abandonment and adoption impacted the development of gender and sexuality in her latency-age, adopted, psychoanalytic patient.

she pasted the cutout onto her paper and began coloring the background behind the serene head in bright yellow, she told me her art teacher's father had died and that her teacher was sick. I said, "You feel bad about what has happened to your teacher and want to help her feel better by taking her something of the work that you do with me." She agreed and began to draw orange lightning-bolts on the background behind the scowling head and then colored the background in red. She labeled the yellow side "happy" and the red side "anger," asking, "See, doesn't she look angry?" I said she did look angry, especially with all that red and the lightning-bolts around her, adding, "You didn't say why she's so angry." She said she didn't know why. I said, "Maybe she's so angry because she lost a parent. Sometimes people can feel pretty angry about that." She said she didn't know why, but added, "Maybe it's because she was raised in hell." I wondered what it meant to be raised in hell. She said, "Maybe she wanted to kill someone." I said, "Maybe she feels bad about the killing feelings and so feels like she should be punished by being in hell. But maybe she wouldn't feel as bad about her own feelings if she understood more about why she felt that way. For example, she may have been hurt herself and mistreated, and reacted to that by being very angry. And also, losing a parent can bring up very upsetting feelings." She seemed pleased, and took the collage with her as she was leaving at the end of the session (prior to a weekend). I said, "Since we didn't see each other for many weeks this summer, perhaps you also want some supplies from my office to help you with feelings of missing me." She smiled and left.

Sleeping as a Compromise Formation

Nikita now age seventeen, has not taken Ritalin for five years since the end of the first year of the analysis and even without the Ritalin was able to maintain her honor roll status at her school for learning disabled children. The tantrums and oppositional behavior the Ritalin helped to contain had been both symptomatic of her rage and anxiety and a defensive adaptation against the passivity of past traumas. The ADD was misdiagnosed. She has been attending a competitive high school for several years, maintaining a B average with occasional A's, and has plans to attend college. While aspects of the learning disabilities have persisted, she has gained many tools, including hard work, to compensate and achieve academic successes. Analytic work with her was no longer so difficult, as we were both reaping the rewards of all of the work done previously.

A major defensive shift occurred in the analysis from an acting out of aggression toward my body and my office to a more withdrawn (though engaged) stance including much sleeping in the sessions as both a resistance to and evidence of her comfort with me. (As she said, "You don't make demands on me and I can rest here.") The sleeping also represented a regression to wishes/memories of being with her biological mother and a recreation of that "blissful" state in the transference. This defensive shift occurred some months following the discontinuation of Ritalin toward the end of the first year of analysis and coincided with onset of puberty around age twelve and a half. Her sleeping served to control her aggression toward me in the transference and toward her adoptive mother who was extremely demanding of her, especially with regard to academics. Angry verbal attacks on me as she came and went from the consulting room often marked off the ensuing sleep of the session.[4] Niki also inhibited (while gratifying) sexual impulses with sleep. I learned this when she responded to my comment that she left out dreams in what we talked about. She said, "I don't have nightmares anymore. Now I dream about sex and I don't want to give that up; I like it." Her parents also reported ongoing play with Barbie and Ken dolls at night that could be so compulsive that it interfered with her getting a full night's sleep. This play seemed to be a masturbatory equivalent and may have included masturbation, unbeknownst to her parents and unspoken to me. In the beginning of the fourth year of analysis (age fifteen and a half) she frantically called her mother and, though embarrassed, pleaded with her mother to remove the dolls from under her pillow so the new cleaning people coming later that day would not find them. She has at times stayed up much of the night talking on the telephone with one of her many boyfriends. Sexuality was another area of conflict with her adoptive mother, although they seemed to be negotiating this with less struggle as her mother had allowed her to begin to date on turning sixteen.

INDEPENDENCE AND LOSS IN GROWING UP

For several years Niki had looked forward to her sixteenth birthday. Turning sixteen held promise of gaining her mother's approval to

---

4. Like 38-month-old Sophie, reported by Mayes and Cohen (1993) p. 160, Nikita's verbal attacks were often "provoked" by eye contact with me as she entered and left the consulting room. She projected onto me the aggressive intent of looking, as though the very act of visual contact would hold us too dangerously close.

date boys and to begin learning to drive, another mark of growth and independence. This reflected much analytic work that allowed her to be comfortable with and excited about growing up. Nikita's ability to mourn the multiple losses of her childhood and move on in life through adolescence with her parents at her side showed the tremendous gains she had made thus far.

She also connected the idea of independence from her parents with her independence from me and "set a date" (which she ultimately revised) for termination, several months later in the summer. She would have completed tenth grade and have reached her sixteenth birthday. To mark the specialness of this birthday, her parents agreed to Niki's going on a class ski trip despite their regrets that she would, for the first time, be away from them for her birthday celebration. The trip ended badly as Niki fell while snowboarding and broke her wrist. She also felt disappointed that her classmates seemed "uninterested" in her birthday celebration. I have wondered, though Niki denied it, if the fall represented continuing conflict about her many successes and growing up, the injury resulting from turning the aggression against the self. She did not wear her wrist guards due to some "confusion" and in this way at least, she had set herself up for injury.

For Nikita, deeply ingrained conflicts about success, having something of value, and being in an enviable position had inhibited her from using her good mind to learn and had interfered with making use of the nurturing relationships her parents offered. These inhibitions also contributed to fears about growing up into a lovely, physically developed, and competent young woman, while others less fortunate were left behind. Defense interpretations about these fears were essential in strengthening ego capabilities allowing for mastery and growth through developmental thrust.

The wrist injury at age sixteen reminded me of another injury to her wrist at age thirteen and a half following a longer than usual summer break of six weeks and her move to a new and academically better school in September to start eighth grade. Niki, feeling guilty and anxious about outpacing her friends academically and faced with new potential opportunities, cut her wrist multiple times in a superficial, yet dramatic fashion. At first I was concerned that this severe regression might portend further regressions that could lead to a psychotic depression. As we came to understand the conflicts leading to this self-destructive action, I was heartened by her strength and resilience when it became clear that the self-mutilation represented an identification with a severely troubled friend, and a defensive regression from the enviable position Niki had advanced to. I responded, "You feel bad that 'Kate' has such trouble in her life and that she doesn't take care of herself and puts herself in harm's way. It's hard to see yourself as having more and doing better than your friend. So you cut yourself, the way Kate has done in the past, so you can be like her and then don't feel so bad about getting ahead." Crying, she said, "Kate just doesn't care about herself and her parents don't take care of her, they think she's okay, but she's not." I said, "And maybe you feel angry, too, that your parents expect a lot of you and you want to punish them for that by hurting yourself and to let them know you want to be taken care of." Still crying, she agreed, "Yes, my mother just doesn't listen to me. All she cares about is work, work, work. I want to do well, but it's too much." I added, "And you're angry with yourself that you too are putting demands on yourself to do well in school just as your mother puts demands on you. And angry with me that I wasn't here this summer at a time you were preparing to go to a new school and I wasn't available to help with all the feelings that came up about that. But you also want to protect me and your parents from all those angry, sad feelings by turning the feelings against yourself in such a self-destructive way." She talked more calmly, but still in a torrent, about the difficulty of adjusting to the new school, feeling lost without her old friends, and the increasing academic as well as social demands. This difficult period took several months of analysis to understand and work through, but there were no further incidents of self-mutilation.

Later that same fall Niki and her parents also moved to a new and larger house, leaving behind their familiar neighborhood as well. Struggles with her mother over demands for academic achievement escalated to several incidents in which Niki physically lashed out and hit her mother. Filled with regret, remorse, guilt, and fears of abandonment, she revealed first to her mother, her father, and later to me, the rape at age five by her then adoptive mother's boyfriend. She told of his repeatedly hitting her, raping her, and of his jealousy and envy of her closeness to the "mother." She requested to return to the orphanage, several days following the rape, leaving her potential new home and family behind. The mounting internal pressure she experienced in the current context of multiple losses sustained while moving on to better circumstances and the raging battles with her mother also connected with achievement, seemed to contribute to these memories of past loss and abuse coming to the surface. Her physical attacks on her mother were, in part, an identification with the aggressor/rapist. Working through the emotional storms took much effort and many months. I was able to interpret to Niki, as the material came up in the sessions, that the pressure of the emerging memories of the rape and loss of the adoptive mother, with all the accompanying rage, sadness and feelings of guilt, had contributed to her self-destructive wrist cutting.

Growing mastery of conflicts around envy and competition was evident in year five of the analysis as Nikita told me a story of a friend she'd known for many years who was able to expertly and efficiently draw animated people figures. Nikita felt sad that her friend devalued her talent, saying it was "no big deal" and "they're just drawings." Nevertheless, Niki vowed to work all day on Saturday (notably in my absence) to perfect her technique because, in contrast, she *could* value her friend's talent. Furthermore, she was envious of it and felt competitive with her. Continuing in the displacement and not commenting on the clear transference implications, I said, "If you practice animation drawing, you can achieve something of value and improve your talent that you are having some trouble with. It seems useful to put yourself in competition with your friend to help motivate you to work hard." She agreed, excitedly anticipating not only the outcome, but also the hard work itself that she now so proudly enjoyed. No longer drawing her animal creatures of the early years of the analysis, her focus shifted to drawing animated people in keeping with Japanese animation films like *Sailor Moon*. It was the nuances of emotions, in particular, that she meticulously and proudly captured in her drawings, reflecting both her identification with her analyst and her competition with her in "labeling" emotions.

Niki has more directly voiced transference feelings of competition and envy in her criticisms of my "fashion sense" and of my office décor, particularly since moving to my home office mid-year five of the analysis. Notably, the barbs were launched as she entered or left sessions, for example greeting me with, "Eeew, those shoes don't go with that dress at all. What were you thinking?!" I have remarked: that it seems she wants to push me away just as she is coming into the office, perhaps to distract both of us from missing feelings since we last met; or that she likes to see herself as the only one of the two of us who knows about fashion, so that I might feel envious of her abilities and feel inadequate about my own, as perhaps she has felt about me at times; or that she has an idea there is only one way to put clothes together and if I don't do things her way, I must be wrong. Her tolerance for our differences grew, as she increasingly valued her own talents and saw me in a less idealized light (which I inferred from her less frequent need to devalue me). She even occasionally paid me a compliment or in a friendlier, more helpful way "taught" me about fashion.

Talk of termination disappeared as we approached the summer date when she had initially insisted on ending and Niki seemed motivated to understand more about her relationships with her peers and to successfully negotiate adolescence. She was also more comfortable talking directly about her memories of the abuses she suffered in Russia, though many of the memories were also now successfully repressed. Occasionally there were references to pleasant memories of life in Russia as well. Sleep was no longer needed as a defense and she was actively working to understand what interfered with her progression toward maturity and independence, including independence from her analyst.

Instead of ending the analysis Niki forged a compromise by attending a camp that required a prolonged summer break from the analysis and from her parents. Proud of her successful camp experience, on her return she shared with me news about a boyfriend she had met there. This was the first boyfriend who was kind, generous, attentive and affectionate toward her without being abusive, abandoning, cold, passive or submissive. As she told me, "He's like you. I can say anything to him and he doesn't get mad." I said, "Maybe spending time with him over the summer break also made it easier to be away from me."

Conflicts over bisexual feelings continue to make relationships with girlfriends difficult as these feelings contribute to her feeling alien and also threaten a longing for closeness she fears will overwhelm her. As she grows more confident in her ability to modulate the feelings aroused by separations and closeness, relationships with girls and boys are becoming more mutual and supportive.

CONCLUSION

Many questions might arise from this material including questions about resilience, analyzability, capacities for developmental growth, and therapeutic change. I have addressed questions about diagnosis and analyzability of Nikita's severe character pathology and symptoms of impulsivity, poor self-esteem, and problems with affect regulation as an example of a severe psychoneurosis. Her emotional/psychological difficulties were precipitated by the pre-oedipal trauma of losing her mother at seventeen months, and the subsequent exposure to various physical and emotional abuses compounding the early trauma. Diagnostically, Niki also fit the group of children described by Fonagy and Target (1998) for whom intensive psychoanalytic treatment was "remarkably effective" (p. 89). These children "show intense, even dramatic, affect and hunger for social response. Clinginess, hyperactivity, and temper tantrums are common features of their early development" (p. 91). They suffer from severe, long-standing and complex psychosocial problems (e.g. Niki was diagnosed with ADD at age nine) with the presence of at least one emotional disorder (for Niki, anxiety disorder). Analyzability was directly related to the child's capacity for mentalization, a reflective function and "developmental acquisition that permits children to respond not only to another person's behavior, but to the child's conception of others' attitudes, intentions, or plans" (p. 92).

Nikita's capacity for mentalization or self-reflection was evident in our initial consultation sessions as she told the story, using play and words, of her difficult life experiences and internal conflicts. Her resilience in surviving the multiple traumas of her life and her capacity for developmental growth and therapeutic change were due, in large part, to her early successful attachment to her mother. This early mother-infant relationship endowed her with the requisite foundation to acquire and develop a reflective function, a protective synthetic ego function. The traumatic disruptions at seventeen months and thereafter led to internal conflict inhibiting her ability to integrate perceptions of reality and fantasy. As a result of the trauma and internal conflict, she was intermittently unable to access her mentalizing capacity, and therefore unable to make use of an awareness of her own and others' thoughts and feelings.

Furthermore, the aggression of the eighteen-month old infant serves the development of individuation and "the very separateness fostered and facilitated by the child's early aggressivity allows the child the capacity to be close without losing his hard won, separate sense of self" (Mayes and Cohen 1993, p. 148). At the same time, whether the child's moves toward autonomous functioning and mastery come to be experienced intrapsychically by the child as exciting and pleasurable or as aggressive and harmful greatly depends on the parents' experience and reaction. Baby Nikita's hard won autonomy was at the cost of leaving her mother in the cold, dark prison cell. The unconscious guilt over this sense of herself as murderous, the "killing feelings," and conviction of deserving punishment, abandoned and raised in the "hell" of the orphanages, compounded her self-destructive behavior (Modell 1971). It is also possible that speech functions were sacrificed by her to compensate for the unconscious guilt in saving herself by moving toward autonomy (Osman 2000) and complicated the learning difficulties she later struggled so hard to overcome. This early traumatic loss of her mother and the ensuing conflict of guilt for her "successfully" achieving separation became the prototype of her survivor guilt worked through in its many incarnations in the analysis. Her guilt-laden superego also significantly interfered with her capacity to mentalize (Sugarman 2003). Defense interpretations leading to awareness of the guilt as part of her inner world allowed for greater self-reflection without interference from guilty self-recriminations.

Issues that arose in the termination phase will be discussed in another paper, but it is useful for this discussion to briefly describe an interaction early in the termination phase of the six year long analysis. Niki, after several consecutive sessions of having very little to say, complained of feeling "bored" being with me. "I can't wait to get out of here," she said, "it's like being in prison." I responded, "Like a mother and her child, trapped in a prison cell." Shooting me an annoyed, disapproving look, she then laughed, saying, "Sorry, Dr. Novak, it's every girl for herself here and I'm getting out." I said, "Maybe you're worried that I can't manage without you." Pausing to reflect, she answered, "No, you can take care of yourself."

No longer overwhelmed by guilt and anxiety that her autonomous and successful functioning would harm me, reflecting her now established self-object differentiation, it was clear that much therapeutic change had occurred in the course of our work together. That she had a theory of her own mind and of others' (in this case the mind of her analyst), reflecting different beliefs and states of being, was evident in this brief interaction. The early mother-infant relationship was revisited in the termination phase, in part, because her relationship with me, both in the transference and as a real developmental object, paralleled the early reflective capacity learned by observing her mother's mind. Her exquisite sensitivity and attention to my facial expressions throughout the analysis was reminiscent of the locked gaze of a cooing, mother-infant pair. The labeling of feelings and the attempts to contain the physical expression of her overwhelming libidinal and aggressive drives in the context of the sadomasochistic struggles served not only to reflect her internal state, but also to re-present it as a manageable image, something both bearable and understandable. Defense interpretations of resistances allowed integration of repressed ideational content by the now accepting ego, facilitating psychic reorganization. Much of the cognitive awareness of her insight was repressed again in the process of psychic reorganization, but the new emotional freedom was maintained (Moore and Fine 1990, p. 99). The expanded awareness of her thoughts, feelings, and motivations, as well as those of others, removed obstacles to her developmental capacity to mourn.

In ending I would like to comment on theoretical frames for understanding therapeutic change in analytic treatment. In his article, "Little Orphan Anastasia, Part Two: Developmental Growth, Love, and Therapeutic Change" (2002), Downey outlines two major frames for analytic treatment. In the first, the interpretive dyadic frame, therapeutic change ensues by making use of interpretation to remove neurotic and traumatic arrest of development in the context of a new object relation. In the second frame, the less object-specific maturational frame of developmental growth, it is sufficient for the analyst to "sit Shiva" over the suffering, loss, and rage for the person to reactivate processes of mourning necessary for a developmental recovery. Borrowing from the Jewish custom of mourning, the analyst metaphorically "sits Shiva" as the child engages in activities allowing the mourning of past losses to proceed. In his article, "Early Object Relations into New Objects" (2001), Downey goes on to say "by and large, the structure and functions of the ego that have been impeded in their exercise by traumatic circumstances in the environment are reactivated by a generalized holding environment, rather than a relationship. In the practice of psychoanalysis, this means that the child analyst may be more relaxed about the nonverbal play and relational aspects of the work; he need not fear that dynamics not captured in secondary process are lost to change" (p. 62). Others (Cohen and Solnit 1993; Scott 1998) agree that play, in the context of an understanding relationship with a child psychoanalyst, need not be interpreted to promote development.

These ideas have helped me to feel much more relaxed about the many hours spent by Nikita with her creations of over 100 anthropomorphized animal/creatures meticulously drawn, colored, cut out, and preserved in a notebook in my office. Countertransference feelings of helplessness increasingly gave way to an understanding of how essential these activities were to her ultimate recovery. Sometimes there were clearly associated transference fantasies connected with these creations that I interpreted as we worked together. Oftentimes, the creations were Nikita's alone as I "sat Shiva," in a sense, silently offering witness to her vital activities. These animal figures were extremely important to her as she transformed her sense of self from that of a wild animal to a competent, accomplished, adolescent.

Environment, in this case the involvement of loving, relatively consistent parents, played an essential role in providing a nurturing opportunity from which Nikita could fashion new objects for internalization leading to growth and developmental change. The rescue fantasies of her adoptive mother seemed to contribute to her ultimate recovery, while also threatening loss. For Nikita, her mother's unrelenting demands that she perform with competence in academic endeavors led to her internalization of these expectations so that they were now her own. Wishes to please her mother, fear of loss of love and loss of the maternal object, as well as identifications with both parents helped to motivate Nikita to these achievements against great odds. The adoptive mother's unconscious fantasies leading to rescue, while also threatening abandonment if expectations went unmet, matched well with her adoptive child's nascent potential and resilience. Her father offered steadfast support of the analysis and also alternative approaches to her mother's academic demands, helping Niki to relax in the face of these demands and to better negotiate her relationship with her mother.

This match of expectation and response is also extremely important in the relationship with the analyst. Nikita seemed to possess an ability to select good objects and use them to catalyze her growth, though a sexual assault made it difficult for her to put her trust in a male therapist. She had refused to attend sessions with the male psychiatrist evaluating her prior to her referral to me. In contrast, she reacted with hopeful anticipation of therapeutic help following her first session with me. Her initial trust of me allowing us to begin the work reflected her relatively secure early mother-infant attachment. Mourning the loss of her mother, and the humiliations, losses and abuses of her early life, enabled Niki to secure her attachment to her adoptive parents with whom she ultimately worked out her loving and hating feelings.[5]

While I agree with Downey's assessment of the two major frames of analytic treatment, the interpretive dyadic and the maturational frame of developmental growth, I think we also have to be cautious not to lose sight of the drives and defenses, even as they sometimes threaten to overwhelm us. I have tried to show how ego-oriented interpretive work served an equally important function in Niki's development of greater ego strength and mastery of trauma as she expanded her awareness of her thoughts, feelings and motivations. Niki's presenting history and symptoms made her seem a most un-

---

5. For further discussion of the necessary mourning of the biological parents to secure attachment to the adoptive parents, see: (Brinich 1980; Cohen 1996; Frankel 1991; Sherick 1983).

likely candidate for psychoanalysis. That psychoanalysis became the treatment of choice for her was made possible by a number of things, including: careful initial and on-going diagnostic assessment of her functioning; use of psychological testing while keeping in mind the limitations of that data and not losing sight of her ability to progress intellectually; trial interpretation; containment of aggressive outbursts in order to minimize disruptions in the analytic task of exploration and understanding; thoughtful monitoring of regressions; and careful attention to drives and defenses throughout treatment.

BIBLIOGRAPHY

BRINICH, P. (1980). Some potential effects of adoption on self and object representations. *Psychoanal. Study Child*, 35:107–133.

COHEN, P. M., & SOLNIT, A. (1993). Play and therapeutic action. *Psychoanal. Study Child*, 48:49–63.

COHEN, S. (1996). Trauma and the developmental process. *Psychoanal. Study Child*, 51:287–302.

DOWNEY, T. W. (2000). Little Orphan Anastasia: The opening phase of the analysis of a five-year-old encopretic adopted Russian girl. *Psychoanal. Study Child*, 55:145–179.

DOWNEY, T. W. (2001). Early object relations into new objects. *Psychoanal. Study Child*, 56:39–67.

DOWNEY, T. W. (2002). Little Orphan Anastasia, part two: Developmental growth, love, and therapeutic change. *Psychoanal. Study Child*, 57:218–244.

DOWNEY, T. W. (2005). Little Orphan Anastasia, part 4: Psychoanalysis and the unexpected. Manuscript in preparation.

FONAGY, P., MORAN, G., EDGECUMBE, R., KENNEDY, H., & TARGET, M. (1993). The roles of mental representations and mental processes in therapeutic action. *Psychoanal. Study Child*, 48:9–48.

FONAGY, P., & TARGET, M. (1998). Mentalization and the changing aims of child psychoanalysis. *Psychoanal. Dial.*, 8:87–114.

FRANKEL, S. (1991). Pathogenic factors in the experience of early and late adopted children. *Psychoanal. Study Child*, 46:91–108.

GREENACRE, P. (1967). The influence of infantile trauma on genetic patterns. In S. Furst (ed.), *Psychic Trauma*. New York: Basic Books.

MAYES, L., & COHEN, D. (1993). The social matrix of aggression—enactments and representations of loving and hating in the first years of life. *Psychoanal. Study Child*, 48:145–169.

MODELL, A. (1971). The origin of certain forms of pre-oedipal guilt and the implications for a psychoanalytic theory of affects. *Int. J. Psycho-Anal.*, 52:337–346.

MOORE, B., & FINE, B. (1990). *Psychoanalytic terms and concepts*. New Haven: Yale University Press.

OSMAN, M. (2000). The Adam and Eve story as exemplar of an early-life variant of the oedipus complex. *JAPA*, 48:1295–1325.

PROVENCE, S., & LIPTON, R. (1962). *Infants and institutions*. New York: International Universities Press.

SCHECTER, M. (1960). Observations on adopted children. *Arch. Gen. Psychiat.*, 3:21–32.

SCOTT, M. (1998). Play and therapeutic action: Multiple perspectives. *Psychoanal. Study Child*, 53:94–101.

SHERICK, I. (1983). Adoption and disturbed narcissism: A case illustration of a latency boy. *JAPA*, 31:487–513.

SPITZ, R. (1945). Hospitalism—An inquiry into the genesis of psychiatric conditions in early childhood. *Psychoanal. Study Child*, 1:53–74.

SPITZ, R. (1946). Hospitalism—a follow-up report on investigation described in Volume I, 1945. *Psychoanal. Study Child.* 2:113–117.

SUGARMAN, A. (2003). A new model for conceptualizing insightfulness in the psychoanalysis of young children. *Psychoanal. Q.*, 72:325–355.

WIEDER, H. (1977a). On being told of adoption. *Psychoanal. Q.* 46:1–23.

WIEDER, H. (1977b). The family romance fantasies of adopted children. *Psychoanal. Q.* 46:185–200.

Early Vulnerability in the Development of the Sense of Maleness

Castration Depression in the Phallic-Narcissistic Phase

SILVIA M. BELL, PH.D.

This paper considers Brenner's (1975, 1979, 1982) modification of Freud's theory that anxiety is the only signal affect. Brenner introduced the notion that castration depressive affect also can trigger psychic conflict, defense, and symptom formation. Clinical material from the first year of treatment of a three-year-old boy who suffered a regression in daytime bladder control is presented. The focus is threefold: First, to show that the often cited but poorly studied symptom of regression in bladder control may be an indicator of the child's struggle with the three calamities of childhood (object loss, loss of love, and castration); second, to present data that support the importance in early symptom formation of both anxiety and depressive affect tied to the ideation of castration as well as of object loss; third, to suggest that vulnerability to castration depression is a concept more pertinent to the stage presently labeled the phallic-narcissistic phase, rather than to the oedipal phase of development. The discussion addresses the importance of castration depressive affect as a concept in guiding therapeutic intervention. Vulnerability to castration depressive affect is postu-

Training and Supervising Analyst; Associate Supervisor in Child and Adolescent Psychoanalysis, Baltimore-Washington Institute for Psychoanalysis.

The Psychoanalytic Study of the Child 59, ed. Robert A. King, Peter B. Neubauer, Samuel Abrams, and A. Scott Dowling (Yale University Press, copyright © 2004 by Robert A. King, Peter B. Neubauer, Samuel Abrams, and A. Scott Dowling).

lated to be more prominent in the phallic-narcissistic phase because phallic self representation is not yet consolidated.

IN 1975, CHARLES BRENNER INTRODUCED A REVISION OF FREUD'S (1926) theory that anxiety is the only affect that triggers conflict and defense. Brenner asserted that unpleasure of two kinds, anxiety and depressive affect, can initiate psychic conflict, defense, and symptom formation in connection with infantile instinctual wishes (Brenner, 1975). He distinguished between the two affects by stating that whereas anxiety is associated with an impending calamity, depressive affect results from ideas about a calamity that has already happened (Brenner, 1975, 1979). Thus, the difference between them relates to a temporal factor: whether the calamity is to occur in the future or is believed to have occurred in the past. Moreover, he states that evaluating the relative contribution of both affects is of primary importance to the understanding of a patient's conflicts.

In his paper "Depressive affect, anxiety and psychic conflict in the phallic-oedipal phase" (1979), Brenner further expands his theoretical contribution. Object loss, loss of love, and castration, what Freud (1926) called "the typical dangers of childhood psychic life" and what Brenner labels "the calamities of childhood," are not only the ideational content of anxiety aroused by drive derivatives but also the ideational content of depressive affect. Depressive affect has been amply documented in the clinical and research literature as a prominent danger associated with object loss and loss of love in both sexes by the time the child has reached the oedipal phase. The relation between depressive affect and castration (Brenner, 1982) is a significant modification of psychoanalytic theory since, heretofore, depression was linked exclusively with object loss.

Whereas developmental research and the psychoanalytic treatment of adults and children attest to the centrality of castration anxiety in the oedipal phase for both sexes, depressive affect that results from castration as the ideational content has been poorly recognized in conflict and symptom formation. Brenner (1982) states, "It is true that for boys in the oedipal phase castration is, in fantasy, a real and imminent danger (Hartmann and Kris, 1945), but it is not always only a danger, a thing of the future. There are instances when reality and fantasy combine to convince an oedipal boy that castration has actually happened, that it is a fact, not a danger." He cites data obtained from boys with penile deformities or testicular abnormalities, who experience their physical defects as a symbolic castration, and boys with a strong feminine identification who, in their defensive use of the fantasy of being female, are "vulnerable to the conviction that the very calamity . . . (they) . . . so feared has actually befallen . . . (them)" (Brenner, 1982). Brenner indicates that we have inadequate data at present to establish the importance of castration depressive affect relative to anxiety as a signal that mobilizes defense in boys, and assumes that it is much more prevalent in girls, who interpret their lack of a penis as a castration that has already occurred. Developmental studies of girls in the preoedipal period offer evidence of the relation between bladder control, castration reaction and mood. Parens (1977), in a study of the girl's entry into the oedipus complex, reports on a 30-month-old girl who manifested anxiety about loss of sphincter control. He believes that the regression in toilet training suffered by this child, which was accompanied by tearfulness and panic-like feelings, was tied to her castration complex. Galenson and Roiphe (1971) described a girl with a congenital defect who developed a basic depressive mood in connection with profound castration reaction in her second year of life. The findings from other studies by these authors (e.g. Galenson and Roiphe, 1977) indicate that girls, more often than boys, suffer these reactions in the early genital period. This lends support to the idea that depressive affect, in the sense described by Brenner, is prevalent in the psychic life of girls, who tend to experience their recognition of the absence of the penis as a castration that has already taken place. In a more recent study of the early development of the sense of femaleness, which refers to observational and clinical data, Olesker (1998) describes that, in girls between 29 and 33 months of age, feelings of being genitally damaged are acutely evident. Girls in this period reacted with "constriction, inhibition, and depression, reactions suggesting castration depressive affect" (p. 282). She differentiates castration anxiety and castration depressive affect (i.e. threats of damage to, versus reaction to the injury or loss of the fantasied phallus) from female genital anxieties, a term that refers to the girl's specific fear of penetration and hurt of her female genital, which also becomes manifest at the entry into the oedipal phase. Others (e.g. Kulish, 2000) clarify the need to distinguish in the case of girls between reactions to damage or loss of female body parts, and similar worries about fantasied male attributes, thus suggesting that girls can also experience specific female genital depressive affect.

While there are frequent references in the psychoanalytic literature to battles associated with toilet training, and to the regressions in bladder and bowel control that result from object loss and childhood trauma, there are few studies of the treatment of children whose primary presenting complaint is failure to achieve daytime bladder control. Serota (1969), in a cleverly titled paper, "Urine or you're in," discussed the toilet inhibition of a two-year-old boy as related to castration anxiety. His young patient's avoidance of the toilet was tied to the ideation first that a lion would come out of the toilet and bite his penis and, later, that he would be engulfed by the toilet, a danger apparently exacerbated by the ambiguity of meaning embodied for him in the word urine. Katan (1946), directly connected nocturnal enuresis with the three calamities of childhood. She observed that bedwetting often results from trauma, and listed object loss, loss of love, birth of a sibling, illness, and surgery, as well as anatomical comparisons between the sexes and with adults, as precursors of loss of nighttime bladder control. Moreover, she stated specifically that there is a connection between this symptom and the ideation of being damaged, thus predating the relation between enuresis and what Brenner would later define as depressive affect. "In all cases of enuresis we find the fantasy that the genitals are damaged and, like a broken water-tap, cannot retain urine" (Katan, 1946, p. 244).

This paper presents evidence from the psychotherapeutic treatment of a three-year-old boy who suffered a regression in daytime bladder control to invite the consideration that this often-cited but poorly studied symptom is an indicator of the young child's struggle with castration issues. Clinical data from the first of a four-year psychotherapeutic intervention is discussed to elucidate the importance in early symptom formation of anxiety and depressive affect tied to the ideation of castration as well as object loss. However, while Brenner refers to vulnerability to castration depression in the oedipal phase of development, the work reviewed in this study indicates that castration depressive affect is a concept more pertinent to the pre-oedipal phallic, or what is presently labeled phallic-narcissistic phase of development, rather than to the oedipal phase.

CLINICAL DATA

Adam was referred by his pediatrician at 39 months of age because of regression in daytime bladder control. The parents stated the toilet training had been accomplished quickly and uneventfully by 32 months. At 37 months, he started wetting his pants. He remained dry at night, and continued to use the toilet regularly for his bowel movements. At the time of the evaluation, Adam was urinating on himself whenever he had to empty his bladder. He refused diapers and resisted being changed after wetting. All attempts to coax, reward, or discipline him had been to no avail.

Adam was the product of a normal pregnancy and delivery, the much-longed-for only child of a couple who had waited many years for his arrival. His mother had left a lucrative position to dedicate herself exclusively to her infant son. She described with pride his early achievement of motor and verbal milestones, and conveyed her sense that Adam was an unusually well-developed child, physically and cognitively. Careful questioning about his infancy, however, revealed that Adam seemed to have certain kinesthetic and auditory hypersensitivites (Bergman and Escalona, 1949). He disliked the feel of certain clothing, did not tolerate being confined, and cried easily in response to sound. The mother acknowledged that he was temperamentally "high strung," and recalled that pediatric visits had always been "horrendous experiences." She seemed, however, to have been able to accept this somewhat difficult infant. In fact, she appeared to be a mother whose own exquisite sensitivity had permitted her to achieve an attunement with her infant (Stern, 1985) in the first year of life. The father, a busy professional who did not share in the daily caretaking of his son, lacked his wife's skill in understanding Adam's cues. As a result, their interaction was not always harmonious. Presently, he felt confused and angered by Adam's wetting. Nevertheless, both father and son expressed a wish for greater closeness with each other. Adam asked that his father join in his activities. The father, recognizing his own dissatisfaction with the somewhat exclusive quality of the mother-child dyad, responded by dedicating more time to being with his son.

Adam was bottle fed, and was gradually weaned to a cup and solid foods by 9 months of age when his mother observed that he appeared to want to feed himself. He had used a pacifier in the first few months of life, and had "given it up on his own." There was no history of an attachment to a transitional object. At 10 months, he started walking. His second year was marked by rapid gross-motor development and an exuberant wish to explore the world. Between 18 and 24 months there was a marked spurt in his language development. In this period he also became more reliant on his mother, who recalled his constant requests for explanations and need to maintain verbal contact with her. "It seems to me that I was talking to him nonstop at this time," she said. Apparently, Adam was attempting to re-establish in the verbal sphere the special closeness that he had experienced in physical contact with his mother. She did not recall other manifestations of an increase in separation anxiety. However, she was careful to keep separations to a minimum. He was left only occasionally during the day at the home of his little girl friend, or in the evenings with one of three carefully selected baby sitters.

At around 24 months Adam became aggressive toward his peers. He was possessive of his toys, and hit or pushed his playmates when he felt threatened by them. The mother was upset by his anger, and responded by removing him temporarily from the situation. When the behavior persisted, the parents became increasingly concerned. They decided to coax him into controlling his impulses by telling him that his behavior was "unacceptable," and by offering him material rewards for good conduct. His aggressiveness appeared to subside at about 30 to 32 months, coinciding with his compliance with toilet training.

Adam had developed an interest in his body and his body products late in the second year of life. By age two he had labels for his bowel movement ("poo") and his urine ("pee"). In the months that followed, he was seen to masturbate when his diaper was removed, and wanted his mother to admire his penis. This exhibitionistic behavior paralleled an interest in doing things with and like his father. The mother stated that she did not initiate toilet training until she obtained cues from her son that indicated his readiness to be trained. He showed curiosity when he observed other children his age on the toilet, and was encouraged to observe his three-year-old girlfriend, who was a frequent playmate. When he became interested in his parents' bathroom activity, he was permitted to see his father, but not his mother, urinating. The parents tended otherwise to maintain privacy. When Adam was 30 months, the mother decided to make a more concerted effort to toilet train him. She read a book with him about a boy and a girl who had learned to use the toilet, and she encouraged him to wear underpants. After a couple of days, he agreed to wear them but clearly without connecting this to his use of the toilet. The mother described his first attempt as "a catastrophe." Following this experience, he wore diapers for a few days while still being encouraged to use the toilet. The mother decided to let him spend part of the day naked so she could direct him to the toilet when he started to urinate. Several days later, he asked to wear underpants again. This time he kept himself dry, and used the toilet appropriately. When he was getting ready for bed he announced to his mother "No more diapers." He gathered his diapers, put them in the trash and sang a "bye-bye diapers" song to them. During the subsequent four months, he had complete bowel and bladder control. He was dry at night, and seemed generally delighted with his new skill.

This feeling clearly paralleled his mother's, who took pride in this accomplishment and generally placed a premium on his developmental milestones.

At 36 months, Adam started nursery school, five mornings per week. Despite having been well prepared for this event, he soon began to show a marked change in his behavior. He was subdued, withdrawn, and lacking in enthusiasm after school. He also became aggressive and angry at school. The teachers complained to the parents that he was uncooperative and hit other children. In his second week of attendance, he had an episode of day wetting at school. This was the first such experience since he had decided to wear underpants, and it recurred several days later. Observation of Adam at school convinced his mother that the environment was a poor match for him. Adam seemed overwhelmed by the noise, the size of the room, the group of children, and the structure, which required that he transition from one activity to another to keep pace with the group without consideration of his personal wishes. The mother worried that the teachers disliked Adam, and that they had been insensitive to his needs. He was removed from the setting, and placed instead in a co-operative nursery school setting which his mother also attended on a part-time basis. He did not mention his first nursery school again. Adam adjusted well to the new situation, separated easily from his mother when required to do so, and established a satisfactory rapport with one of his teachers.

Adam's behavior at home, however, began to deteriorate. He was often unhappy and angry. He started wetting himself, at first occasionally and then constantly. He was upset if this was pointed out to him, and he did not allow his mother to change his clothes. He, apparently wishing to deny the occurrence of his wetting altogether, seemed oblivious to his urination, but still announced proudly whenever he used the toilet to have a bowel movement. The mother tried to encourage his wish to regain control over his bladder by rewarding him for the use of the toilet, and bought him underpants made of a Superman-print fabric.

Adam regressed in his overall behavior and became defiant toward his parents: he refused to brush his teeth and to cooperate with the usual routines; there were battles over his demands for sweets and ice cream; he refused to get dressed and wanted to spend the day at home in his pajamas; he had temper outbursts in response to minor frustrations, such as any limits that might be placed on his behavior. His heightened ambivalence toward his mother was openly expressed. He angrily yelled at her "I hate you! Go away!" only to dissolve in tears and need to be cuddled and comforted by her. His expressions of anger also were directed at himself: "I am a bad guy"; "I was bad the day I was born." As his anger mounted, his fear of losing his mother was heightened. "I hate you! I want you to go away! I'm going to tie you up and lock you away," he said to her, poignantly verbalizing his attempt to defend against the dreadful loss he feared would befall him. Although the parents had curtailed his exposure to violence in the media, he developed a preoccupation with guns and shooting. He talked about "bad hunters" who shoot animals. His worry about his ongoing lack of bladder control finally surfaced as well: "Maybe the pee can be taken out of me," he said to his mother sadly, for the first time giving voice to his misery in the hope that something might be done to help him find relief. Bewildered and alarmed, the parents finally requested a consultation when Adam, having spent himself weeping, despairingly cried out "I do not like me!" as he banged his genitals with his fist.

In preparation for his appointment with me, Adam was told by his parents that they were aware that he "has a big worry," and that they would take him to see a doctor "who understands worries." We had agreed earlier that the mother would come into the playroom with him if he showed signs of separation distress. Adam appeared tense as I approached him in the waiting room. He displayed an initial shyness but, after a few minutes, left his mother's side to walk with me into the playroom. He had brought with him a raccoon, his favorite stuffed animal. Showing it to me, he said with much feeling "Look, it has a tail!" He proceeded to swing it by the tail to make it "fly in the air," in a gesture that reminded me of the Superman underpants. There was no pleasure in this activity; he seemed tense and sad. He added, "He won't pee," poignantly addressing the internal and external conflicts that were oppressing him. I responded that I knew raccoon was having trouble with peeing, and that it made him sad and worried. Adam turned to a family of plastic giraffes. He twisted all of their tails so they would stick up, and made them prance about. Noticing that one of the giraffes, which had loosely jointed legs, kept on falling over, he twisted all of the legs to make them stick up as well. He tried to balance the giraffes in an upright position, sitting on their bellies. As he was unable to do so, and they fell on their sides, he gave up and seemed forlorn. He moved to the clay. "I made a big snake," he said, but quickly rolled it into "a snail." He returned to the giraffes, this time using a dinosaur to eat the animals' tails. At that point he stopped his play and said to me "You are close to Dr. T" (a reference to his pediatrician, whose office was located in close proximity to mine). I took this as an opportunity to address more openly the reason for our meeting. I replied that I knew that he went to Dr. T for help when he did not feel well, and that now he had come to see me for help because he has a big worry. I added that I understood how good the animals feel about having a tail, a tail that can go up and down, and what a big worry it is to think that a dinosaur might take it away. Adam turned to the plastic elephant and told me that Babar's mother had been killed by a "mighty hunter." With this, Adam proceeded to pretend he was the big hunter. Again, he seemed tense and joyless.

The content of this hour presaged the themes he would work on for the next ten months, in twice-a-week sessions, as we gradually uncovered the conflicts that were impeding him from exercising control over his wetting. Through Adam's play we understood the wishes and impulses, and the past and present dangers (calamities, to apply Brenner's term) involved in his suffering which, shaped by his endowment and personal history, resulted in a regression that prevented developmental progress. To clarify the relative contributions of anxiety and of depressive affect in Adam's conflict, the clinical evidence of anxiety manifestations is presented first in this paper, followed by a detailed account of the work on depressive ideation as it unfolded in the treatment.

In the first months of treatment, Adam played almost exclusively with the plastic animals. He elaborated his anxiety about separation and his conflictual feelings about his mother. He started the session by putting each baby animal together with its mother. This was the good mother, that protected and comforted the baby. The theme of vulnerability, represented in the play as the babies were attacked when they strayed from their mothers, was repeated in different contexts. Not even a hasty return to the mother would save the babies from the "big danger," the biting dinosaur. The particular dinosaur he selected, which had itself been labeled "the mother," was a hollow plastic Stegosaurus with no underbelly who pounced without warning and bit off the upturned tails and legs of baby and mother animals alike. Stegosaurus had dual roles. While at times she offered refuge to the baby giraffe who went inside her body cavity in search of complete safety, at other times she chased menacingly after him in an attempt to bite him and clip onto him, thus forcibly subsuming him within her body. The dinosaur seemed to represent both the nurturing and the evil, castrating mother who could engulf him as a punishment for exercising his autonomy. As "the mighty hunter," Adam could safeguard his phallus and his autonomy, but at the dreadful risk of destroying his mother.

Adam's ambivalent posture toward his mother found expression, early in the treatment, in his preoccupation with the story of young Babar. Adam focused on this story in a dyadic way characteristic of a child who has not yet progressed to the oedipal phase of development. He seemed identified with Babar as the helpless baby of a powerless mother who was abandoned when she succumbed to the mighty hunter. This regression to an early, non-phallic position seemed to originate from his need to defend against the dangers of his phallic, aggressive wishes which might result in object loss. Adam's verbalizations also highlighted that this regressive position was strengthened by a defensive identification with his non-phallic mother. "Babar was a baby. He didn't have a gun. He didn't know how to fly. His mommy didn't either. Dumbo could fly. Then he was safe," he said in one session. He added, "Babies pee on the floor. I'm not a baby. I'm the ringmaster," and he proceeded to lash the baby elephant with a string. Adam was expressing, in the displacement, his feeling that the regressive posture of being a baby, symbolic of not being phallic, kept him safe from the danger of hurting mother and being hurt by mother. However, moments later, in his identification with the aggressive ringmaster who contemptuously lashed the weak baby, Adam indicated both his need to defend against a castrated posture which was untenable, and his angry turning against himself because of his perceived helplessness.

In his play, Adam manifested his conflict about the expression of his active strivings, specifically his worry that if he were the one with the powerful gun he might, like the hunter, use it to damage or destroy his mother. Neither being phallic nor giving up his strivings offered a safe solution. In a later session, after enacting a dangerous/exciting game about hunters and powerful guns, he said anxiously, "Babar wants a big gun too, but then his mommy would be very scared. He could smash her." I replied, "Babar could feel so happy to have a big gun if he didn't worry about hurting his mother with it." That night, allowing himself to feel more phallic in response to the interpretation earlier in the day, he also broached his anxiety in a question to his mother: "My pee comes right out of my penis and goes in the toilet. Mom, how strong is our house? Are you safe inside this house?" His mother replied that the house was indeed very safe, and that she was also quite strong and able to keep herself safe. He added, "I'm going to keep you safe." Still later on in his treatment, when he was closer to achieving object constancy and the consolidation of self-representation, he revisited this theme. Now using the dollhouse figures which more closely represented himself and his family, he made a boy drive a jeep with his mother in the passenger seat. He drove wildly, and soon she was knocked out of the car. The mother was unharmed, and helped the boy by stopping the engine from outside the car. Then the boy made a pee and a poo in the toilet. We were able to understand that when the boy feels that his mother won't be hurt or angry because of his exciting/hurting thoughts, he feels safe to grow up and be a big boy who uses his penis to pee in the toilet.

It became apparent that Adam's castration anxiety and anger at his mother was reactive also to his awareness that she did not have a penis. In the early sessions, he dramatized in his play with Stegosaurus (made of non-segmented molded plastic) that she threatened to bite off the baby giraffe's upturned tail because she didn't have one. As the treatment progressed, Adam explored his heightened castration anxiety in recognition of the anatomical differences between the sexes. In the first of several sessions during which this theme was elaborated Adam, after showing off his gymnastic prowess, looked at the genitals of the plastic horse. "Is it a boy or is it a girl?" he asked. I said that he was looking to see what the horse has because the difference between boys and girls is confusing for him—if it has a penis, it is a boy horse, but he is not so sure about the girl horse, and what she has. He said, "My mom does not have one; yes, she has one too!" and moved to less threatening play with clay. I added that he seemed to wonder whether his mother does or does not have a penis, and that sometimes he was worried about having a penis if she doesn't. In a subsequent session, he made two pipes with clay. He said that one is closed and the other one is open. Then he urinated on himself. I commented that when the pipe is open, the pee runs out. He then pulled up the leg of his pants, showing me his wet calf as he simultaneously denied the occurrence of his wetting, and said, "Look, I have hair on my legs. Who gave me this hair? My father has hair; my mother has no hair. My father has a bald spot. What about your mother?" and, answering his own question he added, "No, she has hair." I said that he knows that mothers and fathers are made different. Fathers and boys both have hair, and also a penis, because they are boys and that is how boys are made. I added that, even though he knows that girls are made differently and do not have a penis (something he had previously told me), sometimes he still worries that something has happened to the girl's penis. I said that I thought he worries too that something has happened to his pipe, like what he thinks happened to the girl's penis, and that the pee runs out because there is something wrong with it. In this session, we explored his complex identification with both parents, and elaborated his thought that having hair on his legs, like his father, helps him to feel less worried about something being wrong with "his pipe." A fuller description of the therapeutic work around the theme of the damaged pipe, which connotes castration depressive affect, follows the ensuing discussion of castration issues as they were manifest in relation to the father figure.

In the early sessions, Adam used the shark, a rubber figure many times the size of the other plastic animals with prominent teeth, to express his ambivalent feelings toward his father. He alternated between playing with the shark as powerful and assaultive (the counterpart to the vicious Stegosaurus mother), or as toothless (which he accomplished by bending the rubber teeth into the mouth cavity) and protective of the smaller figures. The "good" (i.e. toothless) and "bad" (i.e. toothy) shark stories, turned into play where armed hunters could be either good or bad. In this period, approximately six months into the treatment, Adam turned increasingly to his father as the work of consolidating a phallic sense of his identity proceeded. He expressed in many ways his wish to be close to his father, and to be loved by him. He began to ask many questions of his father in an attempt to enlist his support and reassure himself of the similarities between them: Did his father shower or take a bath? (which led us to consider his worry about urination: "is it safer to urinate standing up or sitting down?"); could his father build with him, and help him make a gun with Legos? (that is, would his father approve of, and indeed promote his attainment of a gun/penis he could use without fear?). He cried when his father left for work and asked that they have lunch together. He sought reassurance from his father after having an anxiety dream where a threatening witch/teacher/mother reacted angrily to his phallic strivings. In his dream he was "an engineer, driving an engine." His nursery school teacher was chasing him; "she was very angry." Soon afterward, Adam revealed to his father the frightening experience at nursery school that resulted in his wetting. The teacher had yelled at him to stop playing and clean up the blocks which he had strewn about. "I was very bad and hit a child," he said to his father. He spoke of the teacher restraining him and isolating him from the group. He berated himself. "I used to hit, I was a bad guy. I was born bad." This was the first time that Adam had made mention of the feelings of helplessness and fear that were so traumatic for him. While one can only speculate about the full content of his fantasy regarding the episode with the teacher, it seems that the image of an angry, punitive mother was attached to fantasies about his phallic strivings. Moreover, Adam seemed to experience his rage in reaction to the restrictive teacher/mother as bad and punishable. As the clinical material unfolded, it became clear that the regressive wetting induced by this experience became symbolic of "being broken," and that the ideation of being damaged triggered regressive defensive maneuvers (being the baby) that safeguarded the union with his mother and protected him from the risks inherent in his phallic wishes.

The multiple feelings Adam began to experience in the course of treatment—his wish to be like the powerful father; his fear of father as threatening rival; and his defensive compromise—were expressed in a drawing he made to give to his father during one of the therapeutic sessions. It was a drawing of himself as Superman, with a little slash on the groin area to indicate that he did not have a penis. "Daddies have penises. Superman flies; he has a cape," he said. I said that when a boy knows that daddies have penises he worries that his dad might not be happy if the boy wants to be Superman and have a penis too. I added that I understood that he likes feeling big and strong, and also wants his daddy to like him very much. In the following session, now in the seventh month of treatment, he played with the dollhouse. The boy wanted to take a shower like the father. "The father knows when to turn the water on and off," he said. I added that the boy wants to do like father, he too wants to know when to turn the water on and off. "The father is in a wet house, there is water all over," he said. Then the mother doll tried to enter the shower, but the boy pushed her away and went in with the father. I verbalized that the boy wants his father all to himself; then they could choose together whether to be in a wet house or not. In this session, Adam was also beginning to express his excitement relative to passive feminine wishes toward his father. In the course of our work, as Adam understood his conflicts and was able to consolidate his body image in identification with his father, he was able to adopt a phallic posture less imbued with dangerous hostility, symbolized in his own creative ending to the story of Babar: Babar would grow up to be a mighty hunter himself, and thus would be able to protect his weaker mother as he reasserted his own integrity.

The clinical material presented so far corroborates the importance of castration anxiety in the development of symptom formation but it also introduces evidence indicative that defense did not initiate exclusively in reaction to anxiety. Castration depressive affect resulting, as defined by Brenner, from the idea that the calamity has already happened played a significant role in Adam's conflict; one that had to be addressed in the treatment in order for him to resume developmental progress.

The first episode of regression in urinary control at the nursery school had occurred under conditions of heightened separation anxiety and, as we learned from his dream, in reaction to demands from a teacher Adam perceived as attacking. The nursery school experience seemed to repeat the demands of the toilet training situation itself—in both, Adam seems to have experienced demands to comply with expectations that required he exercise powers that, like Superman's, felt superhuman. At stake was a sense of himself as worthy of his mother's pride, versus a sense of himself as a catastrophic failure (to paraphrase her description that his first day in underpants was "a catastrophe"). The history obtained from the parents provided dramatic evidence that, subsequent to the wetting episode, the child suffered a dramatic regression, which was coupled with a progressive intensification of self-directed anger. Once, after wetting, Adam lashed out angrily at his mother. "I am a baby. Babies pee on the floor." Then he burst into tears and said, "I'm sorry, I feel so bad inside." Although this moment elucidates Adam's anger at his mother for her demandingness, it is also a harbinger of feelings he would later elaborate in his story about Dumbo's ringmaster, who lashed at the inadequate Babar because he couldn't fly. Adam had displayed to me in our first session that his raccoon had a tail, and he could fly, apparently in an attempt to defend against the mortifying sense that he, like Babar, was defective and lacked that which would make him phallic. This defectiveness also made him "bad," deserving of punishment. Adam often expressed feelings of uncertainty in relation to his phallic wishes. In the beginning of the treatment when, in a fleeting expression of his wish to identify with his father, he had announced to his mother, "I will be a dad!" he burst into tears and said, "no, I'm going to be a mom." In the course of the treatment, it became evident that the expression of his phallic wishes was risky not only because of fantasied castrating consequences, but because of his dread that he was defective and unable to meet the challenge. His increased separation anxiety from his father during his treatment seemed tied to his need for his father's presence not only as evidence that he was not a dangerous rival, but as a supportive presence that reassured Adam of his maleness. He could urinate in the toilet for his father, but wet himself when the father was away. He struggled with a mood of basic sadness. He called himself "a bad son," an image which again included both aspects of his worry—that his impulses were bad and would be punished, but also that he was damaged and

would not live up to the phallic requirements of being a son. He refused to play with his friends—"I do not want to go anywhere," he
said—in an attempt to defend from his misery by keeping away the
stimuli that would stimulate the expression of his wishes thus trigger-
ing overwhelming conflict. Adam made no lasting progress in his use
of the toilet until his fear that he was damaged was understood in the
course of our therapeutic work.

This aspect of Adam's conflict was revealed in our first session,
when he had so quickly rolled up the clay snake to turn it into a snail.
The most evident explanation of this behavior pointed to Adam's
need to defend from the dangers attending to having a snake. However, as we explored the meaning of his behavior in subsequent sessions, a more complex picture emerged. The snake had a hole; in
fact, it was no snake at all, but just "a pipe with a big hole" which
could not hold the water or the pee. At this point in the treatment,
Adam acknowledged to his mother his fear that he would run out of
his body contents: "my apple juice comes right out of my penis," he
said helplessly. In the office, his play elucidated his wish to be a baby
so he would not have to confront the possibility of being damaged
and unable to control his urine. He routinely removed his shoes and
socks upon arriving for these sessions and often spent the early part
of the hour rolling aimlessly on the floor. "I am a baby. Babies throw
their food on the floor. They are wet all over," he said. I commented
that if he were a baby, then he wouldn't have to worry about keeping
dry. At the end of a difficult session, when he had dramatized his
recognition of the anatomical differences between the sexes and his
fear of being like the castrated female who does not have a penis to
hold the pee, he ran into the waiting room, climbed into his
mother's large canvas bag and demanded that she carry him home in
it. "I am little Roo," he said. "I need my mommy." Our work addressed that by being baby Roo, who is held and carried by his
mommy, he was trying not to think about his worry that big boy
Adam would not be able to hold and carry his own pee. Later that
week, he ran out of his yard abruptly. When his mother called anxiously after him, he yelled, "I'm going to Christopher Robin's house
to get help for a broken pipe." In this period his vocal expressions of
anger and hopelessness to his parents became intensified: "I am bad;
I want to keep my wet pants on; I will live in a house all by myself; I do
not care about anybody; I do not want anybody to care about me."
Adam began requesting that his mother tell him stories about when
he was a baby. This activity proved to be at times the only way to
soothe him.

As we worked to understand the reasons for his regressive posture, Adam's play elucidated more clearly his ideation about the connection between his excitement and aggression, and his sense that his penis was damaged. In the early months of the treatment, Adam let himself express phallic-aggressive wishes only in displacement. The super heroes knocked the chimney off the house as they flew wildly around the room in the dark; the car lost a wheel as he rubbed it vigorously back and forth on the rug; the legs of the plastic animals came off in his excited play. Interpretations aimed at focusing on his worry that damage would result if he let himself act out his wishes did not seem to impact the conflict sufficiently for his symptom to abate. It became evident that Adam's exciting damaging acts were defensive against the misery of feeling that his equipment was defective, inadequate to the phallic task. When he had gained enough confidence to begin to display his exhibitionism in the office, and he let himself show me directly his use of his body and his strength, we had an opportunity to observe together the fragile quality of his self-representation. He had seen some older boys playing ball outside the office, and he was visibly excited when he came in. He decided to play a target game, where he tossed velcro balls at a felt board that had pictures of four Smurfs. "I am strong," he said as his excitement mounted seeing the balls stick to the target. He took off his shirt. He asked me "to talk for the Smurfs." "Tell me what they are saying." I answered, "They are saying, 'This is a strong boy who can throw a ball very well.'" Suddenly, trying to catch a ball on the rebound, he tripped, fell down and lost the ball. He started to cry huddled on the floor. I realized that he had wet himself. He said softly, "I want my mommy." I said, also softly, that he wants so much to feel strong like a big boy, and added that when he tripped he felt very sad because it made him worry that the Smurfs would not believe that he can be big and strong. The experience of inadequacy, at the moment when he was fulfilling his wishes to be admired in his phallic display, seemed rudely to bring back his feeling of being hopelessly damaged—a feeling symbolized in the sudden loss of urinary control which he defended against through regressive avoidance. In a later session, he confirmed more directly his awareness that he thought of his penis as damaged. As he poured water into a container he had asked me to hold, he let the water overflow and run onto the floor. I sensed no provocativeness or aggression in this gesture; Adam seemed sad, forlorn. I said that he wanted me to feel what he feels sometimes, that there is nothing he can do to stop his pee from coming out of his penis and going on the floor. He said, "One shoe just slips off; the other

I have to squeeze off." I added, "just like your pee and your poo." He said "My pee just slips off; I am a bad guy," hence expressing his helplessness as the one who has the irreparable bad pipe.

As Adam gained an understanding of his anxiety and depressive affect, his anger at home diminished and he began to re-experience and express more consistently the wish to have a penis he could control. He requested that his parents buy him a pumper-truck with a "real hose." While playing with it, he announced that his penis was a machine: a creative integration of the wish to acknowledge having a penis that is powerful, under his control, and insensitive to damage. He allowed himself increasingly to use the toilet, although he often sat facing the back of the toilet, once again giving symbolic representation to his conflict. He sat (like a girl), facing the back (like a boy), locked still in the negativism of the anal phase, and limited by the anxiety and depressive affect of his castration reaction. But, at last, he was using the toilet. He requested, at first tentatively and then regularly, to water my plants. At first, he spilled much of the content of the watering can on the floor, thus giving us another opportunity to understand his "big worry" that he would not be able to control his water. As we understood the many dangers inherent for him in allowing himself to display that he could be "big and strong," Adam gradually resumed his earlier exhibitionistic pleasure and spent much time in the office showing off his gymnastics skill, his physical strength, and his excellent balance.

An excerpt from one of the later sessions illustrates the marked change in his mood and self-representation, as well as our working-through of his conflicts about urination. He was playing at putting a marble inside his sweatshirt, so it would roll down his arm but be stopped from rolling onto the floor by the cuff of his sleeve. He stretched the cuff, releasing the marble. He repeated this, looking at me with a smile. I commented that the cuff holds the marble until he lets it out, and added that I could tell how happy he was to be the one letting it out. "It's like my penis; it holds my pee," he replied. I said, "I think you are happy now that you know your penis will hold your pee until you decide to let it out." Adam proceeded to tell me about a storybook character who was entrusted with a special teapot, and because he was not careful, it broke. Then he took it to a "fix it" shop, and it was "all good" again. I said that the story reminded me of him, and about his old worry that he had done something that made him broken and that's why he couldn't stop his pee from coming out. I added that he and I worked together to fix that worry about being broken. Now that he knows he is "all good," he can make his penis hold in or let out his pee when he wants, and that makes him very happy.

Masturbation resumed at home as we worked on his guilt regarding this activity. This was his "playing in the dark" phase, when he routinely turned off the lights in the playroom and talked and acted the exciting and dangerous feelings for which he wanted approval and admiration. This period culminated in an episode when, after using the bathroom in my office, he emerged triumphant and naked. He was acknowledging that he is a boy, that he has an intact penis, that he is proud of his body and its functions. Hereafter, he was observed to entertain himself at home with explorations of the arc he could make with his urine, sometimes aimed into the toilet and sometimes not. Once, while walking past a stream with his mother, he asked her whether he could urinate into it. "That is one of the fun things you can do when you have a penis," she said encouragingly. Soon, his use of the toilet became consistent.

DISCUSSION

The achievement of regulatory control over urinary function has significant implications for masculine identification and the development of self-esteem. Based on the treatment of an adolescent boy with lasting enuresis, Gluckman (1986) stated that failure to achieve bladder control can interfere with the normal progression into the oedipal, latency, and adolescent stages. Psychoanalytic research of early development in boys has offered confirming evidence that the psychic component of mastery over the penis that results from successful bladder training, promotes adequate male self-representation and the positive resolution of the oedipal phase. Galenson and Roiphe (1980) state that the emergence of urinary pride is a precursor of genital schematization and a sense of maleness.

The capacity for urinary sphincter control is a maturational achievement leading to a period of increased genital awareness that ushers in the phallic-narcissistic phase of development. This is the stage during which the child develops a sexually differentiated body representation. The narcissistic investment in the phallus becomes paramount: the penis is the main source of autoerotic gratification, becomes the focus of exhibitionistic wishes, and is the confirmation of masculinity in identification with the father. Because of the burgeoning quality of the child's self-representation in this phase, his vulnerability is great. The discovery of the anatomical difference between the sexes, and of the size difference between himself and his father has a momentous impact on the toddler (Edgcumbe and Burgner, 1975). Galenson and Roiphe (1980) report that boys must defend against this recognition through denial and increasing identification with the father.

While many features are involved in a pathological outcome, the focus of this presentation is to detail how conflicts from each phase (arising from instinctual drives and the defenses activated against them) interact to affect the course of development. Adam is presented as a clinical example of a boy who, following an episode of sudden regression in urinary function in response to his perceived vulnerability to attack and intense separation anxiety, developed compromise formations to ward off the unpleasure of anxiety and depressive affect associated with ideation of object loss and castration. Adam was clearly in the phallic-narcissistic phase of development at the time of the first wetting episode in school. The developmental history obtained from the parents highlighted his narcissistic investment in his penis which provided a primary source of autoerotic gratification, his exhibitionism and wish to be admired, his growing awareness of his sexual identity and desire to be more closely allied with his father. His relationship to his parents in this period had a dyadic quality; he was variously and intensely focused on his mother or his father. Our treatment sessions attested to the stresses a child must endure in this developmental phase: the fragility of his self-representation as phallic, the threat associated with the fantasy that each one of his love objects is also an aggressor, and the heightening of hostile aggression in connection with fantasies of threatened and experienced body damage.

Adam's ability to negotiate these developmental vicissitudes was affected by unresolved issues from an earlier phase: the ambivalent struggles of the rapprochement crisis and the anal stage. According to Mahler (1969), the major task of the toddler years (the separation-individuation phase) is the achievement of an integrated self-representation and of object constancy. She states (1969) that the toddler has to come to accept the unreality of his earlier omnipotent feelings and replace it with a sense of enjoyment of his autonomy. He also must replace his expectation of his parents' omnipotence with a realistic trust in their availability. "It is the mother's love and acceptance of the toddler and even of his ambivalence which enable the toddler's ego to cathect his self-representation with 'neutralized energy'" (1969), and to achieve object constancy. Adam's history offered indications that the road toward separation-individuation would be complicated for him. As an infant he had certain sensory hypersensitivities that stimulated in the mother an intensified need to function as his "protective living shield" (Mahler, 1966). Adam's physical endowment supported his ability to move away from his mother to explore his environment in the practicing phase. However, he appeared to have an anxious need to maintain "verbal union" with his mother in the period of rapprochement. He remained vulnerable to strong separation anxiety, and showed heightened aggressiveness in and out of the home environment. The mother, in turn, remained narcissistically over-invested in him, and attempted to control his expressions of autonomy, possessiveness, and anger with disciplinary measures that further compromised the separation-individuation process.

Adam's achievement of bowel and bladder control, while not developmentally early, seemed to be attained without the benefit of "the long back-and-forth way through . . . (a) . . . series of successes, relapses and accidents" (Freud, A., 1965), that result in greater stability of function. It appears that Adam, having internalized parental expectations, had prematurely relinquished anal and urethral pleasures for fear of loss of love. In order to cope with heightened hostility toward his mother, Adam reacted in a way characteristic of the toddler in the anal phase. He developed early defense mechanisms (object splitting and turning aggression against the self) to ward off the fears of object loss and loss of love.

The father's availability in this period is of crucial importance to the development of the boy. His function is to promote the boy's developmental progress by serving as a figure of identification for his son, and by providing support for the genital schematization of the sexual and urinary aspects of his penis. Adam's father, ill-attuned to his son's needs, was not available to ensure the consolidation of his self-representation. The clinical material culled from Adam's sessions shows that rapprochement and anal struggles prepared the way for an intensified castration reaction which, given the vulnerability of Adam's sense of himself as phallic, was marked by depressive affect. The sudden and overpowering loss of sphincter control, which took place when he was separated from his mother in an environment he found overwhelming, became itself a trauma, given the pre-existing feelings of insecurity. The ideational content of being castrated (the one with the broken pipe) which was stimulated by this event led to the experience of depressive affect that necessitated defense. He resorted to regressive maneuvers that turned him progressively into a baby who would not get out of his pajamas or play with peers, in an attempt to protect himself from the sense of being damaged he would encounter if he let himself express his wish to function like a boy. Adam's sustained inability to control his urine was necessitated by his desperate need to avoid acknowledging the existence of his penis so as to ward off the painful threat of confirmation that he was damaged. While the impact of treatment on a child, and indeed on the family, is multifaceted, Adam's case presents evidence of a boy who achieved consolidation of his self-representation and resumed developmental progress in response to therapeutic work that addressed his sense of being irreparably damaged, as well as his fears that harm would befall him in response to his aggressive and phallic wishes. A failure to recognize both components of his castration reaction would have limited the therapeutic intervention, thereby restricting the patient's capacity to address the crucial aspects of his developmental conflict.

This study provides confirming evidence of the importance of castration depressive affect in a boy who did not suffer from physical traumata, major separation, or loss of the mother. Brenner (1979, 1982) discusses the need to identify the importance of castration anxiety relative to castration depressive affect for boys in the oedipal phase. The material presented above, in conjunction with data from developmental studies, suggests that this inquiry would be better served if we expand our developmental focus to include and distinguish between two phases of development, the phallic-narcissistic and the oedipal phase. It is postulated here that vulnerability to castration depression in boys as well as in girls is most heightened in the pre-oedipal phallic phase. Because phallic self-representation is not yet consolidated, the boy is susceptible to the ideation of having lost or damaged his penis. Therefore, castration depressive affect is most characteristic of, and prominent in this phase. Castration anxiety, which implies a feared potential (future) loss, is evident in the phallic narcissistic period but takes on its momentous importance as the dominant concern in the oedipal phase, after the sexually differentiated body image is better consolidated. Further study of children whose primary symptom is early regression in urinary function may prove to be a fruitful avenue of investigation to test this hypothesis.

The concept of depressive affect as a signal function has not received much attention in the clinical literature. Hoffman (1992) addresses the utility of the concept of castration depressive affect in his treatment of an adult male. He presents detailed clinical material to demonstrate the therapeutic benefit of interpretations based on the recognition that castration depressive affect was the operant signal affect that triggered defense. His patient, a man who became promiscuous to defend against intimacy with a woman, did not find relief from his symptom until he understood that intimacy triggered the fantasy that he was castrated—a fantasy rooted in his wish to be father's little girl. In his paper, Hoffman also reviews the literature on depressive affect in an attempt to utilize his clinical material to clarify various conceptualizations of depression. While such an undertaking is beyond the purview of this paper, data from Adam's treatment is relevant to some of the points of argument. In particular, Milrod (1988) considers depression as rage directed against the self, leading to a depressed mood state marked by the loss of the sense of one's worth. Brenner (1979) states, in contrast, that aggression turned against oneself is not the cause of depression, but a consequence of it. Data from Adam's treatment suggest that these controversies are partly complicated by the confusion inherent in the use of the word "depression" to signify two different concepts—a mood state and a signal affect—and underscores the need to distinguish, as Brenner (1979) indicates, between "depression" (mood) and "depressive affect" (signal). Adam's treatment record abounds with examples demonstrating that punitive turning against the self results in a progressively deepening mood of helplessness and hopelessness—the misery we label depression. However, there is also powerful evidence that, prior to the consolidation of self-representation, a child's reaction to sudden, spontaneous regression in function is associated with loss that signals damage. The child experiences himself as having lost something he used to have; in this sense, loss of function is equated with damage to the previously intact organ. The sense of being damaged mobilizes conflict and defense, and so does the threat of future damage. Whether the individual succumbs to the sense of misery we recognize as depression depends on the state of the ego and its capacity to mobilize defense.

Conflict is part and parcel of development, and children normally find in their makeup and environment the necessary ingredients that promote phase consolidation and developmental progress. Failure of normal progression, however, signals the need for an exploration aimed at identifying the features involved in the pathological outcome, with special consideration of the contribution of the conflicts specific to each stage of development. Abrams (1988) states that therapeutic work with children involves a dual task: to help them reach backward to understand the cause of their suffering, and to facilitate the maturational pull forward. The child searches in the therapeutic setting for the ingredients, "the organizing fantasies," necessary to promote and actualize the emerging developmental organization. In order to fulfill his therapeutic task, the analyst "must be mindful of the developmental process so he may attend to the concomitant task of facilitating phase progression" (Abrams, 1988). A detailed evaluation of Adam's vicissitudes along the developmental continuum was essential in order to effect a therapeutic exploration of his conflicts that promoted the resumption of phase progression. A successful intervention requires that the idiosyncratic meaning of the child's communications be uncovered. Adam's particular constellation of symptoms and the feelings associated with them needed to be understood as the product of the interaction of his particular endowment and his personal history. Through the careful labeling of his feelings, wishes and behavior, the child became better able to control and evaluate them. When Adam understood that his behavior, characterized by regression and anger, was an attempt to put an end to his fear and sadness, he gradually evolved more constructive ways to deal with feeling. Despite having dealt satisfactorily with the tasks of the phallic-narcissistic phase, Adam required ongoing therapeutic intervention to ensure the adequate resolution of his oedipal conflicts.

BIBLIOGRAPHY

ABRAMS, S. (1988). The psychoanalytic process in adults and children. *Psychoanalytic Study of the Child*, 43:245–261.

BERGMAN, A., & ESCALONA, S. (1949). Unusual sensitivities in very young children. *Psychoanalaytic Study of the Child*, 3/4:333–352.

BRENNER, C. (1975). Affects and psychic conflict. *Psychoanalytic Quarterly*, 5–28.

BRENNER, C. (1979). Depressive affect, anxiety and psychic conflict in the phallic-oedipal phase. *Psychoanalytic Quarterly*, 177–197.

BRENNER, C. (1982). *The Mind in Conflict*. International Universities Press.

EDGCUMBE, R., & BURGNER, M. (1975). The phallic-narcissistic phase. *Psychoanalytic Study of the Child*, 30:161–180.

FREUD, A. (1965). *Normality and Pathology in Childhood*. International Universities Press.

GALENSON, E., & ROIPHE, H. (1971). The impact of early sexual discovery on mood, defensive organization and symbolization. *Psychoanalytic Study of the Child*, 26:196–216.

GALENSON, E., & ROIPHE, H. (1977). Some suggested revisions concerning early female development. In Blum, H. *Female Psychology*. International Universities Press, pp. 29–57.

GALENSON, E., & ROIPHE, H. (1980). The preoedipal development of the boy. *JAPA*, 28:805–827.

GLUCKMAN, R. (1986). A paradigm of development. *Psychoanalytic Study of the Child*, 41.

HOFFMAN, L. (1992). On the clinical utility of the concept of depressive affect as signal affect. *JAPA*, 40/2:405–423.

KATAN, A. (1946). Experience with enuretics. *Psychoanalytic Study of the Child*, 2:241–255.

KULISH, N. (2000). Primary femininity: Clinical advances and theoretical ambiguities. *JAPA*, 48/4:1355–1379.

MAHLER, M. (1966). Notes on the development of basic moods. In Loewenstein, R., et. al. *Psychoanalysis—A general psychology*. International Universities Press.

MAHLER, M. (1975). *The Psychological Birth of the Human Infant*. International Universities Press.

MILROD, D. (1988). A current view of the psychoanalytic theory of depression. *Psychoanalytic Study of the Child*, 43:83–99.

OLESKER, W. (1998). Female genital anxieties: Views from the nursery and the couch. *Psychoanalytic Quarterly*, 276–294.

PARENS, H., POLLOCK, L., STERN, J., & KRAMER, S. (1977). On the girl's entry into the oedipus complex. In Blum, H. *Female Psychology*. International Universities Press, 79–107.

SEROTA, M. (1969). Urine or you're in. *Psychoanalytic Study of the Child*, 24:252–270.

STERN, D. (1985). *The Interpersonal World of the Infant*. New York: Basic Books.

Motor Action, Emotion, and Motive

HOWARD M. KATZ, M.D.

The experience, imagery, and fantasy of self in motion play a central part in the dreams, aspirations, and affective life of individuals, and in their growth.

Human infants are supplied with an intrinsic drive to move to, with, and against forces and objects in the natural world, for that action maps a developing self into the world. This striving is not derivative from some other drive; it is a motivational force in and of itself, intertwined with other essential strivings of the developing individual.

Clinical observations and recent findings of developmental and neurobiological studies demonstrate that positive aspects of a person's striving in the sphere of motor control imbue a person's sense of self with qualities of energy, agency, and mastery. And, when thwarted, distorted, or unbalanced in relation to other strivings, one's physicality may also be a locus for conflict and maladaptive defenses.

Schemas of self in relation to the world at large and especially to significant others are often encoded in procedural modes of remembering and perceiving, where movement is central. When the analyst is attuned to the experience of motor action in the life of the person he or she seeks to know fully and to help, the appreciation of that person's motives, emotions, and sense of self is deepened and enhanced.

THE MENTAL REGISTRATION OF THE BODY'S ACTION, THE PLACE OF muscle in the mind, has yet to be well integrated into psychoanalytic

Training and Supervising Analyst, The Boston Psychoanalytic Society and Institute; Instructor, Department of Psychiatry, Harvard Medical School and McLean Hospital.

The Psychoanalytic Study of the Child 59, ed. Robert A. King, Peter B. Neubauer, Samuel Abrams, and A. Scott Dowling (Yale University Press, copyright © 2004 by Robert A. King, Peter B. Neubauer, Samuel Abrams, and A. Scott Dowling)

thinking. The importance of motion in the development of emotion and motive is suggested by the linguistic common core and confirmed by emerging scientific evidence. In this paper I will present clinical observations and considerations of developmental and neurobiological research to show how experience, imagery, and fantasy of self in motion play a central part in the dreams, aspirations, and affective life of individuals, and in their growth.

That the self is rooted in the body has long been a core precept of psychoanalysis, beginning with Freud's conception of a primal "body ego." But, while Freud conceived of the experience of the body as forming the first rudiments of the self, his "body ego" was conceptualized largely in terms of its boundaries, intactness, management of intake and excretion, and sexual excitation. The roles of movement and physical exploration received scant attention.

Freud's most basic formulations of the structuring of the mind included the idea that thinking capacity emerges out of the *inhibition* of motor discharge. That inhibition was seen as a principal function of the ego. Because Freud's views so dominated the early development of psychoanalytic thinking, these perspectives overshadowed those that others might have brought to the developing theory. In an example on which I elaborated in an earlier paper (Katz, 2002), Freud's disciple and biographer, Ernest Jones, put athletic efforts in a category, "beyond psychology," even though he was an avid athlete who wrote a long treatise on skating (Dufresne and Genosko, 1995).

Clinical and research observations support the view that a person's striving in the sphere of motor control, far from being "beyond psychology," should be recognized as a central element in imbuing a person's sense of self with qualities of energy, agency, and mastery. And, when thwarted, distorted, or unbalanced in relation to other strivings, one's physicality may also be a locus for conflict and maladaptive defensives. Each of the following clinical vignettes illustrates both the role of physicality in progressive, adaptive expansion of one's sense of self and ways in which the experience and fantasy of motor action may be involved in conflictual, defensive, and maladaptive scenarios.

The vignettes I offer come from varied experiences, working with patients in psychotherapy or psychoanalysis, and with athletes who have sought help more narrowly focused on their pursuits in sport. Each employs a good deal of disguise, but I have sought to stay as close to the data as possible in relation to the core elements of the phenomena to be described.

Two of these examples start with a dream. In an earlier paper

(Katz, 2002), I compared cinematic imagery portraying transcendent motor action to dreams of flying. I suggested that the excitement of the movie-goer is like that of the dreamer, whose dream of flying captures the feeling of a drive toward free and expansive movement. I argued that such a drive is basic and intrinsic, and doesn't require explanation in terms of symbolic links to other aims, as has been common in the literature on dreams of flying. In this paper, the clinical context for understanding dreams which include images of flying will be spelled out more fully. Additionally, dreams may usefully depict the role of motor action in relation to diverse developmental issues, as dreams often portray a scenario with an emotional thread running through several developmental epochs and challenges (Hartmann, 1996).

VIGNETTE 1: BOB

Bob was in his fourth year of psychoanalysis when he began an hour with this dream:

> I was playing basketball, and it started with a scramble for a loose ball. I get it and then pass it to a guy on the team who makes a great move to the hoop. Then he puts it back to me, and I put it through. The whole play baffles the guy guarding me, so I keep repeating it, and each time I'm impressed by the beauty of the ball swishing through the net. I'm mesmerized by that image: I circle the court, dribbling and shooting through the net over and over. Then I'm bounding from one side to the other. Like flying. One step at mid court, then up, to the hoop, and in. I'm astounding the people watching. It gets more and more acrobatic and becomes a show. They arrange more seating, and then there is music. At the end I'm singing.

Bob said it is "a dream of being able to do anything I imagined." But then he noted that it seemed to be the opposite of how he had been thinking lately, always imagining things won't work out. In particular he felt disparaging about the prospects for the analysis to really help. Then he recalled a topic from the previous day: my upcoming vacation and associations he had had to times in childhood when his mother went away. He said, "I woke from this dream this morning wondering: 'What does this have to do with that?' and then thought about my father coming to my basketball games. I don't think I had it straight until now. I had always thought that he had never come. But he had! He came, at least, to some games. But mother never did. But now I recall vividly that my father was there, though I ignored him, didn't talk to him. . . . I'm imagining right now that I was not as bad a player as I thought myself to be."

I inquired about the possibility that he had carried distorted views for all those years, both about his parents' presence and about himself as an athlete. Bob continued, "Maybe I needed to identify with others' worst view of me. Probably the coach was not as down on me as I thought. But I had my own problem. I couldn't think big and then act big. That dream expresses what is probably a common fantasy of that age, starring on the team or in the musical. But I would shrink from it. I do the same thing now, with activities and with relationships, fantasize one thing but do another. I do it with you.—I avoid things, like your vacation. . . . I felt how much you mean to me last week but didn't say anything about it. I think I worry about what I mean to you."

I said, "You don't say what I meant to you, and then you disparage yourself and your involvement in the analysis. You hedge against your wishes that I'll be there to support you as you seek to 'think big and act big,' as you do in this dream."

After a silence, Bob said, "I felt very emotional, like I could burst into tears. It is hard to relate to you that way, to let myself feel close to you. But maybe there is hopefulness in the dream, a feeling I can relate to you that way . . . sometimes we can be lighter, more playful . . . And I hope I can do that with my father and others."

COMMENT:

At age 12 or 13, as a junior high school basketball player, Bob was indeed inhibited. His self-esteem and confidence were undermined when he began to feel growth of his physical capacities but felt that others, particularly his parents, did not admire or encourage his use of them. He felt the same discouragement about expressing his feelings, and could not show his emotion to others.

Bob had been in much that same state at the outset of the analysis. Dream imagery was then, also, often filled with physical action, but of a much different nature than we see in the dream that began this hour. In the earlier phase of analysis, a typical dream placed him on the ocean, entirely alone, struggling against the elements, desperately trying to get back to shore. He had been intellectualized and limited in his scope of affect. He had been distant from his family, especially his father, and had few friends. A growing sense of isolation and depression had led him to analysis.

And Bob was stiff, physically, in that first phase of analysis. His overall posture was rigid, and he would walk into the room, take a position on the couch, and maintain it with little variation until standing to leave at the end of the hour. On a few occasions it was just at that time, as he stood, that he felt able to see or express something new. As time went on, Bob found that I was receptive to listening to what he said after standing up, and then sometimes he began to sit and talk before the hour was out. He was at first tentative about changing his position, wanting to know if it was all right with me. He learned that as far as I was concerned he could move as he wished, and that what was most important for his analysis was to think together about what feelings and thoughts led to the wish to change positions and what his experience was. We both observed that he was often more animated at such times, and not infrequently a "move" into a new area or mode of thought arose when he was moving more freely physically.

In this material one can see how dream imagery of himself in physical action represented and expressed, indeed, literally embodied, Bob's reaching toward a fuller range of feeling. His expansiveness as a person was experienced in terms of physical expansiveness in an imagistic narcissistic fantasy demonstrating deep desires to be loved and admired. The anxiety which had long caused suppression of such wishes (and associated action) was illuminated by further associations in subsequent hours which included his concerns about wanting too much, his jealousy, and his fears of object loss should he become too grandiose. At this mid-point in analysis, Bob was feeling dimensions of himself in relation to me and to others which evoked both transference repetition and new possibilities. They were represented and experienced most graphically, in a way that provided a portal to deepened affect, by imagery of transcendent athletic activity.

VIGNETTE II: AMY

At 16, Amy's struggles on the basketball court were making her feel very bad about herself. When her father called, he seemed more concerned about her performance than her feelings, but he did indicate that Amy was increasingly frustrated, angry, and morose. A year of redoubled effort in basketball camps and physical training seemed not to be paying off as she started her new season with play that seemed, to her at least, worse than the previous year. Her father portrayed the prospect of getting some psychological help in terms of helping her play better, and Amy had finally agreed she could use some help with it. We set up an appointment, but by the time I was to see Amy, things had gone from bad to worse. She had sustained an ankle injury that would put her on the sidelines for much of the season.

So Amy came into my office for a first visit hobbled not only by pain, but by a sense of depression, in her words feeling "blown away." She felt this was the season to show her abilities and now it was thoroughly ruined. She had trained hard as the season approached, was in the best shape of any girl on the team (a premier team in our state), and was intent on showing that she deserved a starting position. That was one side of the story.

Once Amy trusted me a bit, she revealed the feeling that in the first place she was a sham. She sadly suggested that she was never really a good player, always failing to perform in big games. Maybe she could have proven herself this year, but more likely she would have been shown up as no good. Her anxiety about being watched led her to think too much, to be tentative and slow. She was focused on "not screwing up." She didn't feel she ever did her best. Now she wouldn't even have a chance to try. She even blamed herself for her "stupid injury," though her account of the event suggested to me that she had simply been unlucky. It also appeared to me that as Amy worked and worked at conditioning and drills she got further and further from an experience of basketball as play.

Seeing her weekly, I soon could appreciate the pressure she put on herself both on and off the court. I tried to look for the places where she had felt, or could feel now, a greater sense of efficacy and worth. Getting back in shape was terribly important to her. One day we were talking about the feeling she had swimming. Buoyant in the water, she felt lighter. As we talked about it, her mood got lighter, too, and she really lit up when her associations led to skiing. A broad smile came to her face as she recalled first learning to ski the expert trails with her big sister. She had not thought about those days, back in grammar school, in a long time.

As our discussions broadened to include more about her relationships and her intellectual pursuits, Amy revealed the deep uncertainties about herself. She felt she lived in fear, without being clear what the fear was about, "so I hold back . . . I never feel that I really go for it." She put it together that at least since seventh or eighth grade she felt shaky, awkward, and shy with friends, comparing herself unfavorably with her very outgoing and athletic older sister.

I noted that Amy felt things had changed when she was in seventh or eighth grade and asked about the time before. She thought about what it was like when she was ten or eleven years old; it seemed like a more carefree time. I asked what was important to her then. She recalled again her love of skiing. In the midst of this discussion she became emotional, both excited and upset, as she recalled an incident that occurred when she was in seventh grade, when she had had a serious crash on the slopes. (She had been very shaken up, and carried off the mountain, but had sustained no serious injury.) In our next meeting Amy said that before that crash she had had the feeling "I could just do it, ski free, as though I had wings." But she had gone out of control and been hurt. It felt like a rude awakening.

Amy began to think that since that day, she had been ruled much more by fear and had become increasingly controlled and controlling. She could understand over time that her conflicts over freedom and limits, open expression of her desire or passion versus constraint, were not only about skiing or sport. She recognized the conflict first in the athletic realm, but she struggled with fear and control in many other domains, such as in allowing herself to fantasize, to have ambition, or to be outgoing with friends. Moreover, in various realms of action, and most particularly in basketball, she had increasingly shifted her focus from the joy of playing to performance. She could eventually see how much she was trying to please her father, who was himself a basketball player, and who placed great importance on success. He was vocally proud of her big sister, who was by then playing at the college level. Amy realized that she had focused too narrowly on basketball, that too much was riding on it. But without her identity as a successful athlete, she worried, "Who am I, and what good am I, anyway?"

COMMENT:

At the dawn of adolescence, Amy faced familiar developmental issues. Could she give rein to or must she rein in her sexuality and intensified emotions? How could she manage conflicts over wishes to separate from and differentiate from her family? And how could she define herself, establish her own identity? Athletic action, for this girl, as for many others, was a lightning rod or organizer both for expansive wishes and for inhibitions. As a consequence, conflicts over some of her most central desires were being played out in sport. It is also fair to say that many of her conflicts were avoided through her single-minded and increasingly obsessive approach to sport. The potential for growth which attends athletic striving can be distorted when that activity and associated fantasy are drawn into a narcissistic defensive structure. For Amy, fantasies of being great in basketball and admired for that had become a monomania. They obscured or avoided other areas of activity and conflicts over competition with a sibling, revival of oedipal wishes for her father and worries about managing the interpersonal challenges of greater intimacy with peers. What started out as a consultation to help her perform better as a basketball player transitioned into a psychoanalytically informed psychotherapy helping her to feel more fully herself, on and off the court.

Vignette III: Larry

Larry, a man in his fifties, whose depression had brought him to psychoanalysis a few years earlier, began a session with a dream:

> I was a lifeguard at a swimming club, like back when I was in school. I ran into this college friend [he digressed to tell about the friend, who had always been intimidating]. You were in the dream after that, but like a friend, walking down the street, I'm pushing you along, we're shoving each other, rough-housing like teenagers horsing around. Then I'm in the old bedroom I shared with my brother. I'm admiring myself in the mirror—how muscular I am. Then I worry about people seeing me, and I struggle to lower the window shade.

Larry indicated in his first associations a sense of shame about admiring himself, his strong thighs and buttocks, thinking how people must admire his physique. He then talked about how important sports and physical activity were to him before "converting" to a more intellectual/artistic type, and a subsequent feeling of self-consciousness about his body. Then his associations went to his long-deceased older brother, Jay, who had struggled with a disability that evolved from a neurological disorder of childhood. Larry recalled how he and his brother used to "horse around," but as Jay's illness progressed they no longer could. Larry then went on to note what felt like a change over several years of analysis. Whereas he had at first felt intimidated by the position of authority he gave me, "Like that guy in the dream that always made me feel small," now he felt, "Maybe I can horse around with you."

As I listened, knowledge of Larry's relationship with Jay and ways that the transference had evolved underscored some of the themes which were apparent in this densely packed dream imagery and the associations. I was already well aware of the way that homoerotic wishes and fears permeated Larry's images of his own body, that of his brother, and those of other men, including me. To be active and strong, on the one hand, or immobilized and weak, on the other, quickly became a signifier of masculinity versus enfeebled femininity and of a part to be played in a scenario of dominance and submission. Rough and tumble play that could be sublimated and neutralized had long felt impossible, and Larry had commonly portrayed himself as weak and small. So a new element of this dream image was his aggressive way of horsing around with me.

I commented that in the dream he then felt very strong and admiring of himself.

And Larry replied, "But then I had to hide it, lower the window shade. Yeah, first exhilaration at my incredible body, then shame . . ."

A few days later, Larry reported another dream:

> I was with my brother, going to a meeting. I felt sick, and soiled my pants. It was a mess. Then I showed him where he could get fresh clothes—odd, cause I was the one that made the mess.—Then we're back at the meeting, where I should be able to find my brother, but I can't. I'm looking all over, moving faster, and then. . . . I started to fly! A woman applauded and encouraged my flying. And I said "I like to do it this smooth way, don't need to flap wings harder." Then I was flying over a college campus, a festive scene, but then I realized I'd forgotten my brother and felt guilty.

Larry said that he had awakened from the dream feeling sad about forgetting his brother. Then he recalled last week's dream:

> like I had a power. Like I made you into this person I could be equal with, even push around. . . . First I feel all full of myself, then ashamed. Now in this dream I'm in that place of shame, dragged down into the shit, literally. And then I rise above it all. I'm exhilarated, flying. In the first part I'm all mixed up with Jay, sick like him, it's my problem then his problem, all mixed up. . . . Sometimes when I go to work, or when I go to therapy with you I come back from it in a bouncy state, juiced up. There is this sense that I can move stronger, faster and higher. I forget about Jay. And I am happy I leave him behind. Maybe you too. In that dream last week I push you and then you're gone. I'm alone. Some push in me to be alone. Like in dreams I can only be happy, triumphant alone. People might admire me from a distance but I fly by them. . . .

COMMENT:

Larry had other dreams of swimming effortlessly or flying smoothly, expressions of his wish to "escape gravity" (Katz, 2002). There were both adaptive and defensive aspects of his images of rising above the constraints of actual physical forces of gravity, the gravity of his brother's illness, which ultimately killed him, and his parents' grave expressions of concern about Jay, which punctuated his childhood. He wanted to give up the life-long emotional weight of guilt about surpassing his brother both physically and intellectually, which was conflated with his oedipal guilt and anxiety about daring to do more than his father, who was an able but passive and restricted man.

Larry was also gravely concerned about the meaning of his yearning for connection with a man, whether it be his father, his brother Jay, or his analyst. When in the first dream he started to feel he could "horse around," mix it up emotionally or physically with another man, he briefly felt a sense of pride and strength. But the exhibionism, narcissism, and homosexual connotations feel frightening and shameful, and he pulled down the shade to hide. In the second dream he is plunged into a regressive anal and undifferentiated scene of fusion and confusion. The feeling that he can rise above it and fly has progressive elements of escaping the bonds of guilt that have held him down, but it also has elements of a grandiose avoidant/schizoid/narcissistic defense against frightening images of himself that have conflated connotations, for him, of demasculinization, helplessness, passivity, and disability. His dream image of himself with power is a solitary one.

Anxiety about such issues contaminated Larry's physical engagement in the world. As a boy he had had athletic talents and ambitions, but would shrink from competition and from the body contact inherent in the sports he had pursued. This further damaged his sense of himself as a "real man," and a potent person.

In this third vignette, aims in the realm of motor action are not the central or driving element of the material. Yet even in a pair of dreams where the dominant themes have to do with anxiety about yearnings for connection with a man and fears of a homosexual self-image imbued with connotations of demasculinization and submission, the imagery of the athletic use of the body plays an important part in giving definition to the issues at hand.

DISCUSSION

In each of these three cases the imagery and experience of motor action were powerful elements of the sense of self. In each instance, that action and associated fantasy may serve progressive purposes or may be employed defensively or regressively. But, in either circumstance, moving physically mattered deeply, as a real fact of life and as metaphor. This was felt strongly by Amy in her adolescence, by Bob, as a young adult, and by Larry, well into his middle years. I worked with them at different stages of development and some of the experiences they recall may date back to middle and late childhood, but the depth of affective and emotional resonance of the imagery of motion derives from the extent to which motor action is an intrinsic element in the earliest origins of the self. Some of the data to support this notion come from relatively recent developmental and neurobiological findings.

DEVELOPMENTAL CONSIDERATIONS

The driving force of developmental growth is grounded in activity. At the core level, moving, perceiving, and remembering are unified activities. In the earliest phases of development, a primitive self feeling emerges as the child combines kinesthetic, tactile, visual, and olfactory sensations with motor activity and recognition memory in an early form of synthesizing, integrative ego functioning. The baby, at the onset of life, "is impelled to direct attention outward toward events, objects, and their properties, and the layout of the environment" (Gibson, 1988, p. 17). In the service of that need, the baby is supplied with an urge to explore the world physically and to expand that exploration continuously as development proceeds.

Direct observations of the motor activity of children have helped to elucidate its role in development. Among the first important contributions was a series of papers by Judith Kestenberg (1965, 1967) documenting the role of movement patterns in structuring individual developmental trajectories. Kestenberg related children's development of patterns of alternation between free flow of movement and boundaried movement to the broader ego-developmental issues of freedom and control. Filtering her observations through the then-dominant drive model of the mind and the traditional psychoanalytic parsing of stages of development, the patterns of movement she so carefully observed were often described in terms of how they serve other aims. But Kestenberg's observations also seemed to reflect an appreciation of the central importance of mastery of the actions of one's body in and of itself. She contributed a strong image of the child's individually crafted spatial configuration of self in relation to the world, forged from motor patterns. This view was harmonious with an emerging conception of motivation that includes an "instinct to master" (Hendrick, 1942) or a fundamental drive for "effectance" (White, 1959), and also with more recent work on the central role movement must play, if we see a developing child's behavioral repertoire in terms of dynamic self-organizing systems (Thelan and Smith, 1994).

Attention to the locomotor efforts of the child became sharper for psychoanalysts when it was related to an evolving theory of separation-individuation in the toddler phase. Margaret Mahler and her associates suggested how a child's active exploration of sensory-motor experience in relation to caregivers helps to shape the child's images of boundaries and his or her own locus of control. They noted how free movement, especially walking, is an essential aspect of the toddler's effort to discover and test the reality of the world which is under his or her own control (Mahler, Pine, and Bergman, 1975). Through continually testing the limits of magical images of mastery, the child gradually relinquishes magic omnipotence. But in so doing, he or she experiences increasing autonomy, self-sense, and self-esteem. Although Mahler and her colleagues brought much more attention to the motor aspect of development, their particular focus on the process of separation-individuation may have narrowed psychoanalytic views of where active motor striving fits into mental life.

Other lines of observational research on the motivating factors in child development have extended the view of positive emotional states organized around movement. More current studies show that positive emotional activation is sought by the developing child from the very beginning of life. The mind gets organized, in large part, for the purpose of successfully engaging in that activation, alone or with facilitating others. That success, pursued at progressively higher levels of achievement as development proceeds, contributes in an ongoing way to the child's sense of mastery, and the vitality of the self.

It is now abundantly clear that the youngest infant possesses a remarkable degree of pre-adaptive potential for direct interaction with caretakers, interaction that includes a perceptual, *motor-affective* dialog. For most modern theorists of development, affect is the driver of self organization, and positive affects are sought in a mode in which movement is key from a very early stage of life. Robert Emde (1991) suggests, "There is little question that the most basic motive for behavior in development involves *activity*," and he notes the way in which indications of pleasure in the infant relate to motor activity. Daniel Stern's observational data also suggest that affectively important representational "schemas-of-self-being-with-another" are "less concerned with knowledge and more with doing and being" (Stern, 1995).

Core aspects of the self arise out of action, including, prominently, motor action. Human infants are supplied with an intrinsic drive to move to, with, and against forces and objects in the natural world, for that action maps a developing self into the world. This striving is not derivative from some other drive; it is a motivational force in and of itself, intertwined with other essential strivings of the developing individual.

BRAIN, MIND, AND SELF IN MOTION

If motor behavior is intrinsic to the experience of emotion, the development of intention, and the self-sense that accrues around those experiences, then we might expect that neural representation and control of these functions are highly interconnected. This hypothesis is supported by a growing body of evidence from the neuroscience literature. Neuroanatomical and neurophysiological studies demonstrate dense interconnection of networks associated with motor control and affective states. Motor control processes widely distributed in the central nervous system also appear to be an inextricable component of processes of perception and ordering of attention.

Many studies converge on a conception that neural patterns underlying or representing motor action are inextricably intertwined with those associated with a person's most basic aims in spheres of attachment, sexual desires, and aggressive impulses. Panksepp (1998) suggests: "there is general agreement that the extended ascending reticular activating system, including thalamic reticular nuclei, is necessary for normal waking and attentional activities. However, I think we have almost totally ignored one of the ancient foundation processes—a neurosymbolic affective representation of I-ness or 'the self' that may be critically linked to a primitive representation within the brain stem. . . . I would suggest that *the self-referential coherence provided by ancient and stable motor coordinates may be the very foundation for the unity of all higher forms of consciousness.*" (emphasis added)

The brainstem structures to which Panksepp refers now appear to have an integrative role in cognition, motor control, and consciousness. The cerebellum is another brain structure that is newly seen as serving a broadened range of functions. As recently as the 1980s, the cerebellum was considered by most neurologists and neuroscientists to function purely in the realm of motor coordination, the most important structure plotting "stable motor coordinates." But the most recent data suggest that the cerebellum, as central as it is in coordinating movement, plays an important role in self regulation and self recognition.

Whereas the cerebellum was long considered primarily as a center coordinating muscle movement which was initiated in "higher" cortical centers, in essence taking its orders from the cortex, more recent studies demonstrate information pathways which involve much more intensive two-way traffic from cortex to pons to cerebellum and back through thalamus to the cortex (Schmahmann and Pandya, 1997). The thalamus is not only a way station from cerebellum to cortex, it is a centrally located subcortical structure well connected to many other areas of the brain including, prominently, limbic structures associated with emotion. The thalamus has also been shown to play an important and necessary role in consciousness. When these anatomical data are combined with data coming from careful neuropsychological assessment of patients with cerebellar pathology and from lesion studies of animals, they suggest that the cerebellum's function still has to do with coordination, but in spheres of experience and action well beyond the motor system. It appears that the cerebellum serves a central role in ordering and coordination of perceptual processes, of orientation in space, of language, and of cognition. The role of the cerebellum in affect regulation also is increasingly suggested by the evidence of psychopathology related to cerebellar dysfunction (Schmahmann and Sherman, 1997; Leroi et al., 2002).

Some primatologists have speculated that the cerebellum played a central role as evolving non-human primates needed to integrate an expanded motor repertoire into what may be a precursor to or primitive form of the sense of self. In this view it became essential for our primate ancestors to have increasingly refined knowledge of their own motor capabilities and limitations as they navigate through space in changing environments. Primatologist Povinelli has been one of the strongest proponents of the idea of an "ecological self" evolving in the course of primate evolution. He has been a champion of a "clambering hypothesis," which puts motor activity at a central place in processes of self recognition, not only for the non-human primates which have been the subject of his research, but for humans, especially at early stages of development (Povinelli and Cant, 1996). In this view, the human mind's distinctive capacities for self-reflective consciousness have co-evolved with sophisticated motor capacities and gestures. The idea follows that the emergent self can only be fully experienced as it moves and physically places itself in the world. This leads some cognitive scientists (e.g. Gibson, 1979; Neisser, 1995) to use the concept of ecological self to elucidate the intrinsic role of motor action in the mental registration of the procedural knowledge that gives first form to that self structure. This procedural knowledge and associated affect states serve as constant background to the social organism's experience of situating itself in the world at large and in relation to others.

MOVING ON

As physical activity is so important in the formation of the core of the self, the experience of movement carries motivational and emotional significance throughout life. An athletic dimension of living is repeatedly invoked and drawn into a wider range of experience as development proceeds and the complexity of mental life deepens. In some cultures the physicality of daily work and play insures that for most individuals the challenges and rewards of life are persistently imbued with a prominent motor cast. In modern industrial and post-industrial society, experiences of individuals are more varied. While some maintain athletic action as a valued aspect of life, now more commonly in leisure pursuits rather than work, others de-emphasize physicality, as language-based and aesthetic pursuits take center stage. But I would submit that muscular action persists as a background structuring element of perception and fantasy in each individual. For many people it may often move to the foreground.

The clinical data I offered illustrate ways in which that embodied self-experience is invoked in the representation and expression of diverse needs and wishes that unfold throughout development.

Bob's basic need to have his strivings for excellence and efficacy encouraged and admired were prominently experienced (mostly frustrated) on the basketball court in his pre-adolescence. The imagery associated with that experience continued to live within him many years later. Early in his analysis his posture and movement, the play of facial expression, the flow of thought and the experience of affect were all restricted. As he felt he could "move" freely with another person, from one thought to another, and from thought to feeling, the imagery of movement in dreams and his actual posture and movement in the analyst's consulting room became more free and expansive. This clinical experience is resonant with the developmental and neurobiological data suggesting the degree to which these diverse modes of movement—muscular, cognitive, and affective—are interrelated.

Bob's dream of expansive athletic action shaded into images of flying. In it he experienced entirely free movement, freedom from gravity, and total control of the space of the gymnasium. The capacity to imagine such freedom and the actual use of space in play are related, as can be seen particularly well in play therapy with children (Loewald, 1987). It may be more subtle in an adult analysis, but even so, we could see that Bob's increased sense of freedom included more full and easy movement through the space of my consulting room.

The imagery of Bob's dream was a sharp contrast with his previous image of himself. In his experience growing up, expansiveness, the feeling "I can do anything," was regularly rebuffed. To the extent that he could muster a grandiose feeling of being able to do anything, indeed to fly, he would have repeatedly had the Icarus-like experience of being doomed for the grandiosity of his fantasy.

And Icarus, no doubt, was a teenager. In material Bob shared with me, but which is not reported here, there was ample evidence that his experience of being thwarted occurred in early, middle, and late childhood, and in multiple domains of action. But the most poignant and vivid memories of such experience dated back to his early adolescence. Adolescence presents an invitation and a challenge to expand one's horizons, to live in a bigger world, a world that encompasses more space, literally and figuratively. As Bob entered adolescence, the experience he had already had in his family disposed him to distance himself from his wish for his father's approval, so that he disregarded his presence. He was also disposed to a negative transference to a coach, who probably valued Bob more than he thought. Too easily discouraged because of the interpersonal conflict involved, he quit playing a sport for which he was well suited. That experience contributed further to his already diminished sense of himself as an able and admirable person.

Amy's story similarly focuses attention on the developmental challenge of moving into a wider field of action as one becomes independent of parents and feels the emergence of a body equipped for more speed, more power and for a more adult form of sexuality. The confrontation with the limits on her freedom was acute and concrete in her skiing accident. But it was only a very identifiable example of a number of clashes between expansiveness and constraint any adolescent must encounter. The importance of such a setback in early adolescence may be heightened, as growing capacities raise the stakes on the interpersonal conflicts inherent in wishes to please her father, compete with her sister (and, one imagines, her mother). Partly in reaction to a traumatic setback, which probably collected some of the affect encountered in other setbacks that may be less dramatic and tangible, the sense "I can do anything" was replaced with a competing sense of being unable to do anything well. Moreover, her capacity for play was diminished, further contributing to the depressed and anxious sense of herself that Amy conveyed soon after we met.

The competitive conflict contributing to Amy's matrix of feeling about her athletic activity is akin to that which Larry, a man much further along in life, still carried with him from childhood. His brother's disability and his perception of his father's limitations imbued his aggressive and expansive motor activity with heightened oedipal conflict. Shengold (1994) reminds us that Oedipus and his father clashed over the control of space and the right to locomotion. Larry's particular worries about triumph over his weakened older brother and his father were intermixed with feelings of loss and yearnings for closeness to a man, yearnings that had homosexual connotations he experienced as regressive and shameful. In the context of the psychoanalytic relationship he mobilized imagery of his own body in action which demonstrated both positive strivings for mastery and defensive activity. The flight in Larry's dream may be as much an avoidance of real contact with the messy feelings involved in interaction with his brother, and his analyst, as it is a transcendent move beyond inhibition of his more ambitious strivings.

The strong basic desire to move with strength, grace, and freedom is set against resistance, both by the forces of nature, limits imposed by gravity and time, and by the forces of others who may thwart rather than facilitate our movement. In the conflict that ensues, one may fear injury to self or others. The structure of sports and many physical games allow an arena for playing out these conflicts. The players permit or impede movement, vie for control of space, propel a projectile through space to an intended target. In such games, our most basic conflictual strivings about separation, control, competing for resources or connection with others are played out.

It also follows that if the capacity for and freedom of movement is critically important for the development of a strong and vibrant sense of self, and plays a part in working through developmental conflict, profound restrictions on motor action will have a deep negative impact on narcissistic equilibrium. And, indeed, some psychoanalytically oriented observers have noted the deficit in the sense of self that ensues when free movement is lost or restricted. On the basis of a number of reviewed cases, Bernal (1984) noted, "Loss of the ability to move freely, whether due to illness, trauma, or confinement, threatens to shake the person's sense of vitality and self-esteem." Rabenu and Rabenu (1995) examined the role of free movement in the development of self through a special case of its absence, in a man who had been paralyzed through most of his development. The qualities of his narcissistic disequilibrium led them to conclude: "The dual role of the motor system in regulating and nurturing the self is maintained throughout life."

Schemas of self in relation to the world at large and especially to significant others are often encoded in procedural modes of remembering and perceiving, where movement is central. Expressive therapies, especially dance therapy, have recognized the importance of tapping into these constellations of thought, affect, and memory through motor action, in ways that are being articulated verbally in some recent literature (e.g. Siegel, 1995, Shahar-Levy, 2001). The importance of the imagery of motor action is finding its way into some recent conceptualizations of largely verbal process as some investigators (e.g. Stern, et al., 1998) bring observations of infant research, research on procedural memory, and the traditions of play therapy to bear on adult analysis. When the analyst is attuned to the experience of motor action in the life of the person he seeks to help, the appreciation of that person's motives, emotions, and sense of self is deepened and enhanced.

BIBLIOGRAPHY

BERNAL, W. (1984). Immobility and the Self. *J. Med. Philos.*, 9:75–91.

DUFRESNE, T., & GENOSKO, G. (1995). Jones on Ice: Psychoanalysis and Figure Skating. *Int. J. Psycho-Anal.*, 76:123–133.

EMDE, R. N. (1991). Positive Emotions for Psychoanalytic Theory: Surprises from Infancy Research and New Directions. *J. Amer. Psychoanal. Assn.*, 39S:5–44.

GIBSON, E. J. (1988). Exploratory behavior in the development of perceiving, acting and acquiring of knowledge. *Annual Review of Psychology*, 39:1–41.

GIBSON, J. J. (1979). *The Ecological Approach to Visual Perception*. Boston: Houghton-Mifflin.

HARTMANN, E. (1996). Outline for a Theory on the Nature and Functions of Dreaming, *Dreaming*, 6:2:147–170.

HENDRICK, I. (1942). Instinct and the Ego During Infancy. *Psychoanal. Q.*, 11:33–58.

KATZ, H. M. (2002). Escaping Gravity: Movie Magic and Dreams of Flying. *Psychoanalytic Study of the Child*, 57:294–304.

KESTENBERG, J. S. (1965). The Role of Movement Patterns in Development—Ii. Flow of Tension and Effort. *Psychoanal. Q.*, 34:517–563.

KESTENBERG, J. S. (1967). The Role of Movement Patterns in Development—Iii. The Control of Shape. *Psychoanal. Q.*, 36:356–409.

LEROI, I. ET AL. (2002). Psychopathology in Patients with Degenerative Cerebellar Diseases: A Comparison to Huntington's Disease. *Am. J. Psychiatry*, 159:8:1306–1314.

LOEWALD, E. (1987). Therapeutic Play in Space and Time. *Psychoanalytic Study of the Child*, 42:173–192.

MAHLER, M. S., PINE, F., & BERGMAN, A. (1975). *The Psychological Birth of the Human Infant: Symbiosis and Individuation*. New York: Basic Books.

NEISSER, U. (1995). Criteria for an Ecological Self. In P. Rochat, ed., *The self in infancy: Theory and research.* Amsterdam: Elsevier.

PANKSEPP, J. (1998). *Affective Neuroscience.* New York: Oxford.

POVINELLI, D., & CANT, J. (1996). Arboreal Clambering and the Evolutionary Origins of Self Conception. *Q. Review of Biology,* 70:393–421.

RABENU, P., & RABENU, T. G. (1995). The Role of Free Movement in Separation-Individuation. *Psychoanalytic Study of the Child,* 50:150–167.

SCHMAHMANN, J. D., & PANDYA, D. N. (1997). The Cerebrocerebellar System. *Int. Rev. Neurobiol.,* 41:31–60.

SCHMAHMANN, J. D., & SHERMAN, J. C. (1997). Cerebellar Cognitive Affective Syndrome. *Int. Rev. Neurobiol.,* 41:433–440.

SHAHAR-LEVY, Y. (2001). The Function of the Human Motor System in Processes of Storing and Retrieving Preverbal, Primal Experience. *Psychoanalytic Inquiry,* 21,3:378–393.

SHENGOLD, L. (1994). Oedipus and Locomotion. *Psychoanal. Q.,* 63:20–28.

SIEGEL, E. V. (1995). Psychoanalytic Dance Therapy: The Bridge between Psyche and Soma. *Amer. J. Dance Ther.* 17:115–1128.

STERN, D. N. (1995). *The Motherhood Constellation.* New York: Basic Books.

STERN, D. N. ET AL. (1998). Non-Interpretive Mechanism in Psychoanalytic Therapy, *Int. J. Psycho-Anal.,* 79:903–921.

THELAN, E., & SMITH, L. B. (1994). *A Dynamic Systems Approach to the Development of Cognition and Action.* Cambridge, Mass: MIT Press.

WHITE, R. (1959). Motivation Reconsidered: The Concept of Competence. *Psychol. Rev.,* 66:297–333.

TECHNIQUE

Counter-Responses as Organizers in Adolescent Analysis and Therapy

M. BARRIE RICHMOND, M.D.

The author introduces Counter-response *as a phenomological term to replace theory-burdened terms like counter-transference, counter-identification, and counter-resistance. He discusses the analyst's use of self (drawing on the comparison with Winnicott's use of the object) in processing the expectable destabilizing counter-reactions that occur in working therapeutically with disturbed adolescents and their parents. Further, he discusses the counter-reaction to the patient's narrative, acting-out, and how re-enactments can serve as an organizer for understanding the patient's inner life when the analyst formulates his/her counter-response.*

Chair, Child and Adolescent Analysis Program, Institute for Psychoanalysis, Chicago; Child and Adolescent Supervising Analyst, Institute for Psychoanalysis; Training and Supervising Analyst, Institute for Psychoanalysis; Faculty, University of Chicago Department of Psychiatry.

Sam Abram's (New York) comments on earlier drafts contributed to the central thesis of this paper. I am deeply indebted for his continuing encouragement, wise counsel, and wonderful sense of humor.

Several Chicago colleagues made important contributions to earlier drafts, for which I acknowledge my appreciation: Mark Berger, Herb Cibul, Mark Gehrie, Arnold Goldberg, Meyer Gunther, Richard Harris, Adele Kaufman, Robert J. Leider, Barbara Rocah, Sanford Weisblatt, and Cliff Wilkerson.

Marie Lamia (San Francisco) arranged for a presentation of an earlier version at the Wright Institute in Berkeley, California. Her comments provided an important perspective on working with parents.

Josh Richmond edited the pre-final draft. He helped clarify the premise and brought out the essential ideas in a clear way for both author and reader.

The Psychoanalytic Study of the Child 59, ed. Robert A. King, Peter B. Neubauer, Samuel Abrams, and A. Scott Dowling (Yale University Press, copyright © 2004 by Robert A. King, Peter B. Neubauer, Samuel Abrams, and A. Scott Dowling).

Emphasis is placed on the therapist forming his or her own narrative with the adolescent that takes into account the evoked counter-reaction. For this purpose, the author recommends the use of a combined counter-response and metaphor-orienting perspective to acknowledge and work with the denial, illusions, reversal of perspective, and catastrophic anxieties experienced with these adolescents. The counter-response perspective permits the emergence of the disturbed adolescent's novel narrative; however, since these experiences can be destabilizing or disruptive, the author also recommends the use of a personal metaphor to anticipate the reluctance to examining, processing, and formulating the analyst's dysphoric counter-reaction. With the use of the counter-response, the analyst's therapeutic ideal is to achieve a more optimal balance between using accepted narrative theories and exploring novel enactment experiences. His swimming metaphor stratagem is designed to keep the analyst in these difficult encounters.

Counter-Responses

ANALYSTS REGULARLY ENCOUNTER COUNTER-TRANSFERENCE PROBlems while treating emotionally disturbed adolescents. In this paper, I introduce the term "counter-response" and discuss using a personal metaphor to prepare for and frame potentially disruptive reactions evoked by disturbed adolescent patients. I prefer the theory-neutral term "counter-response" as compared to "counter-transference" for a number of reasons: First, it allows me to differentiate between the analyst's evoked counter-reaction and his formulated counter-response. I want to emphasize the importance of the analyst's experiential processing, which allows him to become more attuned to the severely disturbed adolescent through the better processing of the evoked counter-reaction. Second, there is considerable confusion concerning the empirical referents for transference and counter-transference. Our embedded theories often obfuscate rather than illuminate empirical data. The current loss of specificity in the use of the term counter-transference is largely due to the widespread current practice of using the terms counter-transference, counter-resistance, and counter-identification indiscriminately.

For these reasons, I try to strike a balance and start with the premise that my evoked reactions and experiences should be examined as empirical phenomena, rather than being linked in a theory-influenced pre-packaged way. My primary consideration in assessing what has transpired in interactions with these disturbed adolescent patients is: What am I feeling or thinking in relation to what I comprehend?

Having made my assessment, I then try to reach a genetic-dynamic formulation (Hartmann and Kris, 1945) that takes into account the role of genetic antecedents and developmental transformations in reconstructing the adolescent's psychological life (Abrams, 1978). Also, I make a distinction between novel evoked reactions based on my experiences with these disturbed adolescents, as compared to the analyst's *a priori* clinical intuitions. Granted, years of experience pave the way to clinically intuitive-based conclusions. I don't doubt that our theories place me on paths before I'm aware that I'm on them. Nonetheless, my goal is to hear the patient first, not race to premature closures.

I find it useful, sometimes necessary, to use a personal metaphor to prepare for the aggressive assaults regularly encountered with this sub-group of disturbed adolescents. In these trying encounters, one wants to grab whatever tool is in sight, whether it's appropriate or not, and get out! This adolescent sub-group is prone to acting-out their enactment behavior of destructive, homicidal, and suicidal fantasies and impulses. This strategic approach for processing the analyst's evoked counter-reactions with the use of a personal metaphor as a frame to contain dysphoric reactions, rather than grabbing onto whatever theory feels most appropriate for "getting out" of these tough situations, can help the analyst to be more innovative, and thereby facilitate the disturbed adolescent's discovery of his own personal meanings and to achieve a greater sense of his own agency. Our job is not to get out, but to get into the adolescent's world.

COUNTER-TRANSFERENCE LITERATURE: A BRIEF, SELECTIVE REVIEW

Following Freud's views concerning the patient's influence on the analyst's unconscious feelings, it is generally accepted that no analyst can go further than what his own (neurotic) complexes and internal resistances permit. Freud dismissed the analytic capacity of those who couldn't overcome or manage their counter-transference (Waksman, 1986). Following the Zurich School and then in 1922 the International Psychoanalytic Association, the training analysis became a compulsory training requirement, linked to Freud's "Recommendations to Physicians" paper (1912).

In re-tracing this history, Waksman points out there was no unanimity as to what to do with these feelings. On the one hand, it was acknowledged that the counter-transference existed as a product of the analyst's unconscious, and had to be overcome. And after Winnicott's (1949) "Hate in the Counter-transference," it became more clear that as the target of the disturbed adolescent's aggression, the analyst's fears about his own aggression, along with the ongoing narcissistic assault—all contribute to serious, expectable difficulties in working with such patients. (This probably explains a significant part of the casualty rate among analysts who choose to avoid working with these patients.)

Paula Heimann's contributions (1950, 1960) answered this question about what to do with these feelings. She wrote: "My thesis is that the analyst's emotional response . . . represents one of the most important tools for his work" (See Waksman, p. 406). And a decade later, in her 1959 paper, she elaborated on her views, stating the importance of overcoming the difficulties of the counter-transference by self-analysis (or consultation or additional analysis) and as complete as possible training: only then would analysts be able to use their counter-transference productively in analytic work (Waksman, p. 407).

A large, varied literature has helped to clarify the difficulties the analyst faces with such experiences. Nevertheless, Erna Furman (2002) in her comprehensive review of the use of the terms transference and counter-transference commented that counter-transference is used in inconsistent and different confusing ways. She also noted that Anna Freud never enlarged on the counter-transference concept.

Racker's (1953) depiction of the analyst's counter-identification with his patients, and Bion's (1957) writing about the patient's unconscious envy and related attempts to destroy meaning by attacks on linking, which the analyst's attempts to facilitate in the analytic dialogue, eventuated in different views being proposed to clarify the use of the analyst's counter-transference in working with such difficult patients.

In the context of the changing intellectual climate of psychoanalysis (Jacobs, 1999), two factors have been largely responsible for the increased interest in the analyst's management of his unconscious reactions and his counter-responses to his patients: (1) that the analytic process increasingly has been described in a relationship context; and (2) the analyses of more severely disturbed children and adolescents have resulted in a better understanding of enactment phenomena and the analyst's evoked reaction.

In proposing a theory neutral-viewpoint, my purpose is to facilitate the analyst's use of his own evoked reactions to achieve a better understanding of the disturbed adolescent's inner world and novel narrative. Reviews of the counter-transference literature reveal clear splits along ideological lines. Not uncommonly, representatives of classical analysis and ego psychology either don't index references to the counter-transference literature (e.g. Eagle, 1984) or make only very brief comments about its role in the analytic process—e.g. Marshall Edelson (1988, p. 181) and Paul Gray (1994). Jacobs's (1999) review emphasizes how the changing intellectual climate within and outside of analysis, as well as alterations in the analytic establishment, were the necessary background for the full exploration of the concept of counter-transference that has occurred, especially during the past thirty years. He also credits Strachey (1934), earlier, for both facilitating the recognition of the inter-subjective aspects of analysis (Jacobs, p. 579) and pointing out that the analyst's emotional participation (largely through his counter-transference influenced response) is indispensable in the therapeutic action of analysis.

Klein (1921–45), Winnicott, and many other object-relations theorists pointed to the analyst's subjectivity as a way to access the unconscious of the patient. Fromm-Reichmann (1950) supported Winnicott's view that counter-transference plays an essential role in work with seriously disturbed patients. On the other hand, Jacobs points out that it was [primarily] Annie Reich's influence (1951) that resulted in the term counter-transference continuing to carry a certain stigma.

Jacobs concludes his review by commenting that recent investigations of counter-transference and the larger issues of the mind of the analyst at work have expanded our understanding of the analytic process: "Counter-transference not only exerts a continuous influence on the analytic process, but constitutes an invaluable pathway for the investigation of that process." He highlights the importance of the analyst's subjectivity and the inter-subjective aspects of analysis for understanding the patient's intra-psychic world.

Along with Winnicott, Racker, and Bion, the French psychoanalytic counter-transference literature has strongly influenced and reinforced my own thinking. I especially like the idea that the unconscious bodily resonance experienced by the analyst is the only authentic form of psychoanalytic communication (Pontalis, 1977). Along with the emphasis on bodily tensions, I would include subjectively distressing tension-inducing affects: i.e. the impact on *both* the analyst's mind and body, felt in the actuality of the session, as the most authentically psychoanalytic form of unconscious communication. I include both poorly differentiated affect states elicited by the adolescent's undifferentiated aggression, as well as inchoate body experiences that reflect important but un-metabolized counter-responses. If the reader agrees that these distressing experiences are unconscious authentic communications, then I posit our goal should be to work to stay with these feelings, rather than escape them through some "understanding," which can turn out to be nothing other than an escape route.

COUNTER-RESPONSE VS. COUNTER-TRANSFERENCE

I use the term "counter-response" to include: (1) the analyst's evoked counter-reaction to the adolescent's transference, and (2) the range of reactions and responses stimulated by the adolescent's enactments, acting out, and other actions and behaviors. Further, the term counter-response has the important advantage of addressing clinical phenomena rather than confusing conceptual issues, and is closer to empirical data and the analyst's subjective experience. Thus, the use of the term counter-response is less likely to be blurred by theoretical intrusions that have robbed "counter-transference" of its original specificity.

Some may argue that counter-response is simply a matter of emphasis, or renaming counter-transference, a coming up for air and then going back in, but I beg to differ. I think counter-response goes beyond emphasis: We are talking about a different approach and a different technique with different results. I'm not simply renaming counter-transference. I find counter-response to be a more active, less reactive tool to keep me in these uncomfortable feelings and sensations. Furthermore, I find that the term "counter-response," as compared to "counter-transference," has several advantages: Most importantly, my counter-response permits me to feel more allied with a real person, rather than a subject who has been distanced by a theoretical barrier.

Moving on to the second part of the term "counter-response," the "response" part of counter-response looks specifically at the analyst's evoked emotional reactions and feeling states. As is well known, the analyst's responses to disturbed, acting-out, aggressive adolescents can start with raw, emotionally charged feelings of anger, hatred, or erotic and narcissistically charged excitement states. Nonetheless, viewing the counter-response for its therapeutic potential for forming a connecting alliance better enables me to identify with the adolescent's internal life. How to sustain that connecting alliance is at the heart of counter-response.

We know these feeling states, although evoked by the disturbed adolescent, come in large part from the analyst's repressed, ego-dystonic psychological past and present character. Further along this continuum of counter-reactions lies a more modulated set of contained responses that the analyst needs to take into consideration. When he formulates these evoked thoughts and feelings, he can find a key that lets him into these adolescents' inner lives vs. being shut out by his own feelings and preferred theory.

The counter-response perspective provides an orienting approach to what can often be described as destabilizing and disorganizing clinical events. Dealing with these disturbed adolescents often leaves the analyst feeling uncomfortable, embarrassed, psychologically disorganized, or frightened. On the other hand, when an analyst anticipates the disruptive impact of these adolescent patients, and thus uses his counter-responses as an organizer, i.e. as an orienting approach, he can then find important links to their inner lives.

In addition to introducing the term counter-response, I am promoting the thesis that relates the use of metaphor to the solution for reaching an optimal state of equanimity and total responsiveness when dealing with the evoked counter-response. Since a treatment process can stand or fall depending on how regressed moments are understood and managed with these disturbed adolescents, it is important that the analyst's counter-response be recognized and used analytically to clarify the disturbed adolescent's unconscious life.

Previously (Richmond, 1992), I discussed the analyst's use of his counter-response—using the term counter-identification—as a valuable means for understanding these disturbed adolescents and their parents. Nevertheless, as helpful as this perspective was, I found that contemporary "Counter-Transference Theory"—mainly ideas about projective identification and various counter-reactions—led me to become overly focused on a narrow orientation: my counter-identification with the adolescent's (or parent's) enactment. On the one hand, the counter-identification form served well as an organizer for processing the emotional impact of the adolescent's enactment; yet, something was lost in my sense of immediacy and specificity: the patient's inner narrative or drive escaped me.

The central issue is not so much the narrow focus on the counter-identification, or the loss of immediacy; rather, it's whether this mode of processing has the drawback of limiting the analyst's focus solely to the counter-enactment. This could constrain the analytic ideal of activating the exploration of the adolescent's inner life by searching out his or her novel narrative. These considerations led to my preference for the descriptive phenomenological term "counter-response," which I find the to be most beneficial for dealing with counter-reactions evoked in the analyst.

THE DEVELOPMENT OF THE COUNTER-RESPONSE VIEWPOINT

Having outlined the insufficiencies of dealing solely with counter-identification and how it fails to activate the analyst's pursuit of the patient's inner-narrative, I now want to elaborate on how counter-response provides access to the adolescent's inner narrative.

Two issues about the analyst's counter-response prove to be beneficial for facilitating the therapeutic work with these adolescents: (1) how the evoked reaction in the analyst can be used as an organizer, and (2) the value of creating and using a personal metaphor. Both of these ideas can help the analyst better understand his patient's inner narrative.

(1) The first idea is that the analyst's dysphoric feeling state or over-excited counter-response, when properly contained, and then formulated, can be used constructively to serve psychoanalytic purposes. The evoked feeling state can be used as an organizer to access otherwise inaccessible psychic realities of these disturbed adolescents.

(2) The second idea, which is aligned with the first, adds a guiding perspective: I use a personal swimming metaphor to anticipate and help contain the emotional impact of the disturbed adolescent's enactment, and then use the resultant sense of being destabilized in a constructive manner. For example, the use of the swimming metaphor has helped to anticipate my potential for splitting the (evoked) negativity in my counter-response. I refer to a tendency to over-identify with the adolescent, while being overly critical of the parents. This form of splitting can result in an unwarranted negative attitude toward the parents, while missing the severity of the adolescent's psychopathology (Personal communication, Robert Koff, M.D.). A look at the development of these tools leads to a proper understanding and use of them; it was the tools themselves that gave birth to the term counter-response.

Before proceeding further, I think it's important to share with the reader three formative experiences that specifically led to my interest in using the counter-response as an organizer for strongly evoked emotional reactions:

(1) An early interest in the role of identification in parallel process phenomena, which, in turn, led to my interest in Racker's (1953) writing on counter-identification counter-transferences. This per-

spective led to my realization that what is referred to as "counter-transference" in many instances has more to do with the analyst's ego-dystonic problems with his own aggression and hatred, which I elaborate on further in the body of this paper.

(2) An experienced Child and Adolescent Analyst's report of a stormy evaluative session with an adolescent girl.

(3) A not-to-be-forgotten clinical experience with a pre-adolescent twelve-year-old boy: what I refer to as my "Italian Couch" case.

Read the first two examples with an eye as to how they first formed a notion of the potential value of the analyst's counter-response:

EXAMPLE ONE: TWO FORMS OF IDENTIFICATION IN THERAPY OR ANALYSIS WITH ADOLESCENTS

Following a strong interest in the role of the processes of identification in the psychological lives of my patients, I became aware that my initially unexpressed, ambivalent feelings to the supervisor paralleled the analysand's ambivalent questions, criticism, and doubts about me. Accordingly, my interest in counter-identification processes naturally followed, especially the central role of identification in the parallel process phenomena. This became the precursor to my use of the analyst's counter-identification, and later the counter-response as an organizing idea. By feeling free to express my (negative) ambivalent feelings to the supervisor (who later became a valued mentor), I was able to eventually grasp parallels in the analysand's hatred and disappointment.

At that time, I had little understanding of the potential role of counter-responses for my clinical work. As difficult a step as this was in my own emotional learning curve, I stress that the originally suppressed ambivalent feelings to the supervisor were ego-syntonic, not ego-dystonic thoughts. At no time did I think they were unacceptable feelings, and so I had relatively little trouble in being able to identify with the analysand and understand his feelings toward me.

I am drawing a contrast between these ambivalent feelings and the kinds of ego-dystonic feelings evoked by the disturbed adolescents to which I refer in this paper. The apparently simple distinction between my suppressed (but ego-syntonic) thoughts and feelings vs. the repressed ego-dystonic hating and monstrous thoughts and feelings will be illustrated with the third formative example below. But before discussing this example, another key step was necessary: the idea that the analyst's evoked dysphoria could help to clarify the therapeutic situation.

EXAMPLE TWO: THE USE OF EVOKED DYSPHORIC FEELINGS

About thirty years ago, in a teaching seminar at the University of
Chicago, a Child and Adolescent Analyst reviewed psychoanalytic criteria used to assess analyzability for adolescents. In short, he discussed his use of interviews to clarify his ideas about analyzability of
adolescents. Specifically, he reported that a sixteen-year-old, over-
weight young woman, whom he'd evaluated a few years ago in a clinic
setting, had very low scores in each category of his rating scale for analyzability. But after cautioning about the traumatic impact of asking
questions, since adolescents often experience them as attacks, something un-anticipated occurred: he reported to us that the young
woman, who was in the clinic room with him, interrupted the interview. Feeling attacked by his questions, she interjected: "Doctor, why
do you hate me?"

Suddenly and inadvertently, the analyst captivated us with his
shared reactions about his bodily discomfort and feelings of self-
loathing. The class came alive. In retrospect, this provided an introduction to the evoked dysphoria that often occurs when dealing with
emotionally disturbed adolescents. After collecting himself, he responded: "No, I don't *hate* you, but I do have some hating feelings,
which I'll have to think about."

The links between the young adolescent's psychopathology and
the analyst's self-loathing and despising feelings became clearer in
the classroom discussion. He discussed with us his own weight problems and self-despising feelings in conjunction with hers. In effect,
he introduced the two-person psychological interplay between the
analyst's and the adolescent's issues. He also confided to us that he
had trouble with his own self-despising feelings, especially about
"body contours." When thin, he despised anyone unable to control
his or her weight.

By introducing the world of "counter-transference"—what I now
consider to be the analyst's (evoked) counter-response—he gave me
permission (as compared to my psychoanalytic training experience)
to consider using my evoked emotional reactions as another means
to establish a connection with the adolescent's unconscious life. As a
result, I now possessed an alternative mode for understanding and
promoting the treatment process. By being encouraged to process
and formulate the content of my counter-response, i.e. by identifying
and working self-analytically with my evoked feelings, I could access
an otherwise unavailable sector of the adolescent's unconscious life.
To be sure, this was extremely helpful. However, at that time I was not

ready to compare and contrast what he had related to my clinical experience with my supervisor, nor did I realize its potential for serving as an organizer for working with disturbed adolescents.

Thirty years ago the experienced analyst, anticipating the world of self-disclosure, in effect, told his adolescent patient that he needed to identify and regulate his despising, hating feelings. Currently, my own counter-responses in working with very disturbed adolescents and their parents include the potential for (self- and other-) despising feelings, anxiety-laden confusion states, dysphoric boredom states, and being temperamentally prone to moderate bursts of emotional intensity.

EXAMPLE 3: MY "ITALIAN COUCH" CASE

Before I understood anything about enactment phenomena, or developed a personal swimming metaphor as a containing protective buffer, a younger colleague referred a 12-year-old pre-adolescent boy. His two professional parents (the mother, a lawyer, the father, a surgeon) said their son received a beneficial amount of "quality time" from both of them. Highly articulate, the parents could be described as workaholics and affable; but left me feeling "on empty." When unprepared, here's what—unfortunately—can happen:

Session #1: The boy, a hurricane, bursts through my office door, catapults onto my couch, and is soundly asleep in less than five minutes! Without knowing why, I feel strangely "at sea." I try—unsuccessfully—to recall an analyst's paper about whether I should try to wake him.

Session #2: is better. The boy—whoever he is—actually speaks. Can he use my desk for his homework? I try to engage him—no response. This doesn't feel like "quality time" to me! He does his homework and leaves. "Bye," I say.

Session #3: This next session was neither pretty nor cute. He repeats the pattern of Session #1, but with a twist, or more accurately, he awakens and starts to rip my couch. My *Italian* couch!

Thus, a supervisor added a new phrase to my counter-response vocabulary: "furniture feelings." It so happens I *do* have furniture feelings and I, therefore, reacted badly. Really badly! Caught in my own tidal rage, I grabbed the boy, rationalizing to myself I was restraining him and making a therapeutic intervention, I said: "Who the hell do you think you are?"

He looked at me in sheer terror—a monster, a savage had bullied, worse, ravaged him, and I was that monster. This, I was not prepared for. Suffice to say, I felt horrible, beyond guilty, horribly guilty. (Also, my usually "reliable" *dry* sense of humor was nowhere to be found.)

At this stage of my (pre-swimming metaphor) analytic career—which my prescient mind thought might be coming to a sudden, unempathic, and premature litigious closure—I had no idea that this could be a counter-enactment driven by catastrophic anxiety. Clearly, it was a reaction I wasn't prepared to formulate to promote the treatment at that time. Nonetheless, whether aware or not, what happened was decidedly informative about this boy's external reality and inner life.

Because of the evoked panic, I thought, in effect: "Damage control!" I called his mother, drowning in my catastrophic fear, and preparing for the worst: would she be litigious? I left a voice mail, saying it was important that we talk as soon as possible. I thought she'd sense my urgency—perhaps about as well as she sensed the urgency in the boy, whom by the way, at that time I could tell you next to nothing about; something, I didn't appreciate myself for either. Not only was I a bully, but I told myself in a self-critical way that I was an uninformed bully, and so proceeded to continue to bully myself with an internal conversation: "You know nothing about this kid, neither his development, interests, friends, nor his thoughts and feelings about his parents, school, etc." How effective this bullying was for the analytic process, you can guess.

Back to the voice-mail and his parents. I had left a message for the boy's mother. A prolonged agony of silence emerged and lasted for three days. I thrashed about not knowing what to do. For three whole days, seventy-two hours, no one responded to my urgent call. Finally, the boy's mother called. *She* sounded awful. She said, "I have something I must tell you." She paused and then continued: "My husband committed suicide last night! He took barbituates." "Oh my God, I'm so sorry," came out, but in a controlled voice. Later, she added: "I didn't tell you that he'd been physically violent and abusive before. . . . I just never thought *this* [*the suicide*] could happen." After meeting her that afternoon, I referred her to an analyst at the local Barr Harris center with experience in acute grief reactions.

I immediately sought consultation. In the consultation, we concurred: this pre-pubertal adolescent clearly made me feel the two sources of his terror: the terrorized victim of the father's monstrous, violent behavior and his terror in his identification with the father's monstrous violent behavior. He became his destructive monster-father via his "identification with the aggressor," and also let me know what it felt like to be the victim when his father went on a destructive rampage in the home.

But he also identified the source of the danger. If I'd been properly prepared, perhaps I could have made sense of the feelings he evoked in me. He experienced me as the father-monster, just as he'd experienced the disruptive effects of his disturbed father's violence. And he wanted me to see this monster. Could there be a better way to throw light on the danger than conjuring the monster into the room? In effect, that's what he did. He introduced me to the monster, both by his own behavior and through experiencing my own monstrous reaction. As a result, I could comprehend being both the terrorized victim and the monster aggressor.

Naturally, I've thought a lot about this clinical experience. I've wondered: Was the encoded act the *carrier* of his experience, consistent with Hans Loewald's (1976) idea about enactive remembering?

A supportive colleague volunteered that an analyst cannot stop being a human being: these kinds of intense emotional reactions inevitably occur. I soon realized that unless one is prepared for such hostile aggressive enactments, especially with such disturbed adolescents or their parents, they can be extraordinarily painful and disruptive. Conversely, when properly anticipated, they can be used as an organizer for clarifying unconscious themes that profoundly influence the adolescent's psychological life. In short, the boy worked hard to make me (and my couch!) see what threatened him. The swimming metaphor, along with its containing function, provided choreography for otherwise difficult to depict, distraught emotions: as a result, organizer and metaphor co-joined to create the concept of counter-response.

METAPHOR: ITS VALUE AS A COUNTER-RESPONSE TOOL

And now the second part of counter-response: I discuss how I think about and use my personal swimming metaphor as a counter-response tool with these adolescent patients and their parents. This will provide the contrast to my state of un-preparedness. In my view, the use of metaphors is intricately linked to anticipating and processing the analyst's evoked dysphoric reactions.

One additional perspective, an example from the world of literature: Henry James's short story "The Middle Years," captures how we live in illusion and denial, especially his aphorism: "It was the abyss of human illusion that was the real, the tideless deep." James understood the dominance of illusion on human experience, its disguise in the form of the *apparent* tideless deep, as well as the depths of repression *containing* a person's hidden psychic reality.

THE VALUE OF CREATING A METAPHOR

The value of creating a metaphor to counter denial and illusion and cope effectively with the aggression of this sub-group of disturbed adolescents forms a key part of my thinking about the analyst's counter-response. My use of a swimming metaphor serves both as my own personal container function and also provides evocative (associative) imagery. The analyst's personal metaphor(s) may be created spontaneously, or as part of a well thought-through stratagem. Metaphor facilitates a way of listening. My swimming metaphor facilitates attending in these difficult therapeutic encounters.

Metaphors can function in two important ways: as a container and as an evocative means. As we know, Freud once likened the analytic situation to a surgical procedure, and compared the analytic relationship to the discourse of a pair of traveling companions; he also considered therapeutic action as akin to archeology: Finding treasures in an archeological dig proved to be an important metaphor for Freud.

In working with disturbed adolescents, metaphor provides both time and a therapeutic space to process the disorganizing and destabilizing effects of the patient's affective intensity. Many analysts unwittingly use their personally preferred metaphors, but may not have considered the value of reflecting much about their choice of metaphor. My choice of a swimming metaphor has personal roots: the swimming metaphor functions evocatively and as a container function to monitor, organize, and regulate my emotional responses; while, at the same time, facilitating and providing a holding environment to frame and help contain the expression of the disturbed adolescent's warded-off affects and enactments. Its evocative imagery helps me with the adolescent's narrative and enactments, and the non-verbal ambience in the room. Accordingly, I'm proposing as a strategy for analysts working with disturbed adolescents the use of their own personal metaphor to help prepare for anticipated disruptive experiences.

To illustrate the use of the swimming metaphor: when engaging this particular group of disturbed adolescents with severe problems with their aggression and affect regulation, I prepare myself by evoking an image of treading water, waiting expectantly in anticipation of unpredictable sea changes from two sources: the adolescent's expectable, provocative behavior and my own evoked counter-response. Moreover, by already imagining that I am treading water, in which dramatic sea changes are the expectable course of events, I'm in a state of greater anticipation than what is implied by the traditional analytic term "free-floating attention." I'm in this greater state of vigilance, because I fear being destabilized by an evoked counter-response, which can turn a merely ambiguous setting into a chaotic one.

If the analyst can anticipate the affective content of the counter-response, this may promote the treatment by being better able to create a more neutral therapeutic space. By so doing, he can then try to process and formulate both the adolescent's narrative and enactment, gaining access to otherwise inaccessible aspects of his patient's unconscious inner life: the adolescent's novel narrative. Hence, the importance I give to the dual function of the swimming metaphor.

In brief, the use of the swimming metaphor creates several advantages: it facilitates attention to my clinical observations; differentiates these perceptions from clinical inferences, linked to my theoretical biases; and holds the analyst closer to descriptions of clinical phenomena. It does this by avoiding the premature introduction of theoretical formulations, which obfuscate through the reductionism they introduce. In short, the swimming metaphor—being theory neutral—can serve as a guardian against the reductionism tendency: an ongoing desire to fit clinical experiences into theoretical casts, and thereby undermine the potential for deeper empathic closures.

THE USE OF METAPHOR AS A PROTECTIVE BUFFER

A well-chosen metaphor can serve as a semi-permeable buffer, allowing the patient's unconscious communication to get through. This helps the analyst clarify the clinical situation and facilitates his processing his counter-response, without it becoming too much of an obstacle. In addition to understanding how a metaphor can be useful for keeping the analyst alert, what becomes clear is the usefulness of metaphor as a protective buffer. In retrospect, the "Italian couch" clinical experience, which both formed and evolved my understanding of counter-responses, made the necessity of having a protective buffer clear: specifically a metaphor to be used as a counter-response tool.

As stated, my swimming metaphor's "treading water" imagery creates, in my mind, a state of preparedness. Since a destabilizing interference should be anticipated with these disturbed adolescents, I can now assume a vigilant stance with my metaphor activated. This may not prevent me from being rocked, or acting inappropriately, at times, but I rarely, if ever, capsize.

In a similar vein, Richard Almond (2003) recently discussed the holding function of theory to help analysts regulate their tension states in ways similar to my ascription for a personal metaphor. He writes: "The holding function of theory is a major way in which these affects are recognized, contained, and utilized therapeutically" (p. 148). Referring to the more familiar function of theory (p. 132)—to orient and guide the analyst's listening, formulating and interpreting—Almond cautions "theory can only provide general guideposts for *approaching the individuality of a patient and the uniqueness of any one patient-analyst interaction*" (p. 134) (italics mine).

To summarize: I find the swimming metaphor especially helpful in a combined container/symbolic way for grasping the unique qualities of these disturbed adolescents. By combining the container function of the metaphor with its evocative images, I am less prone to shutting off my analyzing antennae and affective reaction. As I've indicated, the swimming metaphor serves as a systematic method for organizing my state of attentiveness and as an emotional buffer to avoid being "swept up" in difficult-to-manage affective currents. Also, the swimming metaphor establishes imagery that helps convey the emotional tenor and depth of the treatment experience. For example "darkly troubled waters" evocatively suggest the "sea changes" that occur with the destabilizing impact of a sea of deep undercurrents. With storms or deep undercurrents, you need to do more than tread water if you want to avoid a precarious sense of danger, the dread of drowning. The sense of storminess or ominous undercurrents may signal the analyst's potential for fragmenting tensions or disintegrative fears in navigating such uncertain waters: the counter-response impact of unconscious communications with these adolescents.

In both therapy and analysis, I've found this metaphoric orientation especially useful for anticipating and clarifying clinical happenings and phenomena. Perhaps, most importantly, it facilitates working self-analytically with my evoked feelings. By labeling emotional dangers and difficult intense feelings in metaphoric terms, I am brought closer to "awareness" without being so overwhelmed, rather than being taken by surprise due to the disturbed adolescent's generated affective intensity.

As mentioned, psychoanalytic training did *not* prepare me for these destabilizing experiences; hence, I fret that I can get lost, or suffer even worse fates in these "uncharted waters." So by organizing my state of attentiveness in this way, the swimming metaphor conveys the contrasting "silent" danger of drowning in unimaginable and unmanageable depths. In short, I fear I won't be able to modulate the evoked tension state. Hence, why the swimming metaphor works for me.

COUNTER-RESPONSE AND METAPHOR WITH DISTURBED ADOLESCENTS AND THEIR PARENTS

Counter-response and metaphor can be helpful with both disturbed adolescents and their parents. First, the adolescent: An adolescent's boredom, alienation, depression, or repressed rage can create intolerable feeling states in the analyst when no discernible direction is present in the narrative content. Since many analysts need stimuli for their own reasons, a bored adolescent who removes such stimuli can evoke all sorts of responses, including states of apathy, depression, or counter-enactments by the analyst to avoid feeling emptiness or deadness. Often, the interview process deteriorates into either long silences, or at the other extreme, the agonies of "drowning in a sea of words" (Modell, 1984). These draining experiences represent a sharp contrast to adolescents who can form a therapeutic alliance and eagerly explore their experiences.

In dealing with these alienated, deeply depressed adolescents, with their chronic boredom problems, I anticipate and prepare myself for misery. I worry that I'll be *unable* to continue to stay afloat; will sink into a counter-response in reaction to the perceived adolescent's emotional "emptiness"; won't be able to find direction at all; or will be swept up by a disruptive tidal wave and wreak havoc. In working with my counter-response, I try to comprehend the paradoxical absence of feeling, which can occur in a clinical setting fraught with such difficulties.

Also, by purposefully creating a vocabulary, using evocative terms like Bion's "catastrophic anxiety," or "reversal of perspective" to convey "psychotic anxieties," I experience a concrete sense of either a personal, or bodily threat, including the fear of becoming (temporarily) disorganized psychologically. Engaging these difficult feelings brings me closer to the emotional turmoil, which is where I need to be in order to reach the tumultuous inner world of these disturbed adolescents. Introspectively, I look for hidden feelings of deadness, or deeply suppressed rage in this compromised self-state, as both a way of observing my experiences and maintaining some control over the experienced dysphoria. But when I find myself feeling forced into making self-restitution attempts to counter my fragmenting emotional and bodily tensions, I have to acknowledge that, whatever has been touched off in me, I am failing to cope with it and may sink into a defensive counter-reaction state of boredom.

COUNTER-RESPONSE AND METAPHOR WITH THE DISTURBED ADOLESCENT'S PARENTS

When treating disturbed adolescents' parents, similar dysphoric feeling states arise in the analyst. In a previous paper, I emphasized how a parent's dependency conflicts, deep competitive envy, or unconscious identification with the aggressor can undermine the analyst's attempts to effect therapeutic change (Richmond, 1992). While writing that paper, I realized that the parents' acting out, or enactment behavior, provided an important source of emotionally charged information about the disturbed adolescent's psychological world. The parents' undermining behavior can feel like ominous clouds closing in, create an unexpected storm, or evoke the feeling of damp and chilling waters—as when alone in a dark and desolate space.

Accordingly, from a parent's first phone call, I try to anticipate, observe, and formulate the parent's emotional impact. With parents of disturbed adolescents I expect to re-experience important traumatic events that the adolescent had to contend with when he or she was a child. The counter-response approach that I use permits me to actively look for the parent's destructive envy and deep dependency conflicts with their hostile, undermining impact on the analytic process. So, along with the standard interest in the disturbed adolescent's relevant genetic antecedents and developmental transformations, I ask myself: how are these parents affecting me?

To be sure, this counter-response perspective can overemphasize a parent's psychopathology. Also, it may miss the reciprocal impact of the adolescent's psychopathology on the parents, or conceal how creative modifications in parenting helped the disturbed adolescent. To remain alert to the full extent of an adolescent's psychopathology, and *not* overlook multiple interacting causes, I try to counter the not uncommon tendency of splitting the ambivalent feelings that I experienced in my counter-response: so that my negative or ambivalent (despising and hating) feelings about the adolescent are not displaced to the parents.

In our attempts to understand the adolescent's psychic reality, it is useful to differentiate between transient identifications with patients that serve empathy as compared to those repressed unconscious ego-dystonic identifications that are so disruptive to the treatment. The latter I regard as counter-responses evoked by these adolescents. In short, it's crucial for the analyst to stay attuned to his feeling state with the idea of using these evoked emotions to deepen his understanding of the adolescent's psychic reality. I realize that my swimming metaphor, with its state of vigilance or anticipation, may not be suited for everyone, but I find it useful for my own analytic work, especially when the adolescent is seriously disturbed.

Some Limitations Using Counter-Responses and Metaphor

I want to make some brief comments about the inherent limitations in counter-response. For example, how can we differentiate expectably painful and destabilizing reactions in this kind of work, as opposed to idiosyncratic reactions, requiring consultation or more self-analysis? Also, as I've indicated, potential problems may arise in prematurely introducing theoretical biases into our observations, i.e. the tendency to *find* observations that validate our theories and help reduce the emotional discomfort with these disturbed adolescents.

It's been increasingly accepted among psychoanalysts, since Winnicott's seminal paper (1949) and the early 1950s (Heimann), that *containing* the feelings evoked in the analytic encounter is an essential first step in dealing with the analyst's evoked reactions. Paula Heimann denounced the erroneous image of the detached analyst; instead, she set the stage for a change in the prejudicial pejorative view of counter-transference (Reich) with the idea that it was important to use the counter-transference by containing the emotional response. By 1960, Heimann's earlier lead had established the view that the analyst's capacity to sustain vs. discharge the evoked feeling state was a crucial issue in evaluating an analyst's work (with his counter-response). Over the years, theoretical, reductionistic explanations of the analyst's counter-responses have failed to satisfy. As an illustration, the phrase "my maternal counter-transference" may contain chaotic emotions and so the analyst's secondary process "true confessions" often conceals more than they reveal.

After containing the analyst's emotional response, the steps that lead to productive self-analytic work, with the content of the counter-response, undoubtedly vary among analysts. While processing my counter-response to access a teenager's nightmarish apprehension about his destructive rage and monster fantasies, or the bleakness of being alone with deep dependency fears, I often experience uncertainty about how to proceed in order to further explore the patient's experience. As one guiding idea, I find it helpful to look for a (painful) body-affect shift to find direction, especially when I feel convinced that my evoked counter-response is the result of the patient's projection, enactment, or acting-out.

As a strategic approach to anticipate and deal effectively with the destabilizing impact of the disturbed adolescent's aggressive enactments, I recommend the use of a combined counter-response and metaphor perspective to facilitate processing the analyst's evoked counter-reactions. Creating a metaphor counters denial and illusion with this sub-group of adolescents, and provides a buffer function and evocative imagery for the analyst. My swimming metaphor stratagem, as a theory-neutral construct, keeps me in these difficult encounters and permits the emergence of the disturbed adolescent's novel narrative; it also anticipates the resistance to examining, processing, and formulating the analyst's evoked counter-response. Working with the counter-response helps these disturbed adolescents achieve a greater feeling of their own agency and their own unique inner life.

In addition to my own steps, I fall back on Racker (1953) who provided guidelines for understanding the counter-transference difficulties that invariably occur, based on the introjective and projective propensity in the analyst. Additionally, the elaboration of the use of the concept of "projective identification" illuminated the interpersonal interaction between patient and analyst. Among many contributors, Bion (1957) continued his emphasis on the analyst's learning to understand the impact of the patient's competitive envy, as evident in the patient's need to attack the linking in the patient's thought process that leads to meaning in the analytic situation. In this perspective, the analyst's counter-identification form of counter-response would be viewed as an evoked reaction due to the patient's projection of intolerable affective experiences.

With regard to the use of the analyst's counter-response, sometimes analysts have been criticized for their tendency to over-emphasize the importance of self-observation as being more informing about therapeutic actions than it might be. As I have indicated, I have found that the psychoanalyst's use of organizers, while providing a necessary (transient) scaffolding, can pose a threat to an adolescent's individuation process, sense of agency, or struggles, to achieve an autonomous self (with maturing self-object relationships). When analysts give up the tool of broad in-depth introspection (as the basis for their constructions and interpretations) for formulaic or theoretical constructs, as with the use of pre-conceived theoretical formulations that may foreclose the possibility of a fuller understanding of the clinical situation, they risk forfeiture of the most valuable implement they possess in the pursuit of understanding these adolescents: their own clinical intuition, creative imagination, and self-awareness, including an awareness of their own emotional turmoil.

In this paper, I've tried to show how important it is to anticipate the evoked dysphoric reactions in order to create a more neutral and usable therapeutic space. In my view, the use of the analyst's counter-response with a personal metaphor provides the necessary context for achieving a more optimal balance between using accepted narrative theories and exploring novel enactment experiences. The effective use of the analyst's counter-response allows the analyst to reconstruct the adolescent's narrative and enactment, thereby gaining access to the patient's unconscious inner life and novel narrative. This constitutes an important criterion of technical competence: it has an essential part in our continued striving to provide what is best for these very disturbed adolescents patients.

BIBLIOGRAPHY

ABRAMS, S. (1978). "The genetic point of view: Historical antecedents and developmental transformations." *Journal of the American Psychoanalytic Association*, 25:417–426.

ALMOND, R. (2003). "The holding function of theory." *Journal of the American Psychoanalytic Association*, 51:131–154.

BION, W. R. (1957). "The differentiation of the psychotic from the non-psychotic part of the personality." *Int. J. Psycho-Anal.*, Vol. 38, Parts 3–4.

EAGLE, M. (1984). *Recent Developments in Psychoanalysis*. New York: McGraw Hill.

EDELSON, M. (1988). *Psychoanalysis—A Theory in Crisis*. Chicago: University of Chicago Press.

FROMM-REICHMANN, F. (1950). *Principles of Intensive Psychotherapy*. Chicago: Univ. of Chicago Press.

FURMAN, E. (2002). "On the concepts of transference and counter-transference and their use." *Child Analysis: Clinical, Theoretical and Applied*, 13:113–188.

GRAY, P. (1994). *The Ego and Analysis of Defense*. Northvale, N.J.: Jason Aronson.

HARTMANN, H., & KRIS, E. (1945). "The genetic approach in psychoanalysis," *Psychoanalytic Study of the Child*, 1:11–20, New York: International Universities Press.

HEIMANN, P. (1950). "On counter-transference," *International Journal of Psychoanalysis*, 31:81–84.

HEIMANN, P. (1960). "Counter-transference," *British Journal of Medical Psychology*, 33:9–15.

JACOBS, T. (1999). "Counter-transference past and present: A review of the concept," *International J. of Psycho-analysis*, 80:575–594.

JAMES, H. (1992). "The Middle Years." In *The Oxford Book of American Short Stories*. New York: Oxford Univ. Press, pp. 170–189.

KLEIN, M. (1948[1921–45]). *Contributions to Psychoanalysis*. London: Hearth Press.

LOEWALD, H. (1980[1976]). "Perspectives on Memory." In *Papers on Psychoanalysis*. New Haven: Yale University Press.

MODELL, A. (1984). *Psychoanalysis in a New Context*. New York: International Universities Press.

MORRIS, H. (1993). "Narrative representation, narrative enactment, and the psychoanalytic construction of history," *Int. J. of Psychoanalysis*, 74:33–53.

PONTALIS, J.-B. (1977). "From counter-transference: The quick and the dead interlaced." In *Frontiers in Psychoanalysis*. New York: International Universities Press, pp. 170–183.

RACKER, H. (1968). *Transference and Counter-transference*. New York: International Universities Press.

REICH, A. (1951). "On countertransference" *International Journal of Psychoanalysis*, 32:25–31.

RICHMOND, M. B. (1992). "Counter-transference problems in dealing with severely disturbed parents: Their potential value for understanding the adolescent patient." In *Residential Treatment for Children*. Haworth Press, pp. 61–80.

STRACHEY, J. (1934). "The nature of the therapeutic action of psycho-analysis." *International Journal of Psychoanalysis*, 15:127–159.

WAKSMAN, J. D. (1986). "The countertransference of the child analyst," *International Review of Psycho-analysis*, 13:405–415.

WINNICOTT, D. W. (1949). "Hate in the counter-transference." In *Collected Papers*, London: Tavistock Publications, pp. 194–203.

Inhibition of Self-Observing Activity in Psychoanalytic Treatment

LAWRENCE N. LEVENSON, M.D.

The author examines the topic of inhibition of self-observing function in some patients arising from conflicts over aggression. The author's thesis is that conflicts over aggression can interfere with the patient's task of shifting from passively reporting spontaneously occurring associations to actively reflecting on his thoughts in an analysis. This can result in the patient remaining in the role of passive reporter of his associations while ceding to the analyst the role of aggressive interpreter of the patient's psychic functioning. The active ego functions necessary for understanding and integration are inhibited, compromising the potential for growth and change. Clinical vignettes illustrate a close process analytic process to this phenomenon.

EARLY IN HIS ANALYSIS, A PATIENT VOICED CONCERNS THAT HE MIGHT be too familiar with psychoanalytic theory to be able to benefit from psychoanalytic treatment. A well-educated and well-read man, he worried that his knowledge would prevent him from being un-self-conscious enough to make the most of an analysis. He recalled that when he and I had discussed psychoanalysis during his consultation, I had mentioned at one point that in analysis it might be helpful for us to pay attention to those times when there appeared to be some interference in the flow of his associations. Since beginning analysis,

Assistant Clinical Professor, Department of Psychiatry, Yale University School of Medicine; Training and Supervising Analyst and member of the faculty at Western New England Institute for Psychoanalysis.

The Psychoanalytic Study of the Child 59, ed. Robert A. King, Peter B. Neubauer, Samuel Abrams, and A. Scott Dowling (Yale University Press, copyright © 2004 by Robert A. King, Peter B. Neubauer, Samuel Abrams, and A. Scott Dowling)

he had been aware of several occasions when his thoughts had changed or stopped, and he worried that his awareness of such moments interfered with his letting go and saying what came to mind. He added that he assumed that only if he were unreflective on the couch would his unconscious thoughts emerge so that I could notice things about him. I commented that he seemed to assume that in analysis I would be the only one who would be noticing things about the way his mind worked. The patient replied that he thought that he was supposed to say what came to mind, or "spout like a fountain," and that I, the analyst, would interpret what was emerging from his unconscious. He then added that he found it interesting that he thought of analysis in this way, because since he had been in psychotherapy, he often had made important connections on his own.

In converting patients from psychotherapy to psychoanalysis, I have been struck that patients sometimes assume that as analysands their role is to be much more passive than it had been in psychotherapy. Upon moving to the couch, many patients seem to adopt a kind of "topographic attitude" in which they see their task as attempting to free associate in order to bring forth unconscious material for the analyst to interpret. Such patients seem to lay down their observing egos when they lay down on the couch, leaving it to the analyst to "notice things," as my patient put it.

One reason for this, cogently discussed by Paul Gray (1994), is that analysts have not consistently helped patients to be aware of their capacity to notice things for themselves about their minds in conflict. Gray argues that most patients have to learn—but can learn—that they possess self-observational skills which can be put to much advantage in the analytic situation. Without being made aware that they possess such skills and how to use them, however, patients might assume that their role is to free associate while leaving the analyzing to the analyst. A major thrust of Gray's work has been to develop a methodology aimed at helping the patient become aware of, and learn how to use, their objective self-observing functions.

Because he feels strongly that traditional analytic technique has not sufficiently taken into account the relatively autonomous, rational ego of the patient, Gray has placed particular emphasis on the advantages of engaging the patient's conscious ego throughout an analysis. In attempting to remedy this underestimation of the patient's ego in clinical practice, he has highlighted the ego's capacity to engage in active, conscious participation in the analysis and has written relatively little about the ego's resistances to the use of self-observing function. Gray has noted that such resistances do occur, however, and that at such times "the analyst may have to turn the analytic attention away from the study primarily of what the analysand has been saying to take up an examination of the very function, the 'tools,' which the patient is neglecting" (Gray, 1994, p. 71). Busch, who also has made important contributions to current understanding of the role of the analysand's conscious ego in the psychoanalytic process, has similarly emphasized the necessity for the analyst to pay attention to "the analysand's interest and ability to reflect back upon his thoughts, *or his resistance to doing so*" (Busch, 1994, p. 372. Italics added).

Resistance to self-observation is the subject of this paper. The analysand's capacity for autonomous self-observation is a complex and important topic which has received increased attention in recent years from a variety of points of view, including developmental perspectives (Fonagy and Target, 2000). My purpose in this paper is to focus specifically on inhibitions of self-observing function arising from psychological conflict. As analysts have come to recognize the importance of the patient's ego in the analytic process and have begun to modify technique to include the active, conscious participation of the patient's ego in observing intra-psychic activity, it has become possible to attend to patients' resistances to active collaboration with the analyst and the dynamics underlying such resistances. What may appear to be a misunderstanding of the methods of analysis or a deficit in ego function may in fact constitute an important and analyzable unconscious resistance to ego participation. The patient mentioned above, for example, had been invited during preparatory discussions about analysis to notice shifts in the flow of associations once analysis began. These discussions were intended to educate the patient about the methods of observing evidence of conflict and defense during an analytic hour that he, along with the analyst, could employ. The patient, however, feared that with this information he would become too self-conscious to be able to reveal freely his unconscious wishes for the analyst to interpret. In my view, this was not a misunderstanding in need of correcting but a meaningful misunderstanding to be analyzed.

What are the dynamics of resistance to self-observing activity in analysis? The thesis which I shall attempt to develop in this paper is that such resistances frequently reflect conflicts over aggression stirred when patients attempt to shift from passively observing and reporting their spontaneously occurring thoughts to actively reflecting on the significance of their thoughts. Sterba, in his classic 1934 paper, argued that the distinctive characteristic of the psychoanalytic method is that "the subject's consciousness shifts from the center of affective experience to that of intellectual contemplation" (Sterba, 1934, p. 121). This, Sterba stated, is the fate of the ego in psychoanalysis. Enlarging upon Sterba's views, Gray has discussed that in addition to the well-known task of observing and saying what comes to mind, analysands have a second observing task, "that which is necessary as the patient attempts to perceive in close retrospection the phenomena which occur as manifestations related to intra-psychic conflict" (Gray, 1994, p. 66). When patients move from the first to the second observing task, they move from a relatively passive ego state—observing and saying what is coming to mind—to an active ego state requiring higher level cognitive processes such as reflection, rationality, and synthesis. Since in the analytic setting these ego states operate not in private but in the presence of the analyst, the patient's ego is passive or active in relation to the analyst. Passivity and activity bear a close relation to vicissitudes of aggression and, consequently, conflicts over aggression may encumber the patient's ability to perform both observing tasks and move effectively from one to the other.

Most literature on resistance is related to resistances to emerging drive material during the process of free association. Freud pointed out, however, that there are resistances not only to id contents but also "resistances to the uncovering of resistances" (1937, p. 239)— that is, resistance to awareness of the ego activity of resistance. Pray, in a comparative study of methods of analyzing defense, refers to an observation by Anna Freud about defenses operating not only against id derivatives but also against ego functions: "dangerous impulses . . . are more difficult for the child to combat when they are perceived, acknowledged, and remembered . . . defense turns not only directly against the id derivatives themselves but simultaneously . . . puts the relevant ego functions at least partially out of action" (Pray, 1996, p. 69). To this, Pray adds, "she [A. Freud] implies that we will see a patient's sharp, direct, incisive observations become softened, or blurred, or contradicted when the ego objects to the 'sharpness' or 'aggressiveness' of the observation . . . defense includes 'impairment' of the ego function that might recognize the impulse—self-perception is blocked" (Pray, 1996, p. 69). Anna Freud is pointing out that the ego may defend against its own ego functions, and Pray is suggesting that this may occur when those ego functions involve aggressive energy.

There is another way in which patients may defend against the assertive connotations of reflective activity (Gray's second observing task) besides putting relevant ego functions out of action. In the presence of the analyst in the analytic situation, the patient may remain as the passive reporter and experience the analyst as the aggressive interpreter of the patient's mental functioning. Assigning insightfulness to the analyst, deferring to the analyst's ego as the predominant ego that notices things, the patient may put himself on the receiving end of the analyst's aggression in the form of the analyst's interpretation. The patient freely associates and leaves the interpreting to the analyst. This constitutes a manifestation of transference of superego defense, a form of defense transference which Gray has described in detail in his papers on the superego. Gray has shown that patients project images of authority onto the analyst which serve to inhibit impulses, particularly aggressive ones, emerging in the analytic situation, turning the impulses around onto the patient resulting in feelings of guilt, shame, self-criticism, etc. I suggest that these are not just static images of authority projected by the patient but are key elements in the dynamic interaction between patient and analyst, whereby patients unconsciously invite the analyst to take on the active interpreting role with the patient on the receiving end of the interpreting. A clear example of this process is the patient whom Gray mentions telling his analyst, "I don't want to look at that, just zap me with an interpretation" (Gray, 1996, p. 91).

The zap of aggression is inherent in many conceptualizations of interpretative activity. Freud, particularly in his earlier writings but to some extent throughout his work, depicted the analytic situation as the patient engaging in unconscious resistance which the analyst must overcome by use of a counter-force greater than the force of the patient's resistance in the form of interpretation. The well-known adage, "to make an omelet one must break a few eggs," and Freud's predilection for military metaphors in describing the interaction between patient and analyst are indicative of a therapeutic approach which involves the analyst's aggression in the service of cure. In recent times, the conceptualization of effective interpretations as disturbing the patient's equilibrium also suggests that the analyst's aggression is involved in the act of interpretation (Arlow and Brenner, 1990). Raphling has formulated interpretation explicitly in terms of the analyst's aggression and has argued that it is important for analysts to be comfortable with the aggression involved in making an interpretation. According to Raphling, "Interpretation, in order to convey insight, of necessity assaults or challenges patients' psychic equilibrium." (Raphling, 1992, p. 354). Part of the appeal of humanistic techniques such as empathy, support, and holding, Raphling feels, is the avoidance of interpretive aggression. Fogel (1995) goes one step further, proposing that for many, if not most, patients, interpretations must be traumatizing to be effective.

In my view, analysts must be comfortable with aggression primarily to tolerate the *patient's* expression of aggression toward the analyst and others. Analysts must be alert to the patient's difficulties with aggression being dealt with by inviting the analyst to direct interpretive aggression against the patient. When this occurs, the analyst may be providing insight but also may be participating in, rather than analyzing, the patient's masochistic defenses in which aggression is turned around onto the patient.

While interpretation has long been regarded as the analyst's central technical procedure, some analysts have advanced the idea that the analyst's activity should be in the nature of interventions rather than interpretations. Gray (1994) has argued that when analysts interpret latent conflict that is not readily recognizable to the patient, they inevitably exploit their transferential authority in reaching across a barrier of unconscious defense. If the patient accepts the interpretation, the acceptance may be based on the authority with which the patient has endowed the analyst. To this, I would add that an interpretation also may put the patient on the receiving end of the aggression that is inherent in interpretive activity. Set against interpretation is Gray's conceptualization of intervention where the analyst attempts to make the patient aware of his ego's defensive activity in response to emerging drive derivatives in the immediate present of the analytic hour. Since the analyst is pointing to what just happened as the patient was talking, the analyst primarily uses observation, not authority or aggression, to show the patient how his mind is responding to conflict. Such interventions are observations about processes at the surface of the patient's mind; in making observations at the surface, the analyst is helping the patient become aware that he, too, is capable of making such observations. No special intuitive skills are required; minimal aggression is required; what the analyst observes, the patient can observe, too, although Gray emphasizes it takes practice and experience for analysands to develop their self-observational capacities.

I do not mean to suggest that the analyst's interpretations always, or even usually, represent unthinking collusions with masochistic defenses. Analysts would seem increasingly to be in agreement, however, that it is advantageous to the analysis when the patient's rational observing ego forms a co-partnership with the analyst in recognizing evidence of conflict. When an analyst is poised to make an interpretation, he might want to pause and consider why the analyst and not the patient is making the observation about phenomena that also are potentially observable by the patient. At least on some occasions, the patient's resistance to observing for himself what has transpired at his mind's surface may be important for the analyst to point out to the patient. The analyst may want to ask himself: Why am I and not the patient on the verge of making this observation? While there may often be good reasons for the analyst to make the interpretation, there may also be times when the analyst's interpretive activity reinforces the patient's unconscious masochistic defenses.

If the patient's achieving independence in observing intra-psychic activity is an outcome goal in analysis, then analysts will want to pay attention to patients' resistance to pursuing such independence. Gray's technical modifications, including his advocacy of interventions over interpretation as a baseline for treatment, are based on the premise that many patients possess an ego capacity for neutral, independent observation of their intra-psychic activity. Thus, Gray speaks of helping patients "to become familiar with their autonomous 'tools' of observation" (Gray, 1994, p. 70) and "realizing and developing their skills for observation of certain crucial intra-psychic activities" (p. 74). The crucial intra-psychic activities are those moments in the flow of associations when the patient institutes unconscious defenses in response to emerging conflictual material. The analyst attempts to adopt a stance of neutral, non-judgmental observation of the analysand's working mind and invites the patient to adopt a similarly neutral non-judgmental attitude of *self*-observation. While the analyst's neutrality often is portrayed as safe and reassuring to the patient, Gray has pointed out that, to the contrary, it is quite disturbing to the patient since it challenges superego projections which have provided a safe, if neurotic, equilibrium by blocking or distorting the conscious experience and expression of certain instinctual wishes. Gray writes, "Just as the pre-internalized view of the judging parental authorities was necessary for instinctual control, so the patient now needs to distort the otherwise disturbingly un-authoritarian reality of the neutrality and permissiveness (only action is restrained) the analyst provides" (p. 122). In distorting the analyst's neutrality by developing transference of superego defense, experienced as the analyst's criticism and disapproval, the patient inhibits awareness and expression of conflicted impulses, albeit at the cost of experiencing guilt, shame, lowered self-esteem, and other neurotic restrictions on his psychological life. The distortion of the analyst's neutrality for defensive purposes is commensurate with the analysand's defensive distortion of his own capacity for neutral self-observation: by analyzing transference of superego defense which distorts the analyst's neutrality, the analysand's unconscious superego defensive activity is analyzed, enabling the analysand to realize his potential for neutral, independent self-observation.

I suggest that patients may also defensively inhibit their ego participation in the analytic process via superego defense transferences, eschewing the opportunity to observe evidence of psychological conflict and integrate these observations. Patients may maintain a passive role, producing associations while making themselves the recipients of the analyst's interpretive activity and thereby protect themselves from the assertive/aggressive implications of demonstrating ego mastery to the analyst. In other words, as a component of superego defense transference, patients may project active analytic skills onto the analyst and remain passive reporters of the passing intra-psychic scenery. Instead of *therapeutic* dissociation as described by Sterba (1934), in which the ego is split into an affectively experiencing ego and an observing ego followed by a process of assimilation or synthesis, a dissociation may occur which serves defensive purposes and is not accompanied by assimilation of the conflictual issues. A variant of this resistance involves projecting knowledge and authority onto a reified "unconscious" while the patient experiences himself as waiting for the unconscious to reveal its wants and purposes. The patient sees his task as attempting to talk freely so that unconscious desires will become recognizable to the analyst. The patient experiences himself as the medium for expressing the unconscious to the analyst rather than owning his inner life, including its unconscious aspects.

In a paper on the questions of the analyst, Boesky (1990) includes a clinical example of a patient who developed the kind of transference resistance I am discussing here. Boesky's patient saw it as her task to talk and the analyst's to make sense of her talk. When the patient returned for a second analysis after a recurrence of her symptoms, the analyst realized that they had not dealt adequately with her fear of taking responsibility for understanding herself. The analyst had been unconsciously colluding with her resistance by offering interpretations such that it continued to be her job to associate and his job "to say what it all means." When the patient brought a dream to a session, the analyst was on the verge of making an interpretation of the dream, hesitated, and instead asked her what she thought about the dream. The patient proceeded to report an extensive addendum to the original dream. In his discussion, Boesky observed that what was most relevant at that moment was the resistance to self-inquiry rather than the dream analysis and added that if he had understood matters more clearly at the time, he might have said, "It doesn't sound as though you feel you have a right to be interested in your own dreams." By asking questions, Boesky concludes, we hope to teach our patients to be more curious about themselves.

A few clinical examples are now presented to illustrate these points.

CLINICAL EXAMPLES

EXAMPLE #1

Mr. B., a 38-year-old single man, began the hour by reporting a dream in which he was climbing up the corner of the gym building where he had attended college. He thought the dream had something to do with wanting to "climb higher" with erections by having sex with women rather than his usual masturbating. The dream also reminded him that in college he'd always felt too weak to climb the rope in the gym all the way to the top. He then commented that he was feeling weak in the hour and had an image of the analyst standing over him with a neutral expression. He thought his weakness was a way to keep himself from feeling stronger and more masculine than the analyst. There followed several minutes in which Mr. B. described an article he'd once read about a young man who hung himself after having intercourse for the first time. Next, he commented that he was having thoughts of calling the analyst a phoney and filing a lawsuit against him for incompetence. He then reported having an image of himself at the bottom of the rope in gym preparing to hang himself.

> *Analyst:* The image of being at the bottom of the rope and hanging yourself took the place of the image of climbing to the top that was in the dream and occurred right after you mentioned your angry fantasy about me.
>
> *Patient:* Well, I'm trying to push through to the ugly, painful feelings to be free of this stuff. But now I'm thinking there's a meeting of my music group tonight and I'm planning to ask out this woman. (He had not dated since his divorce six years earlier.) But why does this crap about hanging myself flare up in proximity to sex or romance? Is it to keep myself with my mother? Or remain under my parents or you? I wonder if you have any ideas why I do this to myself (brief pause). Now I'm having a cloudy feeling in my head, like a panic attack coming on. It's like, for our uncovering the repressed associations to asking a woman for a date tonight I'm on the verge of punishing myself

with anxiety for that insight. I'm looking for you to come up with something here to stop me from getting a panic attack.

Analyst: If I provide the insight, instead of you, then you won't punish yourself?

Patient: I'm realizing that I'd assumed you'd made the connection to my asking out a woman tonight. Yeah, I need to pawn off the insight onto you. Pawns: my father and I would sometimes play checkers. I sometimes won—my father must have let me. Winning with his permission. Or having insights only with your permission.

Analyst: It could only be that way?

Patient: Well, I was only 8 years old when I played checkers with my father. And in here, you're the analyst, the expert on neuroses. I'm thinking now that it was only a few years later that my father died. I won at something and my father went away. As if I blame myself. If I have sex tonight, will you go away?

In this session, Mr. B. and I turned our attention not only toward moments of unconscious conflict and defense in the content of the patient's associations but also toward moments of conflict and defense related to the patient's exercising self-observing functions. Working *within* the content of his associations, we observed how he turned sexual ambition and anger into self-debasement and defeat. He had thoughts of climbing—becoming bigger in various ways including in a phallic, sexual sense—and then had thoughts of his analyst standing over him and of a young man killing himself after sex. Similarly, following a sadistic fantasy about his analyst, he had thoughts of hanging himself. But, in addition to listening for these defensive shifts in Mr. B.'s associations, the frame of listening included listening for the patient's defensive reactions to having demonstrated autonomous self-observation in the analyst's presence. For example, at the beginning of the hour, after having some preliminary ideas about the dream, he reported feeling weak just as he once felt weak as a youth when it was his turn to rope climb in gym. Later in the hour, after he noted a possible connection between his self-debasement in the session and his intentions to ask out a woman that evening, he began feeling anxious and turned to the analyst to provide the understanding ("I'm looking for you to come up with something here to stop me from getting a panic attack"). As we understood it, his depression was a consequence not only of *what* he had had an insight into (self-attack for sexual intentions) but *that* he'd had the insight on his own in the presence of the analyst. His unconscious defensive response was not only to turn aggression onto himself resulting in self-disparagement and anxiety but also to seek out the analyst's taking charge by providing the insight—as he put it, pawning off the insight onto the analyst. He realized that he had not even been aware that the insight had been his and not the analyst's. For Mr. B., analysis, like checkers, was a competitive game that he felt he could win only if permitted to do so which assured the continued superior status of his father or his analyst. Freed to self-analyze as a result of this analytic work, if only for the moment, the patient was then able to provide meaningful genetic material bearing on the opposition between his sexuality and his father. In this hour, focussing on the here-and-now microdynamics of the analytic situation also included the microdynamics related to exercising self-analytic capacity in the analyst's presence.

EXAMPLE #2

For several minutes at the beginning of the hour, Mr. C. spoke about feeling he had solved an important psychological problem the previous night in realizing that many of his anxieties derived from feeling threatened by his father because of his oedipal love of his mother and wishing his father dead. He then mentioned that he had had a phone call with his mother just before his session in which his mother had told him that she was going to sell her house and move to the area where Mr. C. was living.

> *Patient:* Now I'm hearing your voice saying my mother wants to remain involved with me but that it's not good for me and that I'm angry about it. Even though that's not something you would say. I don't know what it means that I hear it as your voice. Am I wanting a suggestion from you?
>
> *Analyst:* It's safer in my voice?
>
> *Patient:* I wonder if unconsciously I still want my mother—it's hard to admit my attachment to her so better for it to come as your voice. I was reading Freud this morning where he says that if a love is frustrated it turns to anger. And the anger then turns into anxiety. I become afraid my wishes won't be fulfilled and my fear becomes anxieties. When I hear things in your voice, then I feel inhibited from directing things myself—I start thinking that you need to be in control and have your ego stroked.
>
> *Analyst:* Knowledge about yourself should come from Freud or me, not yourself?
>
> *Patient:* Yeah, that you or Freud see things that I don't. Hunger for knowing—maybe it's sexual hunger turned into hunger for knowledge. I'm thinking now of going to the gym to exercise. I'm fantasizing taking my tee-shirt off in front of women. Now I'm thinking about the shirt I'm wearing in here, that it's a shirt a friend gave me because he didn't want it anymore.

Analyst: Your thoughts went to wearing your friend's shirt instead of displaying your chest. And just before, you thought of hearing my voice instead of your own.

Patient: I began the session with the thought I'd solved something but then I started hearing your voice. And then I thought of wearing my friend's hand-me-down shirt, not my own. I'm so inhibited I need everything to come from without, from other people. We hammer away at ways I inhibit myself, but what's the solution? I guess I'm looking for the source—the pill or something—if I could find the underpinnings, the book knowledge, the complex, so I wouldn't have to pick away slowly at inhibitions.

Analyst: Picking away slowly is more uncomfortable than coming up with a general, over-arching theory of your difficulties?

Patient: It's a habit: this need to appeal to an authority has a life of its own, I can't stop it. I'm not sure what it means to talk in such alienated terms—habits, other people's clothes or voices—as if it's not me. It's like having a life where my conscious self watches machinery it can't control. Looking at things second hand. Things have a life of their own that I can't control. I'm thinking if I stop associating, then you'll say something. Or I've come to a point where I'm blocked and when I feel blocked, it's safe to proceed by waiting for you to talk or to discuss what Freud says. I'm having a clear image of looking to others, or to my habits. Maybe I'm defending against the idea that I'm the actor. Is this free associating or a speculative monologue?

In this session, Mr. C. was able to discuss a general theory about himself (his oedipus complex) in his own voice, but when his thoughts turned to a recent, affectively charged event, his phone call with his mother just before the session, he reported thoughts of hearing my voice, not his own, describing his reactions to the phone call and a few minutes later hearing Freud's voice rather than his own. My comments ("It's safer in my voice," "Knowledge about yourself has to come from Freud or me, not yourself") attempted to make him aware of those moments in the analytic exchange when he replaced his voice with mine or Freud's for defensive, safety-seeking purposes. Elaborating on my interventions, the patient described the fantasy that I needed to be in control and have my ego stroked, a fantasy which he recognized had the effect of defensively inhibiting himself from directing things. Instead of demonstrating self-observation and expressing insight in his own voice, he reported feeling that Freud and I saw things about himself that he wasn't able to see. It was possible to demonstrate a similar microdynamic of assertion turned into self-deprecation a moment later when the patient went from describing a fantasy of displaying his chest to stating that he was wearing a shirt that his friend hadn't wanted anymore. Toward the end of the hour, he noted that he experienced his conscious self as a helpless, passive spectator of his free associations. He also noted that an aspect of becoming blocked in his associating was looking to me, an external authority, to take over the talking, act against him, rather than be the actor himself.

By projecting his voice onto me, Mr. C. disowned not only *what* he understood but *that* he could understand important matters about himself and his life. Here and elsewhere in the analysis, I made interventions intended to make him aware that important, here-and-now conflicts over assertion frequently were manifested in inhibiting his active voice about what he was understanding about himself. As this manifestation of conflict was progressively analyzed, it opened the way for Mr. B. to achieve real understanding and insight about the operation of similar conflicts in other areas of his life.

EXAMPLE #3

Earlier in the hour, Mr. D., a 28-year-old college professor, had mentioned that he had asked out a woman the previous night and that she had accepted. He briefly mentioned a dream about marrying a female relative and wondered if the dream really was about marrying his mother. He then remarked that he thought women had this magic intuition to understand men, while he was in the dark because he made himself blind to what was going on. This reminded him that he had had lunch with a male friend, J., who was not living up to his potential, and had thought about trying to help his friend by sharing with him what he had been learning in analysis about his own tendency to diminish himself. He commented that he realized that he was not so dumb and blind to his problems and that maybe he could help his friend by talking to him. His thoughts then went to his work on his book which recently had been going better.

Patient: I have insights about J.'s problems that could help J. And I'm aware of having ideas in my book that other scholars never thought of. Do I sometimes have thoughts about myself, or perhaps even you, that you hadn't thought of? (pause) Is it time to stop for today?

Analyst: It seems as if you wanted the session to end after you had the thought that you might know something about yourself that I don't know.

Patient: Yeah, get away from the idea that I might see things that you don't, or that I could benefit you—make you aware of things—rather than your always benefiting me. I can be smart myself, even be helpful to you. (pause). Do you have any thoughts about my dream of marrying a female relative?

Analyst: Any thoughts why you're asking?

Patient: I guess I'm feeling like you would know something about a dream that I don't know.

Analyst: You seem to be re-instating me as the smart guy right after thinking about your being smart and helpful to me.

Patient: Yeah. I took my shoes off when I came in today, feeling a sense of prerogative, but the whole session I have been thinking that my feet stink. And I feel that I stink if I'm smart. So I subordinate myself to you.

In this hour, it was possible to track an aggressive drive derivative, here expressed as the patient's sense of growing social and intellectual competence, enter consciousness and gain in strength until it generated conflict anxiety resulting in defensive activity. After mentioning the social success of asking out a woman, Mr. D. described feeling that he really wasn't a psychological blind person, as he tended to see himself, but in fact was insightful and could have been helpful to his demoralized friend, J. He then commented that he was working better on his book and realized that he had many original ideas in it. At this point, he expressed the thought that he sometimes had original insights in his sessions, insights which I hadn't had, about himself and me. Experienced in the here-and-now of the analytic situation and in relation to me, his sense of competence now encountered conflict as evidenced by a defensive shift: a pause, asking me a question, wanting time to be up. I pointed out the sequence which had just occurred. This enabled him to go a bit further, tolerate the drive derivative a little more, and be able to say that he thought he was smart and helpful to me sometimes. This, in turn, produced conflict which he now dealt with by attempting to put himself on the receiving end of my interpretive powers by asking me to tell him the meaning of a dream he'd mentioned much earlier in the session; he was now back to feeling that I, like women, possessed magic intuition and knowledge while he was blind. In this session, he had had moments when he felt a sense of prerogative, not only about taking his shoes off, but also about observing and understanding himself, but these moments had activated superego defenses represented by attempting to make himself the target of my interpretive aggression and by attacking himself with the thought that he stunk.

DISCUSSION

A premise in traditional psychoanalytic methodology is that a repression barrier prevents the patient from being able to become aware of the mind's conflicts. It therefore falls to the analyst to help the patient become aware of these unconscious conflicts by making interpretations. In Gray's work (1994), one discerns the very different premise that manifestations of conflict appear in the patient's conscious mind, however briefly, where they may be observed by both the patient and the analyst. In Gray's methodology, helping the patient become aware of his capacity to observe intra-psychic phenomena related to conflicts are central aspects of the analytic work. Evidence of conflict is there in the hour, in the vicissitudes of the associations, for the patient to observe in collaboration with the analyst. The analyst shows the patient that the conflicts contributing to the difficulties in his life are manifest in the here-and-now associative process for the patient, as well as the analyst, to observe. Instead of interpreting unconscious drive content, the analyst points to observable phenomena at the surface of the patient's mind, in particular unconscious defensive activity in response to emerging drive derivatives, which the patient is also capable of noticing. Since this is not a familiar activity to the patient, it takes time and practice and repeated demonstration by the analyst for the patient to learn how to exercise his autonomous self-observing capacities. Lack of familiarity with this activity is very different, of course, from inability to engage in such activity.

When this ego activity itself becomes embroiled in conflict, however, it will not be enough for the analyst to familiarize the patient with his self-observing skills; the conflicts interfering with self-observation must also come under analytic scrutiny. If one agrees with Gray that many patients possess such skills and that greater therapeutic gain accrues when patients understand their psychological conflicts by observing the evidence themselves rather than relying on the analyst's expertise, then an important task for the analyst is to listen for when and how patients inhibit self-observation.

Another important contribution by Gray has been to highlight the special difficulties in analyzing conflicts of aggression, especially related to its destructive aims, a subject which Bird (1972) called attention to thirty years ago. Aggressive conflicts do not arise only in connection with angry affect but also may occur in connection with derivatives of aggression, including efforts toward autonomy, initiative, and self-assertion. The intra-psychic mechanism of turning aggression against the self has an interpersonal counterpart of adopting a passive, masochistic orientation in relation to others which, in the analytic setting, can result in patients turning moments of autonomous self-observation into placing themselves on the receiving end of the analyst's observing activity. Instead of moving between being passively and actively observant of their thought processes, patients may retreat to the passive role of free associating while looking to the analyst to do the active observing. This conflict over autonomous self-observation then becomes the relevant conflict for the analyst to demonstrate to the patient rather than conflicts over material entering the patient's consciousness.

Since patients often are particularly uneasy about becoming aware of conflictual wishes when they are experienced towards the analyst, these conflicts over the assertive/aggressive connotations of ego autonomy may not be accessible to the patient during the earlier stages of the analysis. The exercise of active ego capacities can feel to some patients like a particularly profound display of psychological strength in relation to the analyst, in part precisely because it *is* an action by the ego rather than a "mere" verbal report of the patient's subjective state. In the case of Mr. B., for example, considerable analysis of defensive responses to the awareness of aggression toward others preceded effective analysis of aggressive strivings in relation to the analyst. Only after the patient had achieved a greater tolerance of an aggressive/assertive stance with the analyst, however, was he able to "own" and integrate conflict-laden issues which already had emerged in the treatment. Before that, the analysis proceeded under the shadow of the superego in which important material emerged into consciousness and was verbalized in compliance with superego demands transferred onto the analyst. It was as though the material had been offered to the analyst for his approval and interpretation rather than for the patient to own and master. Change for this patient began not with the emergence of previously repressed material but at a later point when the patient developed a greater capacity for self-observation, integration and synthesis which enabled him to own and master this material.

Holmes (1996) recently has proposed that along with resistances to libidinal and aggressive drive derivatives there is a third kind of resistance, resistance to ego expansion. It is unclear, however, why the ego should resist its ego expansion per se. The ego may resist growth of certain ego functions, however, if those ego functions are associated with libidinal or aggressive drive which generates conflict. I am suggesting that in the analytic setting, the patient's autonomous use of self-observing capacities in the presence of the analyst may have assertive/aggressive connotations which the patient may defend against in a variety of ways, including becoming the passive recipient of the analyst's interpretive aggression.

For some patients resistance to self-observation may supplant the "usual" resistances to exposing conflictual drive derivatives. There are patients who appear to say everything; they are paragons of free associating for whom nothing is too distressing to say to their analyst and whose trust in their analyst's acceptance of their associations appears absolute and unwavering. Gray views this phenomenon as involving transference of affectionate approval, a defense transference in which patients form the illusion of a permissive, accepting analyst to defend against anxieties aroused by the opposite image of a critical, disapproving analyst (Gray, 1994). By "saying everything" to an approving analyst, the patient is resisting the analysis of resistances, a process which inevitably generates some anxiety. Because the patient appears to be participating earnestly in the task of free association, the resisting aspects may be easily overlooked. For his part, the analyst must strive to maintain analytic neutrality, even as he is inviting a collaborative exploration with the patient, in order to be able to point out those moments when the patient turns to a transference fantasy of the analyst as a nice, benevolent, approving figure to defend against the expression of aggressive feelings. I suggest that resistance to self-observation can occur in concert with transferences of affectionate approval to create a situation in which full disclosure conceals usual resistances and limits the possibility of gaining an understanding of the resistances. In such situations, the patient has dealt with his aggressive conflicts by removing aggressive derivatives from the analytic exchange, both his aggressive/assertive efforts at understanding himself and the feared counter-aggression of the analyst. The patient is a passive reporter of his passing thoughts and is talking to an analyst whom he experiences as benign and approving.

Relevant to this point is Landau's observation that consciousness can serve defensive purposes when ideas enter consciousness before important resistances have been analyzed. "If we think of consciousness as an ego function that can become embroiled in conflict," writes Landau, "then we can think of the ego using that function according to its multiple purposes, including those that serve mastery and integration, as well as those that serve defense" (Landau, 1996, p. 285). Consciousness, Landau points out, is not equivalent to mastery and integration and may even act to defend against mastery and integration. The crucial variable is not whether the ideas are in consciousness or not but the amount of conflict the ego experiences in integrating the ideas. In making the ideas conscious and verbalizing them, the patient may avoid becoming aware of the threat to the ego and the associated anxiety; only when the resistances to the ideas are analyzed is the patient able to become aware of the imagined threat and thereby able to integrate the ideas. Thus, a patient may observe and verbalize what is coming to mind in accord with the fundamental rule but this can be an aspect of resistance rather than growth if the patient does not also employ active ego skills to integrate the material and instead looks to the analyst to be the active interpreter.

The question arises whether these resistances to self-observation and integration reflect conflict over the active ego skills required for such tasks, as I am suggesting here, or conflicts over the material which is pressing towards consciousness. For it is clear that often when patients bring conflictual ideas into consciousness but resist integrating them, "know but don't know" as Freud put it (1895, p. 117), a dissociation is taking place to defend against accepting ownership of the ideas. I suggest that these resistances may operate together: for it is when the emerging material represents an opportunity for real gain that the ego's activity of observing and understanding the material constitutes a true demonstration of the ego's strength and mastery which the patient may experience as an aggressive challenge to the analyst. For example, in the second clinical vignette, Mr. C. was able to discuss a general theory about himself without difficulty; when his thoughts then went to a phone call from his mother just before the session and his anger at her—a live anger generated by the recent phone call—he promptly inhibited self-inquiry, instead "heard" my voice in place of his own and looked to me to take charge and provide understanding.

Psychoanalysis seeks to strengthen the autonomous ego of the patient, including the autonomous ego's capacity to recognize and resolve psychological conflict. By attending to the patient's ego activity in observing one's mind, analysts have the opportunity to follow the patient's autonomous ego in action. Renik has cautioned that "there is a danger of analysis becoming a sequestered, self-sustaining, escapist exercise—a separate reality, so to speak" (1998, p. 581). Renik sees this as occurring in patients who have strong passive wishes and magical fantasies that free-floating investigation will yield therapeutic benefit. In such circumstances, Renik argues that it is important to emphasize to the patient that the intent of the analysis is to enable the patient to manage better in reality and at times to confront the patient on the need to "get real" about the analysis, that is, to take seriously the need to work out problems in reality. This stance seems to be a challenge to the traditional view that the purpose of analysis is to help the patient understand himself better while leaving the management of the patient's life to the patient. When analytic listening includes attending to the patient's ego participation in observing psychological conflict, however, there need not be Renik's concern about patients' escapist proclivities if reality is left up to the patient, since the patient's real involvement in the task of understanding himself is part of the ongoing analytic work. In other words, an added benefit to involving the patient's ego in the analytic work is that it provides a basis for assessing the resistances that Renik is referring to but in connection with what is taking place inside the analysis.

Part of the analyst's attention must be on the patient's ego participation in comprehending evidence of psychological conflict. Employing the kind of methodology proposed by Gray and Busch to give patients the opportunity to exercise autonomous ego participation does not assure that the patient will take advantage of the opportunity offered him. In some cases, patients may lack sufficient ego strength to participate in observing their defending minds in action. My interest in this paper is in those patients who do possess the requisite ego capacity for self-observation but present resistances to exercising self-observation. The operation of these resistances may be so tenacious that they may be mistaken for evidence of ego deficit with the result that the analyst modifies his technique in the direction of including ego-supportive measures instead of consistently and patiently interpreting these resistances. Alternatively, the very seamlessness of the patient's free associations along with the pleasures for the analyst of providing the insights which are gratefully received may result in the analyst's failure to recognize the patient's resistances to self-observation at work. Since, as Gray pointed out in his landmark essay "Developmental Lag in the Evolution of Psychoanalytic Technique," there are strong counter-resistances to analyzing the patient's resistances, especially in connection with aggressive wishes, the analyst's task in recognizing and analyzing the patient's resistance to self-observation can be a formidable one indeed.

In analytic practice, analysts meet all kinds of patients who present with all manner of conflicts. There are patients who respond with little evidence of conflict to the opportunity to engage in an active collaboration with the analyst to observe and understand their resisting minds in action. For such patients, it may come as a relief that their autonomous, active ego skills are counted upon and that the analytic process will not result in a passive reliance upon the analyst's authority. Other patients, such as the ones described here, may manifest conflict over employing active ego skills in analysis and for defensive reasons may present a passive, enfeebled, dependent ego to the analyst. Josephs, in a thoughtful critique of the concept of working at the surface, has expressed puzzlement that little has been written about patients' resistances to the close process approach developed by Gray and others (Josephs, 1997). I have attempted to demonstrate in this essay that such resistances do occur and can and should be analyzed by the same close process approach. The appearance of conflicts over the employment of active self-observational skills does not constitute a shortcoming of the technique, as Josephs seems to suggest, or even that the technique must be modified for that particular patient but that self-observation, like almost every constituent of the analytic situation, can act as a stimulus for conflict and resistance.

CONCLUSION

More than sixty years ago, Searl emphasized the importance of exploring "the dynamics about the patient's disability to find his own way" (Searl, 1936, p. 479). Many contemporary analysts, Gray being foremost, share Searl's underlying assumption about many patients being able to find their own way if shown how to do so. Patients are not always inclined to exercise their objective ego capacities to find their own way, however, even when given the opportunity to do so. While the dynamics underlying interferences with objective self-observation are myriad, I have highlighted the role of conflicts over aggression in undermining the deployment of the active ego functions involved in self-observation, understanding, and integration. When such conflicts develop, patients may engage predominantly in the relatively passive task of free association, eschew the second, more active task of observing and understanding their working minds, and place themselves on the receiving end of the analyst's interpretations. In doing so, the active ego functions necessary for understanding and integration are inhibited, compromising the possibility for growth and change.

BIBLIOGRAPHY

ARLOW, J., & BRENNER, C. (1990). "The psychoanalytic process." *Psychoanalytic Quarterly*, 59:678–692.
BIRD, B. (1992). "Notes on transference: Universal phenomenon and hard-

est part of analysis." *Journal of the American Psychoanalytic Association*, 20:267–301.

BOESKY, D. (1990). "The psychoanalytic process and its components." *Psychoanalytic Quarterly*, 59:550–584.

BUSCH, F. (1994). "Free association and technique." *Journal of the American Psychoanalytic Association*, 42:363–384.

FOGEL, G. (1995). "Psychological-mindedness as a defense." *Journal of the American Psychoanalytic Association*, 43:793–822.

FONAGY, P., & TARGET, M. (2000). "Playing with reality: III. The persistence of dual psychic reality in borderline patients." *International Journal of Psychoanalysis*, 81:853–873.

FREUD, S. (1937). Analysis terminable and interminable. *SE* 23.

FREUD, S. (1895). Studies on hysteria. *SE* 2.

GRAY, P. (1994). *The Ego and the Analysis of Defense*. Northvale, N.J.: Jason Aronson.

GRAY, P. (1996). "Undoing the lag in the technique of conflict and defense analysis." *Psychoanalytic Study of the Child*, Vol. 51, pp. 87–101.

HOLMES, D. (1996). "Emerging indicators of ego growth and associated resistances." *Journal of the American Psychoanalytic Association*, 44:1101–1119.

JOSEPHS, L. (1997). "The view from the tip of the iceberg," *Journal of the American Psychoanalytic Association*, 45:425–463.

LANDAU, B. (1996). "Consciousness as a beacon light," in *Danger and Defense*, Goldberger, M. (ed.), Northvale, N.J.: Jason Aronson, pp. 263–290.

PRAY, M. (1996). "Two different methods of analyzing defense" in *Danger and Defense*, Goldberger, M. (ed.), Northvale, N.J.: Jason Aronson, pp. 53–106.

RAPHLING, D. (1992). "Vicissitudes of aggression in the interpretative process." *Psychoanalytic Quarterly*, 61:352–369.

RENIK, O. (1998). "Getting real in psychoanalysis," *Psychoanalytic Quarterly*, 67:566–593.

SEARL, M. N. (1936). "Some queries on principles of technique." *International Journal of Psychoanalysis*, 17:471–493.

STERBA, R. (1934). "The fate of the ego in analytic theory." *International Journal of Psychoanalysis*, 15:117–126.

THEORY

A Reconsideration of the Concept of Regression

A. SCOTT DOWLING, M.D.

Regression has been a useful psychoanalytic concept, linking present mental functioning with past experiences and levels of functioning. The concept originated as an extension of the evolutionary zeitgeist *of the day as enunciated by H. Spencer and H. Jackson and applied by Freud to psychological phenomena. The value system implicit in the contrast of evolution/progression vs dissolution/regression has given rise to unfortunate and powerful assumptions of social, cultural, developmental and individual value as embodied in notions of "higher," "lower," "primitive," "mature," "archaic," and "advanced." The unhelpful results of these assumptions are evident, for example, in attitudes concerning cultural, sexual, and social "correctness," same-sex object choice, and goals of treatment. An alternative, a continuously constructed, continuously emerging mental life, in analogy to the ever changing, continuous physical body, is suggested. This view retains the fundamentals of psychoanalysis, for example, unconscious mental life, drive, defense, and psychic structure, but stresses a functional, ever changing, present oriented understanding of mental life as contrasted with a static, onion-layered view.*

"In rivers, the water that you touch is the last of what has passed and the first of that which comes; so with present time."

—Leonardo da Vinci

Training and Supervising Analyst, Cleveland Psychoanalytic Center, Cleveland; Ohio Associate Clinical Professor of Child Psychiatry, Case-Western Reserve University, Cleveland, Ohio.

This paper is a revision of the Melitta Sperling Memorial Lecture of 1997.

The Psychoanalytic Study of the Child 59, ed. Robert A. King, Peter B. Neubauer, Samuel Abrams, and A. Scott Dowling (Yale University Press, copyright © 2004 by Robert A. King, Peter B. Neubauer, Samuel Abrams, and A. Scott Dowling).

REGRESSION, "A RETURN FROM A POINT ALREADY REACHED TO AN EAR-
lier one" (LaPlanche and Pontalis, 1973), has long been an important explanatory concept in psychoanalytic theory and clinical practice. Although Freud noted early instances of the notion of
regression in the works of Albertus Magnus (thirteenth century) and
Hobbes (1651) (Freud, 1900, p. 542), there were powerful currents
in scientific thought in the late nineteenth century that provided the
intellectual foundation of regression and the related concept, fixation. This foundation consists of two related axioms—"progressive
evolution" and "regressive dissolution"—first enunciated by Herbert
Spencer (1867) and then elaborated by John Hughlings Jackson
(1884). Freud (1891) in *On Aphasia* utilized Jackson's application of
the concepts to neurological disorders. Freud was the first to apply
them to purely psychological phenomena. As will be described below, the axioms of regression and progression carry a heavy load of
value judgment, some of which has been carried over to psychoanalytic theory.

One alternative explanation of clinical phenomena attributed to
regression will be presented. This explanation views mental life as
analogous to the physical body, a singular present reality, related to
the past and to the environment but not consisting of or containing
either. Instead of layers of content extending into a psychological
deep, this alternative suggests that psychological life is best viewed as
a complex and largely unconscious "horizontal" present. Again, the
analogy is with the physical body, constantly renewing and modifying
itself but never quite the same as it was before and certainly not consisting of "layers" of "past bodies" with the possibility of return to past
body states.

In a "horizontal" psychology, mental accessibility is limited by defensive barriers within a "horizontal" present, not by being buried in
"vertical" layers of varying accessibility. This approach has similarities
to Freud's theory of a dynamic timeless unconscious; it is unlike that
conception in seeing all of mental life, including unconscious mental
life, as constantly, interactively "emerging," thus never the same as at
some past time. It is a broad application of *nachtraglichkeit*, or de-
ferred meaning, the idea that what is continually rewrites what has
been. The approach I am suggesting is therefore "constructivist" in
that it recognizes the dynamic interaction of a variety of internal and
environmental factors in determining the path of an ever changing
mental life.

Psychology in this view includes a set of functions that regulate the
construction of conscious and unconscious experience from a con-

straining but ever changing internal and external world. The present, both conscious and unconscious, is always emerging, always new, yet also always the outcome of the past. It is defined by the patterning and content of what has gone before and by ongoing perception, fantasy, and affect with no warehouse of unmodified relics of all that has gone before. In fact, most contemporary psychoanalysts do not think in terms of buried fixed remains and static structures, though they often do continue to use a language of things, places, and forces. To describe work within a horizontal present requires casting psychoanalytic concepts in terms of alterable patterns, fantasies, and affects. "Unconscious," in both dynamic and non-dynamic senses, becomes a description of a relationship to consciousness rather than a place or a collection of events. And it does require thinking of mental life as horizontal and immediate, linked to the past and to present experience through a process of "construction."

This approach will be illustrated by a psychoanalytic theory of object choice that avoids some of the more value laden pitfalls of traditional theory. The approach will also be illustrated in a consideration of the goals of psychoanalysis.

Types of Regression

Freud spoke of three types of regression: topographic, temporal, and formal. Topographic regression assumes a topography of levels of structure or organization that can be traversed in a forward or reverse sequence, as exemplified by Freud's description of dream formation (1900). Temporal regression is a return to earlier, simpler, more primitive psychical structures or contents. Within temporal regression, Freud (1916, pp. 340–44, 357) distinguished regression of object relationships, of libidinal stage, and of ego functioning. Formal regression, he stated, is a return to more "primitive methods of expression and representation" (1900, added 1914).

My concern will be with temporal and formal regression. Although the two are quite different, the first emphasizing a return to an earlier stage of life and the latter a revival of earlier forms of psychical functioning, they are not distinguished from each other in most psychoanalytic writing; "earlier" is usually assumed to be less adequate because it is "more primitive." It is temporal/formal regression that is most often linked with theories of pathogenesis and theories of development; it pervades present day clinical thinking. I question the clinical utility of temporal regression, a movement backward to an

earlier, "less mature," time in life. The suggested constructivist view
includes a version of formal regression that is free of the values implicit in such words as "primitive," "mature," or "advanced." Formal
regression in this revised sense will include the possibility of using
forms of defense or expression acquired at a younger age as part of
the individual's present day, horizontal repertoire of functioning and
content.

The pervasive assumption of temporal regression is linked with the
success of psychoanalytic developmental theory. Freud's own use of
the concept grew with his increasing understanding of the levels of
psychosexual organization (1905, added 1915), of the phallic phase
(1905, added 1923), and of subdivisions within psychosexual stages
(Abraham, 1924). As a result, it became, and remains, common to
speak in terms of "regression to the oral phase," or to some other psychosexual phase; similarly we speak of regression to a "level" of drive
expression, for example, to "oral aggression" or "phallic narcissism";
and to a particular type of object relations, for example, to dyadic
preoedipal, relationships. Finally, we speak of other forms of selective ego regression, for example, to soiling or wetting, to anal messi-
ness and so on.

As particular interpretations of development gained ascendancy,
corresponding forms of temporal regression entered the psychoanalytic vocabulary. Kleinians speak of regression to the depressive or
paranoid positions and the regressive use of "primitive" defenses
such as splitting; Mahlerians, of regression to the symbiotic, rapprochement, or other phase of self/object differentiation; Ko-
hutians, of regression to the early organizations of narcissism; Kern-
bergians, of regression to early self/affect/object formations or to
"primitive defenses." Mainstream analysis has its own signature forms
of id, ego, or superego regression, best articulated in the works of
Anna Freud.

This familiar and traditional theory implies a three dimensional
temporal psychology of both the preconscious and unconscious
mind. The result is a layered past of archaic or "primitive" levels, potentially accessible through regression and the effects of fixation. For
descriptive convenience, this near infinity of potential levels is
grouped into phases or stages, not only as a useful depiction of ongoing development but as a persisting, active and potentially dynamically active and conscious concretion of the past. This multiplicity of
levels or "moments-in-time" coexists with the present moment which
soon becomes yet another "moment-in-time" to be succeeded by another "present."

EXAMPLES OF REGRESSION

Two clinical vignettes will provide common examples of regression and orient you to the questions I am asking. One concerns a young adult patient, the second an adolescent.

> Case #1: David, a twenty-two-year-old man was referred because of maladaptive behavior in all aspects of his life. He was variously viewed as strange, anxious, depressed, or psychotic. He experienced anxiety with entry to college, calling home frequently and only gradually finding his way into the academic and social life of his new environment. Following David's first year in college and at a time when his parents were returning from a trip abroad and unavailable, his older brother died suddenly and inexplicably. For a day, until his parents returned to the U.S., David was the family member in charge. The funeral director turned to him for instructions, authorities spoke to him, and it became his responsibility to break the news to his parents on their arrival. He felt overwhelmed, then profoundly "numb" with an absence of all feeling. With psychotherapy and with transfer to a school nearer to home these symptoms gradually eased during the following year. Renewed interest in school, in sex, and in social life blossomed with hypomanic plans for school abroad, impulsive sexual behavior, and intense inner challenges to religious, occupational, and social expectations. His parents remained prostrate with grief and guilt; the physical and psychological relationship between parents and son became intense and conflictual. Suddenly he again became "numb," this time to an extent that made him unable to recognize needs, feelings, or ambitions. He progressively withdrew, failed college, was unable to date, and returned to the parental home and to dependency, inactivity, and to an intellectual obsessive preoccupation with his "numbness." He did not hallucinate, nor was he delusional. He felt "blocked" and "stuck," terms which he physically assigned to his neck ("my neck feels blocked and stuck") and which paralleled his constipation ("my bowels are blocked").

Using common psychoanalytic terminology, we could say that David showed a marked regression in all aspects of personality functioning. Intrapsychic conflict concerning age appropriate sexual and aggressively ambitious interests and pathological mourning with paralyzing guilt became unbearably intense following the ambivalent victory that resulted from his brother's death. After a year of partial recovery, he experienced symptomatic return of repressed, regressive attitudes and behavior. He experienced psychosexual regression to preoedipal oral and anal sexual organizations together with ego and superego regression.

Psychosomatic or psychophysiological symptoms such as head-aches, skin rashes, and a variety of autonomic disturbances of respira-tory and gastrointestinal function are often viewed with alarm as in-dicating regression to early, preverbal modes of expression and body experience. A striking example, one of many from my own practice, is

> Case #2: John, a seventeen-year-old boy in residential treatment, threw his head back and clutched his hands over (but not on) his throat while recounting a vivid recollection of being beaten and choked at age eleven by his sadistic father. As he poured out his an-guish in sobs and words, erythema and localized linear wheals ap-peared over his neck.

In our usual terminology, John experienced a regressive psy-chophysiological expression of an early experience in the midst of an intense affective reliving of repeated abusive attacks by his father.

THE PHENOMENOLOGY OF REGRESSION

Why do we think of these phenomena as "regressive"? The intuitive answer is that we recognize regression as a result of direct clinical ex-perience. We see it happening before our eyes and ears. We see David return to levels of expression and relationship characteristic of a much younger child while John shows us a literal return to a previ-ous bodily state. In these and other, less dramatic, instances, we rec-ognize a return to the issues, object relationships, and forms of drive expression of the past, often from the repressed past. We recognize a revival of old libidinal forms of expression through the twin influ-ences of the pull of fixation and the push of present frustration or anxiety; we see a falling back of ego functioning to earlier levels in re-sponse to dysphoric affect.

But there are counter examples that should give us pause. When, as adults, we drink from a cup, ride a bike, write a note, walk, sing a nursery rhyme, perform a somersault, or tell our grandchildren a riddle, and much less when we are making love with mouth, skin, and eyes, we do not usually consider that we have "regressed"; we are drawing on and selecting from a potential repertoire of actions, atti-tudes, and varieties of pleasure which have been a "part of us" since childhood. My thesis is that access to physiological responses to affec-tive events, defensive splitting, baby talk, dependent attitudes, and most other phenomena that are usually termed "regressed" have also been a "part of us" since childhood and are available to be utilized by our more adult personalities for specific, adaptive purposes. The difference between the two groups of phenomena is that the former group is less apt to be connected with conflict or stress, whereas the latter group is more apt to be conflictual or designated by society as aberrant. It is simpler, more direct, and equally explanatory to consider the actions or attitudes part of the available repertoire of the individual in both instances. In both groups, the attitude or action is not the same as the original, childhood attitude or action; its performance and meaning are changed by the constructive, modifying, transforming effects of ongoing experience.

THE CONCEPTUAL BACKGROUND OF THE CONCEPT OF REGRESSION

What is the origin and history of our concept of regression? It is a commonplace that however evident or common-sensical an idea may be, it is most often the outcome of prior thinking, an application to new material of a form of organization or a metaphor which has proved useful elsewhere. The metaphor often carries unintended baggage to the new application. More extensive discussion of the historical aspects can be found in papers by S. W. Jackson (1969) and H. Blum (1994).

Freud's use of these terms is an extension of John Hughlings Jackson's ideas concerning evolution and its opposite, dissolution, taken from the evolutionary theories of Herbert Spencer (1867). Spencer, the nineteenth century philosopher, sought to extend the insight of Darwinian evolution of species to a broad set of phenomena. From evolution as a technical biological term that explains the formation of species, Spencer extended its application to patterns of change in inorganic, organic, and social contexts and hypothesized an opposite force, dissolution, to explain instances of disintegration or degradation. Evolution was "forward" or "upward;" dissolution was "downward," more "primitive" or "backward." Evolution and dissolution are patterns of concentration and decay and apply throughout the natural world. Evolving matter moves from diffuseness to concentration with lessening of motion, reduction of organization, and with increase in integration; in dissolution it moves in the opposite direction, that is, toward diffuseness, increase of organization, and decreased integration.

J. H. Jackson (1884) applied Spencer's formula to the "ascending development in a particular order" of individuals. In each individual there is "a passage from the most to the least organized, from the most simple to the most complex and from the most automatic to the

most voluntary." The so-called lowest nervous centers are well organized, simple, and automatic, while the highest are relatively unorga-
nized, complex, and voluntary in their functioning. This implies a
continuity of development without discontinuity from early automa-
tisms to later, more complex, less organized psychological states.[1]

Dissolution, in Spencer's view, is the reverse of the process just described. Thus, "to undergo dissolution," means to return or be reduced to a lower, earlier level of evolution. J. H. Jackson applied this
formulation to illness. Disorders of the nervous system initially affect
the portion of the system with the most recently evolved functions
and only later affect portions with older functions, a pattern which
was applied by both Sigmund and Anna Freud in descriptions of ego
regression. There is a notable conceptual leap in this formulation
which J. H. Jackson, and later Freud, did not hesitate to make: the
claim of an equivalence of ontogenetic "early and later" with phylogenetic "early and later." The well-known formula, "ontogeny reca-
pitulates phylogeny," is a statement of this Jacksonian belief. J. H.
Jackson extended the conceptual leap further, applying the evolu-
tion/dissolution model to rhythmic events of daily life. Thus he
spoke of "a rhythm of evolution and dissolution" in the daily sequence of wakefulness, sleepiness, sleep with dreaming, and deep
sleep (and the reverse).

In J. H. Jackson's system, an evolving higher level of functioning
supplanted and inhibited lower levels. Dissolution is a "taking off of
the higher" and "at the very same time a letting go, or expression, of
the lower." The so-called "lower levels" are both lower in a hierarchical sense and characteristic of temporally earlier stages; they are simpler, more automatic, more organized. To avoid confusion, it is important to know that Jackson never spoke of "dissolution or evolution
of the mind"; he did not apply this system to strictly psychological
phenomena considered separately from brain functioning. It was in
this physical sense that Freud applied Jackson's ideas about evolution
and dissolution of central nervous system functioning in *On Aphasia*
(1891).

Freud, in *The Interpretation of Dreams* (1900), applied these formulations to mental phenomena within a purely psychological system
when he posited regression from thought to image in dreams—

---

1. Organization, for Jackson, implies fixity, a lack of flexibility of response. This is
quite different from Hartmann's (1958) emphasis on organization as the outcome of
coordinated differentiation and integration, a capacity for adaptation.

though still within a quasi-physical "topographic system." More relevant to the topic of this paper is his envisioning temporal regression in dreams from adult to infantile interests and modes of thought. Although expressed in energic terms, he recognized primary process as infantile mentation that evolves into secondary process mentation of adults and is regressively revived in dream thinking.

Over the next decade Freud (1910a, 1910b, 1911, 1912) progressively articulated his theory of pathogenesis based on frustration of libidinal wishes with retreat, or regression, to a predetermined fixation point.

Alongside these formulations, Freud also declared (1896) that fantasies are central to psychoneurotic development, a subtly different notion than shifting libido. A fantasy is a scenario with particular persons and actions, whereas shifts of libido describe an energic condition. A castration fantasy describes a possible experience, e.g. the thought of mother or father, or a displacement object representing them, physically attacking the sexual body. Thus, regression came to have a meaning other than a return to earlier conditions of libido; it is also the evocation of previously important, affectively meaningful fantasies.

To summarize, Spencer and Jackson extended the Darwinian hypothesis of adaptive evolution of species to include a broad range of physical, social, individual, and developmental phenomena, joined by notions of "progress" or "forward motion." They then added the hypothesis of dissolution, a return down the ladder of development, the counterpart of evolution as movement up that ladder. Not only did normal embryological development, the march of civilization, and social progress mirror the progress of evolution, but atavism, compromised brain function, cultural primitivism, and social degradation result from development failing to advance or following a reverse course. Evolution and dissolution are impersonal forces, acting outside the possibility of active intervention.

Spencer and Jackson add a value judgment to Darwinian evolution, with dire results. For Spencer and Jackson, evolution is positive or progressive; dissolution is negative or regressive. Evolution and dissolution are inevitable qualities of an ordered universe, albeit with more than a whiff of righteousness for the evolved (you and I) and disdain for those who are yet to be evolved or have undergone dissolution ("the others," whether because of their culture, race, gender, or form of sexual expression, and the sick). Freud was a part of this cultural milieu in his assumption of the evolutionary inferiority of blacks and of "primitive" American culture and in his struggle to understand the hierarchical place of men and women, biologically, psychologically, and socially. In practice, Freud was ahead of his time in his empathy for the social plight of homosexuals and in his recognition and appreciation of the intellectual power of women.

Freud made special use of the idea of an ordered return to the past, extending Jackson's neurological application of dissolution to purely psychological phenomena, now termed "regression." He did so initially to explain the formation of dreams within the topographical system or, alternatively, by following back along the line of temporal progression.

The theories of Spencer, Jackson, and Freud represent biological or psychological events as the expression of fundamental and impersonal forces, tendencies or principles, a characteristic of nineteenth-century science that is more explicit in Freud's later theories concerning Eros and Thanatos, the death instinct. These forces are not accessible to individual influence, are not analyzable. This is a powerful value laden current in Freud's thinking, noticeable in his assumption of phylogenetic causation and in the cultural assumptions noted above. The Oedipus complex, castration anxiety, and latency are the most obvious examples of developmental characteristics that Freud believed are impersonally, "biologically" transmitted from one generation to the next. Yet Freud and all subsequent analysts recognize another origin of psychic life; they have always recognized the importance of individual fantasy, meaning, and motivation. Analysis is only possible because that is so.

An important characteristic of the classic view of regression is its spatial imagery. Regression is always "back," "inward," or "down," never "forward," "outward," or "up." It is also never "sideways" or "parallel." There is more than a tinge of "worse" or "bad" that comes with this nineteenth-century spatial imagery of regression, just as there is in the application of similar notions to social and cultural issues. In the twenty-first century, we have learned the inaccuracies inherent in this approach to social or cultural issues; it is an approach that *a priori* terms Inuit or Tasaday society and culture "backward" or "simple" compared with Western European society and culture; black African society or music "less advanced" than European society or music; and polytheistic religions "immature" compared to Judeo-Christian-Islamic monotheism. In each instance the older and the earlier are not just "different" or "parallel," they are always "backward" or "inferior" in one or many respects and have evolved into later "progressive" and "superior" forms. The mutual slaughter of

Jews and Muslims while Christians egg them on should cause the most convinced believer to question monotheism as religious progress.

Psychological regression has levels, corresponding to the distance "down" or "back" it goes. One useful way we have of labeling these levels is according to psychosexual development. Other ways of labeling correspond with our particular formulation of development, for example, Kleinian, Kohutian, Sternian, or other. In addition we sometimes speak of regression in terms laden with unstated values and prognostic significance, for example, "primitive," "infantile," or "archaic."

There are two established modifications of these "back" and "down" metaphors that are corrective of their possible abuses. They were introduced by Heinz Hartmann (1958) and Ernst Kris (1951) and are closely allied with ego psychology; the first modification is the adaptational point of view; the second is regression in the service of the ego. The adaptational point of view recognizes that regression occurs in a broad setting of psychological functioning; it is not simply an abandonment of mature functioning but part of an attempt to stabilize and retain functional capacity. Regression in the service of the ego, a controlled regression as in play and artistic expression, attempts to provide a value neutral explanation of regularly observed phenomena such as play, creativity, and the daily fluctuations in ego and drive expression. But these modifications are "add ons" and do not remove the implications of the basic directional metaphor with its inherent prejudices.

A key Freudian metaphor for regression is an advancing army making a tactical retreat when it meets strong resistance. It falls back to previously established strong points (fixation points) where a more adequate defense can be established.

THE HYPOTHESIS OF A CONTINUOUSLY CONSTRUCTED PRESENT

Suppose for a minute a different kind of metaphor, one of an ever advancing, horizontal cross-section of time, each moment expressing the past in a form that is unique; each moment an epigenetic, multi-determined, individual expression as fleeting as a snowflake, as permanent as the flow of time. Now complicate the metaphor by watching an individual over cross-sectional time, seeing the relative simplicity but brilliant intensity of her early appearance (infancy), her greater complexity and greater fixity at later times (latency), her renewed brilliance and complex turmoil at a later time (adoles-

cence) and her greater stability but flexible responsiveness to external circumstance still later (adulthood). Suppose you have come to
know the dominant patterns of expression at different times of life
and recognize that all are present, all variably accessible, all richly
contributing to the typical patterns that follow while altering those
that have already been. All previous patterns are present or potentially available yet always modified through the impingements of
later experience, all subject to *nachtraglichkeit*. Functionally, there is
only the pattern of the moment, drawing upon but distinct from all
that preceded it. Now one past pattern contributes more strongly to
the unique, age determined pattern of the moment, now another,
and now another.

What does the term "the past" bring to mind? Don't we usually
think of an experienced actual scene, most often a visual scene? By
"the past" we mean something real, actual, now reproduced in memory. But we know enough about perception and about memory to
know that when we perceive a complex scene, what we perceive is not
a point by point reproduction of something out there but a construction built from the building blocks of individual sensory input as
shaped into perception by individual motivation, needs, and fantasy.
All of us occasionally indulge in negative hallucinations, removing
what we do not want to see. All of us, all of the time, lend significance
to what is before us on the basis of our moment-to-moment individual needs, wishes, and fantasies. The past that influences us is whatever has been previously made of the perceptions of that time, now
reinterpreted by the conscious and unconscious needs, wishes, and
fantasies of the present moment. The term most of us use for this interpretation of past experience is "meaning." The present meaning
of the past experience shapes what we recall and have in mind. The
memory today is not the same as the memory of yesterday which, in
turn, is not the same as the initial experience. Do we then have, over
time, an infinite multiplicity of "memories" of the same event, each
determined by renewed processing of what went before? I suggest
that we have only the present memory, determined by what has been
previously present as well as by immediate circumstances.

These ideas seek to provide a frame, however hazy, that will convey
what psychoanalytic work teaches us: there is endless complexity, endless over-determination, and endless multi-dimensionality of meaning
in every human experience. One-dimensional static formulas help
only schematically; they do not convey the pulsating reality of ever
changing but ephemeral psychological life.

Granted the ultimate defeat of all efforts to convey the full multi-dimensionality of psychological life, I'd like to explain less metaphorically and more conceptually what I have in mind. Then I will apply these thoughts to the two patients I described at the beginning of the paper and finally bring these ideas to bear on two important issues, one clinical—our present day approach to same-sex object choice; the other very general—the goals of psychoanalysis.

I am suggesting that there is no such thing as a regressive return to the past, no falling back to old garrisons. I can see and feel only from a present vantage point, through the mind and heart of who I am today to a past that has been shaped and reshaped by my past psychology and now is shaped again by my psychology of today. A simple example is the experience of a growing and eventually grown child with his parent. They have reached apparent resolution of past conflicts and view each other as respected adults of different generations. Looking back on painful and pleasurable events of the past, they revise their understanding of those events; they see them in a larger context. Although they can "recall" the pain and pleasure of the past, can taste and sample what it has been, can remove many (but never all) of the barriers of repression, neither parent or child can be there again; the perspective of their newfound maturity, which does not necessarily add factual accuracy to the scene, is the only way they can view that past. They may or may not be able to experience affects associated with the past to a greater extent than was true at other points in their relationship. At each point, including the present, they are limited by the perspective of the moment though influenced by the perspective of past times.

Though this is self-evident in the changing relationship of parent and child, it is less evident that this is true of every recollection of the past. All memory is constructed within the framework of the psychology of the immediate present. It is false to consider the present memory as a factual reproduction of another time and place. This is the point made long ago by Kris in pointing out that we never know what actually happened "under the staircase." We have another kind of fact, a very important one—the fact of the meaning to us, at this time, of that event. The meaning is contained in the expressive and defensive aspects of the memory and its associated affects. And it is, in every event, that *meaning* or those *meanings* that is relevant to our primary task in analysis. That task is the recognition and resolution of intrapsychic conflict and distortions of development.

The word "meaning" frightens those who sense that a relativistic hermeneutics is lurking just around the corner whenever the term is used. Hermeneutics means "the methodological principles of interpretation" and is commonly used to indicate the study of meaning. Meaning can be dealt with as psychological fact equal to the factual nature of wish, need, or fantasy and with more security than when speaking of a cathectic shift or a level of object relationship despite the reassuring apparent reference to objective science.

Thus, the mind contains an ever-shifting sense of past and present reality. The pattern of memory derives not only from the psychosexual stages but also from equally familiar forms of object relationship and affect expression. It also derives from the changing forms of cognition—the concept-free sensorimotor thinking of the infant and young toddler; the diffusely conceptual, affectively dominated thinking of toddlers and preschoolers; the perception, fact bound thinking of the elementary child; and finally, the wide ranging propositional thinking of the adolescent and adult.

Our moment-to-moment daily lives call upon all psychosexual levels, all past experienced forms of object relationship and, significantly, a variety of cognitive forms. We don't *return* to these forms of object relationship and cognition, we *use* them as available vehicles for the expression and defensive remodeling of meaning. Unconscious content and the effects of repression and other defenses find a comfortable home in this present oriented scheme with its foreground-background relationship to present and potential content. This view does maintain that the expression of the unconscious is invariably influenced by the present psychology of the individual. In sleep, for example, our unconscious thoughts are viewed or formed by our sleeping consciousness, with its own repertoire of defensive, expressive, and cognitive characteristics.

We do not *return* to some earlier epoch during regressive episodes, we do not become, as adults, a preoedipal child, a preadolescent, or an adolescent. Neither do we "pass through" or "travel a great distance" in acting or feeling according to the patterns of early childhood as compared to later childhood. It is a matter of daily experience to find preoedipal patterns and content used to defend against expression of oedipal patterns as well as vice versa. Intensity of repression rather than distance in time determines the accessibility of psychic events; chronology cannot be equated with *depth* or availability. Psychic content with particular meaning may be more defended against, more anxiety provoking. There may be as much as or more anxiety about and defensiveness against preadolescent patterns as against preoedipal ones. In every instance we are our adult selves, making contact with those patterns. We grasp the world within the framework of drive, defense, and cognition. We draw upon discrete content and organizational forms from our available repertoire to deal defensively and expressively with our present. It is in this sense that I would understand David's (Case # 1) mental processes. His symptomatology was initially an ego (executive) response to near unbearable levels of anxiety following the death of his ambivalently viewed brother and an assumption of forced responsibility; this response consisted of the adaptational use of available early forms of defense, cognition, and expression together with obsessional and intellectualizing techniques of containing anxiety and constructing a tolerable world. These efforts failed to contain his anxiety and were followed by a further effort at establishing inner stability by denial and manic defenses including an expansion of social and intellectual skills. Months later, when this second set of efforts at inner harmony and synthesis also faltered, David utilized a set of defensive attitudes and affective distortions (dependency, somatic expression, resignation, passivity) with little value in his interactions with the environment but providing adaptation (felt harmony of inner life) with control of anxiety. I chose this case as an illustration because strikingly "early" modes of defense, cognition, and expression are used, intermixed with "later" modes, providing a unique individual mix in his struggle to control anxiety associated with feelings of grandiosity, erotic stimulation, and aggression.

It follows from this rather extreme example and from many others where the individual mix of "early" and "late" techniques are used in the control of anxiety from a variety of sources that we need not assign degrees of pathological significance to psychological content considered "early" vs. "later." Whatever the time of developmental origin of a particular defensive posture, it does not have to be "dug out" from the depths to be used at later times. The belief that we regress down a slope to "later" or "earlier" forms of response depending on the maturity or primitiveness of our minds is inaccurate; we *select* for mutidetermined reasons from our individual repertoire of content, defensive repertoire, forms of cognition and psychosexual organization.

Psychosomatic or psychophysiological symptoms are another challenging case in point. Classically considered a marker of regression to the first year of life, physical symptoms are ubiquitous among all age groups and are accompanied by all degrees of severity of accompanying psychological illness.

John, Case #2, is not a typical case but does illustrate the common features of psychophysiologic disorders. He used available sensorimotor as well as verbal means of expressing the experience of abuse.

The most common psychophysiologic symptoms: headaches, alterations of intestinal motility, transient skin rashes and pruritus are alternate modes of expression of affect or fantasy. Issues of somatic compliance and of irreversible physical complications are relevant to the outcome of psychophysiologic disorders, particularly those disorders that can result in irreversible tissue damage. But in the majority of cases effective analytic and psychotherapeutic treatment is possible as defended affect and fantasy content become available to a strengthened, more flexible ego (Dowling, 1973).

APPLICATION OF THE HYPOTHESIS OF A CONTINOUSLY CONSTRUCTED PRESENT

I would like to apply these considerations to two topics: first, our understanding of same-sex and opposite-sex object choice and second, our definition of the goals of psychoanalysis.

In the psychoanalytic past, heterosexuality (opposite-sex object choice) was "normal;" homosexuality (same-sex object choice) was a deviant "immaturity," the result of regression and/or fixation at an early stage of sexual development. We have chosen, as individuals and as members of the American Psychoanalytic Association, to revise our former view of "homosexuality" as pathology, to recognize same-sex object choice as a mode of sexual expression compatible with psychological health. We now welcome men and women with same-sex and opposite-sex orientation to our training programs, to our faculties, and to the ranks of training analysts. We know there is a vocal minority and probably a much larger, non-vocal group that opposes this position, pointing to the regressive origin of same-sex object choice. Those of us trained within the framework of mainstream analysis face a paradox in accepting the new position. We understood that "homosexuality," though variable in the details of its psychological origin, invariably includes a developmental arrest or regression to a narcissistic, preoedipal, dyadic, or negative oedipal position. It was at such a level that same-sex physical love has its origin and it is to then that the afflicted patient returns in his "regression to same-sex object choice," "pushed" by the pressure of castration anxiety or conflicted positive oedipal impulses and "pulled" by negative oedipal libidinal fixations. The image of "backward," "primitive," "undeveloped," or "infantile" pervades these formulations. I think it helps us to understand that same-sex object choice is none of these if we set aside regression in favor of a multi-determined, emergent present.

The emphasis of such a formulation is on the place of individual needs and wishes in the totality of present psychological organization. I am quite willing to consider object choice, whether same-sex or opposite-sex object choice, as in need of treatment when object choice is part of a patient's network of pathology, when, for example, it is the nidus of maladaptive ego restriction with pain or anxiety, when it leads to destructive behavior, or when it is part of a pattern of psychological disorganization.

In this instance "to treat" is not equivalent to "get rid of." Treatment is to establish balance, gain access to personal potentiality and expression, and achieve relative freedom in making judgments. Same-sex object choice in such a context is not "regressive," in the sense of "undeveloped, immature, primitive behavior out of the past"; it is an adaptive outcome of past conflicts, choices, and defensive maneuvers. It can be respected as such, analyzed as such and left to the patient to determine its fate. In equal measure, opposite-sex object choice is not "undeveloped, immature, primitive behavior out of the past" though it is equally the outcome of past conflicts, choices, and defensive maneuvers and may be equally in need of treatment.

Two examples will illustrate my point. Many men who choose other men as sexual objects are part of a society hostile to same-sex marriage with children and that also values opposite-sex marriage with children. Men often share these "straight" values and seek an outward compliance through the accouterments of "straight" living while maintaining their sexual and personal commitment to same-sex partners with shame and guilt. It is the duality, the inevitable hypocrisy, often with associated sadistic and masochistic behavior, that is the organizing frame of the analytic work with these men. Analysis seeks to attain inward balance, acceptance of self and others, and recognition and assumption of personal responsibility through analytic, not judgmental, intervention.

There are others for whom a sexual connection is the means through which isolated, rejected, sometimes repressed, unacceptable impulses are expressed. Same-sex or opposite-sex cruising with repeated seduction, exploitation, and rejection can be the means through which oedipal aggression is channeled. The partners, whether same-sex or opposite-sex, are not recognized as individuals with respected and valued minds and bodies; instead they are simply displaced representations of another, including, possibly, rejected, or idealized aspects of themselves. This configuration can occur in a personality that is stable and productive in many respects. Such individuals, if conflicted, can be helped, through analysis, to recognize and redirect their aggression to other aims and to acquire less narcissistic relationships with others and with themselves.

The goals of psychoanalysis can be viewed in a very different light if we set aside the metaphors associated with the concept of regression, in particular the image of an embedded, fixed archeological past that is below or down and is approached by digging through intervening layers. The goal of psychoanalysis can then be summarized in the simple formula, "to broaden the domain of the ego." "Broadening" has traditionally included temporal broadening by making contact with earlier times of one's life, and a penetration to the depths of psychological content. It has also, of course, included analysis of defense and resistance. A setting aside of the guiding archeological images of depth and time leads to an equal or greater awareness of defense and resistance and an equal or greater recognition that the transference is central to our work. It leads also to an emphasis on the interconnections, the links, in the present between varieties of content that originated at different developmental eras and an emphasis on a reduction of intrapsychic barriers. The goal then becomes *intrapsychic accessibility* and *capacity for choice.*

No one has complete freedom to decide among his or her potentialities for knowing, experiencing, doing, or choosing. Potential for knowing includes accessibility to both content and to the variety of modes of knowing, that is, sensorimotor, preconceptual, conceptual, operational, and propositional (Piaget, 1960); potential for experiencing includes unimpeded awareness of reality within the limits of individual talent and capacity and unimpeded access to previous experience; potential for doing includes access to the full range of possibilities for action, that is, in thought, movement, speech, and artistic modes, each within the limits of individual talent and capacity; and, finally, potential for choosing includes freedom to recognize and act upon available standards and values. The palette of possible modes of knowing, experiencing, doing, and choosing varies for each individual based on inherent capacity (e.g., ego apparatus and drive intensity), on developmental limitations (e.g., the foundations of the personality [A. Freud]), and on psychological accessibility (e.g., limited by neurosis, character neurosis, or ego limiting defenses).

It is my intent that this rather awkward statement of potentials contains no value judgments or implications of better or worse about particular modes of knowing, experiencing, action, or choosing.

A few examples will make two points: (1) earlier is not necessarily less (or more) and (2) only prejudice can construct a hierarchy of value based on patterns of knowing or action.

From an analytic point of view, sensorimotor knowing, when part of a pattern of choice and interconnection with the rest of the personality, is not of lesser value than abstract propositional knowing. Those who choose to express themselves through movement are of equal value as those who choose to express themselves through speech or writing. Sensorimotor knowing, initially seen in young infants, allows for skills in depth perception and intermodal perception never equaled in later life and the poetry of motion is not less than the poetry of words. Sensorimotor knowing reaches an apogee of finesse, control, and expressiveness in professional dancing and athletics.

Preconceptual knowing, initially seen in toddlers, is expressed later in life in artistic imagination as well as in neurotic symptom formation. Concrete operational knowing provides the young latency child with skills in spatial memory as in playing the game of Concentration, and the older latency child's skills in constructing and recalling lists that are rarely equaled in adult life aside from the professional baseball statistician.

Analytically we make no distinction of value between those who choose to be professional weightlifters and those who choose to be professional physicists. Analysis offers to both a pathway to greater freedom and a broadening of the domain of the ego. Whatever the occupational, sexual, or educational choice of the analysand, the analytic task is to open a path to understanding and the opportunity for greater psychological freedom.

CONCLUSION

This paper considers the historical origin and logical basis of the classical understanding of regression together with the epistemological and value-laden consequences of the assumptions that underlie that understanding. It is my belief that value judgments antithetical to analytic intentions are the result of those assumptions. I have suggested an alternate view of the phenomena we term "regressive," and have applied this alternate view to analytic consideration of sexual object choice and to the goals of psychoanalytic treatment.[2]

---

2. I wish to thank Murray Goldstone, M.D., for his assistance in clarifying my ideas and for his sensitivity to value judgments that impair analytic neutrality.

BIBLIOGRAPHY

ABRAHAM, K. (1924). A short study of the development of the libido, viewed in the light of mental disorders. In: E. Jones, Editor, *Selected Papers on Psychoanalysis*. London: Hogarth Press, pp. 418–501.

BLUM, H. P. (1994). The conceptual development of regression. *Psychoanal. Study of the Child*, 49:60–76.

DOWLING, S. (1973). Psychosomatic disorders of childhood. In: S. Copel, Editor, *Behavior Pathology of Childhood and Adolescence*. New York: Basic Books, pp. 203–239.

FREUD, S. (1891). *On Aphasia, a Critical Study*. London: Imago (1953).

FREUD, S. (1900). The interpretation of dreams. Part II. *S.E.*, 5:542.

FREUD, S. (1905). Three essays on the theory of sexuality. *S.E.*, 7:130–243.

FREUD, S. (1910a). Five lectures on psycho-analysis. *S.E.*, 11:9–55.

FREUD, S. (1910b). Leonardo da Vinci and a memory of his childhood. *S.E.*, 11:63–137.

FREUD, S. (1911). Notes on an autobiographical account of a case of paranoia. *S.E.*, 12:9–82.

FREUD, S. (1912). On the universal tendency to debasement in the sphere of love. *S.E*, 11:179–190.

FREUD, S. (1916). Introductory lectures on psychoanalysis. *S.E.*, 16:340–341.

HARTMANN, H. (1958). *Ego Psychology and the Problem of Adaptation*. New York: Int. Univ. Press.

JACKSON, J. H. (1884). Evolution and dissolution of the nervous system. In: *Selected Writings of John Hughlings Jackson*, 2:29–44. New York: Basic Books, 1958.

JACKSON, S. W. (1969). The history of Freud's concepts of regression. *J. Amer. Psychoanal. Assn.*, 17:743–784.

KRIS, E. (1952). *Psychoanalytic Explorations in Art*. New York: Int. Univ. Press.

LAPLANCHE, L., & PONTALIS, J.-B. (1973). *The Language of Psychoanalysis*. New York: W. W. Norton, 386.

PIAGET, J. (1960). *Psychology of Intelligence*. Totowa, N.J.: Littlefield, Adams and Co.

SPENCER, H. (1867). *First Principles*, 2nd Edition. London: Williams and Norgate.

Latency and the Capacity to Reflect on Mental States

JOHN M. JEMERIN, M.D.

The development of the capacity to reflect on mental states has its origins in the mother's function of accepting the infant's projections of unbearable states of mind and re-presenting them in a more tolerable form. During the oedipal period, the continued availability of a parent who can take in the child's mental states and represent them from a different perspective results in the emergence within the child of a reflective mode of mental functioning. This mental capacity allows the child entering latency to begin to be able to recognize that her experience is but one perspective among many. Reflection on mental states takes place within an intermediate area of experience that belongs neither to the inner world nor to external reality, but partakes of both. In latency, the capacity to reflect on mental states remains a vulnerable capacity that is dependent on the reflective function of a parent at times of crisis. When a parent who can contain and transform the child's experience is not available, the child's potential space for reflection can collapse, leaving the child unable to differentiate inner from outer reality. The mother's relationship to a loved object other than the child is necessary for her continuing ability to support the child's reflective function. The child's awareness of a parental relationship from which she is excluded is also essential to the child's internalization of the capacity to reflect on mental states because it creates a vantage point from which the child can imagine herself being observed from the outside.

Assistant Clinical Professor of Psychiatry and Pediatrics, University of California, San Francisco School of Medicine, and Faculty Member, San Francisco Psychoanalytic Institute.

The author thanks Stephen Seligman, D. M. H., for his review of an earlier version of this paper.

The Psychoanalytic Study of the Child 59, ed. Robert A. King, Peter B. Neubauer, Samuel Abrams, and A. Scott Dowling (Yale University Press, copyright © 2004 by Robert A. King, Peter B. Neubauer, Samuel Abrams, and A. Scott Dowling).

These points are illustrated with material from a first psychotherapy session with a latency age boy.

DESCRIPTIONS OF DEVELOPMENT DURING THE LATENCY AGE PERIOD often emphasize that the years between six and twelve are a time of relative calm. Latency is seen as an interlude between the gargantuan struggles of the Oedipal period and the seismic upheavals of adolescence during which the instinctual drives are relatively quiescent, and the child is predominantly pliable, well behaved, and educable (Benson and Harrison 1991, Buxbaum 1991, Sarnoff 1976). The transition to latency is marked by substantial growth and alteration of cognitive, language, motor, and ego functions (Shapiro and Perry 1974, Furman 1991, Schechter and Combrinck-Graham 1991). These new competencies permit greater independence from the parents and facilitate learning, the formation of relationships outside the family, and the child's training for participation in the larger culture.

Beginning with Freud, psychoanalytic theorists have detailed the growth and reorganization of the ego that occurs on entry into the state of latency[1] (S. Freud 1905, 1908, 1911, 1922, 1923, 1924a, 1924b, 1924c, 1926; A. Freud 1936, 1965; Furman 1991). Chief among these are the formation of the superego and the ego ideal via identification with the values, standards, and prohibiting function of the parents. Separation from the passionate entanglements of the Oedipal period is achieved in part through these identifications and in part through repression and other defensive functions that have become available to the ego/superego. Mental organization in the state of latency is characterized by a constellation of defenses, including regression from genital to anal-sadistic drive organization, sublimation, reaction formation, and obsessive-compulsive defenses. Preconscious and conscious fantasy are particularly important in maintaining psychological equilibrium during latency (Freud 1911, Sarnoff 1976).

In this paper, I call attention to a particular aspect of the psychology of latency that has received less attention. My contention is that

---

1. Sarnoff (1976) points out the multiple definitions of the term "latency," and suggests that the usage of the term would be clarified if combined with identifying qualifications. Following his suggestion, I will use the term "latency age period" to designate the chronological time period between six and twelve years of age, and the term "state of latency" to designate a psychological state characterized by a particular organization of defenses, behavior, and psychological capacities that may or may not coincide with the latency age period.

one of the most profound differences between the mind of a child who has achieved a true latency organization and that of a prelatency child is the latency child's greatly increased capacity to reflect on her own mental states. In the course of development prior to the entry into latency, the child has started to become aware that she has a mind and that others have minds; and she is beginning to recognize an inner, subjective world that is not equivalent to outer reality. These capacities are greatly strengthened and achieve a new level of autonomy with the transition into a state of latency. The child in latency begins to be able to step back from her immediate experience and grasp that her perspective is only one of a number of possible perspectives. I will argue that these abilities emerge from the child's internalization of the mother's reflective function, and achieve a new level of independence with the resolution of the Oedipus complex.

A capacity for self-reflection has long been recognized as an essential ego function that is central to the development of autonomy and a sense of personal agency (Seligman 2003). The early development of the child's ability to understand the distinction between her own mind and the outside world has received increasing attention from a wide range of developmental and psychoanalytic perspectives, including current attachment theory, infant interaction research, and contemporary psychoanalytic theorists writing from a developmental-intersubjective point of view (for example Seligman 2000, and Fonagy, Steele et al. 1995). These authors have elucidated the origins of the "reflective function"[2] in the earliest interactions between infant and caregiver, and traced the evolution of a sense of subjectivity during the early childhood years. There has also been growing interest in the consequences of a failure to develop a capacity to reflect on psychopathology in adulthood and its implications for psychoanalytic therapy.

In this publication I would like to consider the importance of a capacity to reflect on mental states specifically in relation to the psychology of latency age children. Despite the relative stability of the state of latency, the latency age period is the time when the largest number of children is referred to mental health professionals (Schech-

---

2. As outlined by Seligman (2002) reflective function can be thought of as comprising a number of related capacities, such as the awareness that one has a mind like other people have minds, the ability to distinguish between one's own mind and the minds of others, appreciation of the distinction between intentions and effects, and the ability to imagine that one's own experience of an external reality may be one among many. It is the last of these inter-related capacities that I am most concerned with in this paper.

ter and Combrinck-Graham 1991). In my own work with latency age children, it has impressed me that for many, their problems can be understood as the result of difficulty in the separation of inner psychic reality from the external world. Some of these have been children who I believe had previously achieved a state of latency as characterized by a diminution in the intensity of Oedipal ties and the establishment of a stable but flexible defensive organization, increasing involvement in the peer group, and the ability to engage in learning and organized activities. These children had arrived at an age-appropriate capacity for self-reflection, but their ability to think about their own states of mind had failed them to a greater or lesser extent under the pressure of traumatizing life events. A second group of latency age children, more disturbed and presenting greater challenges in therapy, are those who have not entered a true state of latency and who have not developed an adequate capacity to reflect on their own states of mind.

The capacity for self-reflection has its roots in early experiences of recognition. Infants acquire the ability to tolerate negative states of mind through an intersubjective process in which the mother takes in and reflects back the infant's overwhelming mental states in a way that is at once a representation and a modification of the infant's experience. As this process is repeated over the course of development, children eventually learn to differentiate their subjective mental states from a reality external to themselves. The mother's transformation of the infant's experience takes place within an area of experience that is intermediate between infant and mother. Gradually, this area is internalized to become a potential space between the unconscious mind and conscious experience within which self-reflection, creativity, and play are possible.

The profound psychological integration and reorganization that takes place with the transition from the Oedipal period to latency brings with it greatly increased strength and autonomy of the capacity for self-reflection. The ability to reflect on states of mind remains a vulnerable capacity, however, and continues to be relatively dependent on the mother's ability to recognize and re-present the child's emotional state. Especially when exposed to traumatizing or highly stimulating life events, latency age children require the support of a parent's reflective function to manage overwhelming feelings. The sustained absence of an adult caregiver who can help a child to represent and think about her own states of mind leads to the loss in the child of a potential space for reflection and play, and the failure of the child's own capacity to reflect on her subjective experience.

In the sections that follow, I will discuss the normal development of a capacity to reflect on states of mind by highlighting the contributions of major theorists who have contributed to an understanding of this mental faculty. I will begin by presenting a first session with an eight-year-old boy who had achieved an adequate state of latency but whose reflective function had secondarily failed him in a time of crisis. My purpose in presenting this material is not to suggest that a focus on the child's ability to reflect on his own mental states is the only, or the best, perspective from which to view the material. Rather, my intent is to provide an illustration of the theoretical issues I will be discussing, and to suggest how consideration of a child's ability to reflect on his own states of mind can be useful in thinking about a particular illness episode as well as the moment-to-moment process of a clinical encounter.

SCHOOL REFUSAL IN A LATENCY AGE BOY

> But to go to school in a summer morn,
> O! it drives all joy away;
> Under a cruel eye outworn,
> The little ones spend the day,
> In sighing and dismay.
> —William Blake, *Songs of Experience* (1794)

At our first meeting on a hot day in September, Todd looked at me apprehensively in the waiting room, looked back at his mother ruefully, and trudged into my office like a child being sent to bed without dessert. His parents had sought out a referral when he had panicked on the morning of his first day at a new school. When it was time to drop him off, he had clung to his mother like a baby monkey cowering before a predator, crying wildly and refusing to separate.

His parents had told me that Todd is a very bright boy who is way ahead in reading, yet he had had an extremely difficult time the year before in second grade. His teacher had been unrelentingly critical of Todd because of his sloppy work, and he felt abused by her persistent dissatisfaction. Only in the second half of the year and after much distress did he begin to see a learning specialist who recognized that Todd had a learning disability that affected his written work. Todd's parents, ordinarily well organized and closely involved with their children, had been under great stress that year as well. In February, his father had lost his job following a false allegation of sexual harassment by a co-worker. In the aftermath of her husband's crisis and the ensuing financial worries, his mother had become depressed and for several weeks prior to initiating her own successful treatment had spent a great deal of time in bed, with frequent crying episodes. Todd began to experience daytime sleepiness severe enough to lead his pediatrician to consider a diagnosis of Chronic Fatigue Syndrome. He also developed anxiety at bedtime, difficulty falling asleep, and nightmares. He expressed the worry that when he grew up, he would be unable to find a job.

In my office, Todd told me about his favorite computer games and the strategies he employs to avoid losing. There was an amusing contrast between his sagacious, thoughtful demeanor and his eight-year-old enthusiasm that made him instantly likable. After a while, I told him that I understood that he had had a hard time starting school and a hard year in second grade. He said, "I did. My teacher was always accusing me, blaming me, because I have a problem doing some things, like printing. And she didn't believe me, and would say I wasn't doing my best, which I was. My Mom says it's like yelling at someone because they can't see without glasses." I asked him what he had been scared of when school started this year. Todd said, "I was afraid my new teacher would be like the old one and blame me, too. But I'm feeling better now because my new teacher is different. She's strict, but not mean."

I commented that he had started a new school, and that he'd be meeting a lot of new kids. He said that was true, but he had already made friends. Things were going better, but he was worried because next week, he might have to start taking the school bus. He felt scared, and wasn't sure why. Maybe he'd cry a little, and it would be embarrassing for the other kids to see him. Continuing to think about why he was scared to go on the school bus, he told me in a matter of fact way, "My old teacher was fired as a teacher, but was rehired as a bus driver and will be driving my bus."

I was surprised and a bit taken off guard by his certainty. Momentarily confused, I wondered to myself if a teacher *could* be transferred to bus driver duty. I asked him if he really thought that could happen. "Anything is possible," he replied.

I was also a bit surprised by the next thing out of my own mouth. I found myself saying, "Well, it's also possible that a pig could fly. Anything *might* be possible, but some things are a lot more likely than others." After a moment of thought, I added that his former teacher showing up as his new bus driver sounded unlikely to me, but that I could see he was really worried about it.

He responded, "Yes, but if she *were* the driver I'd be O.K. because I could just not get on the bus." "So you could deal with it," I commented. "Yes," Todd said. Continuing to ponder the subject in a worried but subtly playful manner, he continued, "It's as likely as if that plant (pointing to a bundle of dry sticks I keep in a vase) started to grow, turned into a hand, and came and choked me. If it happened, I could just pick up the pot and throw it out the window. Or, if that stick (pointing to a stick-like element in an abstract painting) jumped out of the frame and started to hop around the room and come after me. I could just step on it. But it's not going to happen." I again commented, "You could deal with it." "Yes," he replied. "But it won't happen."

Later in the session he told me that he sometimes can't fall asleep because he's scared. "If I cry, I go to my mother. Or, if that doesn't help, I go to my father and that usually helps." When I inquired about what scares him before he goes to sleep, he explained that it was sometimes what was going to happen the next day, and sometimes that he might have a bad dream. I asked him if he could remember a dream that had scared him. He said, "It was a long time ago. My old teacher came to my new school and was a substitute teacher in my class." He added that he believed he was due for a really bad dream soon, since he hadn't had one for a while. At the end of the session he commented, "I felt scared and thought I wouldn't like to come. But I *did* like being here."

This first visit could be thought about from a range of different perspectives.[1] I will use it here as a platform for a discussion of the relationship to fantasy and the use of reflection by a latency age boy. Todd, who had been an enthusiastic student at the beginning of second grade, has been traumatized both by his own frustration with schoolwork, and by his teacher's unfair criticisms. Under the pressure of his negative feelings, his internal space for reflection had collapsed, and he had lost the ability to entertain more than one perspective on his plight. His experience of himself as stupid and inept had become a reality rather than a feeling. Ordinarily, Todd would have had recourse to his mother's perspective on his internal states when his own capacity for self-reflection was overwhelmed. It has been especially hard for Todd to manage this particular trauma because his parents have been in crisis, and his mother, in particular, has been emotionally less available because of her own depression. Todd's experience of his second grade teacher has a paranoid flavor: at times she takes on the quality of a menacing, persecuting presence that will pursue him wherever he goes. While based in reality, it is likely that this extreme view of his teacher constitutes a projection of a rejecting internal object who will not accept and contain destabilizing experiences of badness.

TOLERATING THE INTOLERABLE: BION'S THEORY OF THINKING

How do children develop the ability to manage overwhelmingly bad feelings? Bion (1962a,b) describes the process, beginning in earliest infancy, by which babies develop the capacity to represent experience and to think. This process depends on two things: the availability of a mother (I am using this term as synonymous with "caregiver") who can take in the infant's intolerable feelings and modify them, and an adequate ability to tolerate frustration on the part of the infant. In Bion's theory, infants perceive negative feeling states such as hunger or the fear of dying as purely sensory experiences, or "things in themselves." The infant does not conceive of an absent and longed-for nurturing breast, but rather experiences the presence of a bad, depriving breast that must be gotten rid of.

Bion modified Klein's theory of what the infant does with intolerable experience in a way that is crucial to our understanding of how children develop and learn. Klein (1946) described projective identification as an omnipotent fantasy in which an unwanted part of the self is split off and projected into an object. The object then "strongly represents one part of the self." Continuing the above example, the bad experience of hunger would, in fantasy, be projected into the good breast. Bion added to this theory with the observation that, "even at the outset of life, [the infant] has contact with reality sufficient to enable him to act in a way that engenders in the mother feelings that he does not want" (1962a, p. 31). Bion's essential modification is that, in normal development, the infant behaves in such a way as actually to produce in the mother a state akin to what the infant is experiencing. For growth to occur, the mother must be able to accept the infant's projections of bad experience and to modify them in such a way that they become tolerable to the infant's psyche. The mother "responds therapeutically: that is to say in a manner that makes the infant feel it is receiving its frightened personality back again, but in a form it can tolerate—the fears are manageable by the infant personality" (1962b).

Bion (1962a, pp. 35–36) refers to the mother's receptivity to the baby's projections as "reverie," and views this state of mind as the essential expression of the mother's love. He uses the term, "alpha function," to refer to the capacity in the mother, analogous to physical digestion, that allows her to transform the infant's experience into a form that is tolerable to the infant. At the beginning, "The infant depends on the mother to act as its alpha function" (1963, p. 27). As a model for the process of projection of raw sensory experience by the infant and its acceptance and modification by the mother, Bion uses the analogy of a container and something that is contained. Over time, the activity of projection, containment, and transformation is itself introjected by the infant, and becomes the basis of the infant's own alpha function. Alpha function, acquired as the precipitate of an adequately attuned mother-infant relationship, is the mental faculty that transforms raw sensory experience into elements that can be stored in memory, represented, and used in dreams and conscious and unconscious processes of thought. It is the prerequisite to symbolization.

Bion's modification of Klein's theory of projective identification is groundbreaking because it conceives of psychological growth as depending on the characteristics of the real mother as well as those of the infant. It is also a modification of Freud's (1911) theory of primary and secondary process, in that it postulates the presence of a reality function operating from the beginning of life, rather than a sequential development of pleasure and reality principles. Development is portrayed as a fundamentally intersubjective process in which fantasy and reality are intertwined from the very start.

In the session under discussion, Todd refers to a moment that bears some resemblance to the process described by Bion. He lets me know early on that his mother is someone who helps him with the all-important task of transforming intolerable experience into something manageable. After telling me about his teacher's unfair accusations, he introduces his mother with the comment, "My Mom says it's like yelling at someone because they can't see without glasses." Todd gives me a snapshot of his mother in the act of taking his experience of humiliation and re-presenting it, but with a difference. He has taken it back inside himself and, much like putting on a new pair of glasses, the experience is now manageable because it has definition. It has become a feeling, and as such, it can be represented and thought about. I think Todd is letting me know something at the outset about how central his use of his mother is in maintaining his mental economy. Yet later in the session, he hints that his mother's reliability to help him in this way is in jeopardy. He tells me that if going to his mother with his bedtime anxiety doesn't help, he goes to his father.

For Todd to be able to make use of this particular comment of his mother's, two things are necessary. First, the moment he refers to must have been preceded by ongoing relational experiences with his mother throughout his life in which his mother has been able to represent his experience to him in a tolerable form. As a result of innumerable exchanges of this kind, Todd has, at least partially, internalized the process by which his overwhelming experiences are metabolized into something manageable. Second, Todd needs to feel that his mother's response is more than just reassurance or blame shifting. He needs to be able to feel that his mother takes in and experiences what he is experiencing, without being wholly taken over by what is so real to him.

I imagine Todd in the past, many times over, interacting with his mother in states of intolerable distress. Recently he has been struggling with painful self-experiences of stupidity and laziness. His state of mind at these moments has elements of despair, because he experiences these attributes as real. At these times, his mother has been able to communicate to him that she "gets" what is going on for him, but has also found a way to express that his experience of reality is not absolute, that it is not the only possible perspective. The awareness of the possibility of a different perspective by itself begins to transform an overwhelming experience into something representable. All of this must have taken place repeatedly at a subtle, nonverbal level throughout Todd's development in order for him now to be able to take in and make use of his mother's verbal reframing of his predicament.

Todd's next comments can be thought of as showing that he has, in fact, internalized a capacity to transform his experience. He says he had been afraid that his new teacher would be like his old one. For Todd to have been in a state of unalloyed panic on the first morning of school, this must have been much more than a worry. On that morning, Todd must have not feared, but known that his new teacher would be the incarnation of the blaming, tormenting mental representation he carries of his former teacher. His unverbalized terror suggests that this awful knowledge was not at this moment capable of being represented, and was not subject to reflection. On the morning of his first day, his expectation of the new teacher's harshness was akin to "a thing in itself." But Todd is able to learn from his experience: having met his new teacher, he recognizes that she is different. With reflection, he is able to differentiate the "cruel eye" of the teacher of his inner world from the "strict" but reasonable approach of his actual new teacher. The persecuting, vengeful teacher has returned to his inner, unconscious landscape; Todd will have to deal with the difficult reality (and opportunity) of an ordinarily demanding teacher and his own limitations.

RECOGNITION AND THE DEVELOPMENT OF REFLECTIVE FUNCTION

Bion's theory is in many ways consistent with current ideas emerging from intersubjective infant research and contemporary attachment theory. As discussed by Seligman (1999, 2000, 2003), this body of work is demonstrating that the experience of being recognized and understood is central to the process by which infants develop the capacity to distinguish between their subjective experiences and the objective world.

Recent research on infant interactions has stressed the intersubjective process through which infants acquire the sense of a subjective self. Referring to Stern's (1985) concept of affect attunement, for example, Seligman (2003) points out that the infant develops "a sense of her own subjective self as she has the experience of being known in the mind of the parent, whose recognition is simultaneously a representation and transformation of the infant's experience. . . . Stern is careful to stress that the moment of attunement rests on the simultaneity of sameness and difference between the two minds of the infant and parent." Unlike Bion's theory, the process described by Stern does not rest on the projection and reintrojection of intolerable parts of the self. The concept of affect attunement is consistent with Bion's theory, however, in viewing the parent's recognition of the infant's states of mind as central to the infant's development of a sense of having a mind that is separate from others' minds. What is crucial to the capacity for self-reflection is the experience of having one's own mental states reflected in the parent's mind, from within the parent's separate perspective.

Working in neighboring terrain, attachment theory has moved beyond earlier conceptualizations of attachment as both a distinctive behavioral system ensuring proximity to the caregiver and an inner sense of security in the caregiver's presence. Current attachment research utilizing the Adult Attachment Interview has focused on the organization and structuring of inner representations of attachment relationships (Main 1995, Fonagy, Steele et al. 1995). A striking and far-reaching finding from this work is that the ability to reflect coherently on one's own experience is the variable associated most strongly with security in attachment relationships, carrying even more weight than the content of the memories themselves. These findings suggest that, in the course of early development, the experience of being responded to in a sensitive and contingent manner is part of the same process by which children develop the ability to reflect on their own states of mind. A further implication, relevant to the question of how therapeutic relationships heal, is that relationships that offer a feeling of being understood in a context of safety have potential throughout life to induce a capacity for self-reflection as well as a fundamental sense of security.

THE TRANSITION TO LATENCY AND THE CAPACITY TO REFLECT

> The night Max wore his wolf suit and made mischief of one kind and another, his mother called him "WILD THING!" and Max said "I'll eat you up!" so he was sent to bed without eating anything. That very night in Max's room a forest grew and grew—and grew until his ceiling hung with vines and the walls became the world all around. . . .
> —Maurice Sendak, *Where the Wild Things Are* (1963)

Bion's theory of thinking refers to very early periods of development and to the elemental processes that underlie increasingly complex levels of psychological organization. Fonagy and Target (1996) have advanced a complementary model of the development of thinking during the Oedipal period focusing on the child's emerging theory of mind. They postulate two modes of psychic functioning during the Oedipal phase. In the predominant mode, the mode of "psychic equivalence," there is no differentiation between the child's experience and external reality. Within this mode of psychic experience, there is no psychic reality, and no subjectivity, because there is no distinction between inner and outer. The authors state, "Ideas are not felt to be representations, but rather direct replicas of reality, and consequently always true. . . . In dramatic distinction to adults, young children appear not to regard their own psychological states as 'intentional' (based on what they believe, think, wish or desire), but rather as part of objective or physical reality" (p. 219). In this mode of experience, thoughts and feelings are not representational: what appears to be real is reality. The possibility of another subjectivity, and within it a different way of experiencing or understanding a given event, does not yet exist.

Psychoanalysts and other child therapists have been more interested in a second mode of psychic functioning present in early childhood that Fonagy and Target refer to as the "pretend mode," the mental functioning typified by a young child engaged in imaginative play. During pretend play, the prelatency child can represent people or other creatures as intentional beings with ideas, desires, and other feelings. A critical feature of play in young children, however, is that there is no perceived correspondence between the pretend world and external reality. The difference between pretend and real must be clearly marked and often exaggerated, because it permits the child in pretend mode safely to give expression to fantasies and desires that would lead to intolerably painful conflicts were they to be examined against external reality. Should the boundary between the pretend world and reality momentarily break down, acute anxiety arises and play is disrupted. As stated by Fonagy and Target, "The small child playing can think about thoughts as thoughts, because these are clearly and deliberately stripped of their connection to the real world of people and even things" (p. 220).

The disconnection between external reality and the world of pretend is illustrated by the fact that young children at play normally have no difficulty moving back and forth between fantasy and fact. This ready ability to distinguish between imagination and perception is conveyed succinctly by A. A. Milne (1924) in the poem, "Nursery Chairs," which begins,

> One of the chairs is South America,
> One of the chairs is a ship at sea,
> One is a cage for a great big lion,
> One is a chair for Me.

The subject of this poem is easily able to separate his use of a chair as a symbol of something bearing little resemblance to a chair, and a chair's actual function in the external world (the world of shared meaning) as a thing to sit on.

Fonagy and Target propose that, during the fourth and fifth years, "the 'psychic equivalence' and 'pretend' modes normally become increasingly integrated, and a reflective, or mentalising, mode of psychic reality is established" (p. 221). This critical developmental achievement permits the experience of a person or situation to be both real and an intensely personal representation of the child's inner experience at one and the same time. The integration of these two modes of psychic experience signals the origin of the child's theory of mind. As Fonagy and Target express it, "With this new way of thinking about his experience, the child not only shows an understanding that his own and his object's behavior makes sense in terms of mental states, but also becomes able to recognize that these states are representations, which may be fallible and change, because they are based on but one of a range of possible perspectives" (p. 221). Put differently, the child begins to develop awareness that she has a mind that experiences and knows, and that other people have minds as well. The fact that a given experience is not reality in itself, but colored by subjective feelings, means that the child's experience of something is not necessarily the same as that of another person.

Paralleling Bion's theory of the infant's internalization of alpha function, in Fonagy and Target's model the integration of the pretend and psychic equivalence modes is a dialectical process that depends on the presence of a caregiver who can take in and represent the child's mental states. For progression to a reflective mode to occur, the child needs to have repeated experience of her own feelings and thoughts represented in the adult's mind, modified by their contact with "the adult's normally reality-oriented perspective." The child reintrojects the image of her own mental state as reflected in the caregiver's mind and "uses it as a representation of her own thinking." This process can go awry when the child, struggling with particularly intense feelings, does not have access to a caregiver who is able to take the child's ideas and feelings into her subjective reality and re-present them. In these circumstances, "the pretend mode may be given up by the child in relation to a particular idea, which is then forced into the mode of psychic equivalence." The idea becomes reality to the child.

The progression to an integrated, reflective mode of psychic reality can be seen as the central task of psychological development during the Oedipal period. The new kind of mental functioning that results from this integration is the platform on which the state of latency rests. Although essential to the state of latency, the reflective mode remains a vulnerable psychological capacity, especially in early latency. This is consistent with Sarnoff's view (1976) that latency is a dynamic state in which the characteristic balance of ego strengths is prone to disruption by a change in the equilibrium between defenses and drives. Unusually intense feelings, and the unavailability of a caregiver who can help the child in representing especially troublesome experience, can result in failures of an adequately established reflective function.

A moment in the session with Todd can be usefully viewed as a transient lapse into psychic equivalence. As he contemplates what frightens him about the school bus, Todd informs me that his former teacher has been fired as a teacher and rehired as a bus driver. Initially, Todd seems to regard this turn of events as a matter of hard fact. He seems not to be relating a fantasy at this point, but a dire reality. Todd's belief that his dreaded teacher will reappear as his bus driver can be understood as a moment when, under the pressure of his anxiety, his use of the reflective mode has failed him. This lapse, and his recovery from it, suggests that he is still very much involved in the task of differentiating inner from outer reality. As portrayed with beautiful economy in the quote from Maurice Sendak, the walls of his room have at this moment become the world all around.

Todd's comments about his dream later in the session can also be thought of as demonstrating that keeping his inner world separate from his everyday, conscious experience is an ongoing effort for him. As if too hot to handle, he needs to place the dream in the distant past. His anxiety about a really bad one happening soon suggests that he lacks confidence that he will be able to know the difference between the dream and reality when it comes.

THE RELATIONSHIP OF THE INNER TO THE OUTER WORLD IN LATENCY

> Benjamin Franklin went to France
> To teach the ladies how to dance
> Heel and toe and around you go
> Salute to the captain, bow to the queen
> And turn your back on the dirty old king.
> —Jump-rope rhyme quoted by H. J. Goldings (1974)

As discussed in the preceding sections, the foundations for a capacity to reflect on mental states have been growing throughout infancy and early childhood as a result of ongoing experiences of recognition. Through repeated experiences of seeing herself reflected in the parent's awareness, the child has begun to develop a theory of mind: she is becoming cognizant that she has a mind and that others have minds, too. Prior to the entry into latency, a subjective sense of self has emerged with the child's growing awareness that she is a self, distinct from other selves, with a unique life story (Stern 1985, p. 174).

The transition to latency is marked by a further stage in the development of self-reflection: the emergence of a reflective mode of mental functioning that makes it possible for the child to imagine that her experience of something in the world is only one of many possible perspectives. Increasingly, the child is able to grasp that her experience of the outer world is colored by what is inside her. She begins to be able to perform for herself a function for which, previously, she had been dependent on a parent: the ability to create enough space around her immediate experience to provide a vantage point from which to consider other possible points of view. This developmental achievement is an outgrowth of the profound changes in the organization of mental life that occur at the end of the Oedipal period, and depends upon a host of perceptual, neurobiological and cognitive changes concurrent with the entry into latency, such as the use of concrete operations with its transformational logic (Shapiro and Perry 1974, Piaget and Inhelder 1969).

An important factor contributing to the qualitative increase in the child's capacity for self-reflection that accompanies the transition into latency is the establishment of repression. The integration of the pretend and psychic equivalence modes of experience that normally occurs at the end of the Oedipal period confers enormous advantages for the child's sense of mastery and independence, yet it is a developmental step that may be powerfully resisted. In part, the child resists this transition because of reluctance to relinquish Oedipal (and pre-Oedipal) illusions: juxtaposition of the world of fantasy with external reality brings home the child's smallness and relative powerlessness and confronts the child with the impossibility of realizing Oedipal desires. Moreover, if the world of fantasy is brought into contact with reality as experienced in the mode of psychic equivalence too rapidly, terrifying conflicts may result because wishes, both the child's wishes toward others and those the child attributes to others, suddenly become frighteningly real. For example, the child's murderous feelings toward a parent, and the retaliation that the child imagines herself to deserve, may precipitately assume the status of reality.

One part of the solution of this dilemma is the establishment of the repression barrier and the restriction of dangerous or unacceptable mental contents to the unconscious, where they continue to have the status of present reality (Freud 1911). Although Freud (1924b) held that, under ideal circumstances, the Oedipus complex is abolished rather than repressed, as reviewed by Sarnoff (1976), in most of his writings on latency he regarded instinctual life as continuing unabated during this period. Loewald (1979) argued that the conflicts associated with the Oedipus complex continue to assert themselves throughout life, in both normal individuals and neurotics.

In concert with this view, psychoanalytic thinking about latency has demonstrated the many ways in which the unconscious, inner world is expressed in the child's relationship to the outside world. Indeed, much of the interest and passion with which activities are invested during latency and throughout life emanates from their connection to unconscious fantasy. For example, the child's pleasure in learning is closely linked to sublimations (Furman 1991, Schechter and Combrinck-Graham 1991), and studies of play during latency have shown how games are shaped by unconscious fantasy (Kaplan 1965, Goldings 1974, Peller 1954). The picture of mental development that emerges from these contributions is that, with the transition to latency, an unconscious, inner world is established that is able to gain expression in derivative form in conscious experience.

With the establishment of repression and the dynamic unconscious, the demarcation between the world of fantasy and consciously perceived reality is no longer absolute. As in the jump rope rhyme quoted above, which is both a chant for keeping time and an excited depiction of genital and pregenital strivings, there now exists an intermediate area in the mind in which a thing can at once be itself and stand for something in the inner world. It is within this mental space that reflection is possible.

TRANSITIONAL PHENOMENA, PLAY, AND THE CAPACITY FOR SELF-REFLECTION

> "What about a story?" said Christopher Robin.
> "*What* about a story?" I said.
> "Could you very sweetly tell Winnie-the-Pooh one?"
> "I suppose I could," I said. "What sort of stories does he like?"
> "About himself. Because he's *that* sort of Bear."
> —A. A. Milne, *Winnie-The-Pooh* (1926)

The internal space at the boundary between the world of unconscious fantasy and conscious experience has its origins in the boundary between infant and mother. Winnicott (1971b) pioneered in studying how infants develop the ability to differentiate between themselves and the outside world. His interest in the infant's first possession and the origins of the experience of "not-me" led him to propose a third area of human experience, an area intermediate between inner reality and the world as objectively perceived.

In Winnicott's model of early development, the "good enough" mother is, at the very beginning, adapted almost perfectly to her infant's needs. The infant experiences the breast as part of herself and subject to her omnipotent control. (Winnicott used the term "breast" to stand for the "whole technique of mothering," not just the actual breast.) The mother's responsiveness gives the infant the illusion of creating the breast: "The breast is created by the infant over and over again out of the infant's capacity to love or (one can say) out of need. . . . The mother places the actual breast just there where the infant is ready to create, and at the right moment" (p. 11).

But Winnicott believed that, second to providing the opportunity for illusion, the mother's most important task was to produce disillusionment. Through experiences of tolerable frustration resulting from its needs being met imperfectly, the infant gradually becomes aware of an object that is real, external, and not under magical control. In the evolution of the baby's growing ability to recognize and accept a reality external to herself, Winnicott described a third state between the subjective and that which is objectively perceived. He introduced the terms "transitional object" and "transitional phenomena" to designate an area of experience that is on the border between inside and outside, belongs to neither, and partakes of both. He wrote, "The intermediate area to which I am referring is the area that is allowed to the infant between primary creativity and objective perception based on reality-testing" (p. 11).

The process of "keeping inner and outer reality separate yet interrelated" is a perpetual human task that must be engaged in throughout life. As Winnicott puts it, "this matter of illusion is one that belongs inherently to human beings and that no individual finally solves for himself or herself" (p. 13). The intermediate area of experience between subjective reality and the external world provides a resting place for the individual of any age from the continuing strain of recognizing and accepting reality. The transitional space occupied by the child's first possessions expands to include artistic creativity and appreciation, religious feeling, and the origin and loss of affectionate feelings for others. I would add that the human capacity for transference, and the experience of falling in love, both belong to this illusory-yet-real, intermediate area of experience.

Winnicott suggests that the use of symbolism within the intermediate area of experience is different from the way symbols are ordinarily used and understood. In ordinary symbol use, as exemplified by the child in "pretend mode," there is clear differentiation between the symbol and that which it represents. The transitional object, on the other hand, is both itself and the thing that it represents at the same time. This kind of symbol use is a stage in the individual's journey from the purely subjective to the objective.

Winnicott (1971a) saw playing as sharing the characteristics of transitional phenomena in that it belongs neither to the inside nor the outside, but rather occurs within the transitional area between infant and mother. Playing takes place on a playground that is a potential space between the subjective object and the objectively perceived object, between omnipotence and actual control, and between creating and finding. He used the term "playing" to distinguish the process of play itself from the content of play, traditionally the main focus of psychoanalytic investigation. According to Winnicott, the immense excitement of play derives not from the involvement of the instincts, but from "the precariousness of the interplay of personal psychic reality and the experience of control of actual objects." What makes playing fun, in other words, is teetering on the boundary between subjective reality and the outside world.

To summarize, the transition to latency can be thought of as the juncture in development when the intermediate area between child and mother is internalized to become an inner potential space between the worlds of unconscious fantasy and conscious experience. It is within this potential space that the capacity to reflect on mental states, newly independent in latency, operates. One can imagine and make use of another point of view precisely in the area where inner reality is neither fully differentiated from nor equivalent to objective reality. Playing is central to processes of growth and change because it balances within the same potential space between self and object, and between unconscious and conscious experience. Playfulness is one way to maintain or restore an internal space for reflection. Moreover, it is in the overlap between two minds at play (mother-child, therapist-patient) that new perspectives can be entertained.

In his recovery from a momentary collapse of the space between his inner world and external reality, Todd demonstrates the use of playfulness in the service of restoring a potential space for reflection. When I first question his conviction about the teacher-bus driver, he steps back from complete certainty a bit without yet relinquishing his belief. After humorously challenging him with my comment about a flying pig, I tell him that I can see how worried he is, although I consider his dreaded scenario most unlikely. Todd affirms his sense of mastery by letting me know that if it did happen, he would find a way to cope.

What happens next is fascinating. In a seriously playful vein, Todd builds on my comments by elaborating two fantasies, both of which he knows to be unreal but which are nonetheless frightening. These brief imaginative stunts could be thought about in a number of different ways. One could point to the presence in both fantasies of a punishing attacker that Todd is able to vanquish. One might also say that Todd is using a humorous strategy of reduction to absurdity as a defense to help himself gain distance from the frightening belief in his teacher stalking him.

I think it is instructive to think about this moment in the session as one in which Todd has entered a playful space poised on the boundary of imagination and reality. His relationship to these fantasies is ambiguous. There is a playful quality, yet he is also anxious and feels a need to plan his defense. The fantasies are his way of considering a different point of view about his teacher: the possibility that her pursuit of him in the form of a bus driver emanates from the same internal world of experience as his thought about a bundle of sticks becoming a choking hand. In playing with the boundary between fantasy and reality, Todd is doing something more than gaining mastery over his aggressive demons. Perhaps more crucially for his developmental progress, he is practicing mastery of the separation of psychic from objective reality. His playing here is an effort to restore a space in which one thing can stand for another without being the same as the thing it stands for: a space within which he can take one step back to consider what sort of bear he is.

The interaction between Todd and myself at this point in the session is also interesting. Todd's conviction about his teacher's new job startled me, and left me feeling subtly off balance. For a moment, I felt not quite sure of my own sense of what was real. I wondered for a moment, "Could a dreaded teacher resurface in a new guise?" My humorous confrontation of Todd with a flying pig is not my idea of ideal technique, nor is it likely I would have made such a remark had I taken more time for reflection. In retrospect, I believe my remark was a half serious, half joking effort to regain my own equilibrium by returning the persecutory projection to him. I think I was also making use of play as my own way of reflecting on the odd turn of events with which Todd had presented me. Todd seemed to respond to the humor in my remark as an invitation to join me on the playground, an invitation that he accepted. I felt this suggested a capacity to make positive use of me, and the beginning of a positive transference. That I risked a humorous comment at this moment reveals a positive countertransference as well: something in Todd's manner made me feel I could get away with it.

My own momentary confusion may have been a necessary ingredient in this interaction. For me to respond in a way that Todd could make use of, I had to experience within myself a bit of the collapse of symbolic space that had taken place for him, and sort it out according to my own resources. Had the distinction between teacher and bus driver remained perfectly sharp for me, I may have responded by maintaining an exploratory stance or perhaps by simply disconfirming his statement, rather than with a more spontaneous (if less ideal) remark that had the effect of stimulating his playful, and thoughtful, response.

POTENTIAL SPACE AND THE SURVIVAL OF THE OBJECT

In summary, Todd's first session presents a microcosm of his efforts to maintain a space within himself for reflection and play. One way of understanding the illness he presents with is as a failure of his capacity to reflect on particular negative states of mind. Under the onslaught of his teacher's criticisms, and in the absence (because of her own depression and sense of loss) of his mother's usual availability, his experience of himself as stupid, lazy, and persecuted has become real.

To sustain a potential space for self-reflection, and for growth and learning to occur, it is necessary that the mother be perceived both as empathically related and as having a separate existence of her own. From the outside looking in, it is through the mother's gradual disillusionment of the child's omnipotence that the child learns about the mother's separateness. Considering disillusionment from the inside looking out, Winnicott (1971c) called attention to the need to destroy the subjective object, the object that is related to as part of oneself, in order to place the object outside the area of the subject's omnipotent control. Only when the object has been destroyed as a purely subjective phenomenon and recognized as an entity in its own right is it possible for the subject (child, patient) to take in "other-than-me substance" from the object (mother, analyst). In this sense, destruction of the object in fantasy is an ongoing necessity for love of a real object to be possible.

But the space for reflection can be maintained only if the object survives. If the object is unable to survive destruction by the subject (and failure to survive does not necessarily mean death or disappearance; it can mean a change of attitude toward the subject), there can be no potential space between a subjective object and an objective object, no reflection, and no play. Winnicott (1971b, p. 9) wrote, "The infant can employ a transitional object when the internal object is alive and real and good enough (not too persecutory). *But this in-*

ternal object depends for its qualities on the existence and aliveness and be-havior of the external object. Failure of the latter in some essential function indirectly leads to deadness or to a persecutory quality of the internal object. After a persistence of inadequacy of the external object the internal object fails to have meaning to the infant, and then, and then only, does the transitional object become meaningless too (italics mine)." In other words, when the external object loses vitality, the potential space between inner reality and the outer world collapses. One way of thinking about Todd's illness is that his mother's loss of aliveness led to the experience of a rejecting, persecutory internal object, and to the loss within himself of a space for imagining more than one perspective on his difficult predicament.

Latency age children in general are engaged in a significant kind of destruction of their parents, as their center of gravity shifts away from the family, toward school, peers, and other adults. Common fantasies of this age period, such as the "family romance," dramatize the de-idealization of parents (Furman 1991). It is critical that parents be able to "survive" this destruction of their centrality to the pre-Oedipal and Oedipal child to be available to the child's continuing and changing needs. Todd's depression in particular can be understood as resulting, at least in part, from the subjective experience of his mother's inability to survive his necessary destruction of her. The crisis for him was more than the loss of his mother's help at a time of need. Her collapse led to the collapse of his internal good and helpful object, and of his capacity for self-refection.

The impact of his mother's "failure to survive" was brought home to me in a session with Todd some weeks later. He told me about his father's losing his job and tearfully described his mother's depression. I asked him if seeing his mother sad was what had made him so tired. Thinking about this, he said something quite striking: "I think it's the big connection." I asked him what he meant by this, and he said, "There's a big connection between me and my mother. I mean, if she died, I think I'd stop eating for a long, long time."

Todd's comment echoes Bion's (1962a) statement of the necessity of alpha-function for the sustaining of psychic life: "A central part is played by alpha-function in transforming an emotional experience into alpha-elements because a sense of reality matters to the individual in the way that food, drink, air and excretion of waste products matter. Failure to eat, drink or breathe properly has disastrous consequences for life itself. Failure to use the emotional experience produces a comparable disaster in the development of the personality" (p. 42).

TRIANGULAR SPACE AND THE CAPACITY TO REFLECT

What allows the mother to survive the child's destruction of her as a subjective object is a loving relationship with an object of her own. (For convenience, I will use the term "father" to refer to the mother's object, although it need not be an actual father or even an external object.) The mother's relationship to the father is necessary for the mother because it allows her to relinquish a position of absolute centrality to the child. Her connection to the father permits her to relate to the child with an attitude of empathy coupled with objectivity.

The parental bond is also necessary for the child because of the fact that it presents the child with the reality that there are relationships from which she is excluded. This is a crucial component of the child's disillusionment as she recognizes that the mother is not wholly her creation. When the child looks in the mother's face, to the extent that what she sees there is not simply a reflection, the mother's relationship to an object other than herself is present.

The "third" is critical to the child's development of a capacity for self-reflection. As stated by Britton (1998), "the perception by the child of the parents' coming together independently of him unites his psychic world. . . . If the link between the parents perceived in love and hate can be tolerated in the child's mind it provides the child with a prototype for an object relationship of a third kind in which he or she is a witness and not a participant. A third position then comes into existence from which object relationships can be observed. Given this, we can also envisage being observed. This provides us with a capacity for seeing ourselves in interaction with others and for entertaining another point of view while retaining our own—for observing ourselves while being ourselves" (pp. 41–42).

As discussed earlier, repression is one factor contributing to greater independence of the reflective function in latency. The capacity to reflect is greatly augmented by a second aspect of the mental organization achieved with the transition to latency: the formation of the superego through internalization of the reality-oriented perspective associated with the father. One reason for this is that the superego strengthens repression. Of greater significance, the establishment of the superego constitutes the child's internalization of the third position, and with it, triangular space. The objective viewpoint represented by the superego includes within it the reality of the parents' exclusive relationship. Formation of the superego means that the child now has internal access to an "objective" perspective, a vantage point from which the child can step back and consider herself as if from the outside.

Todd's history can be viewed as providing an illustration of the failure of reflective function following the disintegration of triangular space within his family. His mother's depression occurred in the setting of his father's humiliating job loss. Beyond depriving Todd of someone to go to when his mother was unable to help, his father's troubles led to a breakdown of the marital relationship. (In a subsequent session Todd drew a picture of his house to show me that his parents no longer shared a bedroom.) The disruption of the tie between his parents constituted the loss of a "third position" for Todd: an objective vantage point from which he could consider his own situation with some degree of detachment.

These observations can be useful in thinking about the intensity of Todd's sense of persecution by his critical teacher. For Todd's mother, the rupture in her marriage coincided with a breakdown of her internal link to a good object beyond the orbit of her relationship with Todd. This left her unable to contain Todd's distress and to help him manage it by conferring with her own internal object. For Todd, his mother's failure of understanding at his moment of need may have been experienced as a hostile attack.

But to experience his mother as hurtful would be a catastrophe for Todd, because he still needs her so much. The badness had to be located elsewhere. Referring again to Britton (1998), "Bion made clear that the inability of the mother to take in her infant's projections is experienced by the child, not simply as a failure, but as a destructive attack by her on the infant's link and communication with her as his or her good object . . . in these circumstances the mother can be retained as a good object in the child's mind only by the child denying the experience of her impermeability and attributing the interference with understanding to another object. This creates a phantasy of a hostile object, or third force, which always threatens to attack the child's communicative link with the mother" (p. 53). Britton states that in the Oedipal situation, the father becomes the hostile force. In this post-Oedipal crisis, Todd, who has come through the Oedipal situation with his father internally established as a fundamentally good object, may have preserved the goodness of both his parents by projecting the failure of understanding onto his teacher.

CONCLUSIONS

The model Bion advances for the acquisition of alpha-function, initial dependence on an adult caregiver leading to progressive internalization of the function itself, can serve as a general paradigm for the development of increasingly complex levels of mental functioning and increasing levels of psychological independence. The concept of alpha-function refers to a fundamental psychological capacity that is basic to consciousness and to psychological existence itself. At the beginning, infants lack the capacity to "digest" raw sensory information into elements usable in thoughts and are dependent on the mother to provide this kind of sustenance. Over time, the digestive function itself is taken in and becomes established in the infant's psyche.

In later stages of development, children continue to depend on parents to provide the psychological functions they have not yet acquired. The process of mental integration during the Oedipal years described by Fonagy and Target is analogous to Bion's concept of the internalization of alpha-function, although at a more complex level of psychological organization. As in Bion's model, the child internalizes the capacity to reflect on states of mind after repeated experiences of seeing her own mental states represented in the parent's mind, modified in some essential way by its contact with the parent's psyche. As Fonagy and Target point out, this model of psychological growth means that the mental capacities we acquire over the course of development are inherently intersubjective.

The mother's transformation of the infant's mental states takes place within an intermediate area of experience where infant and mother overlap. Play also belongs to this transitional area and is the means by which the child explores the differentiation of herself from the external world. With entry into latency and the establishment of repression, the intermediate space between child and mother becomes a transitional area within the psyche where the world of unconscious fantasy overlaps with conscious experience. It is within this potential space between the inner, subjective world and the world as objectively perceived that reflection takes place, and that one can consider alternative points of view.

The child's awareness of a parental relationship from which she is excluded creates another kind of psychic space for self-reflection. The experience of being on the outside looking in creates a third position: a vantage point from which the child can imagine herself being observed from the outside. With the formation of the superego, the third position is set up internally as part of the child's psyche, allowing the child to take an external position with regard to herself. She is now able to observe and think about her own internal experience as if from the outside.

The ability to reflect on one's own and others' mental states, emerging as an autonomous ego function with the transition to latency, is a psychological capacity that is essential to the lifelong task of differentiating psychic from external reality. The existence of this internalized maternal function within the child's psyche is a manifestation of the ongoing internal presence of the mother; it contains within it the mother's tie to the father as well. As we continue to develop, the good and helpful objects inside us become increasingly less dependent for their survival on the presence of good and helpful external objects. None of us ever outgrows the need for actual good and loving objects, however, and our need for real objects to sustain the vitality of our internal objects continues to be particularly great during times of crisis.

In the clinical assessment of latency age children, it is helpful to pay attention to the question of the child's ability to reflect on her own states of mind. Todd was able to make good use of therapy because he had previously established a state of latency and had developed an adequate capacity to reflect on mental states. Many of the latency age children referred for treatment present greater therapeutic challenges than Todd, because they have not achieved a true latency organization. Some are children who have not established an effective repression barrier and who are flooded by the contents of their internal worlds. These children may appear overstimulated and impulsive, and are relatively unable to differentiate elements of fantasy from the world around them. Because they are preoccupied by inner reality, such children are not able to pay sufficient attention to outer reality. As a consequence, their ability to learn is compromised.

A second group of children who are particularly challenging to work with in therapy have achieved a mental organization that resembles a state of latency from the outside. After getting to know these children better, however, one arrives at the impression that the latency they have attained is a brittle structure, allowing little access to affective life and fantasy. This kind of child may not attract attention until a significant breakdown occurs because, on the surface, they meet the expectations of teachers and parents. A child with this type of mental organization can learn skills and may perform well in school, but their activities and relationships have little real meaning because they are cut off from inner life. Their ability to "use" others in Winnicott's sense, to learn from others in a deeper way, is severely restricted.

In doing therapy with children in the latency age range, the first priority is often to help the child restore or achieve a capacity to reflect. The content of play, or fantasy, may be less significant than the way the child does or doesn't use play to create a space for thought. For the child who is impulse ridden, or the child who is rigid and cut off, being able to enter into a shared play space with another person is itself a huge accomplishment, and a necessary prerequisite for further therapy to take place. Interpretation in this kind of work may be of lesser importance than the way in which barriers to reflection and play are managed in the relationship between child and therapist. As Winnicott (1971a) puts it, "Psychotherapy has to do with two people playing together. The corollary of this is that where playing is not possible then the work done by the therapist is directed towards bringing the patient from a state of not being able to play into a state of being able to play" (p. 38). I think the same can be said of the capacity to reflect on mental states.

BIBLIOGRAPHY

BENSON, R. M., & S. I. HARRISON. (1991). The eye of the hurricane: From seven to ten. *The Course of Life*. S. I. Greenspan and G. H. Pollack. Madison, Conn.: International Universities Press, Inc. Vol III: Middle and Late Childhood: 355–364.

BION, W. R. (1962a). *Learning from Experience*. London: H. Karnac, Ltd., 1984.

BION, W. R. (1962b). The psycho-analytic study of thinking, II. A theory of thinking. *International Journal of Psychoanalysis* 43:306–310.

BION, W. R. (1963). *Elements of Psychoanalysis*. London: H. Karnac, Ltd., 1984.

BLAKE, W. (1794). The School Boy, from *Songs of Experience. The Poetry and Prose of William Blake*. Garden City, New York: Doubleday and Co.: p. 31.

BRITTON, R. (1998). *Belief and Imagination: Explorations in Psychoanalysis*. London: Routledge.

BUXBAUM, R. (1991). Between the Oedipus complex and adolescence: The "Quiet" time. *The Course of Life*. S. I. Greenspan and G. H. Pollack. Madison, Conn.: International Universities Press, Inc. Vol III: Middle and Late Childhood: 333–354.

FONAGY, P., STEELE, M., ET AL. (1995). Attachment, the reflective self and borderline states: The predictive specificity of the Adult Attachment Interview and pathological emotional development. *Attachment Theory: Social, Developmental and Clinical Perspectives*. S. Goldberg, R. Muir and J. Kerr. Hillsdale, NJ: Analytic Press.

FONAGY, P., & TARGET, M. (1996). Playing with reality: I. Theory of mind and the normal development of psychic reality. *International Journal of Psychoanalysis*, 77:217–233.

FREUD, A. (1936). *The Ego and the Mechanisms of Defense*. New York: International Universities Press, 1946.

FREUD, A. (1965). *Normality and Pathology in Childhood*. New York: International Universities Press.

FREUD, S. (1905). Three essays on the theory of sexuality. *Standard Edition*. London: Hogarth Press. 7:123–243.

FREUD, S. (1908). Character and anal erotism. *Standard Edition*. London: Hogarth Press. 9:167–176.

FREUD, S. (1911). Formulations on the two principles of mental functioning. *Standard Edition*. London: Hogarth Press. 12:213–226.

FREUD, S. (1922). Group psychology and the analysis of the ego. *Standard Edition*. London: Hogarth Press. 18:67–144.

FREUD, S. (1923). The ego and the id. *Standard Edition*. London: Hogarth Press. 19:3–68.

FREUD, S. (1924a). An autobiographical study. *Standard Edition*. London: Hogarth Press. 20:7–76.

FREUD, S. (1924b). The dissolution of the Oedipus complex. *Standard Edition*. London: Hogarth Press. 19:173–182.

FREUD, S. (1924c). A short account of psychoanalysis. *Standard Edition*. London: Hogarth Press. 17:191–212.

FREUD, S. (1926). Inhibitions, symptoms and anxiety. *Standard Edition*. London: Hogarth Press. 20:77–178.

FURMAN, E. (1991). Early latency: Normal and pathological aspects. *The Course of Life*. S. I. Greenspan and G. H. Pollack. Madison, Conn.: International Universities Press, Inc. Vol III: Middle and Late Childhood: 161–204.

GOLDINGS, H. J. (1974). Jump-rope rhymes and the rhythm of latency development in girls. *The Psychoanalytic Study of the Child*. New Haven: Yale University Press. 29:431–450.

KAPLAN, E. B. (1965). Reflections regarding psychomotor activities during the latency period. *The Psychoanalytic Study of the Child*. New Haven: Yale University Press. 20:220–238.

KLEIN, M. (1946). Notes on some schizoid mechanisms. *The International Journal of Psychoanalysis*. 27:99–110.

LOEWALD, H. W. (1979). The waning of the Oedipus complex. *Journal of the American Psychoanalytic Association*. 27:751–775.

MAIN, M. (1995). Discourse, prediction and studies in attachment: Implications for psychoanalysis. *Research in Psychoanalysis: Process, Development, Outcome*. T. Shapiro and R. N. Emde. Madison, Conn.: International Universities Press. 209–245.

MILNE, A. A. (1924). *When We Were Very Young*. New York: E. P. Dutton and Co., 1950.

MILNE, A. A. (1926). *Winnie-The-Pooh*. New York: E. P. Dutton and Co., Inc.

PELLER, L. E. (1954). Libidinal phases, ego development, and play. *The Psychoanalytic Study of the Child*. New Haven: Yale University Press. 9:178–198.

PIAGET, J., & INHELDER, B. (1969). *The Psychology of the Child*. New York: Basic Books.

SARNOFF, C. (1976). *Latency*. New York: Jason Aronson.

SCHECHTER, M. D., & COMBRINCK-GRAHAM, L. (1991). The normal development of the seven-to-ten-year-old child. *The Course of Life.* S. I. Greenspan and G. H. Pollack. Madison, Conn.: International Universities Press, Inc. Vol III: Middle and Late Childhood: 285–318.

SELIGMAN, S. (1999). Integrating Kleinian theory and intersubjective infant research: Observing projective identification. *Psychoanalytic Dialogues.* 9: 129–159.

SELIGMAN, S. (2000). Clinical implications of attachment theory. *Journal of the American Psychoanalytic Association.* 48:1189–1196.

SELIGMAN, S. (2003). Attachment, intersubjectivity and self-reflectiveness: Implications of the convergence of emerging attachment research with psychoanalysis. Unpublished manuscript.

SENDAK, M. (1963). *Where the Wild Things Are.* New York: HarperCollins.

SHAPIRO, T., & PERRY, R. (1974). Latency revisited: The age 7 plus or minus 1. *The Psychoanalytic Study of the Child.* New Haven: Yale University Press. 31:79–105.

STERN, D. N. (1985). *The Interpersonal World of the Infant.* New York: Basic Books.

WINNICOTT, D. W. (1971a). Playing: A theoretical statement. *Playing and Reality.* New York: Routledge. 38–52.

WINNICOTT, D. W. (1971b). Transitional objects and transitional phenomena. *Playing and Reality.* New York: Routledge. 1–25.

WINNICOTT, D. W. (1971c). The use of an object and relating through identifications. *Playing and Reality.* New York: Routledge. 86–94.

Beneath and Beyond the "Formulations on the Two Principles of Mental Functioning"

Freud and Jung

HAROLD P. BLUM, M.D.

This paper discusses Freud's classic contribution "Formulations on the Two Principles of Mental Functioning" in the historical context of the Freud-Jung relationship, covertly represented by an obscure dream with Freud's interpretation. Freud added the dream and its interpretation to a previous unpublished version of the paper. Freud's analysis of his conflicts with Jung (and earlier with Fliess) particularly regarding parricide and plagiarism, contributed to the incipient psychoanalytic theory of aggression. The paper further explores psycho-biographical issues in the life and work of Freud, exemplified in the latent content of this classic paper. The pleasure and reality principles are re-examined within contemporary psychoanalytic theory.

Clinical Professor of Psychiatry, New York University School of Medicine; Training and Supervising Analyst, NYU Institute; and Executive Director, Sigmund Freud Archives.

This paper was presented as the Freud Lecture, The New York Psychoanalytic Institute, April 9, 2002.

The Psychoanalytic Study of the Child 59, ed. Robert A. King, Peter B. Neubauer, Samuel Abrams, and A. Scott Dowling (Yale University Press, copyright © 2004 by Robert A. King, Peter B. Neubauer, Samuel Abrams, and A. Scott Dowling).

THIS PAPER WILL COMMENT ON PSYCHOANALYTIC THEORY AND HIStory, the interpretation of that history, and Freud psychobiography. It addresses the historical context of Freud's paper, and the covert representation of the highly ambivalent Freud-Jung relationship. The various interwoven strands of the paper are based upon a reexamination of Freud's (1911) complex, multifaceted "Formulations on the Two Principles of Mental Functioning." Freud's analysis of his conflicts with Jung (and earlier Fliess), particularly regarding parricide and plagiarism, contributed to the incipient psychoanalytic theory of aggression. Freud's paper actually emphasized the importance of death wishes as a component of unconscious conflict, parallel to his focus at that time on psychosexual issues. Freud's regulatory principles are reviewed, and correlated with contemporary neuroscience.

Freud's essay "Formulations on the Two Principles of Mental Functioning" has long been appreciated as one of the classics of the psychoanalytic literature. The elegant, concise formulations had been foreshadowed in Chapter 7 of the "Interpretation of Dreams" (1900), and in the earlier "Project" (1895). The paper anticipated many later important developments in psychoanalytic thought and stimulated thinking about reality versus fantasy, object relations, narcissism, and aggression. It was a direct antecedent of Freud's metapsychology papers and "Beyond the Pleasure Principle" (1920).

Freud characterized developmental, clinical, and cultural dimensions of the pleasure and reality principles. In an almost tangential manner, he concluded the paper with his interpretation of a rather perplexing dream. "A man who had nursed his father through a long and painful mortal illness, told me that in the months following his father's death he had repeatedly dreamt that *his father was alive once more and that he was talking to him in his usual way. But he felt it exceedingly painful that his father had really died, only without knowing it.*"

Remarkably, this anonymous dream is apparently a version of a recurrent dream of Carl Jung. Why was Jung's presumed dream incorporated in Freud's paper, and then added to the "Interpretation of Dreams"? What was this dream's function and purpose? The dream is indicative of hidden agenda of the Freud-Jung relationship (Kerr, 1994; Blum, 1998) which influenced the paper's form and content.

The dream was not part of Freud's original presentation of the paper. The original title was "On The Two Principles of Psychic Happenings" which Freud orally presented to the small, eclectic, recently organized Vienna Psychoanalytic Society in October, 1910. Freud was quite dissatisfied with the non-comprehension of the Vienna Society members, and he was sorry that he had not presented the Schreber case instead. Having spoken as usual without notes, he then wrote, enlarged, and finished the paper in its present form in January 1911. Freud had then changed the title and added the dream with his interpretation. A full appreciation of the complexity of Freud's paper requires consideration of its cultural context, its place in the development of psychoanalysis, and its correlation with contemporary psychoanalytic theory and neuroscience.

Freud regarded psychoanalysis as a scientific discipline whose findings and formulations were based upon an objective, verifiable reality, rather than imagination and fantasy. The reality principle was related to the validity of psychoanalytic data and formulation. Freud differentiated between the pleasure-unpleasure principle and the reality principle. The reality principle evolves from the pleasure principle, simultaneously safeguarding and conserving it, and the pleasure principle continues to operate beneath and within the reality principle. The two principles are superimposed on Freud's prior fundamental formulation of primary and secondary processes. Primary process thinking is associated with the pleasure principle, and secondary process logical thought is in the service of the reality principle. The primary process persists concomitant with secondary process thought. In infancy, dreams, and fantasy the pleasure principle is dominant, with the dual goals of achieving pleasure and avoiding unpleasure. The failure to find pleasurable gratification promotes adaptation to reality and initial frustration followed by drive gratification facilitates development. The importance of pleasureable affect exchanges, for example, in holding, in gaze, and in the primary object relationship only gradually emerged in developmental theory after Freud. No advanced form of life could live entirely by the pleasure principle, since without the reality principle, it would be impossible to avoid danger or gratify needs and wishes in the real external world.

Freud noted that instead of wishful hallucination, the psyche had to form a conception of the real circumstances in the external world to be able to alter those circumstances, especially when reality was no longer agreeable but "disagreeable." Humans could adapt to and alter external reality. Whereas the primary process seeks immediate gratification, secondary process thought evolves as trial action. The reality principle imposes delay of gratification, allowing the object or objective to be retained in the mind for a necessary detour. Within the reality principle the object is also recognized as having real attributes, qualities separate from the self; thus the "Two Principles" paper was an antecedent of contemporary Freudian object relations and structural theory. With maturity, the reality principle dominates, but the earlier pleasure principle is prominent in fantasy life and other regressive states. Freud compared this pleasurable preserve of fantasy to Yellowstone Park in one of his rare favorable remarks about America. Freud (1911) quoted George Bernard Shaw to describe the superiority of the reality principle over the pleasure principle: "To be able to choose the line of greatest advantage instead of yielding in the direction of least resistance" (p. 223).

Children require love and approval to even incompletely relinquish infantile pleasures, as well as to internalize disapproval of infantile behavior. Significantly, Freud concluded that the sexual drive could be satisfied autoerotically, and could be dominated by the pleasure principle for life. This was an important contribution to the pathogenesis of neurosis. Although in that era sexuality was a central theme, much of the "Two Principles" paper centers on problems of aggression, death wishes, and their associated unconscious fantasies. Elaborating his earlier formulations of two different mental processes, Freud's paper also reacted to Jung's different formulation of two modes of thought. Freud had responded to Jung's lecture of May 16, 1910, on two kinds of thought, symbolic and verbal, and Jung's notions on the phylogenetic origins of symbolism. Jung had read "The Interpretation of Dreams" (Freud, 1900), and was therefore aware of Freud's conceptualization of primary and secondary processes. Their diverging concepts were apparent soon after Freud's trip with Jung to the USA in 1909. Psychoanalytic journals and local societies were then inaugurated, and Freud and his colleagues were busily engaged in analytic investigations, and devising plans for the psychoanalytic "movement." Psychoanalysis was gaining proponents, yet was boycotted by the academics and often attacked as pornography and quackery. Freud expected that Jung, brilliant, handsome, charismatic, and relatively affluent, would be a champion of psychoanalysis. Freud also assumed that as a Christian, Jung could gain intellectual and social approval for psychoanalysis far more readily than Freud and his almost entirely Jewish adherents. Jung may have initially felt elevated and flattered, but inwardly dependent upon, seduced, and exploited by Freud for the "cause." In the early years, the relationship between Freud and Jung was one of an extraordinary mutual admiration, idealization, and, indeed intoxication with each other, almost love at first sight. Freud was later to be bitterly disappointed by Jung's defection and bigotry. During the 1930s era of Nazi ideology, Jung differentiated between two other forms of thinking, namely Aryan Psychology and Jewish Psychology.

Freud's designation of Jung as his analytic eldest son, successor, and crown prince (letter to Jung, April 16, 1909) was in the background of the "Two Principles" paper, planned in June 1910. Freud had arranged for Jung to become the first President of the newly formed IPA at the Nuremberg Congress, March 1910. Freud promptly introduced the problem of plagiarism in his letter to Jung of June 19, 1910, saying, "Don't be surprised if you recognize certain of your own statements in the paper of mine that I am hoping to revise . . . , and don't accuse me of plagiarism, though there may be some temptation." In this connection, Freud had written to Ferenczi, February 8, 1910, "You should not be surprised if in my Nuremberg lecture you again hear your thoughts and even some of your formulations. . . . I have a decidedly obliging intellect and am very much inclined toward plagiarism." Freud then significantly added, "You must, of course, discover my ideas anew; for the time being they have been relegated to the mute processing of your ucs." Open minded, Freud readily absorbed new ideas, while recognizing his students' difficulty in assimilating Freud's thought.

Freud assured Jung that Freud's "Two Principles" paper was written two days before the arrival of Jung's "transformation and symbols," with Jung's two forms of thought. Freud noted "it is of course a formulation of ideas that were long present in my mind." Writing to Jung on August 10, 1910, Freud then stated, "A number of things, for example, the paper on the two principles of mental functioning are already tormenting me like a blocked bowel movement. (There is good reason for the metaphor too.) I discovered while still in Vienna that I have no need to plagiarize you since I can refer back to certain paragraphs in . . . 'The Interpretation of Dreams.'" On November 12, 1911, Freud wrote to Jung with muted criticism of Jung's "two modes of thought," and his "two modes," in comparison with Freud's classic "Two Principles," have passed into historical obscurity. Conflicted, Freud tried to support Jung's contribution and added, "it is a torment to me to think, that when I conceive an idea now and then, that I may be taking something away from you or appropriating something that might just as well have been acquired by you." However, Freud then formulated a reciprocal exchange, "I have begun several letters offering you ideas and observations for your own use." Jung sharply and quickly replied on November 14, 1911, "You are a dangerous rival . . . our personal differences will make our work different."

There were concerns about plagiarism on the part of both Jung and Freud. Jung once discerned an instance of plagiarism in Nietzsche, and might well have been concerned about plagiarism in his use of concepts influenced by his former patient and probable lover, Sabina Spielrein. Freud had been accused of plagiarism by Fliess in 1904, when Fliess alleged that Freud committed intellectual burglary regarding the theme of bisexuality. Freud had been deeply hurt and exposed to public insult and invective. Yet Freud had acknowledged his own attempt to rob Fliess of originality, though not deliberately. Freud (1901, pp. 143–144) analyzed his slip of memory based on unconscious conflict. But Freud went on to say (Letter to Fliess, July 27, 1904) that ideas could not be patented, and added "there is so little of bisexuality or of other things I have borrowed from you in what I say." Then, just six years later, Freud was reworking the issue of plagiarism with Jung. He was presumably using a version of Jung's recurrent dream without overt permission or attribution, while protecting the anonymity and confidentiality of the dreamer. (There are no known notes of their conversations.) Beyond and beneath the two theoretical principles and their elaboration in Freud's paper are the conflicts between the two powerful principals, Freud and Jung, with reverberations of the Freud-Fliess conflict.

"The Formulation of the Two Principles on Mental Functioning" continued Freud's conflicts with Fliess over plagiarism within the succeeding relationship with Jung. Both identification with Jung and analytic independence of Jung can be discerned in Freud's dream of October, 1910. Freud had congratulated Jung on the birth of his third daughter (September 26, 1910). Freud, who had three daughters, dreamt that they were on his lap, so that he and Jung were identified with each other (Lehmann, 1978). The children were likely a reference to his close disciples, as well as to his (Freud, 1900) earlier dream of the three fates. Freud's statement "you got this from me" in the dream about an object given to his daughter presumably refers to the issue of priority and plagiarism. The theme of plagiarism had appeared in Freud's (1900) associations to the dream of the three fates, indicative of the rift with Fliess. Freud ambivalently desired support and intellectual stimulation from Jung, but, as an independent, innovative thinker, Freud owned his own concepts without giving them to and then taking them back from Jung. His incestuous possession of his daughters in the dream was an oedipal victory; he had symbolically taken what was prohibited. Following this oedipal victory, he could bestow his possessions on his symbolic son, Jung. In this undoing and reversal the competitive, possessive father now encourages and rewards the son. In the same period Freud had written to Ferenczi (October 6, 1910) thinking that he had overcome the trauma of Fliess, "a piece of homosexual investment has been withdrawn and utilized for the enlargement of my own ego. I have succeeded where the paranoiac fails." Certain aspects of the Two Principles paper are a group discourse with Fliess and Jung, with other colleagues, and even with Sabina Spielrein, in the background (Kerr, 1994).

The issues concerning plagiarism are important in the history of psychoanalysis, and in the entire history of thought. So many revolutionary ideas, perhaps all original ideas, have antecedents, precursors, and inspirations or suggestions from other sources. Intellectual influence is hardly the same as innovation and creative transformation. Freud credited the contributions of many authors, such as Popper-Lynkeus, whose similar ideas about dreams preceded Freud's. Freud later commented about cryptamnesia, defined as based on an unconscious identification, and not on deliberate misrepresentation and plagiarism. Group process involved issues of originality and priority as well as those of infantile narcissistic and intra-familial rivalry. Freud's need for and identification with idealized figures was exemplified in the succession of Charcot, Brucke, Breuer, Fliess, and Jung. Anxiety and guilt about being a creator and a "conquistador" could be diminished by sharing discoveries or attributing them to others. Such sharing and idealization relieved the anxiety and isolation of the revolutionary thinker (Blum, 1990). Freud simultaneously both shared his own ideas and consciously and unconsciously incorporated ideas of others, transformed by his own creative genius. He regularly educated his followers, and among them, there were ongoing exchanges of ideas and conjectures. His purported plagiarism was largely an irrational accusation by Fliess, since Freud had radically changed and expanded the concept of bisexuality. Moreover, the concepts of Fliess were steeped in magical numbers and mystical biological connections such as genital loci in the nose. As a narcissistic object, the idealized figure supported aspirations of great achievement and stabilized Freud's self-esteem, giving him added confidence in himself and in the future. The relationships with Breuer, Fliess, and Jung began with mutual respect and affection, but the idealization also defended against the underlying aggression. For Freud, Jung was an idealized self and object, endowed with magical qualities, and for Jung, Freud initially evoked boundless admiration as an idealized father. The idealization of Jung, bringing Jung the paper on "The Formulations of the Two Principles," exchanging ideas and research proposals in many ways recapitulated the earlier intimate relationship with Fliess. Freud's need for their correspondence was intense, and when the correspondence lapsed, its absence was keenly felt. To compensate, Freud then increased his correspondence with other close colleagues.

However, Freud used the conflicted ambivalent relationship creatively, to extract what he needed and found useful, and to expand his own insights. Jung initially unconsciously issued forebodings and forewarnings when he stated, "My veneration for you has something of a character of a religious crush . . . it is disgusting and ridiculous because of its undeniable erotic undertone. . . . As a boy I was the victim of a sexual assault by a man I once worshipped" (Letter to Freud, October 28, 1907, p. 95). Freud had prophetically responded, November, 1907, that a transference on a religious basis could only end in apostasy. The ideal son and ideal father had found each other, but bilateral bitter disappointment and hostility were predictably to ensue. Moreover, Jung had brought a dream to his first meeting with Freud in 1907 which Freud promptly interpreted as Jung's wish to dethrone him, a derivative of oedipal parricide (Binswanger, 1957). This was essentially Freud's same interpretation of Jung's dream included in the "Two Principles" paper. Conflict over death wishes was a red thread throughout the entire relationship, condensing and masking other, for example, competitive, homosexual, and narcissistic conflicts.

When Freud, Jung, and Ferenczi met in Bremen, Germany in August, 1909, for their sea voyage to the United States, Freud remarked that a man who had died accidentally was buried in the basement of the Bremen Cathedral and had thus been preserved like a mummy. But then during dinner Jung discoursed on the recent discovery of preserved peat bog mummies, which were actually in Belgium. Jung refused to change the topic and Freud then fainted and was carried to a couch by Jung. Recovering, Freud inferred Jung's death wish toward him. After boarding the George Washington steamship the same unconscious murderous conflicts continued. To pass the time Freud, Ferenczi, and Jung walked the deck, discussing their ideas. Freud was particularly pleased to note that a steward was reading "The Psychopathology of Everyday Life."

The three colleagues reported and interpreted each other's dreams, a daily analytic exercise and pastime during their historic journey. Jung reported a dream to Freud about skulls in a basement, which Jung later averred initiated his concept of the collective unconscious. Jung dreamt of a house with an upper story, a ground floor, a cellar, and a deep cave. Each of the lower floors was successively a more ancient phase in the history of humanity, without reference to the unconscious depths. In the dream, Jung discovered two very old human skulls and according to Jung's memoir (1989), Freud spoke of these skulls repeatedly. Jung correctly inferred that Freud believed Jung had death wishes toward Freud, but Jung resisted any such interpretation. Jung decided to state that the death wishes were toward his own wife and sister-in-law, whose deaths Jung declared were worth wishing for. Jung acknowledged that he deceived Freud. "I wanted to know what he would make of my answer, and what his reaction would be if I deceived him by saying something that suited his theories. And so I told him a lie" (Jung, 1989, p. 160). Jung revealed his affair with Sabina Spielrein to Freud shortly before their travel together to Clark University, after first being devious and evasive. Jung confessed to Freud (June 21, 1909), about Sabina Spielrein, "In view of the fact that the patient had shortly before been my friend and enjoyed my full confidence, my action was a piece of knavery." This led to Freud's initiating the term countertransference, in his correspondence with Jung, while remaining overprotective of his chosen successor. The layers of history in the dream led Jung to the belief that the two skulls were those of Neanderthal man and Pithecanthropus (Jung, 1989, p. 214). This removed his analysis from his own unconscious conflicts to a collective unconscious and archetypes. From a different perspective, Jung's collective unconscious has been appreciated as an important concept in the psychology of the group and social organizations.

Confusion regarding Freud's two domains of fantasy and reality, especially regarding repressed death wishes, was not altogether uncommon among the analytic novitiates of that time. This can be gleaned from J. J. Putnam's memory of his six-hour analysis with Freud while both were staying with Jung at his home at Kusnacht, a lake a few miles outside Zurich. An eminent neurologist, Putnam readily misconstrued Freud's early, deep interpretation. He stated, "Dr. Freud pointed out to me, in the very first of our few conferences in Zurich, that I was a murderer! . . . Did I suppose he meant that I was to go and jump overboard or give myself up to the hangman? Not a bit of it. I was to be healthier minded from then on and happier, and better able to stop being a murderer" (Clark, 1980, p. 303). The omnipotence of thought and equation of wish with deed did not readily yield to the reality ego. Jung, however, was, not only disowning fantasies of murder and incest, but creating competing theories. Jung assumed that his own analytic psychology and the collective unconscious was far superior to and would supersede psychoanalysis.

The conflicted relationship between Freud and Jung, with Jung's disguised death wishes toward father figures, was represented in the dream within "Formulations on the Two Principles of Mental Functioning." Freud's interpretation was received by Jung, as might be expected, with intense resistance. The unconscious conflicts of both Freud and Jung, over rivalry, homosexuality and death wishes, were major determinants of Freud's two fainting spells in Jung's presence on two historic occasions before and after the publication of the "Two Principles" paper. While Jung's conflicts about death were evident in his dreams, Freud's were expressed in the very fact of his citing the dream in the "Two Principles" paper and the way in which he interpreted it. Freud's two fainting spells in Jung's presence, the subjects of intense psycho-biographical interest, were both particularly connected with manifest and latent fantasies of murder. The issues of priority and plagiarism were in the foreground of the second fainting episode, and both fainting episodes were also related to Freud's unresolved transference and reality conflicts with Fliess.

Freud's second fainting episode in Jung's presence occurred in Munich in November, 1912. Referring to The Pharaoh Amenhotep, who was regarded as the founder of monotheism, Freud identified Amenhotep's oedipal rivalry. Freud regarded Amenhotep's erasing his father's name from public monuments as representative of parricidal wishes. Jung disagreed, stating that this was not parricide but the announcement and consolidation of a new religion. Freud then complained about his own name not being cited by Jung, and Jung's friend Riklin. Jung continued to discourse on Amenhotep, without accepting Freud's interpretation or criticism. Freud had indirectly raised the issue of plagiarism, stressing that his own name had been omitted or deleted in Jung's publication. Freud fell off his chair in a faint and Jung picked him up and carried him into the next room, placing Freud on the couch. According to Jones (1953, p. 317) Freud looked up at Jung and said, "how sweet it must be to die."

This apparent masochistic submission to Jung defended against Freud's own unconscious hate and rage toward Jung. Freud first attributed his fainting to indigestion and lack of sleep, but proceeded to subject the episode to self-analysis (Schur, 1972). He had two years earlier prematurely informed Ferenczi that he had overcome his "Fliess trauma." He later said that he had had similar symptoms in the same Munich hotel room four and then six years prior. Freud further noted the repressed envy and death wishes toward his little brother, Julius, who had died when Freud was a toddler (Blum, 1977). Freud referred to the past figures of Julius and Fliess. But Freud did not overtly refer to bilateral conflict over present death wishes that Freud and Jung apparently had toward each other; nor did Freud cite guilt with an unconscious fantasy of his own death.

Twice placing Freud on a couch after a faint was consistent with
Jung's wish to be Freud's analyst as well his analysand. This fantasy
was symbolically realized in the analyses of each other's dreams.
Probably aboard ship in 1909, or in close temporal proximity while
contemplating his own concepts of symbols and libido, Jung (1989,
p. 163) had a dream which he indicated outlined essential differences between his thought and Freud's thought and presaged their
forthcoming break. The long two part dream referred in the first
part to a customs official who had died years ago, and in the second
part the contrasting figure of a knight in armor with a tunic on which
was woven a large red cross. Analyzing his dream, Jung connected
customs with censorship, and border inspection with the border between the unconscious and consciousness. Jung identified Freud in
the dream as a peevish customs inspector, a defunct still walking
ghost who couldn't die properly. "Could that be the death wish which
Freud had insinuated I had toward him? . . . I had no reason for wishing him dead. . . . the dream recommended a rather more critical attitude toward Freud." Jung (1989, p. 165) contrasted himself as the
knight "full of life and completely real" with Freud who was described as a "fading apparition."

Jung noted "the final sentence of the dream seemed to me an allu-
sion to Freud's potential immortality." His having Freud then fade
away removes Freud from the immortals, Jung's fantasy of defeating
his exalted rival. In a fragment of this dream which Jung reported in
1925, "both the knight and the customs official were dead and didn't
know it" (Jung, 1925, 1989; Kerr, 1988). This dream element is a very
close variant of the last line of the dream in Freud's "Two Principles"
paper, "But he felt it exceedingly painful that his father had died,
only without knowing it." The striking similarity between the ending
of the dreams confirms that they are repetitive variations of Jung's recurrent manifest dream themes. The theme of life after death is consistent with Jung's unconscious fantasy system, and Jung was the first
after Freud to call attention to the importance of unconscious fantasy. It is likely that a version of the recurrent dream in the "Two Principles" paper was also reported to Freud during their joint trip to
America, and Jung definitely disagreed with Freud's dream analysis
of repressed death wishes. Jung's dreams and their respective analyses by Jung and Freud permit graphic comparisons of their two different forms of thought and theory.

Freud's fainting may have been retroactively enmeshed in the issues embodied in the dream which Freud included and concluded
his "Two Principles" paper. In his faint Freud was alive and symboli-

cally dead. Freud recovered, referring to his own death, thus returning to life after death. Indirectly accusing Jung of plagiarism, Freud
was identified with the accuser-aggressor, Fliess, but Freud had also
turned his aggression toward Jung on himself. Plagiarism unconsciously represented murder committed in the act of theft. Freud
also may have been unconsciously communicating to Jung that their
relationship was alive, yet dead. The dream concluding the "Two
Principles" paper may be interpreted as a premonition of the later
termination of their analytic and personal association.

It is not unusual for the denial of death and acknowledgment of
death to be concurrent in both dreams and in waking life. Freud's
appropriation of Jung's dream strongly suggests that for Freud, as for
Jung, the relationship was fated to die. The death in life can be inferred from the aforementioned terminal phrase of the terminal
dream of the "Two Principles" paper. Freud (1911, p. 225) stated that
the only way of understanding this apparently nonsensical dream was
to add that the Father's death was as the dreamer wished. The termination phase of the Freud-Jung relationship was initiated, "only without knowing it."(Termination was probably furthered after Sabina
Spielrein visited Freud in 1911.)

Freud's and Jung's two lines of thought became increasingly divergent. While Freud interpreted the unconscious death wish in the
dream, Jung had been concerned with potential life after death.
Though skeptical, Jung had participated in séances with a female
cousin as medium, and in 1902 had written a medical dissertation on
the occult. Jung associated his repetitive dreams with survival and
mystical communication after death. He was probably also influenced by Sabina Spielrein who was then advancing concepts linking
sexuality with destruction, death with rebirth. Spielrein, Jung's former patient and likely lover, may have also influenced Freud's hypothesis of a death instinct beyond the pleasure principle. Much
closer to clinical experience, Freud had delineated the defense of denial of painful reality, and observed how difficult it was for humanity
to accept the irreversible reality of death. Denial and self-deception,
distortion of reality, and personal myths are critical areas of analytic
work, as are internalized distortions of the ethical principles of truth
and honesty. Freud was disturbed by the spiritual-mystical trend in
Jung's writings, even as he was gratified to have a Christian champion
of psychoanalysis.

Freud, however, harbored his own superstitions but he was aware
of their fantasy basis. Freud was interested in the occult and thought
transference, and discussed telepathy experiments with Ferenczi.

Freud explained mind reading analytically, in that we all betray our thoughts in speech, movements, etc. Freud provided a further psychoanalytic explanatory proposition, which initiated burgeoning discourse on unconscious communication. Freud (1913, p. 157) asserted: "everyone possesses in his unconscious mental activity an apparatus which enables him to interpret other peoples' reactions, that is, to undo the distortions which other people have imposed on the expression of their feelings."

Jung was appropriately critical of the rather exclusive focus on and overgeneralization of psychosexual motivation in the pioneer era of psychoanalysis, and so rejected libido theory as an explanation of schizophrenia. However, Jung dissented from the psychoanalytic discoveries of unconscious incestuous and murderous wishes. While Freud was in the process of re-assessing Jung's ideas, as well as his own idealization of the man and his mind, Jung was writing that the sexuality of the unconscious was merely a symbol and step forward to every goal of life. Jung regarded incestuous conflicts as more frequent and intense in Jews, than in Christians. His anti-Semitic attitudes were a determinant of his arrogance toward Freud and his later flirtation with Nazism. In his memoirs Jung (1989, p. 167) asserted, "Usually incest has a highly religious aspect." But Freud clung to the literal interpretation of it and could not grasp the spiritual significance of incest as a symbol. Like the "Two Principles" paper, "Totem and Taboo" was written in part as Freud's (1913) response to Jung and the first chapter was "The Horror of Incest." Jung's retreat from unconscious fantasies of incest and murder would prove to be typical of departures from psychoanalytic findings over the course of the entire history of psychoanalysis. At the time that the Oedipus complex of the child was first being designated as such (Freud, 1910), some of the first psychoanalytic students, like Oedipus, became blind to the new formulations. The pleasure-unpleasure principle held sway, and the unwelcome repressed "complex," a term first used by Jung, was repeatedly transformed into much more palatable new theory.

Jung's problems with religion and authority had powerful family roots. His father was a minister and there were ministers on both sides of his family. As a youth he had a recurrent blasphemous dream to which he attached great significance: God sits on his golden throne in the heavens and expels a giant turd, which falls on the (Basel) cathedral, smashing its walls (Jung, 1989). His biographers have overlooked his own enactment of this dream. The ordinarily proper, spiritual Jung could empty his chamber pot from the top of the famed tower that he had built, without concern for whoever might be walking below (Hayman, 2001). Deference to authority would be followed by rebellion, devaluation, and residual respect; Jung maintained a lifelong ambivalent admiration of Freud. Jung's rebellion and determined independence reaped their own rewards. Jung was then very popular in America, and his own theories quickly attracted intercontinental adherents. The "need for Aryan patronage" of psychoanalysis was to be overtly dismissed by Freud even while a residue was unconsciously maintained (e.g., Freud's later depiction of Moses as an Egyptian, 1939). The favorable reception accorded Jung and Adler here evoked Freud's displeasure and added to his antagonistic attitude toward America.

The dreams that colleagues reported to Freud and Freud's interpretations of them were vastly over-determined and can be construed as conscious and unconscious communications to each other and their coterie. Freud might have hoped his analysis of Jung's dream would be convincing to Jung (and his readers) even while anticipating the death of the relationship. (When Freud anointed Jung as his analytic son and successor, Freud's actual eldest son, Martin, was twenty years old and entering adulthood. Freud's [1900, p. 559] death wishes toward his eldest son were elucidated in his self-analysis of a dream. Freud's dream about his son is also relevant to the psychology of envy—here the envy of youth by the elder parent.) Identifying and collaborating with Freud while competing with him, Jung's attitudes of analytic and cultural superiority were associated with ideas of supplanting Freudian theory with his own "analytic psychology." Dreams and daydreams of surpassing the master, with oedipal and narcissistic issues, would spur both regressive and progressive change in psychoanalysis.

The propositions in Freud's "Two Principles" paper were much more internally consistent and reality oriented than the later philosophical and imaginative "Beyond the Pleasure Principle." He wanted his paper to educate and stimulate his followers. Freud's correspondence with Ferenczi at the time he was writing "Two Principles" drew Ferenczi into the personal and analytic issues. Freud's "Two Principles" paper was a stimulus for the development of Ferenczi's own reflections. Ferenczi's (1913) "Stages in the Development of the Sense of Reality" followed from Freud's paper and remains an important historical contribution in its own right.

The problem of fantasy vs. reality both preceded and followed from considerations of the pleasure and reality principles. Reflecting upon the strange characteristic of unconscious processes that equate psychic reality with external reality and wishes with their fulfillment,

Freud repeated that this happens under the domination of the pleasure principle. He subsequently noted the problem which has intrigued and plagued psychoanalysis to this day: the difficulty of distinguishing unconscious fantasies from memories which have become unconscious. Freud (1918, p. 103) stated, "I admit that this is the most delicate question in the whole domain of psychoanalysis. I did not require the contributions of Adler or Jung to induce me to consider the matter with a critical eye, and to bear in mind the possibility that what analysis puts forward as being forgotten experiences of childhood (and of an improbably early childhood) may on the contrary be based upon fantasies created on occasions late in life. . . . No doubt has troubled me more; no other uncertainty has been more decisive in holding me back from publishing my conclusions. I was the first . . . to recognize both the part played by fantasies in symptom-formation and also the 'retrospective fantasying' of late impressions into childhood and their sexualization after the event."

Controversy over the conflict theory, unconscious fantasy, and actual trauma prefigured current dispute over false memories, iatrogenic fantasy, suggestion and indoctrination. The reality principle and Freud's interest in unconscious communication provide a background for later interest in the analyst as a real object and participant observer and the concepts of unconscious communication and of projective identification as bilateral shaping influences in the analytic process. Freud's "Two Principles" contrasted reality with the importance of unconscious fantasies in the formation of symptoms. Freud noted the pleasurable sharing of unconscious fantasy by the artist with the audience as well as the artist's return from fantasy to reality in the process of artistic sublimation. The audience could enjoy the artist's disguised fantasy vicariously and without guilt. Foreshadowing the later formulation of the superego, self-reproach could occur on the basis of fantasy rather than an actual transgression, particularly when the relationship with the deceased was intensely ambivalent.

When Freud visited Jung's home in September, 1911, he discussed famous pairs of men in mythology. Freud noted that there was always one who was weaker and fated to die. At the Weimar Congress later that month, Freud presented "A Postscript to the Schreber Case" which can also be interpreted as a postscript to the "Two Principles on Mental Functioning." In the post-script, Freud observed that the eagle forced its young to stare at the sun without blinking, rejecting those who failed. Colleagues like Jung, who had recommended the Schreber Case to Freud, must prove they are legitimate psychoanalytic heirs. Freud could also have referred to others who distanced themselves when he described Bleuler as a genius at misunderstanding. Yet, proof of legitimacy would have regrettable derivatives in later pressures for conformity as psychoanalysis became institutionalized.

CONTEMPORARY THEORETICAL CONSIDERATIONS

Freud proceeded to de-idealize his former crown prince and to further develop the formulations of the "Two Principles" paper. It is difficult enough to define pleasure and there are different forms of pleasure, from drive gratification to heightened self-esteem, to pleasure in thought, etc. Only a few years later Freud (1915) formulated three polarities governing mental life: pleasure-un-pleasure; subject-object; active-passive. Freud (1920) tried to relate increasing stimulation and tension to unpleasure and tension decline or discharge to pleasure, but recognized the limitations of this reductionist formula. It was modeled on Fechner's constancy principle, and Freud did not clearly distinguish between pleasurable affect and a pleasure principle of regulation (Schur, 1972). The psychobiological need in infancy for appropriate stimulation and parental response has superseded constancy and nirvana principles. The pleasure-unpleasure antithesis remains of great psychoanalytic and neurobiological interest. Dominant in infancy and in the infantile unconscious, the primordial power of the pleasure principle, pleasure and pain, exert their influence throughout life. Pleasurable gratification and the avoidance of un-pleasure underlie unconscious wish and defense, components of all unconscious conflict and compromise formation. In this connection, the critical growth during infancy of both psychic structure and brain structure are profoundly influenced by the postnatal experience of pleasure, distress or trauma.

The reality principle subsumes interrelated systems encompassing the various dimensions of the perception of reality, social reality, adaptation to reality, and scientific concepts of reality (Hartmann, 1956), as well as intermediate states between external and internal reality (Winnicott, 1953). Versions of reality are represented by parents and other authorities and taught to children. Though reality is differentiated from fantasy there is no absolute reality without unconscious fantasy components (Arlow, 1969; Brenner, 1982); conversely there is a grain of truth in every delusion (Freud, 1937). Closer to analytic observation and experience, we may prefer to think in clinical parlance of the pleasure ego that Freud introduced in the "Two Principles" paper. The interaction of a number of ego functions, for example, anticipation, delay, and judgment is subsumed within the reality ego. Psychobiological aspects of pleasurable and painful affects are subject to, and reciprocally influence ego and cortical regulation (Heilbrunn, 1979; Schore, 1994).

Freud's instructive dream interpretation in "The Formulation on the Two Principles of Mental Functioning" balanced the then ascendant libido theory with an appreciation of the importance of aggression and universal conflict concerning death wishes. Though not as directly connected with the pleasure principle as sexuality, aggression was encompassed within the pleasure-unpleasure principle. An aggressive drive and related death wishes were ultimately formulated without invoking a death instinct theory, contributing to the clinical analysis of aggression as well as the understanding of death wishes toward the analyst and psychoanalysis. Thoughtful and sometimes aggressive challenges, including contributions of Jung, have in the long run resulted in valuable additions and modifications to psychoanalytic theory, building on the basic findings and formulations of psychoanalysis (Rangell, 2000).

BIBLIOGRAPHY

ARLOW, J. (1969). Unconscious fantasy and disturbances of conscious experience. *Psychoanal. Q.* 38:1–27.

BINSWANGER, L. (1957). *Sigmund Freud: Reminiscences of a Friendship.* New York: Grune & Stratton.

BLUM, H. (1990). Freud, Fliess, and the parenthood of psychoanalysis. *Psychoanal. Q.,* 59:21–39.

——— (1994). *Reconstruction in Psychoanalysis. Childhood Revisited and Recreated.* New York: International Universities Press.

——— (1998). Freud and Jung: The internationalization of psychoanalysis. *Psychoanal. and History,* 1:44–55.

BRENNER, C. (1982). *The Mind in Conflict.* New York: International Universities Press.

CLARK, R. (1980). *Freud—The Man and the Cause.* New York: Random House.

FERENCZI, S. (1913). Stages in the development of the sense of reality. In: *First Contributions to Psycho-Analysis.* London: Hogarth Press, 1955.

FREUD, S. (1895). Project for a scientific psychology, *S.E.* 1.

——— (1900). The interpretation of dreams. *S.E.,* 4 and 5.

——— (1910). Psychoanalytic notes on an autobiographical account of a case of paranoia. *S.E.,* 12.

——— (1911). Formulation on the two principles of mental functioning. *S.E.,* 12.

———— (1913). Totem and taboo. *S.E.*, 13.

———— (1915). Instincts and their vicissitudes. *S.E.*, 14.

———— (1918). From the history of an infantile neurosis. *S.E.*, 17.

———— (1920). Beyond the pleasure principle. *S.E.*, 18.

———— (1937). Construction in analysis. *S.E.*, 23.

The Correspondence of Sigmund Freud and Sandor Ferenczi. Vol. 1. E. Brabant, E. Falzeder, P. Gianpieri-Deutsch, Eds. Cambridge, Mass.: Belknap Press of Harvard University Press.

The Freud/Jung Letters. W. McGuire, Ed. Princeton: Princeton University Press.

HARTMANN, H. (1956). Notes on the reality principle. *Psychoanal. Study Child*, 11:31–53.

HAYMAN, R. (1999). *A Life of Jung.* New York: Norton.

HEILBRUNN, G. (1979). Biologic correlates of psychoanalytic concepts. *J. Amer. Psychoanal. Assn.*, 27:597–626.

JONES, E. (1953). *The Life and Work of Sigmund Freud.* Vol. I., New York: Basic Books.

JUNG, C. (1925). Analytic Psychology/ Notes on the Seminar in Analytic Psychology. (Compiled by C. deAngulo & Approved by C. G. Jung.) Zurich: multigraphed typescript.

———— (1989). *Memories, Dreams, Reflections,* New York: Vintage.

KERR, J. (1988). The devil's elixirs, Jung's "theology," and the dissolution of Freud's "poisoning complex." *Psychoanal. Review,* 75:1–33.

———— (1994). *A Most Dangerous Method.* New York: Vintage.

LEHMANN, H. (1978). A dream of Freud in the year 1910. *Internat. J. Psychoanal.*, 59:181–187.

RANGELL, L. (2000). Psychoanalysis at the millennium: A unitary theory. *Psychoanal. Psychology,* 17:451–466.

SCHORE, A. (1994). *Affect Regulation and the Origin of the Self.* Hillsdale, N.J.: Lawrence Erlbaum.

SCHUR, M. (1972). *Freud: Living and Dying.* New York: International Universities Press.

WINNICOTT, D. (1953). Transitional objects and transitional phenomena. *Internat. J. Psychoanal.*, 34:89–97.

CONTRIBUTIONS
FROM DEVELOPMENTAL
PSYCHOLOGY

Representations in Action

(Or: Action Models of Development Meet Psychoanalytic Conceptualizations of Mental Representations)

GOLAN SHAHAR, PH.D.,
LISA W. CROSS, PH.D., and
CHRISTOPHER C. HENRICH, PH.D.

Integrating psychoanalytic and action models of development affords a rich, detailed depiction of developmental psychopathology. Psychoanalytic models depict mental representations of self and others as unconsciously organizing and regulating affect, cognition, and behavior, in response to both maturational imperatives and drive related conflicts. Action models emphasize the active, reciprocal, and goal oriented nature of person-context exchanges. In linking the two perspectives, we propose that representations serve as the mechanisms through which individuals shape their development, personality, and well-being. This integrative perspective is illustrated using a clinical case of an adolescent female treated for an eating disorder.

Golan Shahar is Assistant Professor, Departments of Psychiatry and Psychology, and the Program on Recovery and Community Health, Yale University. Lisa W. Cross is Clinical Assistant Professor, Department of Psychiatry, Yale University School of Medicine. Christopher C. Henrich is Assistant Professor, Department of Psychology, Georgia State University.

The authors wish to thank John H. Porcerelli and Sidney J. Blatt, as well as the editor and three anonymous reviewers, for their helpful comments on earlier versions of this article.

The Psychoanalytic Study of the Child 59, ed. Robert A. King, Peter B. Neubauer, Samuel Abrams, and A. Scott Dowling (Yale University Press, copyright © 2004 by Robert A. King, Peter B. Neubauer, Samuel Abrams, and A. Scott Dowling).

> "Effective psychotherapy must focus on patients' *project
> relationships* as well as on their *object relationships*"
> (Yalom, 1980, p. 291; italics in the original)

DANA, A SIXTEEN-YEAR-OLD HIGH SCHOOL STUDENT AT AN ALL-GIRL boarding school, presented for therapy with a two-year history of anorexia, dating back to eighth grade. At the beginning of treatment, Dana's weight bordered on the medically dangerous, which was in fact an improvement over her previous, even lower, weight. In her early psychotherapy sessions Dana sat on the edge of her seat, always with her coat on, speaking in a slightly stilted, precise fashion. She wore close-fitting but layered clothing. She looked like a delicate, elegant, wild bird, perched at one's window and ready to fly off if one made any unexpected movement. As the therapy unfolded, it was clear that Dana's world, both internal and external, was divided into dichotomous categories. The first key psychological category was that of absolute discipline, ambition, academic success, calm, and social prestige—all epitomized by thinness. The second and opposite key psychological category was that of laziness, abject social and academic failure, and despair—all epitomized by fatness.

As long as Dana stayed thin she could (just barely) hold onto her view of herself as belonging in the first, all-good, category. Thinness, of all of her "good" categorical qualities, was easier to achieve and easier to measure. It was a guarantor of self-esteem, to a fragile, but exalted, self-image. At times thinness afforded Dana a secret sense of superiority, a quasi-spiritual sense of moral and psychological transcendence. She experienced herself as almost non-corporeal, pure spirit.

At her boarding school, Dana was envied for her thinness. Most of the other girls saw her as "perfect," since they, to a lesser extent, used the same mental categories as she. To them she was mysterious, self-contained, and unflappable, always on top of her work and disciplined in her exercise and dieting regime. Dana and the other girls, in fact, lived in what Goffman (1961) would call a "total" subculture, where psychological stereotypes can reign supreme, with little influence from the larger surrounding social world.

So what were the downsides of anorexia? At first, Dana was convinced that there were none. Increasingly, however, she became cognizant of the price she had to pay for her weight-related triumphs and her iconic social status. Although dieting enabled her to retain her membership in the ranks of the perfect, it only did so precariously. If she did not constantly work on staying thin—and the weight criterion of thinness ever increased in its stringency—her self-image would revert, Jekyll-like, into its complementary reverse. When the number on the scale shifted up even a few ounces, ever more mental and physical energy had to be expended on exercise and meal planning. As a result Dana was often obscurely depressed, only able to say she was inexplicably "upset" or "feeling bad."

Costs were also high in the interpersonal world. Dana's battlements of self-sufficiency and perfection both required and created a moat of social isolation. The girls around her not only felt envy, they also felt alienated from, and often even dislike, for her. In what Paul Wachtel (1977) would call a "vicious cycle," Dana did not have stable, reliable sources of self-esteem through close friendships, because of her anorexic method of self-esteem modulation. She did not get close to others, because they then might see through her, past her perfection, to the ugliness that she felt lay beneath. The impact of the anorexic self on others in turn widened her social isolation, deepening her depression and self-criticism, and requiring her to redouble her efforts to stay thin.

Not only did social isolation have a direct, negative effect on Dana's mood, it also robbed her of opportunities to extend and enrich her views of herself and others. If she could have made some cautious forays into confiding in others, she might have found that some girls were tremendously relieved that she too was human. Their pleasure in her self-disclosures might have created a positive cycle, rather than a vicious one, in which she in turn felt lured into greater intimacy.

Confiding, and being confided in, opens up a more complex, differentiated emotional world, one in which people are not simply categorized as either losers or goddesses. The adolescent practice of "hanging out" creates a kind of interpersonal reverie, a social "transitional space," as Winnicott (1951, 1959) would put it. Dana could not "hang out," because every minute had to serve a purpose, whether to solve an academic task or to seek further strategies of physical perfection. Here once again Dana created a social environment that did not offer her experiences to reconsider her dichotomous view of herself and others. In fact, Dana also could not "hang out" in her own mind, in her own internal transitional space; she could not muse or mentally play with different ways of thinking and feeling.

An additional detriment of Dana's interpersonal style was her perpetual feeling that she was undermined and rejected by other girls. When she was able to identify others' responses toward her as positive and nurturing, she swiftly discounted those others as "losers," as they took their turn as the abased objects—similar to Groucho Marx's famous remark that he wouldn't want to belong to any club that would have him as a member. Either view of others caused her to withdraw further, leading others to see her as haughty or touchy. Needless to say, such reactions consolidated Dana's viciously critical self and object representations.

Did Dana "create," or at least contribute to, the consolidation of her own eating disorder? We believe it to be the case. This and other instances of active generation of ones' own psychological difficulties (Shahar, 2001, in press) pose serious theoretical and clinical challenges. Whereas theoretically the challenge is to identify the intrapsychic structures and processes that propel individuals to create the very social environment that inflicts distress upon them, the clinical challenge is to help individuals short-circuit these vicious interpersonal cycles as well as to embark on positive interpersonal cycles, thereby creating a nurturing, growth-enhancing environment.

The present article represents an additional step in a series of attempts to address these challenges (cf. Shahar, 2001, in press; Shahar, Henrich, Blatt, Ryan, & T. D. Little, 2003; Shahar, Chinman, Sells, & Davidson, 2003). Specifically, herein we address the potential inherent in integrating two markedly independent, yet profoundly complementary, lines of inquiry: psychoanalytic theories of mental representations and action models of human development. We argue that psychoanalytic models of mental representations contribute to this integration the realization that individuals' behavior, cognition, and affect are largely regulated by "mental maps" or interpersonal schemas of self, other, and relationships. In turn, action perspectives of human development contribute to this integration their emphasis on individuals' goals, plans, and life tasks, and their translation into coping strategies and interpersonal behavior.

We explicate our thesis by first presenting a condensed overview of psychoanalytic models of mental representations. Then, we briefly present a family of theories and empirical findings that can be grouped under the umbrella of action theory. Next, we relate the two lines of inquiry, noting points of convergence and divergence. Out of this comparison emerges an integrated formulation of person-environment exchanges throughout development.

MENTAL REPRESENTATIONS IN PSYCHOANALYTIC
THEORY AND RESEARCH

We begin by offering an illustrative, but by no means exhaustive, summary of the history of psychoanalytic object relations theory. By examining the contribution of several key theorists to the understanding of self and object representations, we hope to illustrate the ways in which this remarkably rich, century-long, theorizing has resulted in relatively new, exciting, empirical research on mental representations.

Freud's often cited penchant for dualistic thinking (Holt, 1972; Schafer, 1976) and his tragic vision of human experience (Schafer, 1976) are epitomized in his view that the individual is inevitably at odds with the physical and social environment (Freud, 1930). For instance, Freud envisioned the infant as only being lured, or even compelled, out of hallucinatory instinctual gratification (a state of "primary narcissism") by physical need for food (1911, 1912–1913, 1914, 1926, 1930). The early, crucial stages of development were significantly shaped, in his view, by a biologically predetermined sequence of stages organized around body zones, organ modes and characteristic defenses. This element of Freud's thinking made up a view of human nature as primarily motivated by instinctual drive and only secondarily impelled to connect to others as a result.

In Freud's writings, the fundamental prototype of object-internalization's creation of mental representation is the super-ego (Schafer, 1968; Laplanche & Pontalis, 1973), which is generally seen as prohibitive or punishing, as a result of having originated in fear (Schafer, 1960). Freud did not conceive of the child as having a primary psychological need for the object. Rather, he emphasized physical fear as the motive for internalization, and did not typically stress other functions of the internalized object aside from punishment and critical self-evaluation. Freud did discuss psychological loss (1917, 1923) and admiration of another (1921) as motives for identification, and for ego, not simply super-ego, formation. Nonetheless the primary structural "precipitate" (1923) of object relations for Freud was the super-ego. In addition, the role of internalization in pre-oedipal development remained vague.

There was, however, an object-relational component to Freud's thinking, often most apparent in his clinical writings (Greenberg and Mitchell, 1983), but integrated into some of his metapsychological thinking as well. As soon as "the shadow of the object fell on the ego" in "Mourning and Melancholia" (1917, p. 249), that object was integrated into psychological structure (1923).

Heinz Hartmann extended Freud's description of the defensive functions of the ego by adding another facet: the ego as an innate "organ of adaptation" to the external world (Hartmann, 1939). This enlarged concept of the ego laid the theoretical groundwork for an increased emphasis on the external, social world, rather than on internal, physical drive, and for a less inimical relationship between self and environment in general. Hartmann, Kris, and Loewenstein (1953) underlined "the importance of environmental factors on earliest stages of development in general, and the role of pre-oedipal experience specifically" (p. 119). Elsewhere (1962) they included "object relations" as an important component of "progress in psychoanalytic theory" (p. 143). Hartmann et al. (1946) also emphasized that identification, a key process in object relations, is "one of the major, if not the major, mechanisms contributing to the child's early formation of personality" (p. 46). In this passage he also stated that identification is only secondarily a defense against danger, in contrast to Freud's emphasis.

Hartmann left out in his discussion much of the concrete detail of object representation and relationships, especially the corresponding fantasies and affective content. Such an elaboration was proposed by the British Object Relations theorists, among whom we will focus on are Melanie Klein and Donald Winnicott. *Melanie Klein* retained Freudian drive theory but, in contrast to Hartmann, understood drive as elaborated in pervasive object relational fantasy. Klein enlarged upon Freud's concepts of projection and introjection, and of split and part objects. Moreover, she assigned to these latter concepts a multitude of psychological functions, and described with great color and drama their fantasy landscape. "Internal objects" as discussed by Klein were equivalent, variously, to objects of perception, fantasy images, enduring mental representations, or more superordinate mental structures, such as the ego and super-ego (Greenberg and Mitchell, 1983). This ambiguity in the description of internal objects was a continuing difficulty for later object relations theorists, as well as a stumbling block for empirical researchers on object relations.

In direct disagreement with Freud and Hartmann, Klein insisted that internal objects and fantasy exist even at the earliest phase of development (Klein, 1974). This recasting of the primary narcissism phase constituted a major transformation of developmental theory, from childhood as largely predetermined by a sequence of bodily zone shifts, to an at least equivalent emphasis on the influence of interpersonal connection.

Donald W. Winnicott was brilliantly attuned to subjective experience, especially to that of the early phases of the self. He described the subtle gradations of experience along the ontological continuum of self to other, using his evocative concepts of transitional space and objects. In addition, he depicted other significant self feelings: integration, vitality, authenticity, "going-on-being," and the effects of environmental interference with these. In many passages Winnicott subtly deprecated the role of instinct in early development. At the same time, he consistently highlighted the real personalities of the baby's significant objects, in explicit opposition to Klein (Winnicott, 1969, in 1989), even to the extent of provocatively denying any psychological reality to the baby in absence of the mother. As stated by Winnicott: "There is no such thing as a baby . . . the unit is not the individual, the unit is an environment-individual set-up." (pp. 99–100, 1952, in 1975).

Subsequent psychoanalytic theorizing attempted to integrate tenets of ego psychology and object relations theory. Four integrative approaches will be briefly noted here, that of *Edith Jacobson, Otto Kernberg, Joseph Sandler,* and *Roy Schafer.*

Jacobson sought to differentiate clearly on the one hand between self and object representations, ideal self and object representations, and internalized objects of different levels of sophistication, and on the other hand the more abstractly structural, less phenomenological concepts of ego and self. One of her most significant contributions was in the area of development of self-feelings: shame, healthy grandiosity, self-consciousness, identity. She described how these feelings are intricately influenced from early infancy to adulthood by object relationships and emphasized (before Kohut, 1977) how the parent's necessary and gradual disillusionment of the child gently tempered his self and object idealizations (Jacobson, 1964).

In contrast to Klein's emphasis on phantasy, Jacobson viewed relationships as involving real people, as well as distorted object representations and reprojected internalizations. There is a "receding role of identifications in favor of autonomous thought processes" (Jacobson, 1964, p. 187) as development proceeds. Jacobson systematically laid out the evolution of self-object relationships from fusion, through gross, holistic introjects of concrete, personified images, to more selective partial identifications, and finally to depersonified structures which are integrated into the self and are both flexible and stable. The transformation of grossly idealized self-representations and internal objects into a reasonable, integrated ego ideal through gradual, healthy disillusionments is part of this process.

Elaborating on drive theory, Jacobson emphasized the importance of intrasystemic, rather than intersystemic, conflicts between identifications. Specifically, she described conflicts that are not bound up with the press of instinct (Jacobson, 1964) and that lead to self-feelings of shame or lack of identity. The self-feeling of pride may in fact "develop, in part, independently of the child's instinctual conflicts and the mother's attitudes and reactions" (Jacobson, 1964, p. 102). Similarly, Jacobson explicitly stated that internalization does not always come out of conflict, fear, or loss, but often directly evolves out of "close intimacy" (Jacobson, 1964, p. 90). She rectified the previous, predominantly prohibitive view of the super-ego by describing not only its origins in fear but also in love, and its function in modulating mood, identity, and self-esteem, rather than serving only as moral task-master. In all of this are the seeds of a theory of the development of the self, separate from drive.

Kernberg (1966), like Fairbairn before him, argued that all internalizations are of a specific self-object relationship, and retained Fairbairn's emphasis on splitting. In his comprehensive view of development and pathology, Kernberg (1975) mapped out the essential interconnectedness of levels of defense, affect-modulation, object relationship, and internalization. He delineated as well the cognitive and perceptual framework on which the capacity for internalization relies. This attention to cognitive and perceptual factors was evident in his clinical material, which presented clear descriptions not only of the content but also of formal aspects of primitive internalizations: dichotomous, chaotic, concrete, and variable in projection/reintrojection as a result of poor self-other differentiation.

Kernberg provided a more precise description of the function, form, and development of Klein's notion of projective identification (Klein, 1974). As Kernberg described it, the patient imagines that an aspect of his internal life resides within another person, yet also still feels some emotional link to that disclaimed experience, because of continued fluidity of self-object boundaries. This ineffectiveness of projective identification as a defense changes not only the patient's internal life, but also the way he acts toward the other person, whom he tries to control (Kernberg, 1966). Finally this entire process influences the reactions of the other person, who can feel the impact of the projected experience. Thus, even more than Klein, Kernberg opened the way toward examining how various types of pathology manifest themselves in specific types of interpersonal behavior, and how this can cause others to both feel and act in particular ways in response.

Joseph Sandler addressed the continuing theoretical confusions between self-representation and self-image, object representation and object image, thing representations, ego, and internalized objects. Sandler stated that images, in contrast to representations, are brief, non-stable perceptions. He emphasized that mental representations are not only of objects (e.g., significant people) but also of internal states and external things (Sandler, 1962). In addition, objects cannot be internalized unless they have been perceived and cognitively organized (Sandler, 1962). Sandler also addressed psychoanalysis' tendency to reify internalization concepts. In projective identification, for instance, he observed that theorists speak of "putting an aspect of oneself into another person" (Sandler, 1981, p. 185). Introjects are often described as if they have a life of their own, and identification is loosely referred to as quasi-physical, swallowed internalization of an object, rather than as a mental process of setting up an imagined relationship between one's self-representation and a representation of an object. Sandler believed that such reifications blur our understanding of the phenomenology of these processes.

According to Sandler, people are not only driven from the inside, but actively and planfully seek to satisfy their wishes not only for instinctual satisfaction, but also for security and self-esteem (Sandler, 1976, 1981). As a result, "objects" are not "cathected." Rather than a cathexis there exists a wish, which is always made up of a self-representation, an object-representation, and a representation of the desired interaction between these two (Sandler, 1978)—a concept comparable in structure to Kernberg's self-object-affect internalizations. Thus Sandler made object relationships the center of his theory of human development, relegating instinct to the status of one of several human motivations (Sandler, 1981).

An additional aspect of Sandler's theorizing, which is particularly pertinent to the present discussion, was his notion of "role responsiveness" (Sandler, 1976, 1981). From this point of view, each person not only tries to fulfill in his interaction with the other a wish dating from childhood, but also often succeeds in changing the behavior and feelings of the other, in accordance with this wish. This notion advances a more interactive, complex notion of object relations in contrast, say, to Klein's often solipsistic vision of fantasy dominating one's experience of the external world, or Hartmann's positivist notion of the mind as programmed to a large extent to portray reality veridically (Schafer, 1983).

Roy Schafer shared Sandler's concern with the inconsistencies of psychoanalytic language: its frequent confusion of phenomenological, structural, and metapsychological levels of discourse; and its an-thropomorphizing of abstract functions and structures (Schafer, 1968, 1976, 1983). Similar to Sandler, Schafer believed that we would have a clearer understanding of such constructs as introjects if we could focus on them phenomenologically, rather than locating them in the context of a complex metapsychology. Eventually, Schafer took this argument even further, to dispense with metapsychology altogether within the context of the clinical situation (Schafer, 1976) and to in-sist that, in general, metapsychology is a choice of a particular theo-retical "storyline," not an unquestioned foundation of psychological knowledge (Schafer, 1983). From this perspective, the language of "causes," rather than "reasons," adds nothing to our understanding of the clinical situation (Schafer, 1968). In contradistinction to the dearest hopes of Freud and the Post-Freudians, Schafer felt that, "The biological language of functions cannot be concerned with meaning" (Schafer, 1976, p. 89). In other words, "psychoanalysis is an interpretive discipline, not a natural science" (Schafer, 1983, p. 255). Thus, Schafer may be viewed as one of the early proponents of "post-modernist" psychoanalysis in his emphasis on the truth of the "co-authored" (Schafer, 1983, p. 183) patient/therapist narrative, rather than on historical truth.

As a reaction against what he called an earlier psychoanalytic focus on "the self as it desires the 'object'" (Kohut, 1984; cited in Teicholz, 1999, p. 110), *Kohut* took up an interest in the self as it develops more independently of objects, particularly objects of instinctual desire. The self starts to evolve at birth and has the primary functions of in-tentionality and meaning-giving, as well as the provision, later on, of felt coherence, continuity, and creativity (Kohut, 1977).

Kohut had been criticized for insufficiently stressing relationships with differentiated objects. His focus, however, is on the goals, tal-ents, and ideals of the self, its healthy sense of vitality and pride, and thus on the "selfobjects" (objects that are important in terms of their function for the self), which invigorate and develop the self in these areas (Kohut, 1977). The parents as self-objects mirror the child's healthy exhibitionism and grandiosity, provide an empathic psycho-logical twinship, and offer up idealized aspects of themselves to be gradually internalized in a "transmuting" fashion. The "motor," so to speak, of internalization is gradual and age-appropriate frustrations and disillusionments. Here Kohut's writings take Jacobson's further in elucidating the importance of the function of idealized objects and self-representations.

Hans Loewald's thinking, spanning the 1950s through the 1980s, was an important way station between the traditional ego psychology of Hartmann and postmodernist psychoanalysis, with a stop at object relations in between. Loewald generally spoke in the language of Freud, but claimed to find in the later writings ("Beyond the Pleasure Principle," 1920 and on), and especially in Freud's later concept of "Eros," a different, more object-relational, and less mechanistic Freud (Loewald 1960, 1973, 1988). For Loewald, object relations, rather than instincts, had developmental and causal primacy. As a result, Loewald stated that internalization is of object relationships, rather than simply of objects (Loewald, 1960).

What made Loewald's thought so rich and dialectical, however, is that he also was very critical of what he viewed as ego psychology's overly rationalist de-emphasis of primary process (Loewald, 1960). He thus took issue with what he saw as a contemporary understatement of the importance of both object relations and primary process, in favor of rational adaptation to the environment. Loewald repeatedly stressed that healthy development, in and out of therapy, involved overcoming rifts between primary and secondary process (see Loewald, 1960, p. 53).

Kohut and Loewald thus anticipated postmodernist psychoanalytic thinking by making empathy the analyst's primary "scientific" tool. We conclude our overview therefore with a brief discussion of postmodern psychoanalysis, an over-arching category which is used to denote (a) successors of Sullivan's interpersonal theory (Sullivan, 1953, 1962), such as Mitchell (1988, 2000), Benjamin (1988), Aron (1992), Ghent (1989), and Levenson (1972), (b) intersubjective thinkers, such as Stolorow, Brandchaft, and Atwood (1987; also Stolorow and Atwood, 1997; Stolorow, 1995), (c) neo-Kleinians such as Ogden (1994), (d) social-constructivists, such as Hoffman (1991), and (e) integrative, cognitive-behavioral-psychodynamic thinkers such as Wachtel (1977, 1993, 1997). Although it is beyond the scope of this paper to outline the differences between these authors, it can be argued that they take Schafer's emphasis on phenomenology and interpersonally constructed narrative to an even more extreme position. In this "two-person" psychology (Modell, 1984), the other person in the dyad must be recognized equally, in his or her actions and subjective experience, to the self. The field of inquiry is between two subjectivities, integrating a focus on real behavior in the real world with the private world of representations, internalization, and intrapsychic conflict.

FROM CLINICALLY-BASED CONCEPTUALIZATIONS
TO EMPIRICAL SCIENCE: PSYCHOANALYTICALLY INFORMED
RESEARCH ON MENTAL REPRESENTATIONS

One of the most exciting developments taking place in the past four and a half decades in academic psychology is the advent of rigorous, systematic, and empirically based research on mental representations of self, others, and interpersonal relationships. It is of little surprise that such extensive and rigorous research is pursued by investigators who either received a full-fledged psychoanalytic training or those heavily influenced by psychoanalytic theory. As reviewed above, the evolution of these theories reflects a painstaking struggle to capture the enormous complexity of the way people represent their social environment, that is, the fact that these representations slowly emerge in the context of development, that they are multifaceted, sometimes contradictory, and frequently unconscious, and that they occupy a central position in the human psyche, as regulators of affect, cognition and behavior.[1]

These tenets are all manifested in empirical research on mental representations of self and others. Studies conducted by numerous groups, including those led by Sidney J. Blatt, Peter Fonagy, Linda Mayes, Martin Mayman, Arietta Slade, J. Urist, Drew Westen, and others, have yielded substantial information on the role of mental representations in personality, development, psychopathology, and the therapeutic process. Review of this research, which is highly consistent with psychoanalytic conceptualizations of mental representation as a superordinate regulator of affect, cognition, and behavior, lies outside the scope of this article. The reader interested in such a review is referred to Baldwin (1992), Blatt, Auerbach, & Levy (1997), Kelly (1997), Horowitz, Eells, Singer, and Salovey (1995), and Westen (1991, 1998). Herein we briefly illustrate this literature by focusing on two of the research groups, one led by Blatt and the other by

---

1. In this context it is important to point out the attachment paradigm in mainstream academic psychology. The "internal working models of relationships" originally envisioned by Bowlby (1969, 1973, 1980) have made a major impact on research on internalization and interpersonal relationships. Attachment theory and research is also highly consistent with the notion that people shape their own environment (cf. Muir, 1995). However, although this paradigm is now extensively cited by leading psychoanalytic theories (cf. Fonagy, Steele, Steele, Higgitt, & Target, 1994), the lack of elaboration of unconscious and defensive functioning can be seen as an impediment to this paradigm's integration with psychoanalytic theory (cf. Slade, 1999; Fonagy, 1999; Holmes, 2001).

Westen. These two research groups are notable in their attempts to link research on mental representations with tenets of two principal paradigms of empirical psychology. Specifically, Blatt and his colleagues linked research on mental representations with theory and research on *cognitive development,* particularly with the models proposed by Piaget (1950, 1952, 1968) and Werner (1948). Likewise, Westen and his colleagues connected research on mental representations with *social cognition,* a leading theoretical and empirical paradigm in academic social psychology.

Drawing from psychoanalytic object relations theory, from attachment theory, and from theory and research on cognitive development, Blatt and colleagues (cf. Blatt, 1995; Blatt, Auerbach, & Aryan, 1998; Blatt et al., 1997; Blatt, Stayner, Auerbach, & Behrends, 1996) depict mental representations of self, others, and relationships as cognitive-affective schemas that organize individuals' experiences and interpersonal relatedness. Although the precursors of these schemas are rooted in early parent-child exchanges (cf. Stern, 1985), they continue to develop throughout the life span (Erikson, 1950, 1959, 1968; Blatt & Blass, 1996) while gaining increasing complexity and articulation. The structure of these cognitive-affective schemas of self-and-other follows the trajectory described by Piaget (1950, 1952, 1968).

Similar to Piaget's sensory-motor phase schemas, initial mental representations, formed in early development, focus largely on physical and motor aspects of self and others. As development unfolds, particularly through individuals' immersion in interpersonal relations, these schemas, or mental representations, become increasingly abstract and sophisticated, incorporating not only physical aspects but also complex behaviors, mental and psychological states, and reciprocal and well-coordinated components of human relationships.

Blatt and colleagues (Blatt, Bers, & Schaffer, 1992; Blatt, Chevron, Quinlan, Schaffer, & Wein, 1988; Diamond, Blatt, Stayner, & Kaslow, 1991) developed the Object Relations Inventory (ORI), a procedure that empirically assesses individuals' representations of self and significant others. The ORI asks respondents to describe significant others in their lives (e.g., mother, father, friend, therapist) and rates these descriptions for content and structural dimensions based on the principles put forth by Piaget. More mature representations are not only benevolent and nurturing, but, more importantly, also more articulated, complex (i.e., pertaining to mental states and character traits of self and significant others), and reflect greater differentiation between self and object. Research (cf. Blatt, Stayner, et al.,

1996) demonstrated that changes in mental representations (as assessed by the ORI) among inpatients treated in a long-term psychoanalytically oriented treatment were positively correlated with changes in patients' clinical functioning. Readers interested in research and clinical applications of the ORI are referred to the article by Bers, Blatt, and Dolinsky (this volume).

Similarly to Blatt and colleagues, Westen and his colleagues drew from another mainstream psychological paradigm—that of social cognition. This paradigm is itself an integrative one, linking information processing patterns studied mainly in cognitive psychology with the study of social interactions, the hallmark of social psychology. Social cognition researchers take a cognitive approach to numerous interpersonal processes, including (a) schematic processing (i.e., the use of organized knowledge structures to process information), (b) errors in social judgment and social inferences, (c) "nonconscious" informational processing, and other areas. According to Westen (1991), social cognition and object relations theory complement each other. Whereas social cognition provides an empirically based, detailed description of the cognitive processes through which mental representations of self and others organize individuals' perceptions of their world, object relations theory elucidates the affective, motivated, and unconscious nature of such perception.

In an ingenious application of this theoretical integration of social cognition and object relations, Westen and colleagues (Westen, Klepser, Ruffins, Silverman, Lifton, & Boekamp, 1991) developed the Social Cognition and Object Relations Scale (SCORS), a procedure for analyzing stories that are told in response to the Thematic Apperception Test (TAT) cards. In this procedure, each of the TAT-related stories is analyzed according to four dimensions that capture the overlapping features of the social cognition and object relations perspectives. These perspectives are (1) the affective tone of the characters (i.e., "objects") described in the story (Affective Tone), (2) the extent to which these characters are able to be emotionally involved with other persons (Affective Involvement), (3) the extent to which the these characters are depicted in complex ways, such that their description include intricate psychological states, thoughts, and feelings (Complexity of Representations), and (4) the extent to which the stories convey an adequate understanding of social norms, rules and scripts (Social Causality). An impressive body of research provides support for the reliability, validity, and clinical applicability of the SCORS. For review of this research, the reader is referred to Westen (1991, 1998). Vivid clinical cases are presented by F. Kelly

(1996, 1997), and by Porcerelli, Abramsky, Hibbard, and Kamoo (2001).

ACTION PERSPECTIVES ON DEVELOPMENT: CONTINENTAL AND NORTH-AMERICAN INFLUENCES

In an early, seminal contribution to the understanding of parent-child relationship, Bell (1968) questioned the then-prevalent model of socialization according to which the action of the parent on a child assumes causal priority, whereas the effect of children on their parents are dismissed as only a logical but implausible alternative. Reviewing research on both humans and animals, Bell (1968) demonstrated that the parent effect model cannot account for myriad findings as to the variability of parent behavior across siblings, and that experimental manipulation of animal offspring induced differential responses in parents. To illustrate how features of the child modify parents' responses, Bell (1968) argues:

> Children high in person orientation attend to behavior of their parents and reinforce social responses emanating from them. Children low in person orientation induce less nurturance from parents, and their behavior is controlled less by variation in social response of parents. They are interested in physical activity and inanimate objects. Their stimulus characteristics primarily mobilize those elements in the parent nurturance repertoires pertaining to providing and withholding physical objects and activities. Since love-oriented control techniques are less useful with these children and material reinforcers can not always be flexibly applied, their parents more frequently show further recourse to physical punishment (Bell, 1968, p. 85).

Bell's argument is tantamount to the assertion that children (partly) shape their parenting. Similarly, in his key article, "Children and Adolescents as Producers of Their Own Distress," Richard Lerner (1982) advances the idea that children's physical and behavioral characteristics promote differential reactions in others with whom they socialize (e.g., parents, teachers, and peers). In turn, these reactions feed back, affecting further development. In that sense, individuals can be said to be the molders of their own development. Concurrently with Lerner (1982) various other academic psychologists explored the ways in which individuals shape their development by acting on their social environment (e.g., Brandtstadter, 1998; Bronfenbrenner, 1979; Bruner, 1990; see also the 1984 special issue on action theory in the journal *Human Development*).

An additional support for the view that children, adolescent and adults in part shape their own environment comes from the field of behavior genetics. Reiss, Plomin, and their colleagues, in numerous studies aimed at disentangling genetic and environmental influences on adolescent development, found that genetic factors account for a large part of adolescent social behavior. An unexpected finding was that the environment shared by adolescent siblings had a negligible effect on their social behavior. However, non-shared environmental factors (i.e., factors in the adolescent environment that are unique to each sibling) had a considerable impact on social development, over and above the effect attributable to genetic factors. What might account for this non-shared environmental effect? As reasoned by Reiss (2000), this effect represents the distinctive influence of cumulative and subtle genetic variations in adolescents' social behavior on their significant others.

Consistent with this emphasis in developmental psychology and behavior genetics on the active and reciprocal nature of person-context exchanges, various personality psychologists propose to focus on the ways in which individuals construct long and short-term goals as a viable unit of psychological analysis (Austin & Vancouver, 1996; Brunstein, 1993; Cantor, 1990; Emmons, 1986; B. Little, 1999; J. Smith, 1999). Goals, or Personal Projects (B. Little, 1999) are pertinent units of analysis of person-environment exchanges because they elucidate the motivations that underlie individuals' action on their environment. This is particularly true of key goals, or "Core Personal Projects" (B. Little, 1999). As argued by Shahar (in press), such key goals or personal projects are only partly conscious, and are frequently formed in early childhood, due to painful experiences arising in the context of child-caregiver relationships. As Shahar (in press) suggested: "because these decisions evolve in an effort to alleviate severe mental pain, they have the urgency of desperate measures. Consequently, these core personal projects lead to rigid, albeit 'passionate and persistent' (Harris, 1984, p. 179) interpersonal behavior that precipitates contextual risk factors." In turn, these contextual risk factors are likely to lead to psychopathology.

ATHEORETICAL INTEGRATION: REPRESENTATIONS IN ACTION

The principal thesis of this article is twofold. First, we submit that the developing agent is a purposeful, future oriented subject, who acts on the social environment in order to attain his or her goals. Second, these goals are only partly conscious, and they are always "relational" in the sense that they are crafted in the context of real and fantasized interpersonal relationships and frequently address interpersonal needs, drives, and wishes. Consequently, individuals' goals, plans, and "personal projects" (B. Little, 1999) are intimately tied to the content and structure of their mental representations of self and others (see Cross, 1993; Harris, 1984; and Shahar, in press for clinical illustrations of the intimate ties between mental representations and goals and plans).

To gain a greater appreciation of the unique contribution of psychoanalytic object relations models and action models to this integrative statement, we ask two questions: What is missing in psychoanalytic models of mental representations that can be found in action models of development? And, what is lacking in action models of development that can be supplemented by psychoanalytic models of mental representations?

There are at least four aspects in which action models of development may enrich psychoanalytic models of mental representations. The first and obvious aspect is that action theory enables a better appreciation of the role of the future in the psyche. By definition, psychoanalytic models elucidate the importance of past occurrences, particularly early relationships, in personality development, psychopathology, and the therapeutic process. More recent psychoanalytic models have also highlighted the importance of the present, not only as evoking past traumas, but also as an opportunity for development and growth (Vaillant, 1993, 2000). In contrast, the role of future in people's phenomenology, that is, of setting long-term goals, planning, and proactive coping in people's personality, which has been demonstrated in action-oriented empirical research to have a considerable impact on people's development and well being (Aspinwall & Taylor, 1997; B. Little, 1999), has largely been overlooked in psychoanalytic theory (but see Gedo, 1995, for an exception).

Second, this action-theory depiction of the developing agent as future oriented and purposeful necessitates a focus on the environment, because goals, plans, and personal projects can only be attained through interpersonal relationships (B. Little, 1999; Shahar, in press). Thus, by superimposing an action theory perspective on psychoanalytic models of mental representations, the latter models' focus on intrapsychic processes and only secondary attention to the environment is offset. From an action theory perspective, individuals "create," or shape, their development, personality and well-being vis-à-vis their exchanges with their social environment. It therefore follows that a comprehensive understanding of individual's dynamics entails a particular focus on their salient and explicit environmental exchanges. Put differently, from an action theory perspective, *actual social behavior*, rather than, or in addition to dreams, associations, and fantasies, represents the royal road to their psyche.

As Brinich (personal communication) has noted, "When Freud described how intrapsychic processes (and especially fantasy) played a part in the genesis of neurosis, he did not mean or suggest that we could neglect the part played by environmental factors. He was, however, concerned that his insight about the importance of the unconscious would be dismissed; thus his difficulty in tolerating perspectives that gave more weight to the external world." The purpose of this paper is to argue for a perspective that acknowledges both the internal and the external worlds as co-contributors to development and to suggest the theoretical and clinical advantages of such a perspective.

A concrete illustration of this perspective is the evolution of Dana's actual social relations during early adolescence and their link with her representational world. Although Dana's choice of symptoms had multiple determinants rooted in her conflicts over dependency, individuation, pathological perfectionism, and aggressive and sexual impulses (as intensified by adolescent development), understanding the cumulative impact of these issues requires examining their recursive reverberations in and with Dana's interpersonal world. For example, Dana's father's position in the army necessitated frequent moves. Such moves, demonstrated in empirical research to seriously impede adolescent adaptation (Lopez & Little, 1997), reinforced her already existing tendency to present the world with only a brittle facade. "If you are always the new girl, who is stared at and instantly judged by other girls, you learn to put on a mask that gets you through," she explained to her therapist. As we noted earlier in this paper, she came to learn in therapy that this façade, although seemingly beneficial, had negative social consequences: Sensing both her vulnerability and fear of contact, the girls around her kept their distance, thus depriving her of an opportunity to have rewarding interpersonal exchanges that would, in turn, add some complexity to her overly dichotomous view of self-and-other.

The therapist's selective attunement to Dana's actual social exchanges with peers, parents, school personnel, as well as in the transference, elicited a clear view not only of Dana's inner structure, but also of the culture of her family and the wider army culture in which this family operated. The army's tremendous emphasis on polished performance and façade, as well as its culture of externalized dignity, clear social hierarchy and emotional restraint, helped both cause and perpetuate Dana's emotional difficulties. We have already seen earlier in this paper the effect of the relatively closed culture of a girls' boarding school on Dana.

A third way in which action perspectives on development may enrich psychoanalytic models is by increasing these models' appreciation of the reciprocal nature of person-environment exchanges. Namely, from an action perspective, people not only shape their environment, but are also constantly being shaped by it (Sameroff, 1995). Most psychoanalytic models appear to be based on the assumption that representations, once formed, are difficult to change other than through intensive psychoanalytic therapy.[2] In contrast, an action theory perspective, backed up by empirical research (Mischel & Shoda, 1995; Shahar & Davidson, 2003; Wachtel, 1994) would hold that individuals' mental representations are more malleable than had been previously considered, and that benign or positive environmental occurrences might update, amend, or even change individuals' sense of self and significant others. This view would shed particular light on personality development during transitions such as puberty, entering college, and parenthood.

The fourth and final way in which action models of development might enrich psychoanalytic theories of mental representations, especially the more traditional ones, is that by viewing mental representations from an action theory perspective, a "supremacy of information processing" fallacy is circumvented. This fallacy is highly prevalent in cognitive models of psychopathology (Beck, et al. 1983; Ellis, 1962; Meichenbaum, 1977). Despite various disagreements between these various cognitive models, they all subscribe to the point of view that intact development and mental health are incumbent upon an accurate perception of reality, and that psychopathology, maladjustment, and emotional and behavioral problems ensue as a result of individuals' "distorted" view of the word (cf. Beck, Shaw, Rush, & Emery, 1983). Consequently, remediation of psychopathol-

---

2. Harry Stack Sullivan and Paul Wachtel were important exceptions to this point of view, for instance, in Sullivan's notion of the importance of chumship in late latency and early adolescence (Sullivan, 1953) and in Wachtel's rejection of what he called "the woolly mammoth" notion of the unconscious (Wachtel, 1977, 1997). Loewald also insisted that "The unconscious is capable of change and, as Freud says, is 'accessible to the impressions of life'" (Loewald, 1960, p. 57). Additionally, authors integrating object relations theory with family therapy perspectives (e.g., Scharff & Scharff, 1987) are also attuned to the effect of the social (i.e., family) context on mental representations.

ogy should be focused on improving people's information process-ing capacities, in order to help them to arrive at a less distorted, more realistic, worldview.

These cognitive models, which are largely based on the advent, and overwhelming popularity, of the information processing para-digm in computer science during the 1950s and subsequently, have been repeatedly criticized by leading developmental and clinical scholars from various schools of thoughts (cf. Bruner, 1990; Ban-dura, 1978; Coyne & Gotlib, 1983). In a series of articles, provocative in tone as well as in content, Coyne challenged what he termed as the "spectator" view of the person. Rather than suffering from emotional and behavioral problems because of a distorted view of their world, Coyne argued, people experience these problems because of adverse environmental conditions, such as relational discord and/or social or political inferiority (Coyne & D. A. F. Smith, 1994; Lakoff & Coyne, 1993). In some cases, such as in the case of a loss of a loved one, people have little control of adverse environmental conditions. In other cases, however, people's behavior brings about the very same environmental consequences that contribute to their plight (Coyne, 1976a, 1976b). In other words, according to Coyne and to other investigators following his conceptualization (Hammen, 1991, 1998; Joiner, 1994, 2000), *people are distressed because they accurately perceive the very circumstances that they themselves generated.*

This view, couched in terms borrowed from behaviorism and learning theory, is highly compatible both with action perspectives on development and with psychoanalytic conceptualizations such as that of Sandler's "role responsiveness," Klein's "projective identifica-tion," and most prominently, relational theorists such as Mitchell (1987) and Hirsch (1994). Nevertheless, psychoanalytically oriented *empirical* research on mental representations (e.g., Blatt et al., 1997; Westen, 1991) appears to have been heavily based more on an infor-mation processing perspective. In fact, the tenet underlying such re-search has been that mental representations regulate people's cogni-tive functioning, and that negative, malevolent, and maladaptive representation would lead people to have distorted perceptions and beliefs, in turn leading to psychopathology. In keeping with the criti-cism launched by Coyne and others on this "spectator" view of the person, and in agreement with an "actor" view of the person, we would like to propose an alternative: individuals' mental representa-tions lead them to act upon others in a way that evoke responses which are consistent with these representations (Priel, Mitrani, & Shahar, 1998; Swann, 1983; Joiner, 1994). These actual responses, which are largely negative when provoked by malevolent representations, are often accurately perceived by the person, in turn leading to emotional distress and psychopathology.

Our second question follows: *What is action theory missing that psychoanalytic models can add?* Whereas action theory provides an excitingly vibrant depiction of the developing person, this theory does not emphasize the intrapsychic underpinnings of individuals' action on their environment. Put differently, action theorists appear to focus on actual behaviors and/or interpersonal processes at the expense of personality structures. Psychoanalytic object relations approaches, with their emphasis on mental structures and contents, readily address this gap in pointing to mental representations of self and others as the psychic entities that organize affect, cognition, and behavior, and in our case, goals, plans, and personal projects.

In this context it is worth noting an exception to action theory perspectives, namely, the transactional model put forth by Sameroff (1995). In this model, development is seen as the product of interactions between the individual and the social environment, which exert mutual influences. The transactional model defines environmental influences the "environtype," which is conceived of as an organization of environmental factors that regulates the behavior of the individual, akin to how a genotype refers to the makeup of genetic factors that influence individual characteristics (Sameroff, 1995). Particular environmental emphasis is placed on the cultural code and the family code, which regulate how children's individual characteristics fit with their social environment. According to Sameroff (1995), family stories and myths can be seen as mental representations that regulate development (an empirical application of this model to the problem of child conduct disorder is presented by Sameroff and Fiesse [2000]).

The psychoanalytic point of view also includes the key concept of epigenesis, an unfolding of biologically predetermined phases of development (no matter the extent to which they overlap and never completely replace each other). Key examples of such phases of development are the oral-anal-phallic-genital sequence or Mahler's separation-individuation phases, developmental sequences involving shifts of sensual emphasis, predominant drive derivatives and organ modes, and characteristic conflicts and defensive operations, as well as shifts in relationships and concepts of the self. Attention to maturational phenomena has the corollary that at different developmental epochs the child may evoke different reactions in significant others and in turn may be sensitive to different aspects of others' behavior which acquire changing saliencies in different phases of life. This is illustrated in Reiss et al.'s finding that various environmental (and genetic factors) had different effects in early vs. late adolescence.

In Dana's case, as with other adolescent girls, the move into puberty and adolescence brings to the fore a host of new concerns and conflicts regarding autonomy, aggression, sexuality, and body image, as well as a heightened sensitivity to the responses the adolescent evokes in others around these concerns (King, 2002; Ritvo, 1984). Thus, psychoanalysis's epigenetic emphasis adds an increased complexity to action theory in shedding light on how, at different phases of development, children differentially affect and are affected by different aspects of their environments.

A third important way in which psychoanalytic perspectives on mental representations might enhance action models of development is by doing away with the assumption, frequently implied by action theorists, that people are rational, conscious, informed strategists. The psychoanalytic theorist Adrienne E. Harris (1984), in what appears to be the first attempt to link action theory and psychoanalysis, noted that "it is both ironic and moving to contemplate the development of action theory in a contemporary climate in which people experience a loss of control, a sense of cultural and political forces moving beyond the intent and management of individuals" (Harris, 1984, p. 197; also cited in Shahar, in press). Harris wants us to locate human action in the context of Freud's topographical model of the mind, noting that some goals and plans are conscious while others are not. Building on Harris (1984), Shahar (in press) points out that some of the most meaningful plans or "personal projects" (B. Little, 1999) are formed by people as a response to painful early experiences in the context of parent-child relationships. It is the very painful nature of these experiences that constitute these personal projects as rigid, closed, and unconscious systems, consequently leading to an interpersonal behavior that precipitates contextual risk factors. In addition, psychoanalysis emphasizes that people often have conflicting wishes and plans, which straddle conscious and unconscious experience. Conflict is often due to uneven levels of development, such that some emotional sectors are mature and well-adapted, while others are still dominated by residual childhood fantasies and wishes. Thus, psychoanalytic theory can add much to the full human complexity of action theory's notion of the self. People not only plan rationally; their plans can be in conflict with each other. Their plans can be unconscious, and can sometimes date back to previous developmental periods.

Finally, psychoanalysis' emphasis on epigenesis, conflict, the unconscious, and the continuity of childhood themes, combined with action theory's view of the self as proactive, adaptive, and environmentally oriented, *both* can shed light on Dana's case.

Dana's case, like that of many other adolescent anorectics, can be seen from many perspectives, especially that of a crisis over adolescent individuation, a continuing power struggle with maternal representations, a draconian attempt to control dependent longings, and a repudiation of the burgeoning adolescent body as the bearer and representation of intolerable appetites and desires. In our narrative, however, we have focused on the ways in which these only partly conscious dynamic "projects" were enacted in the context of her social environment whose responses in turn further shaped the elaboration of Dana's problematic feelings and behavior.

With respect to epigenesis, it does appear that Dana was not encouraged, early on, to understand herself in terms of emotions, rather than just in terms of concrete bodily states, and thus had trouble differentiating her self, and her needs, from her mother's. As a result her mother, who was significantly isolated from friends and her husband by the family's many moves (for reasons too complex to discuss here), was able to use Dana as a kind of narcissistic mirror. Dana's mother's response only reinforced her incapacity to reflect on her own mind as a separate entity, with thoughts, feelings, and motives separate from her mother's. Dana's difficulty in interpreting her own internal states also was a contributor to her eating disorder, through which she could cut off entirely her self from her body, while simultaneously only understand herself in terms of bodily states. In therapy she talked about herself and her family members in a kind of one-dimensional narrative. Feelings were very rarely discussed, and when they did force their way to the surface, usually in the form of bouts of inexplicable crying, Dana understood neither their origins nor their consequences. Dana acknowledged neither ambivalence, nor the gap between her attempted self-presentation and underlying self. This illustrates how a child's shaky "reflective self-function" (Fonagy, Steele, Steele, Leigh, Kennedy, Mattoon, and Target, 1995), whose foundation should be set during the separation-individuation period, can cause an early vicious cycle of family relationships.

The many changes of location also stopped Dana from developing latency friendships, or alternative parental figures (such as teachers or extended family members), so key in the child's journey out of the narrow, emotionally charged, oedipal world (Jacobson, 1964). She appeared to travel from country to country always contained in the psychological bubble of her nuclear family, with little constructive input from the outside. Earlier we saw how this "bubble" further alienated her from peers, and thus reinforced her simplistic views of self and other.

We have already discussed the polarized, rigid, and largely unconscious aspects of Dana's internal world, her use of projection and occasional splitting, and the repetition of early emotional themes. The behaviors resulting from these mental processes greatly perpetuated Dana's difficulties.

It should be noted, however, that in certain ways Dana was well adapted to her environment. Her strategies for success were certainly propelling her forward. Indeed, she was accepted by a prestigious university, maintained a level of social and academic prestige at her school, and managed to retain a level of continuous identity despite her many changes of environment early on. She was a jewel in her parents' crown, and could always be relied on to shine when displayed at social events in the military.

In therapy, both representation and action became the arena of change. During transference-countertransference exchanges, she became aware of how her longstanding, rigid views of herself and others were in fact self-perpetuating. As one consequence, she proactively planned to place herself in more nurturing social environments. She found a friend with a more relaxed, open family and spent increasing time with them. By making small forays into intimacy with other girls and then trying to rationally evaluate their reactions without prejudice, Dana embarked on a long, painstaking journey. Hence, representation in action constitutes not only the source of developmental arrest and psychopathology, but also the cradle of hope.

BIBLIOGRAPHY

Aron, L. (1992). Interpretation as expression of the analyst's subjectivity. *Psychoanalytic Dialogues,* 1:29–51.

Aspinwall, L. G., & Taylor, S. E. A. (1997). A stitch in time: Self-regulation and proactive coping. *Psychological Bulletin,* 121:417–436.

Auerbach, J. & Blatt, S. (1996). Self-representation in severe psychopathology: The role of reflexive self-awareness. *Psychoanalytic Psychology,* 13:297–342.

Baldwin, M. W. (1992). Relational schemas and the processing of social information. *Psychological Bulletin,* 112:461–484.

BANDURA, A. (1978). The self-system in reciprocal determinism. *American Psychologist*, 33:334–358.

BECK, A. T., RUSH, J. A., SHAW, B. F., & EMERY, G. (1983). *Cognitive therapy of depression*. New York: Guilford.

BELL, R. Q. (1968). A reinterpretation of the direction of effects in studies of socialization. *Psychological Review*, 75:81–95.

BENJAMIN, J. (1988). *The bonds of love: Psychoanalysis, feminism, and the problem of domination*. New York: Pantheon.

BERS, S., BLATT, S. J., & DOLINSKY A. (2004). The sense of self in Anorexia-Nervosa patients. *Psychoanalytic Study of the Child*, 59:294–315.

BLATT, S. (1995). Representational structure of psychopathology. In D. Cicchetti, S. L. Toth (Eds.), *Emotion, cognition, and representation: Rochester symposium on developmental psychopathology* (pp. 1–33). Rochester: Rochester University Press.

BLATT, S. J., AUERBACH, J. S., & ARYAN, M. (1998). Representational structures and the therapeutic process. In R. F. Bornstein & J. M. Masling, *Empirical studies of the therapeutic hour. Empirical studies of psychoanalytic theories*, Vol. 8. (pp. 63–107).

BLATT, S. J., AUERBACH, J. S., & LEVY, K. N. (1997). Mental representations in personality development, psychopathology, and the therapeutic process. *Review of General Psychology*, 1:351–374.

BLATT, S. J., BERS, S. A., & SCHAFFER, C. (1992). *The assessment of the self*. Unpublished research manual. Yale University.

BLATT, S. J., & BLASS, R. B. (1996). Relatedness and self definition: A dialectic model of personality development. In G. G. Noam & K. W. Fischer (Eds.), *Development and vulnerabilities in close relationships* (pp. 309–338). Hillsdale, N.J.: Lawrence Erlbaum Associates.

BLATT, S. J., CHEVRON, E. S., QUINLAN, D. M., SCHAFFER, C. E., & WEIN, S. (1988). *The assessment of qualitative and structural dimensions of object representations (Revised Edition)*. Unpublished research manual, Yale University.

BLATT, S. & LEVY, K. (2003) Attachment theory, psychoanalysis, personality development, and psychopathology. *Psychoanalytic Inquiry*, 23:102–150.

BLATT, S. J., STAYNER, D. A., AUERBACH, J. S., & BEHRENDS, R. S. (1996). Changes in object and self-representations in long-term, intensive, inpatient treatment of seriously disturbed adolescents and young adults. *Psychiatry: Interpersonal and Biological Processes*, 59:82–107.

BRANDTSTADTER, J. (1998). Action perspectives on human development. In W. Damon & R. M. Lerner (Eds.), *Handbook of child psychology* (pp. 807–863). NY: John Wiley & Sons.

BRONFENBRENNER, U. (1979). Toward an experimental ecology of human development. *American Psychologist*, 32:513–531.

BRUNER, J. (1990). *Acts of meaning*, Cambridge, Mass.: Harvard University Press.

BRUNSTEIN, J. C. (1993). Personal goals and subjective well-being: A longitudinal study. *Journal of Personality and Social Psychology*, 65:1061–1070.

CANTOR, N. (1990). From thought to behavior: "Having" and "doing" in the study of personality and cognition. *American Psychologist,* 45:735–750.

COOPER, A. (1991). Our changing views on the therapeutic action of psychoanalysis. In G. Fogel (Ed.), *The work of Hans Loewald* (pp. 61–76). Northvale, N.J.: Jason Aronson.

COWAN, P. (1978). *Piaget with feeling: Cognitive, social, and emotional dimensions.* New York: Holt, Rinehart, & Winston.

COYNE, J. C. (1976a). Toward an interactional description of depression. *Psychiatry: Journal for the Study of Interpersonal Processes,* 39:28–40.

COYNE, J. C. (1976b). Depression and the response of others. *Journal of Abnormal Psychology,* 85:186–193.

COYNE, J. C. (1994). Possible contributions of "cognitive science" to the integration of psychotherapy. *Journal of Psychotherapy Integration,* 4:401–416.

COYNE, J. C., & GOTLIB, I. H. (1983). The role of cognition in depression: A critical appraisal. *Psychological Bulletin,* 94:472–505.

COYNE, J. C., & SMITH, D. A. F. (1994). Couples coping with a myocardial infarction: Contextual perspective on patient self-efficacy. *Journal of Family Psychology,* 8:43–54.

DIAMOND, D., BLATT, S. J., STAYNER, D., & KASLOW, N. (1991). *Self-other differentiation of object representations.* Unpublished research manual, Yale University.

ELLIS, A. (1962). *Reason and emotions in psychotherapy.* New York: Lyle Stuart.

EMMONS, R. A. (1986). Personal striving: An approach to personality and subjective well-being. *Journal of Personality and Social Psychology,* 51:1058–1068.

ERIKSON, E. (1950). *Childhood and society.* New York: Norton.

ERIKSON, E. (1959). *Identity and the life cycle.* New York: International Universities Press.

ERIKSON, E. (1968). *Identity: Youth and crisis.* New York: Norton.

FAIRBAIRN. W. R. D. F. (1952). *Psychoanalytic studies of the personality.* Boston: Routledge & Kegan Paul.

FLAVELL, J. (1963). *The developmental psychology of Jean Piaget.* NY: Van Nostrand.

FOGEL, G. (1991a). Loewald's integrated and integrative approach. In G. Fogel (Ed.), *The work of Hans Loewald* (pp. 1–12). Northvale, N.J.: Jason Aronson.

FOGEL, G. (1991b). Transcending the limits of revisionism and classicism. In G. Fogel (Ed.), *The work of Hans Loewald* (pp. 153–190). Northvale, N.J.: Jason Aronson.

FOGEL, G. (ED.) (1991c). *The work of Hans Loewald.* Northvale, N.J.: Jason Aronson.

FONAGY, P. (1999). Psychoanalytic theory from the viewpoint of attachment theory and research. In J. Cassidy & P. R. Shaver (Eds.), *Handbook of attachment: Theory, research, and clinical applications* (pp. 595–624). New York: Guilford.

FONAGY, P., STEELE, M., STEELE, H., HIGGITT, A., & TARGET, M. (1994). Theory and practise of resilience. *Journal of Child Psychology and Psychology,* 35:231–257.

FONAGY, P., STEELE, H., MORAN, G., STEELE, M., & HIGGITT, A. (1991). The capacity for understanding mental states: The reflective self in parent and child relationships and its significance for security of attachment. *Infant Mental Health Journal,* 13:200–217.

FONAGY, P., STEELE, M., STEELE, H., LEIGH, T., KENNEDY, R., MATTOON, G., & TARGET, M. (1995). Attachment, the reflective self, and borderline states: The predictive specificity of the Adult Attachment Interview and pathological emotional development. In S. Goldberg, R. Muir, & J. Kerr (Eds.), *Attachment theory: Social, developmental, and clinical perspectives.* Hillsdale, N.J.: Analytic Press.

FREUD, S. (1911). Formulations on the two principles of mental functioning. *Standard Edition,* V. 12:213–227.

FREUD, S. (1912–1913). Totem and taboo, *Standard Edition,* V. 13:1–162.

FREUD, S. (1914). On narcissism. *Standard Edition,* V. 14:67–104.

FREUD, S. (1917). Mourning and melancholia. *Standard Edition,* V. 14:243–260.

FREUD, S. (1921). Group psychology and the analysis of the ego. *Standard Edition,* V. 18:65–143.

FREUD, S. (1923). The ego and the id. *Standard Edition,* V. 19:3–66.

FREUD, S. (1926). Inhibitions, symptoms, and anxiety. *Standard Edition,* V. 20:77–178.

FREUD, S. (1930). Civilisation and its discontents. *Standard Edition,* V. 21:59–148.

GEDO, J. E. (1995). On the psychobiology of motivation. *Psychoanalytic Inquiry,* 15:470–480.

GHENT, E. (1989). Credo: The dialectics of one-person and two-person psychologies. *Contemporary Psychoanalysis,* 25:169–211.

GOFFMAN, E. (1961). *Asylums: Essays on the social situation of mental patients and other inmates.* Chicago: Aldine.

GREENBERG, J. R. & MITCHELL, S. A. (1983). *Object relations in psychoanalytic theory.* Cambridge, Mass.: Harvard University Press.

HAMMEN, C. (1991). Generation of stress in the course of unipolar depression. *Journal of Abnormal Psychology,* 100:555–561.

HAMMEN, C. (1998). The emergence of an interpersonal approach to depression. In T. E. Joiner & J. C. Coyne, *The interpersonal nature of depression* (pp. 21–35). Washington, D.C.: American Psychological Association Press.

HARRIS, A. (1984). Action theory, language, and the unconscious. *Human Development,* 27:204.

HARTMANN, H. (1939). *Ego psychology and the problem of adaptation.* New York: International Universities Press.

HARTMANN, H. (1952). The mutual influences in the development of ego and id. *Psychoanalytic Study of the Child,* 7:9–30.

HARTMANN, H. (1964) Concept formation in psychoanalysis. *Psychoanalytic Study of the Child,* 19:11–47.

HARTMANN, H., KRIS, E., & LOEWENSTEIN, R. (1946). Comments on the formation of psychic structure. *Psychoanalytic Study of the Child*, 2:11–38.

HARTMANN, H., KRIS, E., & LOEWENSTEIN, R. (1953). The function of theory in psychoanalysis. *Psychological Issues: Papers on psychoanalytic psychology*, 4: 117–143.

HARTMANN, H. & LOEWENSTEIN, R. (1962). Notes on the super-ego. *Psychoanalytic Study of the Child*, 17:42–81.

HIRSCH, I. (1994). Dissociation and the interpersonal self. *Contemporary Psychoanalysis*, 30:777–799.

HOFFMAN, I. (1991). Discussion: Toward a social-constructivist view of the psychoanalytic situation. *Psychoanalytic Dialogues*, 1:74–105.

HOLMES, J. (1995). "Something there is that doesn't love a wall": John Bowlby, attachment theory, and psychoanalysis. In S. Goldberg, R. Muir, & J. Kerr (Eds.), *Attachment theory: social, developmental and clinical perspectives.*

HOLT, R. (1972). Freud's mechanistic and humanistic images of man. In R. Holt & E. Peterfreund (Eds.), *Psychoanalysis and contemporary science.* New York: Macmillan.

HOROWITZ, M. J., EELLS, T., SINGER, J., & SALOVEY, P. (1995). Role-relationship models of case formulation. *Archives of General Psychiatry*, 52:625–632.

JACOBSON, E. (1964). *The self and object world.* New York: International Universities Press.

JACOBSON, E. (1971) *Depression: Comparative studies of normal, neurotic and psychotic conditions.* New York: International Universities Press.

JOINER, T. E. (1994). Contagious depression: Existence, specificity to depressed symptoms, and the role of reassurance seeking. *Journal of Personality and Social Psychology*, 67:287–296.

JOINER, T. E. JR. (2000). Depression's vicious scree: Self-propagating and erosive processes in depression chronicity. *Clinical Psychology-Science and Practice*, 7:203–218.

KELLY, F. D. (1996). *Object relations assessment in younger children: Rorschach and TAT measures.* Hillside: New Jersey: Lawrence Erlbaum.

KELLY, F. D. (1997). *The assessment of object relations phenomena in adolescents: TAT and Rorschach measures.* Hillside: New Jersey: Lawrence Erlbaum.

KELLY, G. A. (1955). *The psychology of personal constructs.* New York: Norton.

KERNBERG, O. (1966). Structural derivatives of object relationships. In P. Buckley (Ed.) (1986) *Essential papers on object relationships* (pp. 350–384). New York: New York University Press.

KERNBERG, O. (1975) *Borderline conditions and pathological narcissism.* New York: Jason Aronson.

KERNBERG, O. (1984). *Object relations theory and clinical psychoanalysis.* New York: Jason Aronson.

KING, R. A. (2002). Adolescence. In M. Lewis (Ed.). *Child and adolescent psychiatry: A comprehensive textbook.* Third edition. (pp. 332–342). Philadelphia: Lippincott Williams & Wilkins.

KLEIN, G. (1976). *Psychoanalytic theory: An exploration of essentials.* New York: International Universities Press.

KLEIN, M. (1974). *The psychoanalysis of children,* New York: Dell.
KLEIN, M. (1975). *Love, guilt, and reparation.* New York: Dell.
KLERMAN, G. L., & WEISSMAN, M. M. (1992). The course, morbidity, and costs of depression. *Archives of General Psychiatry,* 49:831–834.
KOHUT, H. (1971). *The analysis of the self.* New York: International Universities Press.
KOHUT, H. (1977). *The restoration of the self.* New York: International Universities Press.
KOHUT, H. (1984). *How does analysis cure?* A. Goldberg & P. Stepansky (Eds.). Chicago: Chicago University Press.
LAKOFF, R. T., & COYNE, J. C. (1993). *Father knows best: The use and abuse of power in Freud's case of Dora.* New York: Teacher's College.
LAPLANCHE, J. & PONTALIS, J-B. (1973). *The language of psychoanalysis.* New York: Norton.
LERNER, R. M. (1982). Children and adolescents as producers of their own development. *Developmental Review,* 2:342–370.
LEVENSON, E. (1972) *The fallacy of understanding: An inquiry into the changing structure of psychoanalysis.* New York: Basic Books.
LITTLE, B. (1999). Personal projects and social ecology: Themes and variations across the life span. In J. Brandtstadter & R. M. Lerner (Eds.). *Action and self-development: Theory and research through the life span* (pp. 169–220). Thousand Oaks: Sage.
LOEWALD, H. (1960). On the therapeutic action of psychoanalysis. In G. Fogel (Ed.), *The work of Hans Loewald* (1991) (pp. 13–60). Northvale, N.J.: Jason Aronson.
LOEWALD, H. (1970). Psychoanalytic theory and psychoanalytic process. In *The essential Loewald* (2000), (pp. 277–301). Hagerstown, Md.: University Publishing Group.
LOEWALD, H. (1973). On internalization. In *The essential Loewald* (2000), (pp. 69–86). Hagerstown, Md.: University Publishing Group.
LOEWALD, H. (1975). Psychoanalysis as an art and the fantasy character of the psychoanalytic situation. In G. Fogel (Ed.), *The Work of Hans Loewald* (1991) (pp. 123–152). Northvale, N.J.: Jason Aronson.
LOEWALD, H. (1978). Instinct theory, object relationships, and psychic structure formation. In *Papers on Psychoanalysis* (1980), (pp. 207–218). New Haven: Yale University Press.
LOEWALD, H. (1979a). Reflections on the psychoanalytic process and its therapeutic potential. In *Papers on Psychoanalysis* (1980), (pp. 372–383). New Haven: Yale University Press.
LOEWALD, H. (1979b). The waning of the Oedipus complex. *Journal of the American Psychoanalytic Association,* 27:751–776.
LOEWALD, H. (1986). Transference-countertransference. *Journal of the American Psychoanalytic Association,* 34:275–389.
LOEWALD, H. (1988). Sublimation. In *The essential Loewald* (2000), (pp. 439–530). Hagerstown, Md.: University Publishing Group.
LOPEZ, D. F., & LITTLE, T. D. (1996). Children's action-control beliefs and

emotional regulation in the social domain. *Developmental Psychology*, 32:299–312.

MEICHENBAUM, D. B. (1977). *Cognitive-behavior modification: An integrative approach.* New York: Plenum.

MISCHEL, W., & SHODA, Y. (1995). A cognitive-affective system theory of personality: Reconceptualizing situations, dispositions, dynamics, and invariance in personality structure. *Psychological Review*, 102:246–268.

MITCHELL, S. (1988). *Relational concepts in psychoanalysis.* Cambridge, Mass.: Harvard University Press.

MITCHELL, S. (2000). *Relationality: From attachment to intersubjectivity.* Hillsdale, N.J.: Analytic Press.

MITCHELL, S. & BLACK, M. (1995). *Freud and beyond.* New York: Basic Books.

MODELL, A. (1984). *Psychoanalysis in a new context.* New York: International Universities Press.

MUIR, R. C. (1995). Transpersonal processes: A bridge between object relations and attachment theory in normal and psychopathological development. *British Journal of Medical Psychology*, 68:243–257.

OGDEN, T. (1994) *Subjects of analysis.* Northvale, N.J.: Jason Aronson.

PIAGET, J. (1929). *The child's conception of the world.* New York: Harcourt Brace.

PIAGET, J. (1950). *The psychology of intelligence.* New York: Harcourt Brace.

PIAGET, J. (1952). *The origins of intelligence in children.* New York: International Universities Press.

PIAGET, J. (1968). *Six psychological studies.* New York: Vintage.

PIAGET, J. (1981). *Intelligence and Affectivity.* Palo Alto, CA: Annual Reviews.

PORCERELLI, J. H., AMBRAMSKY, M. F., HIBBARD, S., & KAMOO, R. (2001). Object relations and defense mechanisms of a psychopathic serial sexual homicide perpetrator: A TAT analysis. *Journal of Personality Assessment*, 77:84–104.

PRIEL, B., MITRANI, D., & SHAHAR, G. (1998). Closeness, support and reciprocity: A study of attachment styles in adolescence. *Personality and Individual Differences*, 25:1183–1197.

REISS, D. (2000). *The relationship code: Deciphering genetic and social influences on adolescent development.* Cambridge, Mass.: Harvard University Press.

RITVO, SAMUEL. (1984). The image and uses of the body in psychic conflict: With special reference to eating disorders in adolescence. *Psychoanalytic Study of the Child*, 39:449–469.

SAMEROFF, A. J. (1995). General systems theories and developmental psychopathology. In D. Cicchetti & D. J. Cohen (Eds.), *Manual of developmental psychopathology: Theory and methods* (Vol 1, pp. 659–695). New York: Wiley.

SAMEROFF, A. J., & FIESSE, B. H. (2000). Models of development and developmental risk. In C. H. Zeanah (Ed.), *Handbook of infant mental health*, 2nd ed. New York: Guilford.

SANDLER, J. (1962). The concept of the representational world. *Psychoanalytic Study of the Child*, 17:128–145.

SANDLER, J. (1976). Countertransference and role responsiveness. *International Review of Psychoanalysis*, 3:43–48.

SANDLER, J. (1981). Unconscious wishes and human relationships. *Contemporary Psychoanalysis*, 17:180–196.

SANDLER, J., HOLDER, A., & MEERS, D. (1963). The ego ideal and the ideal self. *Psychoanalytic Study of the Child*, 18:139–158.

SANDLER, J. & SANDLER, A-M. (1978). On the developmental of object relationships and affects. In P. Buckley (Ed.), *Essential papers on object relations* (pp. 272–292) (1986). New York: New York University Press.

SCHAFER, R. (1960). The loving and beloved super-ego in Freud's structural theory. *Psychoanalytic Study of the Child*, 15:163–188.

SCHAFER, R. (1967). Ideals, the ego ideal, and the ideal self. In R. Holt (Ed.), *Motives and Thought: psychoanalytic essays in honor of David Rapaport*, (pp. 131–174). New York: International Universities Press.

SCHAFER, R. (1968). *Aspects of internalization*. New York: International Universities Press.

SCHAFER, R. (1976). *A new language for psychoanalysis*. New Haven: Yale University Press.

SCHAFER, R. (1983). *The analytic attitude*. New York: Basic Books.

SCHAFER, R. (1991). Internalizing Loewald. In G. Fogel (Ed.), *The work of Hans Loewald*, (pp. 77–90). Northvale, N.J.: Jason Aronson.

SCHARFF, D. E., & SCHARFF, J. S. (1987). *Object relations family therapy*. Northvale, New Jersey: Jason Aronson.

SEGAL, H. (1979). *Melanie Klein*. NY: Penguin.

SELIGMAN, M. E. P. (1995). The effectiveness of psychotherapy: The Consumer Report Study. *American Psychologist*, 50:965–974.

SHAHAR, G. (2001). Personality, shame, and the breakdown of social bonds: The voice of quantitative depression research. *Psychiatry: Interpersonal and biological processes*, 64:228–239.

SHAHAR, G. (in press). Transference-countertransference: Where the (political) action is. *Journal of Psychotherapy Integration*.

SHAHAR, G., CHINMAN, M., SELLS, D., & DAVIDSON, L. (2003). An action model of socially disruptive behavior among people with severe mental illness: The role of self-reported abuse and suspiciousness/hostility. *Psychiatry: Interpersonal and Biological Processes*, 66:42–52.

SHAHAR, G., & DAVIDSON, L. (in press). Depressive symptoms erode self-esteem in severe mental illness: A cross-lagged, three-wave design. *Journal of Consulting and Clinical Psychology*.

SHAHAR, G., HENRICH, C. C., BLATT, S. J., RYAN, R., & LITTLE, T. D. (2003). Interpersonal-relatedness, self-definition, and their motivational underpinnings during adolescence: A theoretical and empirical integration. *Developmental Psychology*, 39:470–483.

SLADE, A. (1999). Attachment theory and research: implications for the theory and practice of individual psychotherapy with adults. In J. Cassidy & P. R. Shaver (Eds.), (pp. 575–594), *Handbook of attachment: Theory, research, and clinical applications*. New York: Guilford.

SMITH, J. (1999). Life planning: Anticipating future life goals and managing personal development. In J. Brandtstadter & R. M. Lerner (Eds.) *Action* and self-development: Theory and research through the life span (pp. 223–255). Thousand Oaks: Sage.

STERN, D. (1985). *The interpersonal world of the infant.* New York: Basic Books.

STOLOROW, R. D. (1995). An intersubjective view of self-psychology. *Psychoanalytic Dialogues,* 5:393–400.

STOLOROW, R. D. & ATWOOD, G. (1997). Deconstructing the myth of the neutral analyst. *Psychoanalytic Quarterly,* 66:431–449.

STOLOROW, R. D., BRANDSHAFT, B., & ATWOOD, G. E. (1987). *Psychoanalytic treatment: An intersubjective Approach.* Hillsdale, N.J.: Analytic Press.

SULLIVAN, H. S. (1953). *The interpersonal theory of psychiatry.* New York: Norton.

SULLIVAN, H. S. (1962). *Schizophrenia as a human process.* New York: Norton.

SWANN, W. (1983). Self-verification: Bringing social reality into harmony with the self. In J. Suls & A. Greenwald (Eds.), *Psychological perspectives on the self* (Vol. 2). Hillsdale, N.J.: Erlbaum.

TEICHOLZ, J. (1999). *Kohut, Loewald, and the postmoderns.* Hillsdale, N.J.: Analytic Press.

VAILLANT, G. (1993). *The wisdom of the ego.* Cambridge, Mass.: Harvard University Press.

VAILLANT, G. (2000). Adaptive mental mechanisms: their role in a positive psychology. *American Psychologist,* 55:89–98.

WACHTEL, P. (1977). *Psychoanalysis and behavior therapy: Towards an integration.* New York: Basic Books.

WACHTEL, P. (1982). Vicious circles: The self and the rhetoric of emerging and unfolding. *Contemporary Psychoanalysis,* 18:273–295.

WACHTEL, P. (1993). *Therapeutic communication: Principles and effective practice.* New York: Guilford.

WACHTEL, P. (1994). Cyclical processes in psychopathology. *Journal of Abnormal Psychology,* 103:51–54.

WACHTEL, P. (1997). *Psychoanalysis, behavior therapy, and the relational world.* Washington, D.C.: American Psychological Association.

WALLERSTEIN, R. (2002). The growth and transformation of American ego psychology. *Journal of the American Psychoanalytic Association,* 50:136–168.

WERNER, H. (1948). *Comparative psychology of mental development.* New York: International Universities Press.

WESTEN, D. (1991). Social cognition and object relations. *Psychological Bulletin,* 109:429–455.

WESTEN, D. (1998). The scientific legacy of Sigmund Freud: Toward a psychodynamically informed psychological science. *Psychological Bulletin,* 124:333–371.

WESTEN, D., KLEPSER, J., RUFFINS, S. A., SILVERMAN, M., LIFTON, N., & BOEKAMP, J. (1991). Object relations in childhood and adolescence: The development of working representations. *Journal of Consulting & Clinical Psychology,* 59:400–409.

WINNICOTT, D. W. (1950–1955). Aggression in relation to emotional development. In *Through pediatrics to psychoanalysis* (1975) (pp. 204–218). New York: Basic Books.

WINNICOTT, D. W. (1951). Transitional objects and transitional phenomena. In *Through pediatrics to psychoanalysis* (1975) (pp. 229–242). New York: Basic Books.

WINNICOTT, D. W. (1952). Anxiety associated with insecurity. In *Through pediatrics to psychoanalysis,* (1975). (pp. 97–100). New York: Basic Books.

WINNICOTT, D. W. (1959). The fate of the transitional object. In *Psychoanalytic explorations* (1989) (pp. 53–58), Cambridge, Mass.: Harvard University Press.

WINNICOTT, D. W. (1969). Contributions to a symposium on envy and jealousy. In *Psychoanalytic explorations,* (1989), (pp. 462–464). Cambridge, Mass.: Harvard University Press.

WINNICOTT, D. W. (1988). *Human nature.* New York: Schocken Books.

WINNICOTT, D. W. & KHAN, M. M. (1953). Review of Psychoanalytic studies of the Personality (W. Fairbairn). In *Psychoanalytic explorations* (1989, pp. 413–422). Cambridge, Mass.: Harvard University Press.

WOLFF, P. (1960). The developmental psychologies of Jean Piaget and psychoanalysis. *Psychological Issues, 2.*

YALOM, I. D. (1980). *Existential psychotherapy.* New York: Basic Books.

The Sense of Self in
Anorexia-Nervosa Patients

A Psychoanalytically Informed Method
for Studying Self-Representation

SUSAN A. BERS, PH.D., SIDNEY J. BLATT,
PH.D., ABPP, and ANN DOLINSKY, M.D.

This paper has two purposes: to study a central psychological feature of anorexia nervosa, the disturbed sense of self, and to demonstrate the utility of an empirical research method to explore a psychoanalytic concept such as self-representation. The aim of the study was to distinguish the sense of self of anorexia-nervosa patients from that of other psychiatric patients, as well as from non-patients. We obtained open-ended self-descriptions, which provide access to self-representations, from 77 young women between the ages of 14 and 24 who made up three groups—anorexia-nervosa patients (n = 15), control psychiatric patients (n = 15), and control non-patients (n = 48). The self-descriptions, when rated on 18 scales that fell into four factors

Susan A. Bers is Assistant Clinical Professor, Department of Psychiatry, Yale University; Staff Clinical Psychologist, Yale University Health Services; and Faculty, Western New England Institute for Psychoanalysis. Sidney J. Blatt is Professor, Departments of Psychiatry and Psychology, Yale University; and Faculty, Western New England Institute for Psychoanalysis. Ann Dolinsky is Assistant Clinical Professor of Psychiatry, Columbia University College of Physicians and Surgeons; and Faculty, Columbia University Center for Psychoanalytic Training and Research.

This paper was presented as a poster at the American Psychoanalytic Association Winter Meeting in January 2004 where it received the 2004 American Psychoanalytic Association Poster Session Award.

The Psychoanalytic Study of the Child 59, ed. Robert A. King, Peter B. Neubauer, Samuel Abrams, and A. Scott Dowling (Yale University Press, copyright © 2004 by Robert A. King, Peter B. Neubauer, Samuel Abrams, and A. Scott Dowling.)

(Agency, Reflectivity, Differentiation, and Relatedness) and two af-
fective scales (Anxiety and Depression), showed that the two patient
groups shared characteristics that significantly differentiated them
from women who were not patients—a lower sense of agency and re-
latedness. What significantly differentiated the anorexia-nervosa pa-
tients from the other psychiatric patients, as well as from the non-
patients, were a heightened and harsh self-reflectivity and more openly
expressed depressive and anxious affect in the self-descriptions. The
implications for treatment and for understanding eating disorders
are discussed.

RESEARCHERS AND CLINICIANS FROM DIVERGENT PERSPECTIVES HAVE
come to view patients with eating disorders as fundamentally having
disorders of the self. In 1980, Sours wrote of some of these patients,
"Their primary disturbance is the perception of the self, not simply
that of the body" (p. 343). Significant problems with self-esteem and
self-perception, ego deficits, a failure to achieve autonomy, as well as
impaired perception of the body, appear to characterize individuals
with a variety of eating disorders from severe forms (anorexia nervosa and bulimia nervosa) to subclinical varieties (e.g. Lerner, 1993;
Vitousek and Ewald, 1993). This paper has two purposes: to study a
central psychological feature of anorexia nervosa, the disturbed
sense of self, and to demonstrate the utility of an empirical research
method to explore a psychoanalytic concept such as self-representation.

Bruch (1962, 1973, 1978, 1988) identified a paralyzing underlying
sense of ineffectiveness and helplessness, as well as a profound lack
of self-esteem, in these patients. At the end of a long career devoted
to the study and treatment of eating-disorder patients, Bruch wrote:

> Deep down, every anorexic is convinced that basically she is inade-
> quate, low, mediocre, inferior, and despised by others. . . . All her ef-
> forts, her striving for perfection and excessive thinness, are directed
> toward hiding the fatal flaw of her fundamental inadequacy. . . . They
> [anorexic patients] feel they have found, in their extreme thinness,
> the perfect solution to all their problems, that it makes them feel bet-
> ter and helps them to attain the respect and admiration they have
> yearned for all their lives. (1988, pp. 6–8)

Goodsitt (1977, 1985), Sugarman, Quinlan, and Devenis (1982), and
Casper, Offer, and Ostrov (1981) emphasized the centrality of the
self-system and the representational world in understanding eating
disorders. Swift and Wonderlich (1988) have delineated the disorders of self-definition and self-regulation observed in these patients.

For example, anorexia-nervosa patients attempt to achieve moral and ascetic perfection through extreme self-negation. Even in mild varieties of eating disorders, identity issues predominate, self-esteem is fragile, self-perception is often fragmented, and self-representations lack cohesion, continuity, strength, and harmony (Lerner, 1993). These formulations focus on the eating-disorder patient's inner experience of herself and others.

Drawing on clinical impressions, many writers have speculated on the psychodynamic causes of the psychopathology of eating-disordered patients. Aronson (1993) found a variety of theories about the genesis of these disorders: conflicts around sexuality (Falstein, Sherman, Feinstein, and Judas, 1956), separation-individuation difficulties (Bruch, 1962; Selvini Palazzoli, 1963/1974), the mother's narcissistic issues and inhibitory response to the female child (Sours, 1980), the child's lack of control and autonomy (Wilson and Mintz, 1982), the absence of a soothing, calming parental presence (Goodsitt, 1983; Sugarman et al., 1982), and failures in empathic connectedness (Geist, 1985). Others have emphasized the defensive function of eating-disorder pathology, for example, as an expression of wishes, aims, and conflicts relating to the object (Ritvo, 1980), a mask for feelings (Bemporad and Ratey, 1985), a response to low affect tolerance (McDougall, 1989), or a manic defense against the depressive position (Joseph, 1982; Lawrence, 2001). Rather than focus on causation, the present study explores a central aspect of that pathology—the experience of the disturbed sense of self, in particular, of patients hospitalized with severe cases of anorexia nervosa. We use an empirical research methodology that articulates the experience of self, a psychological dimension of these disorders, and we hope to provide an example of how research on aspects of the representational world (Sandler and Rosenblatt, 1962) can elucidate clinical phenomena and psychoanalytic constructs.

Though clinical observations of eating disorders clearly point to problems in self-esteem and self-concept as a central aspect of these disturbances, relatively little empirical research has been conducted on the topic. The few empirical studies in this area have generally used poorly operationalized variables to capture and assess the sense of self. Furthermore, disturbances in self-experience are found in many psychiatric disorders. Therefore, if a disturbed sense of self is fundamental to the development, expression, and treatment of eating disorders, it is crucial to delineate the distortions in the sense of self unique to eating disorders as compared to other psychiatric disturbances. Whereas the difference in identity issues between eating-disorder patients and normal adolescent and young adults seems relatively clear, surprisingly the difference between their experiences of self as compared to other psychiatric patients has barely been explored in empirical research or theory. For example, many empirical studies in this area have not compared eating-disorder patients with other psychiatric patients.

In an attempt to remedy these methodological problems, Bers and Quinlan (1992) compared inpatients with anorexia nervosa to both control inpatients and normal controls on a new measure of "ineffectiveness," a self-perception that Bruch (1962, 1978) identified as basic to the experience of the sense of self of anorexia-nervosa patients—that is, a lack of appreciation of their own resources, a lack of confidence in their initiative, an inability to recognize their accomplishments and capabilities, and a feeling that they are not competent to lead a life of their own. Bers and Quinlan found that a disparity between a high interest in various activities and a low perceived ability in these activities significantly differentiated anorexia-nervosa patients from other psychiatric patients of similar age and severity of illness, as well as from normal subjects. This measure of ineffectiveness, "perceived-competence deficit," appeared to capture an important aspect of the impaired self-esteem of anorexia-nervosa patients—the combination of extreme self-criticism and feelings of incompetence so commonly observed in and described by these patients, sometimes even in the presence of lively interests, aspirations, and recognized accomplishments (e.g., Daniels, 2001).

Further empirical investigation of the phenomenology of the anorexia-nervosa patient's sense of self is the subject of the present study. We explored the experience of the sense of self with self-descriptions, a procedure that prior research (Blatt and Bers, 1987, 1993; Diamond, Kaslow, Coonerty, and Blatt, 1990; Bers, Blatt, Sayward, and Johnston, 1993) has indicated is an effective way to systematically assess various important aspects of the sense of self. Three groups of adolescent and young adult females (anorexia-nervosa inpatients, control psychiatric inpatients, and control non-patients) were asked to describe themselves. We assumed, consistent with psychoanalytic assumptions about the interpretation of projective techniques and about the treatment process, that reflections and associations in verbal reports, such as self-descriptions, can provide access to both conscious and unconscious aspects of the representational world.

Studies of development and pathology have increasingly explored representational structures in the functioning of the mind, in psychopathology, and in therapeutic processes. As Blatt and Auerbach (2000) point out, Freud's structural model of the mind (1923/1961), which focused on the balance among the three primary psychic agencies—ego, id, and superego—initiated a broad development in psychoanalytic theory, viz. ego psychology. Hartmann's (1939/1958) adaptive model of the mind was derived from Freud's structural model and emphasized ego functions and processes of adaptation. These emphases on ego functions were eventually extended to an interest in object (and interpersonal) relations as a particularly important dimension of adaptation and of ego functions themselves (A. Freud 1936/1937, 1965; Jacobson, 1964; Mahler, Pine, and Bergman, 1975). Using concepts from developmental-cognitive and psychoanalytic theories, Blatt and colleagues developed several procedures for assessing aspects of mental representations by evaluating the structure and content of descriptions of self and significant others (e.g., Blatt, Chevron, Quinlan, Schaffer, and Wein, 1988; Diamond et al., 1990; Blatt, Bers, and Schaffer, 1993). In this approach, the thematic content and the cognitive-structural organization of self-representations are studied through open-ended self-descriptions that depict the subjects' sense of themselves.

In earlier research in this area, we developed procedures (Blatt and Bers, 1987) for identifying and rating dimensions of self-descriptions which attempted to delineate disturbances in the self-representations of seriously disturbed patients, as well as more adaptive and constructive aspects. With these procedures, we were able to differentiate significantly the self-descriptions of patients from those of non-patients on dimensions of agency, relatedness, affect, developmental level, and differentiation. Patients' self-descriptions, compared to those of non-patients, lacked a sense of both striving and relatedness, were more negative, expressed moderately more depressive feelings, were at a lower cognitive-developmental level, and used fewer dimensions (Bers et al., 1993). Previous studies have also found that changes in a patient's self-description over time (a more positive and effective self-view; more references to affect, relatedness, and agency; more differentiation; and the use of more dimensions to describe the self) corresponded to independently assessed indications of clinical progress (Bers et al., 1993; Blatt, Stayner, Auerbach, and Behrends, 1996; Blatt, Wiseman, Prince-Gibson, and Gatt, 1991; Diamond et al., 1990; Gruen and Blatt, 1990).

In the present study, we used an expanded version (Blatt et al., 1993) of the scales originally developed by Blatt and Bers (1987) to assess descriptions of the self. We applied this expanded version of our rating system to the self-descriptions of anorexia-nervosa inpatients and two control groups of patients and non-patients. The aims of the study were (1) to identify aspects of the sense of self unique to anorexia-nervosa patients, in order to distinguish these patients from other psychiatric patients; and (2) to identify those aspects of the sense of self shared by anorexia-nervosa patients and other psychiatric patients, in order to distinguish patients in general from non-patients.

METHOD

SUBJECTS

Seventy-seven single adolescent females, aged 14 to 24 (M = 18.3 years) participated in this study. The anorexia-nervosa-patient (n = 15) and control-patient (n = 15) groups were all psychiatric inpatients at one of three hospitals in the northeastern United States. The nonclinical-control volunteers (n = 47) were from a suburban high school and a nearby university, and were matched on age with the two clinical groups (Bers and Quinlan, 1992).

The anorexia-nervosa and control patients were selected by a member of the hospital staff because they met criteria for one of the two groups. An investigator confirmed the diagnosis of anorexia nervosa during interviews and confirmed the diagnoses of the control patients by reviewing their medical charts. Ten percent of the patients declined to participate: 3 of 18 anorexia-nervosa patients and none of the 15 control patients. The three anorexia-nervosa patients did not differ significantly from those who participated on degree of weight loss, age, or socioeconomic status.

Anorexia-nervosa-patient group. Fifteen hospitalized young women in the anorexia-nervosa-patient group (mean age of 18.2 years, range of 15 to 24 years) met criteria for a diagnosis of anorexia nervosa as specified by the Diagnostic and Statistical Manual of Mental Disorders (third edition; DSM-III; American Psychiatric Association, 1980) with the addition of Garfinkel and Garner's (1982) recommendation to include individuals who weighed 15 percent or more below the expected weight for their height and age. All of these women scored above the 20-point cutoff on the Eating Attitudes Test (Eat-26; Garner, Olmsted, Bohr, and Garfinkel, 1982), which measures disturbed eating patterns.

Because the anorexia-nervosa patients varied in their level of ability to function during the acute phase of their illness, they participated at different points in their hospitalization. The average age at onset of illness was 14.9 years (range of 12 to 18 years) and the average length of the illness was 2.9 years (range of 6 months to 10 years). The average number of hospitalizations for the anorexia-nervosa group (including the present hospitalization) was 3.2 (range of 1 to 10 times) and the average length of their current hospitalization was 105 days (range of 28 to 415 days). Their average SES (calculated by highest SES of a parent; Hollingshead, 1957) was 1.87, ranging from Class I (upper) to class III (middle). All of the anorexia-nervosa subjects were white.

Control-patient group. Fifteen hospitalized young women in the control-patient group (mean age of 17.3 years, range of 15 to 23 years) met the following criteria: a) never had an eating disorder, b) scored below the 20-point cutoff on the Eat-26, and c) their weight was between 15 percent above and 15 percent below that expected for their height and age. In order to control for severity of illness, none of these patients had a history, or current diagnosis, of a psychosis or an organic brain syndrome. The diagnoses of the control patients assigned by the hospital staff included: adjustment, substance abuse, dysthymic, somatization, conduct, identity, and oppositional disorders.

The average age of onset of illness for the control patients was 14.1 years (range of 11 to 18 years) and the average length of the illness was 3.0 years (range of 3 months to 11 years). They had been hospitalized an average of 1.3 times including the present hospitalization (range of 1 to 2 times); and the average length of the present hospitalization was 61 days (range of 34 to 89 days). The average SES for the clinical controls' families was 2.60, ranging from class I (upper) to class IV (lower-middle class). All of the control patients were white.

Control non-patient group. The control-non-patient group consisted of 47 young women with a mean age of 18.6 years (range of 14 to 24 years) who were recruited from a public high school and a private university. The high school students ($n = 14$) were selected randomly from class lists. A letter describing the project and a consent form were mailed to each student's parents or guardian. The return rate was 26 percent. The college students ($n = 33$) were drawn from an introductory psychology course or recruited from an advertisement in the university community. All these women weighed between 15 percent above and 15 percent below their ideal weight for height and age, and scored below the 20-point cutoff on the Eat-26. The average SES of their families was 2.13, ranging from class I (upper class) to class V (lower class). Seven of the non-patient subjects belonged to ethnic minority groups.

The control-patient and the anorexia-nervosa-patient groups did not differ significantly on age, IQ, level of education, SES of the family, height, age of onset of the illness, length of illness, number of hospitalizations, length of the present hospitalization, and DSM-III Axis V (American Psychiatric Association, 1980), which assesses the highest level of functioning over the past year.

The Assessment of Self Descriptions. The manual for scoring self-descriptions (Blatt et al., 1993) was based on an earlier version (Blatt and Bers, 1987), which was revised to assess a broader range of self-descriptions including clinical as well as nonclinical subjects. This study used scales from this revised manual that assess seven categories of dimensions of self-descriptions:

(1) *Modes of Description.* Three scales assess the different modes used to describe the self, that is, physical and demographic aspects, behavioral qualities, personality features, and inner thoughts, feelings, and values. "Predominant Mode" indicates which of these modes occurred most often in the description. "Substantiality" indicates how many modes were included and integrated in the description. The descriptions of the self were also rated on the highest "Conceptual Level," of the self-description based on developmental-psychological (Piaget, 1954/37; Werner, 1948) and psychoanalytic theory (Blatt, 1974; Blatt et al., 1988).

(2) *Sense of Relatedness.* Two scales assess references to relatedness to others: "Articulation of Relationships," and "Quality of Relationships."

(3) *Cognitive Variables.* Three scales assess cognitive aspects of the self-description: "Self-Reflectivity," "Tolerance of Contradictory Aspects of the Self," and "Differentiation and Integration."

(4) *Self View.* Three scales assess global self-esteem, sense of confidence and strength, and sense of agency: "Negative/Positive Self-Regard," "Self-Critical," and "Striving/Ambitious."

(5) *Developmental Variables.* Four developmental scales: "Level of Relatedness," "Level of Self-Definition," "Balance," and "Integrity" assess the level of relatedness to others, the level of self-definition, and

sense of integrity along a continuum of development. The scale "Balance" assesses whether themes of relatedness or of agency predominate in the self-description.

(6) *Affective Variables.* Two scales assess the extent to which the individual makes references to Anxiety or Depression in the self-description.

(7) *Length.* The length of the description, or verbal fluency, was estimated on a seven-point scale.

These seven apriori categories of scales could have substantial overlap and correlation. Therefore, to delineate dimensions of the self-descriptions in a more parsimonious way, a statistical method called factor analysis was used to reveal underlying commonalities and differences among the self-description scales. A factor analysis was performed on these scales using the scores of 171 nonclinical males and females, and yielded four clear and interpretable factors labeled Agency, Reflectivity, Differentiation, and Relatedness (Blatt et al., 1993). Anxiety and Depression were excluded from the factor analysis because they were less stable (possibly mood dependent) aspects of the sense of self and were used as separate scales in subsequent analyses.

Factor I, Agency, included Negative-Positive Self-Regard, Level of Self-Definition, Integrity, and Striving/Ambitious. Factor II, Reflectivity, included Self-Reflectivity, Conceptual Level, Predominant Mode, Tolerance of Contradictory Aspects, and Self-Critical. Factor III, Differentiation, included Substantiality, Differentiation/Integration, and Length. Factor IV, Relatedness, included Level of Relatedness, Articulation of Relationships, Quality of Relatedness, and Balance. Table 1 shows the self-description factors and scales used in this study with more detailed definitions of the scales.

Two judges independently rated the self-descriptions of 20 subjects, including a proportional number from each group. Interrater reliabilities (Pearson *r*) were at an acceptable level for all 18 scales, ranging from .67 to .95. Then one of these judges rated the self-descriptions of all 77 subjects on each of the 18 scales. Factor scores were computed by adding the scores of each subject on scales composing each factor.

Measure of intelligence. The Similarities subtest of the Wechsler Adult Intelligence Scale-Revised (WAIS-R; Wechsler, 1981) or the Wechsler Intelligence Scale for Children-Revised (WISC-R; Wechsler, 1974) was used as an estimate of intelligence (IQ). This subtest is less reflective of academic experience than others (Allison, Blatt, and Zimet, 1968), and thus may be less impacted by school difficulties that

Table 1: Self-Description Scales and Factors

Factor I: Agency

A. *Negative-Positive Self-Regard:* the extent to which the self-view is critical, harshly judgmental, neglectful, and hateful (1), versus benevolent, accepting, caring, and positive (7).

B. *Level of Self-Definition:* the degree to which the description expresses a clearly defined identity with particular goals and values, on a developmental scale ranging from (1) a lack of articulation, and/or annihilation or fragmentation, to (3) an emerging sense of self, to (7) a more internal definition, to (9) an identity which enables the person to articulate values and establish future plans.

C. *Integrity:* the degree to which the self-description is characterized by a sense of integrity, from (1) a psychic deadness, inner void, and depersonalization, to (5) an emerging ability to sense one's inner continuity and identity, to (9) an emotional integration, cohesiveness, and satisfaction with one's life through both agency and relatedness.

D. *Striving-Ambitious:* the degree of strivings for accomplishment, drivenness, or investment in achieving in areas of one's choice, from (1) non-striving, to (5) strongly striving (no mention of striving received a score at the midpoint, 3).

Factor II: Reflectivity

A. *Self-Reflectivity:* the degree to which the self description itself is introspective and self-reflective, from (1) no introspection to (5) much introspection and reflection on one's subjective experiences perhaps including how one is perceived and experienced by others.

B. *Conceptual Level:* the highest developmental level ranging from global, amorphous descriptions based on action sequences and need gratification (1), to more differentiated descriptions emphasizing part properties (5), and finally to highly articulated, integrated, and complex forms of descriptions which include feelings, thoughts, and values (9).

C. *Predominant Mode:* an indication of which mode of representation is given greatest emphasis, (1) physical/demographic, (2) behavioral, (3) personality traits, and (4) inner feelings, thoughts, and values.

D. *Tolerance of Contradictory Aspects:* the extent of contradictory and opposing aspects of the self and the ability to integrate them, from (1) unidimensional, to (5) diverse and contradictory elements accepted comfortably as part of the personality.

E. *Self-Critical:* the intensity and pervasiveness of evaluations and harsh judgments that reflect dissatisfaction with oneself, from (1) non-critical, to (5) highly critical and driven by standards which one is not meeting.

Factor III: Differentiation

A. *Substantiality:* the extent of the inclusion and integration of four modes of representation (see Predominant Mode), from (1) a flat sense of self with one or

(continued)

Table 1: (*continued*)

two modes included, to (4) a multidimensional description with an integration of all four modes.

B. *Differentiation and Integration:* capacity to view and understand the self across multiple domains, from (1) one domain, to (7) six or more domains which are highly integrated.

C. *Length:* verbal fluency using a seven-point scale to estimate the number of words used.

Factor IV: Relatedness

A. *Level of Relatedness:* the degree to which portrayed relationships are characterized by mutuality, reciprocity, and empathy on a developmental scale from (1) fused, to (4) one-sided, to (8) mutual, reciprocal, enduring, and intimate (no mention of relationships received a score at the midpoint, 4.5).

B. *Articulation of Relationships:* the extent to which people are mentioned in terms of relationships, from (1) no explicit mention of others, to (5) a particular relationship is described with specificity and elaboration.

C. *Quality of Relatedness:* a reflection of the quality of feelings toward and perceptions of others, from (1) cold and negative, to (7) warm and positive (no mention of others received a score at midpoint, 4).

D. *Balance Between Relatedness and Self-Definition:* the predominance of either themes of relatedness (1) or of self-definition (2).

Affective Scales (not part of the Factor Analysis)

A. *Anxiety:* the extent of references to tension, apprehension, fears, worry, and anxiety about the self, others, and life in general, from (1) no anxiety, to (5) severe, incapacitation anxiety.

B. *Depression:* the extent of references to sad, pathetic feelings about the self, others, and life in general, from (1) no depression, to (5) severe depression, possibly including suicidal thoughts and impulses.

---

clinical controls may have had and by the over achievement characteristic of many anorexia-nervosa patients (Bruch, 1978; Selvini Palazzoli, 1963/1974).

Measure of disordered eating behavior. The EAT-26 (Garner et al., 1982), an abbreviated 26-item version of the Eating Attitudes Test (Garner and Garfinkel, 1979), was used to measure the presence of disturbed eating patterns. A cutoff score of 20 was suggested by Garner et al. (1982), above which eating patterns are disturbed.

PROCEDURE

Each participant was interviewed individually, first gathering demographic information, weight history, and (for patients) a brief psychiatric history. For anorexia-nervosa patients, the diagnosis assigned by the hospital staff was confirmed by the interviewer using a series of diagnostic questions from the anorexia nervosa section of the Kiddie-Schedule for Affective Disorders and Schizophrenia-E (Gammon, John, Rostblum, Mullen, Tischler, and Weissman, 1983; Orvashel, Puig-Antich, Chambers, Tabrizi, and Johnson, 1982). All subjects were then asked to describe themselves, and their answers were recorded verbatim. If participants asked questions about the task, they were encouraged to describe themselves in whatever way they wished. Subjects were stopped after 15 minutes if they had not already finished. Table 2 presents prototypic self-descriptions of three subjects one from each group, an anorexia-nervosa patient, a control patient, and a control non-patient. Table 3 shows the scores on the four factors and two affective variables for these three subjects' self-descriptions.

In the final part of the interview, the Similarities subtest of the WAIS-R or WISC-R was administered and participants filled out the EAT 26.

RESULTS

DEMOGRAPHIC VARIABLES AND EATING-DISORDER SYMPTOMS

Group differences in demographic variables and symptoms of eating disorders were assessed with one-way analyses of variance (ANOVAs) followed by post hoc comparisons of the means using the Newman-Keuls test. Table 4 shows the means of the three groups on these variables and the results of these analyses.

As designed, no significant differences were found among the three groups in age, IQ, years of education, and SES of their families. Although the three groups were also not significantly different in height, anorexia-nervosa patients were significantly lower in percentage of expected weight for age and height at the time of the interview and in their lowest weight in the past compared with the two control groups. Also anorexia-nervosa patients' scores on the EAT-26 were significantly higher than the scores of the two control groups. These findings are consistent with the classification of the groups according to criteria and related variables.

Table 2: Examples of Self-Descriptions

Anorexia-Nervosa Patient

I've been depressed all my life. I have no self-esteem. I hate myself. I don't think I'm good enough. I don't think I can meet up to my brothers' achievements. I don't tell anyone how I'm feeling. I punish myself a lot. I don't feel I have any good qualitites even though people tell me I have a lot. I talk to myself a lot, like a repeated ritual, like whenever I eat or do something wrong, I say I hate myself over and over again. I drive myself very hard with little sleep and little food. I have to keep working and doing things. When I'm out in school and out in public, I act totally different and no one knows I'm depressed. My parents just found out that nobody knows anything about me. I don't know. I don't think I'm good at anything. That's it.

Control Patient

Describe myself? That's really hard. You mean what I look like? That's really hard. Artistic, Musical to a point. That's so weird. I don't know. I can't think of what I am. That's hard. Ordinary. Oh, no, I don't know. Nothing comes to mind. I don't dress like anybody I know. Like I don't look like anybody I know. But I'm not especially different from anybody I know. I'm not special or anything. A lot of people say I'm really cold—that's what they tell me. I like watching people. I would probably rather listen than talk, and I don't know. I don't think I think about myself that much. I like being with people and not talking, and I definitely don't like talking about myself.

Control Non-Patient

What I look like? I'm 5'4." I have brown hair and light green eyes. I go to _____ High. I'm really shy. I have plenty of friends though. I just moved from _____. I don't know. My best friends's C. I live in a wee house. I get pretty good grades in school. I'm pretty good friends with my parents. My favorite holiday is the 4th of July. My favorite food is pork roast. My favorite TV show is *General Hospital.* Madonna is my favorite singer. I like to listen to music and I love to dance. I've been to gymnastics and dance for 4 years. Do we have to fill up this whole thing? You're going to write that down! Lots of times I like to read. I miss the kids back in _____. This week I'm going to Great Adventure. My favorite subject is English. That's about it.

SELF-DESCRIPTIONS

Differences among the three groups on the four Self-Description Factors (Agency, Reflectivity, Differentiation, and Relatedness) and the two Affective Scales (Anxiety and Depression) were assessed with one-way analyses of variance (ANOVAs) followed by post hoc comparisons of the means using the Newman-Keuls test. Table 5 shows

Table 3: Scores on Factors and Affective Variables for Three Example Subjects

Factors and Variables (range)	Anorexia-Nervosa Patient	Control Patient	Control Non-Patient
Factor I: Agency (12–25)	14	14	21
Factor II: Reflectivity (8–25)	19	12	12
Factor III: Differentiation (5–16)	10	10	14
Factor IV: Relatedness (3–17)	7	7	15
Anxiety (1–5)	2	1	1
Depression (1–5)	4	1	1

the means of the three groups on these factors and scales with the results of these analyses.

The findings for the self-descriptions are outlined below; their implications will be elaborated in the Discussion Section to follow. The anorexia-nervosa patients and the control-psychiatric patients shared two dimensions of the self-descriptions on which they differed significantly from the non-patients. The two patient groups expressed significantly lower levels of Agency and Relatedness in their self-descriptions than the non-patient group.

The anorexia-nervosa patients differed significantly from the other psychiatric patients, as well as from the non-patients, in three ways. The anorexia-nervosa patients' self-descriptions showed significantly higher levels of Reflectivity, Anxiety, and Depression than the self-descriptions of the two control groups.

No significant differences among the three groups were found on the Differentiation factor. However, the factor scores for Differentiation, shown in Table 3 for the three example subjects, suggest a trend for Differentiation to distinguish the self-descriptions of the two patient groups from those of the non-patients: the two example patients are low on Differentiation compared to the example non-patient.

DISCUSSION

Based on our analyses of the self-descriptions of young women, we were able to delineate statistically significant differences in the sense

Table 4: Mean Scores and Standard Deviations on Classifying Variables for Anorexia-Nervosa Patients and Two Control Groups

Variable (range)	Anorexia-Nervosa Patients ($n = 15$)		Control Patients ($n = 15$)		Control Non-Patients ($n = 47$)		$F(2,74)$
	M	SD	M	SD	M	SD	
Age (years; 14.16–24.6)	18.17	(2.27)	17.29	(1.96)	18.60	(2.57)	1.68
WAIS-R or WISC-R, Similarities Subtest (7–17)	12.20	(1.70)	11.00	(2.59)	11.83	(2.12)	1.28
Level of Education (years; 9–17)	12.07	(1.62)	11.20	(1.42)	12.72	(2.47)	2.92
SES[1] (1–5)	1.87	(0.83)	2.60	(1.12)	2.13	(1.13)	1.81
Height (feet; 4.90–5.90)	5.35	(0.25)	5.36	(0.22)	5.43	(0.23)	0.82
Weight (%; 57.6–114.4)[2]	79.00[a]	(11.00)	98.00[b]	(6.00)	100.00[b]	(7.00)	39.70*
Lowest weight (%; 54.40–108.20)[2]	67.00[a]	(8.63)	91.00[b]	(7.36)	93.00[b]	(6.10)	82.79*
EAT-26 (0–60)	44.93[a]	(11.80)	6.27[b]	(5.15)	6.04[b]	(4.78)	199.79*

[a,b] Means sharing a common superscript do not differ significantly from each other using Newman-Keuls tests. WAIS-R = Wechsler Adult Intelligence Scale-Revised; WISC-R = Wechsler Intelligence Scale for Children-Revised; SES = Socioeconomic Status; EAT = Eating Attitudes Test.
[1]On the basis of Hollingshead (1957): 1 = upper class; 5 = lower class.
[2]Percentage of weight expected for subject's height and age (Metropolitan Life Insurance Company, 1983).
*$p < .001$.

of self between patients and a normal control group, as well as between inpatients with anorexia nervosa and a general, psychiatric-inpatient sample. This empirical investigation of the representational world of seriously disturbed inpatients with anorexia nervosa provides further understanding of important aspects of eating disorders and their treatment.

The sense of self of the psychiatric patients in this study, both anorexic and a general psychiatric sample, shared characteristics that distinguished them from young women who were not patients. These two patient groups, which were matched on demographic character-

ble 5: Mean Scores and Standard Deviations on Self-Description Factors and Affective riables for Anorexia-Nervosa Patients and Two Control Groups

ctors and riables (range)	Anorexia-Nervosa Patients (n = 15)		Control Patients (n = 15)		Control Non-Patients (n = 47)		$F(2,74)$
	M	SD	M	SD	M	SD	
ctor 1: zency (12–25)	15.98[a]	(2.58)	16.00[a]	(2.48)	19.32[b]	(2.54)	16.03**
ctor 2: eflectivity (8–25)	18.53[a]	(4.17)	15.13[b]	(3.70)	15.74[b]	(3.19)	4.44*
ctor 3: ifferentiation (5–16)	10.47	(2.03)	9.73	(2.60)	11.34	(2.61)	2.55
ctor 4: elatedness (3–17)	6.77[a]	(2.28)	7.63[a]	(2.69)	10.26[b]	(3.53)	8.73**
nxiety (1–5)	2.73[a]	(0.80)	1.87[b]	(1.06)	1.53[b]	(0.78)	11.61**
epression (1–5)	2.00[a]	(1.00)	1.40[b]	(0.63)	1.40[b]	(0.68)	3.89*

ᵇ Means sharing a common superscript do not differ significantly from each other in ewman-Keuls tests.
ᵇ < .05.   **p. < .001.

istics and other aspects of their psychiatric disorders besides eating-disorder symptoms, described themselves with less sense of Agency than non-patients—that is, with less investment or direction in chosen areas, a more negative, fragmented self-regard lacking confidence, a relatively unarticulated sense of self, and more despair over defining or becoming the person they wanted to be. The self-descriptions of both clinical groups were also similar in that both contained low levels of Relatedness, indicating more isolation and emotional detachment from others or dependency on others, a feeling of rejection or being judged by others, and a lack of interest in issues of interpersonal relatedness. In addition, we found a trend in which the self-descriptions of the two patient groups were less differentiated than those of the non-clinical group. These results are consistent with previous findings of Bers et al. (1993) who found that patients' self-descriptions, compared to those of non-patients, were more negative, expressed more depressive feelings and less sense of effectiveness, lacked a sense of relatedness, and were less articulated in that they were based on fewer dimensions.

Beyond these findings, it is the differentiation of anorexia-nervosa patients from other psychiatric patients (as well as from non-patients) that provides important insight into aspects of anorexia nervosa. Anorexia-nervosa patients had a heightened Reflectivity, indicating more self-reflection, a less concrete and more internal focus, and an ideational style which was more contradictory and evaluative, containing harsh judgments of the self. While all the psychiatric patients had a negative view of themselves, the negative self-view of the anorexia-nervosa patients occurred in the context of intense self-scrutiny. Their heightened self-reflectivity was accompanied by depressive and anxious affect that was openly expressed in the self-descriptions. These distinguishing dimensions were unique to the sense of self of the anorexia-nervosa patients, and, therefore, appear to be a core issue in their disorder. Anorexia-nervosa patients appear to be engaged in a desperate struggle to feel adequate, worthy, and effective, but in a way that leaves them feeling even more inadequate, unworthy, and ineffective.

Some tolerance of depressive affect in self-descriptions has been found to correlate with signs of progress during the treatment of psychiatric patients; namely, as behavioral expressions of depression decreased, there was a marked increase in the expression of depression in the patient's self-descriptions (Bers et al., 1993; Blatt and Bers, 1993; Blatt et al., 1996). Yet, the sense of self in the anorexia-nervosa patients studied here was colored, and even flooded, with intense negative feelings. In contrast to a capacity for reflection on the self generally found in young women, the high level of "Reflectivity" in the anorexia-nervosa patients pointed to an unmodulated self-reflectivity, a reflectivity gone seriously awry, with a critical, negative, and driven quality.

Although the anorexia-nervosa patients were engaged in an intense pursuit of thinness and a preoccupation with appearance and weight, concrete or physical descriptors and an external focus did *not* dominate their self-descriptions. Instead, the anorexia-nervosa patients displayed an internal focus in the sense of self which provides evidence that the pathology of anorexia nervosa goes beyond the physical and that there are deeper underpinnings to the sense of self of patients with anorexia nervosa than an inaccurate perception of body image or an exaggerated drive for thinness. The anorexia-nervosa patient's treatment of and attitude to her body, the symptoms which make up the DSM criteria for anorexia nervosa (American Psychiatric Association, 1980), then, could be conceptualized as concretization of the self-loathing, endless dissatisfaction, and punishing stance that she takes toward herself.

The findings of this study lead to further questions and point to future research in this area. Do these characteristics of the sense of self pertain only to these severe cases of anorexia nervosa, or would studies of groups other than hospitalized anorexia-nervosa patients—patients with different forms and severity of eating disorders—show similar results? Both replications of these results and similar studies with other eating-disordered patients would be useful. We would expect to find evidence of the same harshly negative and intensely self-scrutinizing sense of self in other forms of eating disorders, as these disorders have been increasingly viewed along a continuum with many patients routinely moving from one form to another (Zerbe, 1992). Longitudinal studies of anorexia-nervosa patients, and other eating-disordered patients, could provide some evidence for other questions: Are the characteristics of the anorexia-nervosa patient's self-descriptions found here a result of the severe, chronic state these hospitalized patients were in at the time of the study? Or are they more stable traits that are precursors to the illness and last throughout the recovery phase, not necessarily correlated with symptoms?

We speculate, based on clinical impressions of eating-disordered patients, that the sense of self might have different functions for different patients and play different roles at different points in treatment. Even among the group of anorexia-nervosa patients in this study, the sense of self we have delineated was present only for a significant number of them. Therefore, some in the group (a non-significant number) showed a sense of self of a different configuration. Other aspects of the sense of self, or other dimensions of the pathology, might be more prominent for the patients who were not among the subgroup leading to the significant finding in this study. Further study of individual cases or other groups of eating-disorder patients might help sort out the defensive, enduring, conscious, or derivative nature of the sense of self, and also the complexity of diverse levels of self beliefs which Horowitz, Eells, Singer, and Salovey (1995) believe are necessary for case formulations and treatment planning.

Based on clinical experiences with eating-disorder patients in treatment, we expected that the sense of self, assessed in this study by self-descriptions, would not be readily accessible at the nadir of their illness when their symptomatology was severe. Indeed we were surprised that the methodology of collecting self-descriptions used in this study was so powerful as to elicit such rich descriptions of self from these severely ill hospitalized patients. Clinically we had noticed that as the troublesome behavioral pattern subsides (e.g. with weight gain, less frequent bingeing and purging, or reduced preoccupation with appearance, eating, and weight), there is more awareness of feelings. A psychological dimension, previously hidden, emerges that patients can begin to talk about and work on in treatment. We then often find a sense of self that is characterized by an intensely anxious and desperate pursuit of self-definition and a preoccupation with introspection, as though the patient is relentlessly, yet hopelessly, driven to achieve a sense of effectiveness and to be very different from the kind of person who she fears she is.

When evaluating, treating, and looking at the outcome of treatments for eating-disorder patients, it is easy to get distracted by changes in weight, eating behaviors, and preoccupations with food and appearance. Though these disruptive and life-threatening symptoms must be attended to, our findings suggest that the nature of and changes in the sense of self must also be an important consideration of the treatment process with anorexia-nervosa, and perhaps other eating-disorder, patients. Attention to the sense of self might, in addition, lead to more understanding of the pathogenesis and maintenance of these disorders and might avoid the replication of these patients' family dynamics by ignoring their inner experience of themselves.

BIBLIOGRAPHY

ALLISON, J., BLATT, S. J., & ZIMET, C. N. (1968). *The Interpretation of Psychological Tests.* New York: Harper & Row.

AMERICAN PSYCHIATRIC ASSOCIATION. (1980). *Diagnostic and Statistical Manual of Mental Disorders* (3rd ed.). Washington, D.C.: Author.

ARONSON, J. (Ed.) (1993). *Insights in the Dynamic Psychotherapy of Anorexia and Bulimia, An Introduction to the Literature.* Northvale, N.J.: Jason Aronson.

BEMPORAD, J. R., & RATEY, J. (1985). Intensive psychotherapy of former anorexic individuals. *American Journal of Psychotherapy,* 34:454–466.

BERS, S. A., BLATT, S. J., SAYWARD, H. K., & JOHNSTON, R. S. (1993). Normal and pathological aspects of self-descriptions and their changes over long-term treatment. *Psychoanalytic Psychology,* 10:17–37.

BERS, S., & QUINLAN, D. M. (1992). Perceived-competence deficit in anorexia nervosa. *Journal of Abnormal Psychology,* 101:423–31.

BLATT, S. J. (1974). Levels of object representation in anaclitic and introjective depression. *Psychoanalytic Study of the Child,* 29:107–157.

BLATT, S. J., & AUERBACH, J. S. (2000). Psychoanalytic models of the mind and their contributions to personality research. *European Journal of Personality,* 14:429–447.

BLATT, S. J., & BERS, S. A. (1987). *The Assessment of Self-Descriptions: A Scoring Manual.* Unpublished manuscript, Yale University, Department of Psychiatry, New Haven, Conn.

BLATT, S. J., & BERS, S. A. (1993). The sense of self in depression: A psychodynamic perspective. In Z. V. Segal & S. J. Blatt (Eds.), *The Self in Emotional Distress, Cognitive and Psychodynamic Perspectives.* New York: Guilford Press, pp. 171–210.

BLATT, S. J., BERS, S. A., & SCHAFFER, C. E. (1993). *The Assessment of Self-descriptions.* Unpublished manuscript, Yale University, Department of Psychiatry, New Haven, Conn.

BLATT, S. J., CHEVRON, E. S., QUINLAN, D. M., SCHAFFER, C. E., & WEIN, S. (1988). *The Assessment of Qualitative and Structural Dimensions of Object Representations.* Unpublished manuscript, Yale University, Department of Psychiatry, New Haven, Conn.

BLATT, S. J., STAYNER, D. A., AUERBACH, J. S., & BEHRENDS, R. S. (1996). Change in object and self-representations in long-term, intensive, inpatient treatment of seriously disturbed adolescents and young adults. *Psychiatry,* 59:82–107.

BLATT, S. J., WISEMAN, H., PRINCE-GIBSON, E., & GATT, C. (1991). Object representations and change in clinical functioning. *Psychotherapy,* 28:273–283.

BRUCH, H. (1962). Perceptual and conceptual disturbances in anorexia nervosa. *Psychosomatic Medicine,* 24:187–194.

BRUCH, H. (1973). Psychiatric aspects of obesity. *Psychiatric Annals,* 3:6–10.

BRUCH, H. (1978). *The Golden Cage: The Enigma of Anorexia Nervosa.* Cambridge, Mass.: Harvard University Press.

BRUCH, H. (1988). *Conversations with Anorexics* (Czyzewski, D. and Suhr, M. A., Eds.). New York: Basic Books, Inc.

CASPER, R. C., OFFER, D., & OSTROV, E. (1981). The self-image of adolescents with acute anorexia nervosa. *The Journal of Pediatrics,* 98:656–661.

DANIELS, L. (2001). *With a Woman's Voice.* Laham, Md.: Madison Books.

DIAMOND, D., KASLOW, N., COONERTY, S., & BLATT, S. J. (1990). Changes in separation-individuation and intersubjectivity in long-term treatment. *Psychoanalytic Psychology,* 7:363–397.

FALSTEIN, E. I., SHERMAN, D., FEINSTEIN, S. C. & JUDAS, I. (1956). Anorexia nervosa in the male child. *American Journal of Orthopsychiatry,* 26:751–772.

FREUD, A. (1937). *The Ego and the Mechanisms of Defense* (C. Baines, Trans.). New York: International Universities Press. (Original work published in 1936).

FREUD, A. (1965). *Normality and Pathology in Childhood: Assessments of Development.* New York: International Universities Press.

FREUD, S. (1961). *The Ego and the Id.* In J. Strachey (Trans. and Ed.), *The Standard Edition of the Complete Psychological Works of Sigmund Freud,* Volume 19, pp. 12–66. London: Hogarth Press. (Original work published in 1923).

GAMMON, G. D., JOHN, K., ROSTBLUM, E. D., MULLEN, K., TISCHLER, G. L., &

WEISSMAN, M. M. (1983). Identification of bipolar disorder in adolescents with a structured diagnostic interview: The frequency and manifestations of the disorder in an inpatient sample. *American Journal of Psychiatry,* 140:543–547.

GARFINKEL, P. E., & GARNER, D. M. (1982). *Anorexia Nervosa: A Multidimensional Perspective.* New York: Brunner/Mazel.

GARNER, D. M. & GARFINKEL, P. E. (1979). The Eating Attitudes Test: An index of the symptoms of anorexia nervosa. *Psychological Medicine,* 9:273–279.

GARNER, D. M., OLMSTED, M. P., BOHR, Y., & GARFINKEL, P. E. (1982). The Eating Attitudes Test: Psychometric features and clinical correlates. *Psychological Medicine,* 12:871–878.

GEIST, R. A. (1985). Therapeutic dilemmas in the treatment of anorexia nervosa: A self-psychological perspective. In S. W. Emmett (Ed.), *Theory and Treatment of Anorexia Nervosa and Bulimia: Biomedical, Sociocultural and Psychological Perspectives.* New York: Brunner/Mazel.

GOODSITT, A. (1977). Narcissistic disturbances in Anorexia nervosa. In S. Feinstein & A. Giovacchini (Eds.), *Adolescent Psychiatry, Developmental and Clinical Studies* (Annals of the American Society for Adolescent Psychiatry), Vol. 5. New York: Jason Aronson, pp. 304–312.

GOODSITT, A. (1983). Self-regulatory disturbances in eating disorders. *International Journal of Eating Disorders,* 2:51–60.

GOODSITT, A. (1985). Self psychology and the treatment of anorexia nervosa. In D. M. Garner & P. E. Garfinkel (Eds.), *Handbook of Psychotherapy for Anorexia and Bulimia.* New York: Guilford Press, pp. 55–82.

GRUEN, R. J., & BLATT, S. J. (1990). Changes in self- and other-representations during long-term dynamically oriented treatment. *Psychoanalytic Psychology,* 7:399–422.

HARTMANN, H. (1958). *Ego Psychology and the Problem of Adaptation,* D. Rapaport (Trans.). New York: International Universities Press. (Original work published in 1939).

HOLLINGSHEAD, A. B. (1957). *Two Factor Index of Social Position.* Unpublished manuscript. Yale University, New Haven, Conn.

HOROWITZ, M. J., EELLS, T., SINGER, J., & SALOVEY, P. (1995). Role-relationship models in case formulation. *Archives of General Psychiatry,* 52:625–632.

JACOBSON, E. (1964). *The Self and the Object World.* New York: International Universities Press.

JOSEPH, B. (1982). Addiction to near death. *International Journal of Psychoanalysis,* 63:449–456.

LAWRENCE, M. (2001). Loving them to death: The anorexic and her objects. *The International Journal of Psychoanalysis,* 82:43–55.

LERNER, H. D. (1993). Self-representation in eating disorders: A psychodynamic perspective. In Segal, Z. V. and Blatt, S. J. (Eds.), *The Self in Emotional Distress: Cognitive and Psycho-dynamic Perspectives.* New York: Guilford Press, pp. 267–298.

MAHLER, M. S., PINE, F., & BERGMAN, A. (1975). *The Psychological Birth of the Human Infant.* New York: Basic Books.

MCDOUGALL, J. (1989). *Theaters of the Body: A Psychoanalytic Approach to Psychosomatic Illness.* New York: W. W. Norton.

METROPOLITAN LIFE INSURANCE COMPANY. (1983). 1983 height and weight tables. *Statistical Bulletin,* 64:3–9.

ORVASHEL, H., PUIG-ANTICH, J., CHAMBERS, W., TABRIZI, M. A., & JOHNSON, R. (1982). Retrospective assessment of prepubertal major depression with the Kiddie-SADS-E. *Journal of the American Academy of Child Psychiatry,* 21:392–397.

PIAGET, J. (1954). *The Construction of Reality in the Child.* (M. Cook, Trans.). New York: Basic Books. (Original work published 1937).

RITVO, S. (1980). The image and uses of the body in psychic conflict—With special reference to eating disorders in adolescence. *Psychoanalytic Study of the Child,* 33:449–469.

SANDLER, J., & ROSENBLATT, B. (1962). The concept of the representational world. *Psychoanalytic Study of the Child,* 17:128–145.

SELVINI PALAZZOLI, M. (1974). *Self-Starvation, from Individual to Family Therapy in the Treatment of Anorexia Nervosa* (A. Pomerans, Trans.). Northvale, N.J.: Jason Aronson. (Original work published 1963).

SOURS, J. (1980). *Starving to Death in a Sea of Objects: The Anorexia Nervosa Syndrome.* New York: Jason Aronson.

SUGARMAN, A., QUINLAN, D. M., & DEVENIS, L. (1982). Ego boundary disturbance in anorexia nervosa: Preliminary findings. *Journal of Personality Assessment,* 46:455–461.

SWIFT, W. J., & WONDERLICH, S. A. (1988). Personality factors and diagnosis in eating disorders: Traits, disorders, and structures. In Garner, D. M. and Garfinkel, P. E. (Eds.), *Diagnostic Issues in Anorexia Nervosa and Bulimia Nervosa.* Brunner/Mazel eating disorders monograph series, No. 2., pp. 112–165.

VITOUSEK, K. B., & EWALD, L. S. (1993). Self-representation in eating disorders: A cognitive perspective. In Segal, Z. V. and Blatt, S. J. (Eds.) *The Self in Emotional Distress: Cognitive and Psychodynamic Perspectives.* New York: Guilford Press, pp. 221–266.

WECHSLER, D. (1974). *Wechsler Intelligence Scale for Children-Revised.* New York: Psychological Corporation.

WECHSLER, D. (1981). *Wechsler Adult Intelligence Scale-Revised.* New York: Psychological Corporation.

WERNER, H. (1948). *Comparative Psychology of Mental Development.* New York: International Universities Press.

WILSON, C. P., & MINTZ, I. (1982). Abstaining and bulimic anorexics: Two sides of the same coin. *Primary Care,* 9:517–530.

ZERBE, K. (1992). Eating disorders in the 1990s: Clinical challenges and treatment implications. *Bulletin of the Menninger Clinic,* 56:167–187.

Index